POPULATION AND RESOURCES IN WESTERN INTELLECTUAL TRADITIONS

POPULATION AND RESOURCES IN WESTERN INTELLECTUAL TRADITIONS

Michael S. Teitelbaum
Jay M. Winter
Editors

Based on papers presented at a seminar held at Pembroke College, University of Cambridge, August 1987

A project of the American Association for the Advancement of Science Committee on Population, Resources, and the Environment

POPULATION AND DEVELOPMENT REVIEW
A Supplement to Volume 14 1988

Cambridge University Press
Cambridge
New York New Rochelle
Melbourne Sydney

Library of Congress Cataloging-in-Publication Data
Main entry under title:

Population and resources in western intellectual traditions.

"Based on papers presented at a seminar held at Pembroke College, University of Cambridge, August 1987."

"A project of the American Association for the Advancement of Science Committee on Population, Resources, and the Environment."

"Population and development review. A supplement to volume 14, 1988."

Includes bibliographies.

1. Population—Congresses. I. Teitelbaum, Michael S. II. Winter, J. M. III. American Association for the Advancement of Science. Committee on Population, Resources, and the Environment. IV. Population and development review. Vol. 14 (Supplement)
HB871.P64 1989 b 304.6 89-878
ISBN 0-521-37538-X

First published in 1989.
The Population Council, Inc.
New York, New York

Printed in the United States of America.

CONTENTS

ACKNOWLEDGMENTS

THIS VOLUME IS BASED on papers solicited under the aegis of the Committee on Population, Resources, and the Environment of the American Association for the Advancement of Science (AAAS).

Established in 1984, this AAAS Program has focused on selected topics at the intersection of population, resources, and the environment, with the intention of clarifying scientific issues and communicating them widely. Committee member Michael S. Teitelbaum suggested that a first order of business should be to trace the intellectual antecedents of today's thinking on population-resource-environment interrelationships. With the assistance of Jay M. Winter of the University of Cambridge, Dr. Teitelbaum undertook the task of initiating, editing, and generally overseeing the project from its inception. The aim has been to explore, and hopefully to clarify, the two-century-long tradition of scientific and nonscientific discussion of such relationships—a convoluted tradition from which, nonetheless, much of significance about present and future debate and research can be learned. A major contribution to the coherence of the finished product was the convening of an authors' workshop at Pembroke College, Cambridge, in August 1987.

In addition to the two editors, the other twelve authors, and the members and staff of the Committee on Population, Resources, and the Environment, all of whom participated actively in shaping this work, the other person who played a special role in producing the resultant volume has been Ethel Churchill, managing editor of *Population and Development Review,* who has imparted extraordinary editorial assistance and encouragement.

Funding for the study has been provided by the Andrew W. Mellon Foundation, through its core support of the Population, Resources, and Environment Program; by the American Association for the Advancement of Science, which also supports the Program; and by the Population Council, which has contributed to publication costs.

Introduction

Michael S. Teitelbaum
Jay M. Winter

This volume of essays surveys the Western tradition of reflection on questions of population and resources. The participants in this ongoing debate have come from diverse fields. Scientists, philosophers, theologians, social scientists, and political actors have all made important contributions. Indeed, social thought and scientific analysis have cohabited, albeit uneasily, for as long as these inquiries have gone on.

This is true despite the pretentions to purity of many of the protagonists in the debate. Scientists have scorned ideology, and then have consciously or unwittingly injected political and ideological elements into their explanations of observed phenomena. Political thinkers who have addressed these problems have rejected the label of "ideologist" for its taint of theory divorced from reality. Like Marx, many political figures have declared themselves scientists, whose views have a sound empirical base: only their opponents are ideologues.

When we consider the mélange of scientific and political judgments in this literature, it is clear that the different sides have shared more than they have realized. Most scientists have not been insensitive to the political undercurrents of their day. Equally, many political writers have been deeply impressed with scientific method and analysis and have striven repeatedly to integrate them into their writing.

The essays that follow show that science and political speculation are part of a spectrum of analysis of population and resources. Individual thinkers and schools of thought along this spectrum can be located in terms of three factors: the purpose of the analysis, the method of investigation, and the language or discourse within which these issues have been discussed.

The first key distinction concerns the purpose of analysis. In the first two sections of this book—on Population in Western political thought and on Population and ideology in modern times—we are introduced to an array of thinkers who addressed the population question not as an issue in its own right, but as it both informed and reflected upon principles of a moral, ethical, and philosophical nature. This was as true of Rousseau and Montesquieu as it was of Proudhon and Marx. And in the twentieth century as well, the population question has obsessed fascists, socialists, and Catholic conservatives alike, because they saw that it enabled them to reaffirm and reinforce the nondemographic elements of their thought.

The third and fourth parts of this book—on Population and natural science and on Population and social science—occupy a somewhat different terrain. Surveys of the natural and social sciences demonstrate that the purpose of analysis has been primarily to uncover and understand in their own terms processes of biological, economic, and social development. In other words, the discourse of these disciplines was slowly (and incompletely) uncoupled from broader philosophical and metaphysical debates. The shift here was away from nineteenth century positivism, which adopted a scientistic (if not scientific) approach to all social questions in the search for universal "laws" of behavior. Instead, a more skeptical and limited approach was fashioned, emphasizing experimentation and observation as the only means to unravel the complexity of the population/resources question. Some scholars in these fields did indeed touch fundamental issues of human values, but to do so was no longer the central purpose of their enterprise.

To be sure, nineteenth century positivism is alive and well in some corners of the social sciences. Some scholars still believe that data contain their own explanation, and if we simply collect enough we will somehow discover the "truth." In some quarters, the rule seems to be: if we do not know how to approach a problem, the best thing to do is to count it. But as the essays in the third and fourth sections show, such unstructured quantification has been bypassed in most areas of biology, ecology, economics, and demography. Scholars in these fields have developed sophisticated approaches—conceptual, statistical, and experimental—that enable them to explore problems of growth, scarcity, and competition.

A primary distinction between various discussions of population and resource questions is, therefore, one of the destination of the analysis. A second divide concerns procedure and methodology. The essays on population and political thought in parts one and two of this volume describe a dazzling array of writings, produced by polymaths and political activists, who studied demography and resources in the same way as they studied all other moral and ethical questions. And this was as it had to be, they argued, since population and resource distribution were but two of many issues that determined patterns of welfare and happiness. The subject of population, they argued, must never become a reified science, studied in a vacuum, taken out of its social context, and divorced from the turbulent political, social, and economic conflicts of the day.

The essays in parts three and four, in contrast, trace the scientific line of development toward analytic isolation of the key variables that govern population and resource dynamics. Many scholars whose work is described in these chapters have strengthened the methodological armament of analysis precisely to restrict, if not eliminate, the extent to which statements of value are mistaken for statements of fact.

Alongside distinctions of aim and method, a third way of separating different approaches to the study of population and resources is to look at the language in which scholars in different disciplines report their findings and speak to one another. Scientific writers adopt the discourse of their disciplines, and follow—or at least purport to follow—rules of evidence, rigorous sets of definitions, and so forth, that are among the distinguishing features of professional academic work. This is not to say that the eighteenth century *philosophes* or twentieth century social democrats were unstructured or undisciplined thinkers; on the contrary. It is rather to suggest that over time, new modes of academic discourse have developed within which important advances have been made toward understanding this set of problems. Indeed, the development of formal tools, such as stable population models or statistical theory, enables us to understand demographic and economic processes in ways denied to eighteenth and nineteenth century thinkers.

The essays in this book suggest, therefore, that over time there has been a change in both the content and the form of debate on population and resource questions. The field of economics, for example, has seen a shift from a concern with the ethics of wealth distribution to the means of wealth creation. This new emphasis has both arisen from and led to new methodologies, new styles of analysis, and new analytical tools.

Sophistication has its price, in this as in other areas. The cost of professionalism is on occasion to yield a desiccated and overly narrow approach to what remain vital human questions. Perhaps inevitably, the growth of science through specialization has increased the risks that the demographic and the economic domains become detached from the social, or indeed the human domain. No one could make such a claim about Montesquieu or Marx, in whose writings population and resource questions, imperfectly analyzed though they were, appeared alongside every other major topic of social study.

Most contemporary writers on these questions abjure, with more than a touch of humility or caution, the universalist approaches of writers from the Enlightenment to Marx. Current wisdom has it that to understand the interaction of population and resources requires its isolation to a large degree from other problems.

But even when such necessary narrowing of vision occurs in contemporary writing, the overlap between what may be called the philosophical and the scientific approaches to the population/resources dilemma remains substantial. This becomes more cogent whenever scholars turn from description to explanation. Today students of demographic, biological, and economic change are able to describe events and phenomena with great, perhaps unprecedented, degrees of precision; it is when they turn to explanation that the affinity between older writings and new approaches appears. Explanation entails causality, which in turn requires comment on a range of variables hard to define or measure. These variables of necessity include the distribution of wealth; the nature of social inequality and the differential resource endowment across nations; and the character of social conflict along gender, ethnic, national, religious, or class lines. When such issues enter the argument, so does political and philosophical language, replete with moral assumptions and a priori beliefs. Since the discussion of population and resources must entail explanation as well as description, the distinction between ideology and science has never been easy or clear. This is inevitable given the nature of the issues involved and the inordinate difficulty in isolating them from political questions of all kinds.

While the subjects discussed in this book encompass many complex and rich intellectual traditions, our treatment is in no sense meant to be comprehensive. In particular, we recognize the disadvantage of limiting our discussion exclusively to Western thinking. We feel nevertheless that there are substantial advantages in concentrating on what is an ongoing and intellectually coherent body of ideas, the echoes of which can be heard in many non-Western debates and developments. Anyone who studies, for instance, Chinese, Indian, and Latin American developments will continue to find a mix of European and indigenous ideas. For example, Chinese Marxists have recently rejected the population optimism of their Marxist-Leninist predecessors, and have embraced instead Malthusian arguments in adopting the world's most forceful program of state intervention aimed at reducing fertility through restraints on marriage (like Malthus), contraception (like the neo-Malthusians), and abortion (like Lenin). In brief, a knowledge of the European intellectual tradition is a necessary, if not sufficient, basis for an appreciation of these and other developments.

Even in the West echoes of earlier debates are still heard today. Some writers on the political right embrace the population optimism of the eighteenth century *philosophes* and the nineteenth century utopian socialists, while sharing the Marxist antagonism to Malthusian ideas, and (at times) rejecting contraception and abortion on moral grounds. These are but two instances of the stubborn survival of earlier modes of thinking about population questions, and of the tendency of today's writers to adopt positions of whose intellectual pedigree they might be largely unaware.

Perhaps reflection on these currents in the European tradition of thinking about population and resources will help bring about a healthy degree of humility in current discussions of these perennial questions. Little that is said today can be described as genuinely new, or free of the difficult choices faced by earlier writers. If students of the political dimensions of these issues are drawn to a more careful and fuller scrutiny of scientific writings in this field, and if scientific writers and workers are made more aware of the political content and context of their work and that of their predecessors, then at least part of the authors' intentions will have been fulfilled.

POPULATION IN WESTERN POLITICAL THOUGHT

Moral Philosophy and Population Questions in Eighteenth Century Europe

Sylvana Tomaselli

O Venus! O mother of love!

. . .

For as soon as the vernal face of day is made manifest, and the breeze of the teeming west wind blows fresh and free, first the fowls of the air proclaim you, divine one, and your advent, pierced to the heart by your might. Next, wild creatures and farm animals dance over the rich pastures and swim across rapid rivers: so greedily does one follow you, held captive by your charm, whither you go to lead them. Then throughout seas and mountains and sweeping torrents and the leafy dwellings of birds and verdant plains, striking alluring love into the breasts of all creatures, you cause them greedily to beget their generations after their kind.

Lucretius, De Rerum Natura, *Book I.1: 1–20, cited by Montesquieu in* De L'Esprit des Lois, *prologue to Book XXIII, ''Of Laws in the Relation they Bear to the Number of Inhabitants.''*

The study of eighteenth century theories of population growth and decline provides an Ariadne's thread to anyone wishing to make his way into the Enlightenment. Pursuing this ubiquitous subject leads not only to the heart of the economic debates of the period, but to writings about somewhat less predictable topics such as toleration, slavery, primogeniture, climate, suicide, duelling, torture, prostitution, celibacy, monasticism, luxury, and the consequences of the development of the arts and sciences. The topic, in other words, impinges on nearly every important aspect of the Enlightenment's evaluation of the morality, manners, and mores of the *Ancien Régime* and of modern commercial society more generally speaking. Nothing short of webbing any set of views or pronouncements on population within the overall assessment of the merit or demerit of the progress of civilization and of the comparative worth of ancient and modern civilizations will go toward placing these beliefs in their proper context, and nothing less than this contextualization will enable one to understand their true nature and content. While rendering this theoretical framework in any detail is an awesome prospect, it affords, even when only very roughly sketched out, some sense of the manner in which the issue of population increase and decline was conceived of in the eighteenth century.

In seeking to comprehend how Enlightenment thinkers came to view the issue of population growth and decline in the way they did, we are not only engaging in a commendable historical exercise. For in addition to achieving a better understanding of the period—something worth doing for its own sake—we open the way for an appreciation of the value of some of the Enlightenment's insights into the subject, insights that are by no means irrelevant to our present-day concerns.

As we venture along these lines, it is well to remember that for all the wealth of reflections which eighteenth century writers produced on the topic and despite the extensive disagreements which otherwise mark the movement of ideas, there seems to have been something approaching a consensus on population growth: it was the object of near-universal approbation just as population decline was unqualifiedly dreaded. Indeed, the general level of agreement on this particular matter is probably the single most important factor in explaining the frequency with which the subject of population comes up in Enlightenment writings. Playing on the fear of population decline in attacking any given social, legal, or political practice or, conversely, emphasizing the extent to which a reform would bring about an increase in population were such standard rhetorical ploys, that it is often difficult to assess the real importance which was given to the issue of population in and of itself.

Moreover, not only was there little dispute as to whether or not population increase was a good and its decline an evil, but population growth was often the criterion by which the value of any social and political proposal or institution was gauged. Why this should have been so in what was after all an increasingly secular age might be puzzling, especially for those of us who are prepared to see the pre-Malthusian era as something other than an unscientific, not to say credulous, age.

Admittedly the Enlightenment consensus on population is not equally perplexing from every possible angle. That the wealth and power of a nation should be conceived in terms of the size and strength of its population may seem somewhat crude, outmoded, or simply mistaken, but it is not altogether incomprehensible to us now. What is less immediately accessible is why someone such as Jean-Jacques Rousseau, who deplored all the consequences attending the advent of commercial society, rejected a predominantly economic mode of analysis in ethical and political issues, and was not particularly exercised by the issue of defense, should have given such inordinate weight to demographic growth. But to approach the Enlightenment debate on population armed with the conceptual divide I have just suggested, namely between the advocates and the critics of modernity, is already to obscure an essential feature of much of eighteenth century writing on population and to ignore a common thread that runs through the texts of proponents and opponents of commercial society alike. Let me illustrate by turning to some of the works of two thinkers who, while not unaware of the real costs of the progress of civilization, were nonetheless appreciative of the distinct advantages this process also brought in its wake, Montesquieu and Hume. In the course of this exposition, we will also touch on the work of Sir James Steuart. Were this discussion to do justice to the wealth of reflections from which Malthus's thought evolved, it would have to consider the work of many other prominent writers (James, 1979). Not least among them are Johann Peter Süssmilch (Süssmilch, 1979 ed.), Victor Mirabeau (Spengler, 1942), Diderot (Wilson, 1972), Millar (Ignatieff in Hont and Ignatieff, 1983), Adam Ferguson (Ferguson, 1966 ed.), Condorcet (Koyré, 1961), and Godwin (Himmelfarb, 1984) as well as the Encyclopedists (Raymond, 1963; Fage, 1951). In the space of a brief essay, we can only hope to highlight certain salient themes that establish the terms of the debate and not its parameters.

Montesquieu's warnings

Montesquieu's *Lettres Persanes* (1721) proved to be one of the most influential treatments of the population question. In this subject, as in all the others he discussed, Montesquieu was to have a profound impact on the thought of the subsequent generation of Enlightenment writers in Scotland as well as on the Continent. Of the 161 letters that constitute this work and that taken as a whole provide a critical examination of modern European, and more especially of French, society, through the eyes of imaginary Persian travelers, 11 are devoted to a discussion of population, namely Letters 112 to 122 (Montesquieu, 1964 ed.). Writing from Paris to Usbek in Venice, Rhedi explains that in the course of his travels, he could not help but notice how depleted Europe was. Where once large populations throve such as in the great cities of Italy or in Greece or again in Spain, there now lived scarcely anyone. The same was true of Northern Europe and such faraway places as Poland, Turkey, and most of Asia. Calculating as exactly as one could in such matters, Rhedi declared that he found the present population of the Earth to be one-tenth what it had been in ancient times. Nor was this decline showing any sign of reversal. At this rate, Rhedi concluded, the globe would be entirely deserted within the next thousand years (Letter 112).

Usbek's reply only goes to reinforce this gloomy vision of the future of mankind. He begins by remarking that nothing in the universe is incorruptible. The Earth was not exempt from the universal laws of change and motion. It was, in fact, the scene of a perpetual struggle between its various forces. Thus the sea and the continents were engaged in an eternal war, and men's natural habitat, far from being immutable, had itself no less precarious an existence than that of its occupiers. Thousands of different causes could destroy the species, diminish or increase its numbers. Twice already mankind had come within a hair's breadth of total disappearance. The Black Death in 1348 had ventured as far as the plains of China, and what Montesquieu called the most shameful of diseases, syphilis, had been so rampant in the sixteenth century that had it not been for the discovery of a remedy, it would have won the battle over human life on Earth (Letter 113).

That the continued existence of the human race could not be taken for granted was a point which was to be repeatedly made in the writings of the *philosophes*. The dreadful Lisbon earthquake in 1755 was to consolidate this apprehensiveness in the minds of many (Gay, 1964: 34). Montesquieu was hence not alone in thinking of the possible end of the existence of mankind. Indeed, David Hume's famous essay "Of the populousness of ancient nations" opened in terms akin to those with which Usbek had begun his letter:

> There is very little ground, either from reason or observation, to conclude the world eternal or incorruptible. The continual and rapid motion of matter, the violent revolutions with which every part is agitated, the changes remarked in the heavens, the plain traces as well as tradition of an universal deluge, or general convulsion of the elements; all these prove strongly the mortality of this fabric of the world, and its passage, by corruption or dissolution, from one state or order to another. (Hume, 1985 ed.: 377)

Much as Hume may have disagreed with Rhedi's letter about the demographic impoverishment of modern nations compared to ancient ones and though the Scottish philosopher explicitly criticized Montesquieu's *Lettres Persanes*, his frame of reference, his language and approach to the issue owed a great deal to the French thinker.

The awareness shown by Montesquieu and Hume that the existence of humanity was very much a contingent matter somewhat undermines the commonplace view that pre-Malthusian writers were unthinkingly or unqualifiedly optimistic in their visions of the future of mankind. However much Enlightenment thinkers may have favored population increase, their reason for doing so was not that they blindly trusted nature or progress or providence to benignly ensure the survival of the species. Certainly well into the eighteenth century, the background against which they expressed their concerns about population was one which highlighted the fact that the shape of things to come could not be taken as given.

Thus Montesquieu not only spoke of great epidemics as the potential exterminators of the human race, he also commented on the fact that not all forms of attack on life were as clearly visible as that of the Black Death. Several parts of the Earth had ceased to provide for human subsistence. Was it not possible, he asked through Usbek's pen, that the globe as a whole had its own slow and imperceptible general laws and that it might grow weary of feeding men? (Letter 113).

Such physical limits to growth or even to life were, however, not Montesquieu's primary concern. In prefacing his discussion of population as he did, he was not only casting some doubt on any possible unreflective optimism, but also drawing attention to the fact that the causes which he saw as affecting numbers were physical or social (or both) as opposed to divine. The discussion, in other words, was explicitly set against cosmic providentialism. This is the force of Montesquieu's and Hume's opening remarks. Though both alluded to the Deluge, they did so in passing and in ways that only go to underline the fact that they were not engaged in a conversation about the Christian projection of the end of the world.

Having thus set the stage for a secular treatment of the question of population, Montesquieu immediately turned his attention to what he saw as the real cause of the decline in numbers ever since the disappearance of the ancient world (Letter 114). It is at this point that one might begin to wonder whether his raising the demographic issue was not simply a ploy to arrest his readership's attention and vent his critique of religion on his captive audience. For we are instantly treated to a tirade against religious interference in the domestic and the sexual sphere. Usbek points to the Church's prohibition of divorce and, for good measure, to polygamy in Islam, as major factors in keeping numbers down. Forbidding married, but utterly miserable, couples to seek their happiness by divorcing and marrying again accounted for the small number of children in many families. It also encouraged prostitution, which was in itself inimical to population growth. The celibacy of Catholic priests and the existence of monastic institutions contributed further to the smallness of numbers in the Christian world. As none of this applied to Protestant countries, one could expect them to have large populations. And indeed, they were blessed with increasing and buoyant populations. As a result, they were inevitably far richer: first, because there were more people paying taxes; second, because the land was better cultivated; and finally, because commerce flourished better in such countries, because there were more people who had the means to engage in its pursuit and because the greater need for commerce meant that there were more resources available to meet this need. An insufficient number of people meant that commerce must wither. Agriculture and commerce were intrinsically linked, each to the other's performance, and both required a large number of people (Letter 117).

But population was a stick with which Montesquieu beat more than Catholicism. In Letter 118, Usbek explains to Rhedi how astonishing it was that North America was almost entirely deserted. Why was it that despite the enormous number of slaves that were taken there from Africa, it continued to have so small a population? The reason was of course very simple and lay in the nature of the labor that was exacted from them and from the American natives. Thousands were dying in the process of extracting gold and silver, which were in themselves utterly useless (Letter 118). The Romans had treated their slaves far differently. In Letter 115, Usbek had argued that the incentives which the slaves had in the Ancient Republic led them to be especially industrious, to engage in various economic activities, to become rich and be enfranchised. Their numbers never ceased growing.

The fecundity of a people could, according to Usbek, depend on very subtle factors. Ideas and convictions could have, or so it is said in Letter 119, a great causal influence on population growth. Thus the Jews survived as a people despite the fact that they were constantly persecuted, Montesquieu reasoned, solely owing to their conviction that a Messiah would arise from among them. Similarly, in the ancient kingdoms of Persia and in China, religion and culture encouraged people to have very large families. In Europe, on the other hand, practices such as primogeniture led fathers to neglect all but their first born.

As he had done and was to do again, Montesquieu used this context to decry the appalling record of the Spaniards in their colonies. Their barbarism had led to the extinction of a population as large as that of Europe. Spaniards, Usbek claimed in Letter 121, would have fared much better by remaining within their own borders. Attacking Spain in this way was a means that the Frenchman often resorted to, as it was but a veiled way of attacking the intolerance of Catholicism and the evil of absolutism.

Such a critique paved the way for an exposition of the view outlined in the final letter on the subject of population, namely, that moderate forms of government were most beneficial to population growth. Usbek thus cited Switzerland and Holland to show that the republican form of government led to population increase. Such a demographic success was all the more impressive given that neither country could be deemed to have fertile soils. Liberty, wealth, and the near equality of citizens were interdependent factors, according to Montesquieu, all of which brought about population expansion, if only because they attracted foreigners. Tyrannical or arbitrary forms of government, on the other hand, were notorious for their concentration of the wealth of the nation in a very few hands while the bulk of the people lived in poverty (Letter 122).

Though Montesquieu admitted that, once married, a peasant was unlikely to limit the number of his children even if he was poor, he did think that, generally speaking, misery held men back from marrying or wanting too many children. In France, however, the fear of conscription, which the wars of Louis XIV had necessitated, had led to very early marriages, which, in turn, resulted in a vast number of children living in dire circumstances and prey to illnesses and famine. Such conditions, he warned in Letter 122, tended to make for the degeneration of the race. Usbek's series of letters on population was thus brought to an ironical conclusion: if this bleak picture could be painted of France, matters could only be worse in less well-governed nations. Coming from Montesquieu, this remark could only be intended sarcastically.

Perhaps somewhat embarrassed by what is conceived as naïveté or error in Montesquieu's discussion of population, commentators have either suggested that Montesquieu should be excused, since he was not really exercised by the issue in and of itself (Shklar, 1987: 46), or they have pleaded extenuating circumstances, such as the infancy of political arithmetic, which they point out had only just been established by Sir William Petty (Shackleton, 1961: 44). Such condescension, though well-intentioned, is not entirely warranted. Montesquieu was as well informed as anyone could be on the subject at the time. His views on population were derived from very extensive readings in travel literature, contemporary social and economic writings, and the Classics. He was familiar with Petty's work, for instance, and even cited him in the chapters dealing with population in *De L'Esprit des Lois* (Montesquieu, 1964 ed.: Book XXIII, chapter 17).

That he exploited the fear of population decline to draw his readers' interest and make them pay heed to his social and political critique seems highly likely. But this in no way trivializes what he had to say about population. The fact that the subject received one of the lengthiest treatments in *Les Lettres Persanes* and was carefully considered again in *De L'Esprit des Lois* must give some indication as to the extent of his own interest in it. More importantly, Montesquieu had a real point to make. Population, he sought to demonstrate, was not a variable that could be taken in isolation from social and political institutions. Nor, for that matter, from physical circumstances either. It was part and parcel of a complete and highly complex causal process, all aspects of which had to be attended to when implementing policies seeking to affect it. Thus while a variety of factors could have detrimental or positive effects on population levels, any attempt to manipulate the latter required changes in all of the other interdependent areas of civil society.

Apart from showing the real impact that certain practices, for instance, religious prohibitions, could have on population growth, it was Montesquieu's apparent objective to convince his readers that the population issue could not be tinkered with haphazardly. To obtain greater revenues, the state could not simply let numbers rise or coerce the youth into early marriages, as he reported had been the policy of the Spaniards in their colonies. A legislator had to take into account a wide number of factors when it came to regulating population levels, including the fertility of the land, the climate, the nature of the economy, the distribution of wealth among the citizens, the relative strength of the agricultural and manufacturing sectors, and, last but not least, a people's mores and religious convictions (1964 ed.: Book XXIII, chapter 16). Whatever Montesquieu may have believed about the demographic decline in Europe since ancient times, the example he gave of Ancient Greece in *De L'Esprit des Lois* shows that his admiration did not extend to polities that increased numbers independently of all other considerations. On the contrary, in Book XXIII, chapter 17, he commended Greece for the many steps that were taken to ensure that its population did not go beyond a fixed level, and he cited Plato and Aristotle as examples of political theorists whose works reflected contemporary social practices as both specified that population was to be controlled.

In 1666, Louis XIV had sought to encourage marriages through an edict and the granting of pensions to families of ten or more children. It was precisely this kind of piecemeal state interference that Montesquieu regarded as not only ineffective in the long run, but very damaging as it necessarily would breed poverty. Increasing numbers was a difficult task in a nation dispirited by the excesses of despotism and the abuses of an intolerant and rich clergy. It could well prove impossible. Nothing short of the most thorough economic reforms would do, according to Montesquieu, who pointed to the example of Rome and its extensive agrarian reform. Only ensuring the proper cultivation of all available land might provide the requisite remedy for so deep a social malaise as that which was the cause of depopulation in France (1964 ed.: Book XXIII, chapters 20–22).

Book XXIII of *De L'Esprit des Lois* made it clear that a government which was concerned to increase numbers had to ensure that there was employment for its subjects. Industriousness was the key to wealth, according to Montesquieu, and the wealth of nations was a subject as dear to him as that of liberty, if only because of their interconnectedness in his view of things. He did not believe that the wealth of a nation consisted in its population any more than he agreed with the Mercantilist view that it amounted to the accumulation of bullion, generated from commerce with foreign nations (1964 ed.: Book XXIII, chapter 22). He did think, however, that where liberty reigned, agriculture and commerce were likely to be flourishing, as was population. Agriculture and commerce needed a thriving population, and the ensuing prosperity favored the spirit of liberty. Only a large population growing in such circumstances was worth having, for it was these factors combined that made for the wealth of society. Like many other theorists in the eighteenth century, Montesquieu was highly critical of idleness (1964 ed.: Book XXIII, chapter 29). He was by no means against governmental or social provisions for those in need and did, in fact, envisage that these would be necessary in a large and complex commercial society, where many different branches of commerce existed, any one of which might temporarily suffer. He did, however, argue against institutionalized and hence permanent schemes of poor relief. These, he claimed, militated against the spirit of industry and all its attendant benefits. Thus, he ended Book XXIII of his magnum opus by pointing to the example of England, where commerce and industry had flourished ever since Henry VIII's reformation of the Church. By destroying monasteries and all related institutions and practices, the King had begun to put an end to the idleness of the gentry and the middle classes, just as he had clamped down on means by which the body of the people found easy subsistence. The moral was clear: wealth would accrue to that nation which took bold means to revitalize its spirit. By the end of *De L'Esprit des Lois*, its reader could be left in no doubt that this necessarily meant moving away from the absolutism of Louis XIV's regime and curbing the power of the Church. It meant following the English example.

Virtue and happiness in the Scottish continuation of the population debate

Not having to wage similar battles, the Scottish political economists' discussions of population did not contain Montesquieu's harangues (Forbes, 1975: 16ff.). Despite this and indeed even given some real disagreements (e.g., Hume, 1985 ed.: 380, 460), there are affinities between their approach and that of Montesquieu, whose writings had a very real impact on the Scottish Enlightenment (Forbes, 1975; Hont and Ignatieff, 1983). Thus, Montesquieu's insistence on the importance of employment to the population question can also be found in Sir James Steuart's *An Inquiry into the Principles of Political Oeconomy* (1767) in which he argued that: "Upon the proper employment of the free hands, the prosperity of every state must depend: consequently the principal care of a stateman should be to keep all employed" (Steuart, 1966 ed.: 81). He added that he considered "multiplication as no otherwise useful to a state, than in so far as the additional number becomes so, to those who are already existing, whom I consider as the body-politic of the society" (ibid., p. 82). The best number of people for any one society was easily gauged, on his view, as it was to be "compatible with the full employment" of every one of its inhabitants. How to keep the population within these bounds was, as Steuart himself declared, by no means so simple. "Every individual," he wrote,

> is equally inspired with a desire to propagate. A people can no more remain without propagating, than a tree without growing: but no more can live than can be fed; and as all augmentations of food must come to a stop so soon as this happens, a people increase no more; that is to say, the proportion of those who die annually increases. This insensibly deters from propagation, because we are rational creatures. But still there are some who, though rational, are not provident; these marry and produce. This I call vicious propagation. Hence I distinguish propagation into two branches, to wit, multiplication, which goes on among these who feed what they breed, and mere procreation, which takes place among those who cannot maintain their offspring.

> This last produces a political disease, which mortality cures at the expence of much misery; as forest trees which are not pruned, dress themselves and become vigorous at the expence of numbers which die all around. How to propose a remedy for this inconveniency, without laying some restraint upon marriage; how to lay a restraint upon marriage without shocking the spirit of the times, I own I cannot find out; so I leave every one to conjecture. (ibid., pp. 155–156)

It is easy to see why Malthus was to list Steuart as one of his precursors in the second edition of the *Essay on Population* (1803), though Montesquieu, I hasten to add, was also among the few cited (James, 1979: 103–106).

Steuart, like Hume before him, was to take exception to Montesquieu's claims that Europe's population had declined since ancient times. He was also critical of Montesquieu's expressed concern that technical improvements would have a detrimental impact on employment and hence also on population (Montesquieu, 1964 ed.: Book XXIII, chapter 15; James, 1979: 105). Speaking of the wit and genius that led to these inventions, Steuart explained:

> The wit I here mention is not that acquired in the closet; for there one may learn, that an equal distribution of lands was favorable to multiplication in antient [sic] times, that it must be owing to a contrary practice, that our numbers now are so much smaller. But he who walks abroad, and sees millions who have not one moment's time to put a spade in the ground, so busily are they employed in that branch of industry which is put into their hands, must readily conclude, that circumstances are changed, and that the fewer people are necessary for feeding the whole of society, the more must remain free to be employed in providing every other thing that can make life agreeable, both to themselves and to strangers; who in return deliver into the hands of their industrious servants, the ensigns of superiority and dominion, money. (1966 ed.: 159)

Much needs to be said about Steuart's sophisticated account of the manner in which, within the network of an international system of trade, the scarcity in one nation could be offset by provisions from another country; how the ever-rising demands of the rich, "who multiply as much as they incline" (ibid., p. 158), encourage agriculture not only in their own nation, but in foreign countries as well; how numbers could come to a standstill, in the absence of an increase in food production, yet commerce go on expanding and wealth increasing; how this prosperity could also be translated into military might as money bought mercenaries as well as everything else; and, finally, how the introduction "of machines into manufactures" (ibid., p. 159) could supply needs, lower prices, and baffle competitors, despite a country's inability to augment the number of its subjects. It will suffice here, however, to show something of the nature of the population debate as it was taken up in the wake of Montesquieu's writings and prior to the treatment of the issue by Adam Smith and Malthus, the subject of the next essay in this volume. Freed from Montesquieu's own parochial, though entirely worthy, concerns with reforming France, Steuart could incorporate some of the former's insights into the nature of the relation between the spirit of a people and its social and political makeup into his system of political economy. Thus he could speak, in a manner that would have astonished Montesquieu, of a British moral incapacity of augmenting numbers, despite the fact that Britain's population did not suffer from the constraints of war, or commerce, or the export of its subsistence (ibid., p. 157). More generally, Steuart's reflections on population illustrate the way in which the Enlightenment's discussion of population placed that subject within a very wide context of related factors and that even an author as cautious about demographic rise as he was saw the question as a moral and ideological issue, no less than an environmental or economic one.

The art of the statesman consisted, in Steuart's view, of successfully triggering a spiral of needs and ensuring that his subjects enter into a web of reciprocal services. Interdependence of this kind, maintained as it needed to be by industriousness, was the key to population growth. "If a society does not concur in this plan of reciprocal industry," Steuart claimed, "their numbers will cease to increase; because the industrious will not feed the idle" (ibid., p. 151). It was this which he called "a moral impossibility of increase in numbers" as opposed to "the physical impossibility," which was imposed by nature when it refused to produce subsistence. For a population to continue growing, it was essential that its agricultural laborers and its artisans exert themselves to the utmost and that the rich continue to desire more and more goods. The statesman had to ensure that the existing members of the society found labor and that the number of laborers was sufficient to meet the needs of rising demand. For Steuart the simple societies of the past, characterized by a subsistence economy and hence not enslaved to the pursuit of superfluities, were unlikely to be the scene of demographic increases. He did, however, agree with Montesquieu that in modern commercial societies idleness placed a very severe constraint on population growth. Indeed, for both authors, an increasing population was the reward, however unintentional, of hard work and, hence, of virtue.

Turning back to Hume's response to Montesquieu's views on population, we find that "Of the populousness of ancient nations," far from challenging the relation between virtue and demographic growth, had wholly endorsed it. As Hume explained,

> every wise, just, and mild government, by rendering the condition of its subjects easy and secure, will always abound most in people, as well as in commodities and riches. A country, indeed, whose climate and soil are fitted for vines, will naturally be more populous than one which is fitted only for pasturage. In general, warm climates, as the necessities of the inhabitants are there

> fewer, and vegetation more powerful, are likely to be most populous: But if every thing else be equal, it seems natural to expect, that, wherever there are most happiness and virtue, and the wisest institutions, there will also be most people. (Hume, 1985 ed.: 382)

Because of his firm commitment to the truth of this last statement, Hume thought the issue of the relative populousness of ancient and modern nations was highly important and tried to prove Montesquieu wrong.

Hume launched his critique by arguing, rather contentiously, that the principal difference between the much-admired Ancients and the Moderns was that, what liberty the former enjoyed was secured by maintaining vast numbers of people in slavery. Nor was this all. The Romans not only kept slaves, but were notoriously cruel to them. If, then, it was true that the slave population of ancient times did multiply nonetheless, it would constitute a very significant exception to the view that "the happiness of any society and its populousness are necessary attendants" (ibid., p. 387). Hume, however, found very little evidence to convince him that this was the case. Indeed, it was his belief that whatever the shortcomings of the master–servant relationship, the checks and restraints were at least mutual and that "slavery is in general disadvantageous both to the happiness and populousness of mankind, and that its place is much better supplied by the practice of hired servants" (ibid., p. 396). To be sure, there were in modern times institutions that also held population back. Hume was no less loath to forfeit an easy opportunity to vent his anti-popery than Montesquieu had been; but he also struck another bird with that same stone:

> Our modern convents are, no doubt, bad institutions: But there is reason to suspect, that anciently every great family in Italy, and probably in other parts of the world, was a species of convent. And though we have reason to condemn all those popish institutions, as nurseries of superstition, burthensome to the public, and oppressive to the poor prisoners, male as well as female; yet may it be questioned whether they be so destructive to the populousness of a state, as is commonly imagined. Were the land, which belongs to a convent, bestowed on a nobleman, he would spend its revenue on dogs, horses, grooms, footmen, cooks, and house-maids; and his family would not furnish many more citizens than the convent. (ibid., p. 398)

Such weighing of the pro and con of modern society did not prevent Hume from fully acknowledging the merits of life in premodern times. But it was important to single out precisely when past societies had been happy and flourishing places. Prior to the expansion of Rome, the world had been divided into small commonwealths, "where of course a great equality of fortune prevailed, and the center of the government was always very near its frontiers'' (ibid., p. 401). This was true of much of Europe and the Mediterranean basin; ''And it must be owned,'' Hume continued,

> that no institution could be more favourable to the propagation of mankind. For, though a man of an overgrown fortune, not being able to consume more than another, must share it with those who serve and attend him; yet their possession being precarious, they have not the same encouragement to marry, as if each had a small fortune, secure and independent. Enormous cities are, besides, destructive of society, beget vice and disorder of all kinds, starve the remoter provinces, and even starve themselves, by the prices to which they raise all provisions. Where each man had his little house and field to himself, and each county had its capital, free and independent; what a happy situation of mankind! How favourable to industry and agriculture; to marriage and propagation! The prolific virtue of men, were it to act in its full extent, without that restraint which poverty and necessity imposes on it, would double the number every generation: and nothing surely can give it more liberty, than such small commonwealths, and such equality of fortune among the citizens. (ibid.)

There was, thus, far more agreement between Montesquieu and Hume than may have been first apparent. That happiness, equality, industry, virtue, and liberty were factors making for growing populations was a view both were committed to. The question simply was when and to what extent these had been or were being exhibited. In other words, it was the facts of the matter and not the principles behind them that were in dispute.

Hume thus conceded that compared to the small commonwealths of the ancient world, ''the situation of affairs in modern times, with regard to civil liberty, as well as equality of fortune, is not near so favourable, either to the propagation or happiness of mankind'' (ibid., p. 402). Wealth was concentrated in the hands of a small number of people and inequality very great. ''Swisserland alone and Holland,'' Hume thought as Montesquieu had, ''resemble the ancient republics; and though the former is far from possessing any advantage either of soil, climate, or commerce, yet the numbers of people, with which it abounds, notwithstanding their enlisting themselves into every service in Europe, prove sufficiently the advantages of their political institutions'' (ibid., p. 403).

But for all the advantages of the past, there were also great forces limiting population increase. First, the small commonwealths had given way to large empires, and this had put an end to the idyllic conditions, including the near equality of fortune, prevailing under them. Second, warfare in that period of human history had been far bloodier. Third, even in peace time, society had been prey to constant and most violent tumults, and hence its commerce and manufactures had been much weakened by the atmosphere of uncertainty and irregularity. For these reasons, it seemed unlikely that the world had been more populous in ancient than in modern times. Having thus argued, Hume set out to show, with the aid of figures drawn from such Classical sources as Plutarch, Polybius, Caesar, Strabo, and Taufus, that his was the correct inference.

However much their calculations differed, Montesquieu and Hume were very much at one about the terms of the debate. Moreover, it is important to recall that Montesquieu believed that there were parts of Europe which were experiencing population growth, among which, of course, he cited England. Nor did he ever deny that given the proper conditions, such growth was within the reach of comparable European countries. Quite the contrary. Though a great admirer of the Ancients, Montesquieu was by no means pining for the world Europe had lost. His concern was, as was Hume's, to comprehend the true nature of modernity and to seek to ensure that his country did not experience its negative aspects without also enjoying its advantages: a position which a Scot, also sensitive to the success of the English, could easily have sympathized with. Both by and large favored the development of modern commercial society. But as indicated above, neither thought of demographic increase instrumentally. The reason they valued it and were keen to show when and where it had occurred was not that they thought it the means toward some specific end, such as the creation of wealth, the expansion of agriculture or of commerce, or again the making of large armies. As with Steuart, population increase was itself the product of other moral and socioeconomic phenomena in modern times. What is more, both Montesquieu and Hume considered that population could flourish in an entirely different, though no less specific, set of circumstances, to wit, in small commonwealths.

Further evidence of the centrality of the notion of felicity to eighteenth century writers may be found in the entry on population in the Enlightenment text par excellence, the *Encyclopédie,* edited by Diderot and d'Alembert. The entry's author, D'Amilaville, pointed to the multiplicity of causes of population changes, which were imbedded in what he termed "the physical and moral order of things." Concluding a discussion drawing on the writings of Wallace, Montesquieu, and Hume, he claimed that there was, is, and always would be roughly the same number of people inhabiting the Earth as a whole. Fluctuations certainly existed in some places, but these variations depended on the level of felicity to be found in them. Thus, echoing Montesquieu and Hume, D'Amilaville noted that all things being equal, the most populous countries were those in which there was the greatest happiness. This was where government was least complex, where equality reigned, where liberty and livelihoods were secure, where toleration and learning throve, where virtue outstripped riches. It was, in effect, the essence of the Enlightenment conception of the idealized commonwealth (*Encyclopédie,* Vol. 13, 1765: 103 ab).

Unraveling Rousseau's views on population

Let us now consider Jean-Jacques Rousseau's views on the subject. *Du Contrat Social* (1762) gives an account of the nature and requirements of an ideal polis, one so constituted as to enable the general will to prevail over all particular wills, including the will of the majority or even the will of all, understood as the mere sum of all particular wills. Alongside mentioning the kind of constitution and laws such a polis would need, the work provides an outline of the geographic, social, economic, and demographic factors that it would no less require. Rousseau is unambiguous. His must be a small state. Using an organic metaphor, he argues that,

> As nature has set bounds to the stature of a well-made man, and, outside those limits, makes nothing but giants or dwarfs, similarly, for the constitution of a State to be at its best, it is possible to fix limits that will make it neither too large for good government, nor too small for self-maintenance. In every body politic there is a maximum strength which it cannot exceed and which it only loses by increasing in size. Every extension of the social tie means its relaxation; and, generally speaking, a small State is stronger in proportion than a great one. (1973 ed.: Book II, chapter IX, p. 199)

To substantiate this claim, Rousseau pointed to the administrative burden that a large state entailed and the way in which this drained the resources of one and all. Less efficacious, manageable, and equitable, a large governmental machinery also led to a diminution in the affection a people should bear for those in executive office. What is even more to the point, given Rousseau's political concerns, is the view that a large state made strangers of the individuals that inhabited it and could but foster heterogeneity. Face-to-face relations and cultural uniformity were prerequisites for the civil society that Rousseau envisaged when writing *Du Contrat Social.* On the other hand, and as he himself remarked, his polis had to be large enough to be capable of sustaining itself (ibid., pp. 200–201).

Several factors were brought to bear in judging the optimum size that any given state should have, in Rousseau's view, and knowing how to weigh them against one another was a crucial political skill, in his estimation. Though he distinguished two ways of measuring a polity, namely by the size of its territory and by the number of its people, the art obviously lay in finding the right balance between them. As he explained,

> . . . there is, between these two measurements, a right relation which makes the State really great. The men make the State, and the territory sustains the men; the right relation therefore is that the land should suffice for the maintenance of the inhabitants, and that there should be as many inhabitants as the land can maintain. (1973 ed.: Book II, chapter X, p. 201)

Such a relation between the size of a nation and the number of people living in it was ideal in the sense that it showed a people at its strongest, both economically and in matters of national security. Economically, it meant that the nation was self-sufficient. This was of the utmost importance. For not to be prey to the vicissitudes of an international market and a network of trade was an essential feature of a polis, given that Rousseau was eager to ensure that his dreamland would be bypassed by the forward march of history and hence free from the endless spiral of artificial needs that, as Steuart and other political economists would have agreed, this march engendered. A country with just enough people inhabiting it, themselves just able to provide for their basic needs, would neither require expansion nor incur the envy of its neighbors. "In this proportion," Rousseau contended,

> lies the maximum strength of a given number of people; for, if there is too much land, it is troublesome to guard and inadequately cultivated, produces more than needed, and soon gives rise to wars of defence; if there is not enough, the State depends on its neighbours for what it needs over and above, and this soon gives rise to wars of offence. Every people, to which its situation gives no choice save that between commerce and war, is weak in itself: it depends on its neighbours, and on circumstances; its existence can never be more than short and uncertain. It either conquers others, and changes its situation, or it is conquered and becomes nothing. Only insignificance or greatness can keep it free. (ibid.)

In speaking in this way and displaying his awareness of the importance of size relative to territory, Rousseau showed himself a pupil of those who, like Montesquieu, had sought to understand the causes of the rise and decline of Ancient Rome and other initially small city-states. Moreover, Rousseau showed himself a disciple of Montesquieu in another way, namely, when he explained that in order to calculate the best possible number of people for any one territory, the quality of the land, its fertility, the nature of its yield, the impact of its climate, the national temperament, and the level of consumption all had to be taken into account. In addition, the fertility of women and the extent to which this last variable could be positively affected by any state measure or institution was also to be carefully considered. A larger territory was clearly called for when dealing with a mountainous region, not only because its population would have to be more thinly spread since forestry and shepherding were not labor-intensive activities, but also because women were more fertile in those areas and the cultivable land very limited. Coastal regions, on the other hand, demanded a far higher density of inhabitants, for the sea was a cornucopia that, in Rousseau's view, easily offset the infertility of the coasts, and a vaster population was required to counter the attacks of pirates as well as to harness the fruits of the water. In any case, any demographic surplus could easily be discharged onto the colonies (1973 ed.: Book II, chapter X, p. 202).

Rousseau did not tackle the issue of scarcity, a condition that, it may be worth recalling at this stage, did not characterize his account of the state of nature, though he did have to introduce it eventually into his conjectural history of mankind, like a *Deus ex machina,* in order to explain the origin of the formation of civil society (1973 ed.: 76–77). He simply begged the question. For having delivered the examples just given, he noted: "To these conditions of law-giving must be added one other which, though it cannot take the place of the rest, renders them all useless when it is absent. This is the enjoyment of peace and plenty" (1973 ed.: Book II, chapter X, p. 202). Granted abundance and peace, a small territory with just enough people for a self-sufficient subsistence economy to flourish, with laws striving toward maintaining as near an equality of wealth between the citizens and as little a division of labor as possible, one had the setting, indeed the only setting, in which men could be free. That such conditions would rarely present themselves was something which Rousseau was first to acknowledge. That most, if not all, nations were too set in their ways and too irremediably engaged on the course of progress to make his work at all relevant to them was made no less clear by him. Only Corsica, he suggested, might prove the exception to the rule (ibid., p. 203).

But this does not exhaust the population factor in Rousseau's thought. Apart from the fact that he believed that agriculture led to demographic growth while trade and manufacture depleted a nation—a view that he was by no means the only one to hold in the eighteenth century (Spengler, 1942)—Rousseau conceived of population as epiphenomenal, as an effect rather than a cause, in yet another way. In a chapter entitled "The marks of a good government," he argued that population increase was the only objective measure of good government. "For my part," he wrote,

> I am continually astonished that a mark so simple is not recognized, or that men are of so bad faith as not to admit it. What is the end of political association? The preservation and prosperity of its members. And what is the surest mark of their preservation and prosperity? Their numbers and population. Seek then nowhere else this mark that is in dispute. The rest being equal, the government under which, without external aids, without naturalization or colonies, the citizens increase and multiply most is beyond question the best. The government under which a people wanes and diminishes is the worst. Calculators, it is left for you to count, to measure, to compare. (1973 ed.: Book III, chapter IX, p. 231)

In a lengthy note, appended to this passage, Rousseau attacked those who pointed to the internal turbulence of the ancient republics as indicative of the undesirability of this form of government. "Long ago," Rousseau argued, "Greece flourished in the midst of the most savage wars; blood ran in torrents, and yet the whole country was covered with inhabitants" (ibid.).

Population increase was thus a phenomenon that Rousseau, like his contemporaries, wholly welcomed. Unlike those of his contemporaries who either favored or were reconciled willy-nilly to the further development of civilization, Rousseau did not value it for its causal properties within a chain of other causes that typified commercial society. For him the choice was between wealth and population. One was not productive of the other. In fact, he did not seem to think of population as anything but an effect, a sign or symptom of well-being, understood in the terms outlined above. Without wishing to sound overly Malthusian at this point, one might nonetheless recognize that Rousseau was liable to the charges that were leveled against Condorcet and Godwin later in the century. They believed—in contradistinction to Rousseau—that progress would sustain population growth. Indeed, the absence of any consideration of what would become of this growing population—as opposed to the optimum number that he seemed to find desirable elsewhere in his book—is a serious weakness of *Du Contrat Social.*

But even if Rousseau's criterion of felicity were entirely consistent with the body of his social and political thought, why should someone so insistent on the need to preserve the highest level of mutual acquaintance between the members of a polis, so emphatic about the necessity of keeping the right ratio between geographical size and the number of inhabitants, and so self-consciously indifferent to the advantages that, say, a pool of cheap labor would secure, why should such a person select demographic growth as the measure of a people's prosperity? That this was, as we have seen already, a gauge which had very wide currency might provide part of the explanation. But to answer the question more fully, we must go back to the indictment of civilization that forms the theme of Rousseau's discourses "Sur les Sciences et les Arts" (1750) and "De l'Inégalité parmi les Hommes" (1755), as well as turn to his pedagogical work, *Emile* (1969 ed.), published in the same year as the *Social Contract* (1762).

Civilized man is a degenerate being according to Rousseau. Addicted to false needs, men become increasingly effeminate, in the entirely negative sense of being weak, sickly, and denatured. The more removed they are from the state of nature, the more this is so. Describing the first few steps toward the making of civilization and culture, Rousseau wrote,

> The simplicity and solitude of man's life in this new condition, the paucity of his wants, and the implements he had invented to satisfy them, left him a great deal of leisure, which he employed to furnish himself with many conveniences unknown to his fathers; and this was the first yoke he inadvertently imposed on himself, and the first source of the evils he prepared for his descendants. For, besides continuing thus to enervate both body and mind, these conveniences lost with use almost all their power to please, and even degenerated into real needs, till the want of them became far more disagreeable than the possession of them had been pleasant. ("Of inequality," 1973 ed.: 81)

Similarly, in his first discourse, Rousseau had claimed that "Richness of apparel may proclaim the man of fortune, and elegance the man of taste; but true health and manliness are known by different signs. It is under the homespun of the labourer, and not beneath the gilt and tinsel of the courtier, that we should look for strength and vigour of body" ("On the arts and sciences," 1973 ed.: 5).

Like many before him, Rousseau deplored the effect of luxury on the health and well-being of those who allegedly enjoyed it. He also added his voice to those who, like his one-time friend Denis Diderot, condemned the working conditions that the production of luxury goods created (Tomaselli, 1985: 116ff.). Rich and poor suffered in their different ways at the hands of modernity. Modernity, moreover, brought illnesses and diseases that were wholly unknown to natural man. Indeed, to write the history of illnesses was, along this view, tantamount to writing the history of mankind (1973 ed.: 51).

Not only did the rise of sciences and the arts emasculate men by weakening their bodies, but the society as a whole was further made effeminate by the literal ascent of women to power. This development was epitomized in Rousseau's time by the flourishing salon culture of Paris. Women were the cause behind the growing empire of luxury and the attendant cultural advancements. But far from using their power like their Roman ur-mothers, to bolster marriage, domesticity, and hence virtue, modern women were loath to forsake the pleasures of society for the duties of motherhood. When they gave birth at all, they were unwilling to breastfeed their children; when they did breastfeed them, they were intent to wean them as soon as possible and that done, to dispose of them by farming them out to nurses, who, in Rousseau's view, were notoriously careless and ill-suited to the task. *Emile* thus begins by addressing mothers and seeking to educate them, before turning to the rearing of children themselves (1969 ed.: 245–248). Indeed, the opening pages of the work read like a diatribe or sermon addressed to women. Focusing on the practice of swaddling, Rousseau could find no other explanation for what he deemed a denatured practice than women's neglect of their first and foremost duty. As long as there was no proof of neglect on the part of the nurse, it mattered not to the mother whether the child died. Women, he continued, rid of their children, and surrendering themselves to the pleasures of the town, did not so much as bother to inquire how their children were treated in the villages. Not only did women refuse to breastfeed their children, but they in fact made every effort not to have any children at all. Added to the other causes of depopulation, namely, the sciences, the arts, philosophy, and modern mores, this new perversion of nature would soon lead to the total annihilation of the species.

A good reason, then, why Rousseau made population increase the index of the felicity of a nation was that in arresting the progress of civilization and placing restraints on the diversification of the economy, society could escape the moral and physical degeneration that followed from the cancerous growth of artifice and artificial needs. These, in his view, eroded domestic values and subverted the natural relation between men and women.

Love, procreation, and happiness

To understand eighteenth century views on population, it is, therefore, essential to think of them within the context of a wider appraisal of the mores of modern commercial society. This is true even of the reflections on population of those who saw the future in a more optimistic light than someone like Rousseau. Thus Montesquieu's first comment in his book on population in *De L'Esprit des Lois* was about women (Montesquieu, 1964 ed.: Book XXIII, chapter 1). The fertility of females in other animal species was more or less constant, he noted. But not so that of women: their manner of thinking, their character, their passions, their fantasies, their capriciousness, their fear of losing their beauty, of the cumbersomeness of pregnancy and of having too large a family, all these perturbed the propagation of humanity. Even Adam Smith wove his partial disdain for the culture of luxury into his comments on population. "Poverty," he pointed out,

> though it no doubt discourages, does not always prevent marriage. It seems even to be favourable to generation. A half-starved Highland woman frequently bears more than twenty children, while a pampered fine lady is often incapable of bearing any, and is generally exhausted by two or three. Barrenness, so frequent among women of fashion, is very rare among those of inferior station. Luxury in the fair sex, while it enflames perhaps the passion for enjoyment, seems always to weaken, and frequently to destroy altogether, the powers of generation. (Smith, 1976 ed.: I.viii.37, p. 96)

Important as the overall framework of the critique of civilization may be, eighteenth century population theories do not just require projection on a grand historical canvas. To be fully understood, the detail of the relations between men and women they either presume or advocate must also be fully investigated. Nor must this stop at the sexual division of labor and power within the family. Many of the pronouncements on population in the period can only be wholly appreciated if one bears in mind the tight connection in the eighteenth century between sexual pleasure and reproduction (Porter, 1985). If our present culture draws a great divide between sex and reproduction, the eighteenth century experienced this conceptual gap but rarely and tended to be critical wherever it saw its emergence.

At the beginning of this essay, I asked why a secular culture should have placed so much emphasis on population growth. It is time now to point out that this question rests on a false paradox. As Theodore Tarczylo (1988) has rightly felt the need to remind historians and as Antoine Prost's remarks elsewhere in this volume suggest, despite the injunction "Be fruitful and multiply," Christianity values chastity far above all else. Marriage is effectively a concession to the weaknesses of human nature. The growing secularism, at least at the level of theory, in the eighteenth century is not relevant to my question. Contrary to what I initially implied, there is no reason to think that secularism would lessen the seriousness with which the population question was tackled. Indeed, secularism, if anything, added to the importance attached to population precisely because of the degree to which it liberated sexuality, especially female sexuality, from the guilt and prohibitions in which Christian dogma surrounded it. This was yet another reason for Enlightenment thinkers to ponder the long-term consequences of modernity for the happiness, virtue, size, and, indeed, ultimately also, the future of humanity.

The prologue to this essay drew attention to the centrality of the theme of love in eighteenth century writing on population. While I do not wish now to conclude on too lascivious a note and to suggest that, by taking population as the measure of happiness in a society, eighteenth century writers effectively conceived of it as the telltale sign of libidinal expression in a given nation, and thus that the felicity it was set to gauge was entirely sensuous in kind, it is not entirely amiss to recall that until the 1780s, the pleasure of a woman was deemed necessary to conception (Porter, 1985). Moreover, Diderot, who in the *Encyclopédie* entry "Puissance" had argued that a nation's strength lay principally in its population (Diderot, 1963 ed.: 38), was to describe, in one of the period's most characteristic sexual fantasies, *Le Supplément au Voyage de Bougainville,* a sexual paradise in which men and women were freed from the European, and hence Christian, restrictions on copulation. There, women's attractiveness was enhanced by motherhood: the more children they bore, the more desirable they became (Diderot, 1964 ed.: 486). There, procreation was not hindered by religious vows, by celibacy, by prohibitions against incest and adultery. Couples remained together only for as long as they wished to do so. Births were always cause for celebration. There was one taboo, namely, that women be sexually active only when and for as long as they were physically capable of bearing children (ibid., pp. 487 and 494). In a fantasy society that measured its wealth in terms of its population level, vice and corruption were conceived of in terms of sterile sexual acts and encounters (ibid.). The work of the Marquis de Sade clearly belongs to an entirely different age.

Not so that of Malthus. His very language, his interest in such topics as climate, luxury, the nature of sexual attraction, marriage, idleness, and mores, his comparisons between primitive and civilized nations, his assessment of the changing condition of women, his discussion of the relation between civic liberty and the growth of manufacture reveal him to be the quintessential Enlightenment figure he was. Most of all, however, he never lost sight of the issue of happiness. Indeed, he too believed that

> The happiness of a country does not depend, absolutely, upon its poverty or its riches, upon its youth or its age, upon its being thinly or fully inhabited, but upon the rapidity with which it is increasing, upon the degree in which the yearly increase of food approaches to the yearly increase of an unrestricted population. (Malthus, 1979 ed.: 118)

Rather than the nature of his conclusion about the limits to growth, it is only his attempt to place his theory of population within a providential framework that makes him stand somewhat apart from the rest of the movement we call the Enlightenment.

References

Cassirer, Ernst. 1979. *The Philosophy of the Enlightenment,* trans. Fritz C. A. Koelln and James P. Pettegrove. Princeton, N.J.: Princeton University Press.

Condorcet, M.-J.-A.-N. 1970. *Esquisse d'un Tableau Historique des Progrès de L'Esprit Humain.* Paris: J. Vrin.

Diderot, D. 1951. *Oeuvres,* ed. André Billy. Paris: Gallimard.

———. 1963. *Oeuvres Politiques,* ed. Paul Vernière. Paris: Garnier Frères.

———. 1964. *Oeuvres Philosophiques,* ed. Paul Vernière. Paris: Garnier Frères.

———, and d'Alembert (eds.). *Encyclopédie ou Dictionnaire Raisonné des Sciences, des Arts et des Metiers par une société de gens de lettres.* Paris and Neuchâtel; 17 vols. of texts, 11 vols. of plates (1751–1772).

Fage, Anita. 1951. "Les doctrines de la population des Encyclopédistes," *Population* 6: 609–624.

Ferguson, Adam. 1966. *An Essay on the History of Civil Society 1767.* Edited with an introduction by Duncan Forbes. Edinburgh: University Press.

Flinn, M. W. 1975. *British Population Growth 1700–1850.* London and New York: Macmillan.

Forbes, Duncan. 1985. *Hume's Philosophical Politics.* Cambridge: Cambridge University Press.

Gay, Peter. 1964. *The Party of Humanity: Essays on the French Enlightenment.* New York: Alfred A. Knopf.

Glass, D. V., and D.E.C. Eversley. 1965. *Population in History: Essays in Historical Demography.* London: Edward Arnold.

Godwin, W. 1976. *Enquiry Concerning Political Justice,* ed. Isaac Kramnick. Harmondsworth: Penguin Books.

Goldberg, Rita. 1984. *Sex and the Enlightenment: Women in Richardson and Diderot.* Cambridge: Cambridge University Press.

Himmelfarb, Gertrude. 1984. *The Idea of Poverty: England in the Early Industrial Age.* London and Boston: Faber and Faber.

Hont, I., and M. Ignatieff. 1983. *Wealth and Virtue: The Shaping of Political Economy in the Scottish Enlightenment.* Cambridge: Cambridge University Press.

Hufton, O. H. 1974. *The Poor of Eighteenth-Century France 1750–1789.* Oxford: Clarendon Press.

Hume, David. 1985. *Essays, Moral, Political and Literary,* ed. Eugene F. Miller. Indianapolis: Liberty Classics.

James, Patricia. 1979. *Population Malthus: His Life and Times.* London and Boston: Routledge & Kegan Paul.

Koyré, Alexandre. 1961. "Condorcet," in *Etudes d'Histoire de la Pensée Philosophique*. Paris: A. Colin, pp. 95–115.

Kriedte, P., H. Medick, and J. Schlumbol. 1981. *Industrialization before Industrialization*, trans. Beate Schempp. London and New York: Cambridge University Press; Paris: Editions de la Maison des Sciences de l'Homme.

Levine, David. 1977. *Family Formation in an Age of Nascent Capitalism.* New York and London: Academic Press.

Lucretius. 1975. *De Rerum Natura*, trans. W.D.H. Rouse. Cambridge, Mass.: Harvard University Press.

Malthus, Thomas Robert. 1979. *An Essay on the Principle of Population*, ed. Anthony Flew. Harmondsworth: Penguin Books.

———. 1986. *The Works of Thomas Robert Malthus*, 8 vols., ed. E. A. Wrigley and David Souden. London: William Pickering.

Montesquieu, C.-L. Secondat, Baron de. 1964. *Oeuvres Complètes*. Paris: Seuil.

Porter, Roy. 1985. " 'The secrets of generation display'd': Aristotle's Master-piece in eighteenth-century England," in *Unauthorized Sexual Behaviour during the Enlightenment*, ed. Robert P. Maccubin. Special Issue of *Eighteenth-Century Life*, n.s., 3, Vol. 9 (May).

Raymond, Agnes. 1963. "Le problème de la population chez les Encyclopédistes," *Studies on Voltaire* 26: 1379–1388.

Rousseau, Jean-Jacques. 1969. *Emile*, in *Oeuvres Complètes*, ed. C. Wirz and P. Burgelin, Vol. IV. Paris: Gallimard.

———. 1973. *The Social Contract and Discourses*, trans. with an introduction by G.D.H. Cole, revised by J. H. Brumfitt and John C. Hall. London: J. M. Dent & Sons Ltd; New York: E. P. Dutton.

Shackleton, Robert. 1963. *Montesquieu: A Critical Biography.* Oxford: Oxford University Press.

Shklar, Judith N. 1987. *Montesquieu*. Oxford: Oxford University Press.

Smith, Adam. 1976. *An Inquiry into the Nature and Causes of the Wealth of Nations*, R. H. Campbell and A. S. Skinner, general editors; W. B. Todd, textual editor. 2 vols. London and New York: Oxford University Press.

———. 1978. *Lectures on Jurisprudence*, ed. R. L. Meek and D. D. Raphael. Oxford: University Press.

Spengler, Joseph J. 1942. *French Predecessors of Malthus: A Study in Eighteenth-Century Wage and Population Theory.* Durham, N.C.: Duke University.

Steuart, Sir James-Denham. 1966. *An Inquiry into the Principles of Political Oeconomy: being an Essay on the Science of domestic policy in free nations*, ed. with an introduction by Andrew S. Skinner. Edinburgh and London: Oliver and Boyd, Ltd; Chicago: University of Chicago Press.

Süssmilch, Johann Peter. 1979. *'L'Ordre divin': aux origines de la démographie*, original trans., with critical studies and commentaries edited by Jacqueline Hecht. 3 vols. Paris: Institut National d'Etudes Démographiques.

Tarczylo, Théodore. 1988. "Lascivious erudition in the history of mentalities," in *The Sexual Underworld of the Enlightenment*, ed. G. S. Rousseau and R. Porter. Manchester: Manchester University Press.

Tomaselli, Sylvana. 1985. "The Enlightenment debate on women," *History Workshop Journal* 20 (Autumn): 101–124.

Wilson, Arthur M. 1972. *Diderot*. London and New York: Oxford University Press.

The Limits to Growth: Malthus and the Classical Economists

E. A. Wrigley

Adam Smith is sometimes regarded as the herald of a new and expansive age in which great advances in output per head were to be achieved. The concatenation of formerly isolated markets through more efficient transport and more sophisticated commercial networks was to liberate the productive powers whose nature was exemplified in the parable of the pinmakers. Robert Malthus, in contrast, tends to be pictured as a man oppressed by the implications of the intriguing contrast that he set out early in the first *Essay on Population* between the tendency of population to grow geometrically if left unchecked and the inability of societies to expand their production of food faster than by arithmetic progression at best. Gertrude Himmelfarb (1984), for example, has recently remarked that the effect of the publication of the *Wealth of Nations* "was to give technology and industry a new and decisive role not only in the economy but in society. The division of labour . . . became the harbinger of a social revolution as momentous as anything dreamed of by political reformers and revolutionaries." The book created "a political economy that made the wealth and welfare of the people dependent on a highly developed, expanding industrial economy and on a self-regulating 'system of natural liberty.' " She went so far as to claim that the industrial revolution was "presumably reflected" in Smith's great work (p. 44). Himmelfarb then turns to consideration of the publication 20 years later of the *Essay on Population*. "The 'principle of population,' " she writes, "subverted the whole of Smith's theory, starting with his views on industrial productivity and high wages and culminating with his predictions of economic and social progress. It is hard to imagine a more thorough reversal of thought, short of a return to mercantilism" (p. 100).

In my view this reading of Smith and Malthus does them both a serious injustice, and fails to take into account the degree to which they shared a common viewpoint about the limits to growth and the implications of the necessary relationships between population, resources, and environment, a viewpoint also shared by David Ricardo.

The prospects for living standards

It is convenient to approach the subject by considering the views of the classical economists about the prospects for real wages. If a single defining characteristic had to be specified to denote the occurrence of an industrial revolution, it would probably be a majority view that it should be the achievement of a sustained, progressive, and substantial rise in real wages per head. It is attainable only if output per head makes equal strides, and, given the differing elasticities of demand for different types of consumer expenditure, this implies many of the changes—in occupational structure, in the rates of growth in output of different industries, in the scale of urbanization, and in other related matters—that are regarded as the normal concomitants of an industrial revolution.

On this issue the three greatest classical economists were unanimous. In their view the secular tendency of real wages was likely to be flat, if not tending downward, because any increase in the funds available to pay wages would be matched by a proportional rise in the number of wage earners. There might be a time lag between the economic change and the associated demographic response. The enhanced fertility and reduced mortality resulting from greater economic opportunity would take time to produce an increased labor force. In the meantime both fuller employment and a higher daily wage might improve the living standards of the average family, but eventually the balance would be restored. The existence of this equilibrating mechanism did not mean that real wages must be close to the level of bare subsistence even when labor was in abundant supply. Social convention rather than physiological necessity prescribed minimum acceptable standards of living, which in the case of some West European countries might be well above bare subsistence. But the prospects were nonetheless bleak so far as the trend, as distinct from the level, of real wages was concerned.

Although Adam Smith recognized that real wages in England had risen during the eighteenth century (1976, i: 78–91, esp. 85–88), he was not sanguine about their future course either in England or elsewhere. This was essentially because "the demand for men, like that for any other commodity, necessarily regulates the production of men; quickens it when it goes on too slowly, and stops it when it advances too fast" (i: 89). Periods of rising real wages occurred only when the stock of capital was rising so fast that the demand for labor temporarily outstripped its supply. But the increase of stock reduced the return to be had from its employment, as opportunities for profitable investment were gradually exhausted. Hence profits, for which the prevailing rate of interest might serve as a proxy, were substantially lower in England than in France or Scotland, and lowest of all in Holland. The gradation in interest rates from high to low was an indication of the distance between the present state of a country and its state when it would have "acquired that full complement of riches which the nature of its soil and climate, and its situation with respect to other countries, allowed it to acquire; which could, therefore, advance no further, and which was not going backwards." As a result, "both the wages of labour and the profits of stock would probably be very low" (i: 106).

Countries with high and with low standards of living alike were subject to the same constraints. Smith insisted, for example, that there was a wide gulf in living standards between the common people in Europe and the Chinese masses, remarking, "The poverty of the lower ranks of people in China far surpasses that of the most beggarly nations in Europe" (i: 80–81). But he thought that both China at one end of the spectrum of real wages and Holland at the other displayed some of the characteristics associated with the acquisition by a country of its "full complement of riches" (i: 80–81, 102–103, 106).[1]

Malthus initially reiterated several of the lines of argument already developed by Smith, although he explored them with a new precision by developing the implications of two postulates that he thought would be readily accepted: that food was necessary to the existence of man, and that the passion between the sexes could be regarded as a constant (1986a, i: 8). In a world that employed no contraceptives, the second postulate implied that marital fertility might be supposed invariant, and that therefore in the absence of any influences tending to alter prevailing levels of nuptiality or mortality, population would grow at a constant rate. Hence the plausibility of the view that in the absence of constraints population would rise geometrically. In contrast, Malthus suggested, the supply of food could not be expected to grow faster than arithmetically, even on the most optimistic assumptions about agricultural expansion. Given the properties of geometric and arithmetic series, there must therefore always be an ineluctable tension between man's formidable powers of reproduction and his much more modest powers of production. The tension might be resolved at any point on a spectrum of possibilities where the operation of the positive check alone represented one extreme, while the exclusive dominance of the preventive check stood at the other extreme. The two alternatives were associated with very different levels of real wages, but in both cases the presumptive trend was flat.[2]

Later, Malthus added sophistication to his treatment of the constraints that prevented a rapid and indefinite rise in production by providing one of the earliest analyses of the law of declining marginal returns, an exposition given its classical form a few years later by Ricardo (1951, esp. chaps. 2, 5, and 6).

Declining marginal returns on the land

One of the three factors of production in terms of which the classical economists conducted their analyses of the economic system was land. Unlike the other two, the supply of land was fixed, except in areas still in the course of settlement, and the bulk of the land suitable for agriculture was normally already in use. In such circumstances, at both the extensive and the intensive margins of cultivation additional units of output could only be secured by a greater than proportionate increase in the inputs of labor and capital. Technological advance might offset this tendency for a substantial period; indeed increasing returns might even be secured for a time, but in due course decreasing returns must prevail and both profits and real wages must fall.[3] This formulation was both more compelling than an assertion about an arithmetic growth rate as the best that could be expected in the supply of food, and more depressing in suggesting that it would prove difficult not merely to sustain real wages but to prevent them from falling.

The law of declining marginal returns on the land implied deepening problems in increasing food supplies in step with population growth, but its gloomy implications extended more widely. In all preindustrial economies land was the principal source of industrial raw materials as well as food. Wool, cotton, flax, silk, leather, hair, grain, straw, fur, and above all wood were the raw materials used by the vast majority of those engaged in manufacture. Spinners, weavers, dyers, fullers, tailors, shoemakers, glovers, carpenters, cappers, hatters, knitters, coopers, bakers, butchers, brewers, millers, and those engaged in the building trades formed the bulk of the industrial labor force, and looked to the land for all or almost all their raw materials. Even those employed in occupations using mineral raw materials were indirectly subject to the same constraints. For example, inasmuch as the smelting of ore or the further working of metals depended on the use of charcoal, the scale of metal production was conditioned by the supply of wood, and this in turn, therefore, by the productivity of the land.

Much the same applied to the sources of mechanical energy and heat. Human and animal muscle and wood fuel were the preponderant means of converting raw materials into useful products and transporting them to places convenient for their subsequent use or consumption. The energy needed for production processes and transport, therefore, was also largely derived from organic sources. The productivity of the land set limits to the scale of industrial activity no less than to the level of food consumption. A growing population that also aspired to rising living standards would therefore exert a double pressure on a factor of production whose supply could not be significantly expanded. The demand for food would rise but the demand for non-food products would rise even more rapidly, given that the income elasticity of demand for food was less than unity. The attempt to satisfy both types of demand through an increasingly intensive use of an unvarying land surface by a process subject to declining marginal returns could scarcely fail to be viewed somberly by the classical economists, who were conscious of the extent to which an organically based economy was subject to constraints upon the increase in industrial output as well as upon food supply (Smith, 1976, i: 401; Ricardo, 1951: 117–118; Malthus, 1986c, v: 114–115; Wrigley, 1987: chap. 2).

The same point can be made using a different paradigm. It was a defining characteristic of all preindustrial economies that they were negative feedback systems. Movement away from an equilibrium relationship between the main elements of their economic and demographic systems tended to provoke changes that restored the balance. In particular economic growth, if long sustained, produced increasingly severe problems associated with a rising intensity of land use. Thus, even though important sectors of the economy might be able to secure increasing marginal returns, as in Smith's parable about the pinmakers, the economy as a whole could not long tread a positive feedback path, where each step taken made the next easier to take. At some stage pressure on the land would entail such severe difficulties in such a substantial proportion of the economy that negative feedback would prevail in its functioning as a whole.

The classical economists shared a common view of this issue. None appreciated the revolutionary possibilities for the scale and speed of expansion in industrial output (and at a later date in agricultural output) made available to an economy that switched from sole reliance upon organic raw materials to an increasing dependence upon mineral raw materials (Wrigley, 1988). It transpired not merely that through the use of mineral raw materials industrial production could be expanded massively without provoking conflict over land use with those engaged in food production, but even more importantly that heat energy and mechanical energy could be harnessed for productive purposes on a scale that dwarfed anything previously possible when coal was substituted for wood as a source of heat and the heat was converted into mechanical energy by the steam engine. The world of the classical economists was a bounded world where the growth path traced out by a successful economy might at best be asymptotic; it could never assume the exponential form that became the hallmark of economies that had experienced an industrial revolution.

The stationary state

It is symptomatic of their attitude to growth possibilities that all the classical economists supposed that economic development must tend toward a condition that came to be termed the stationary state. Smith's views are visible in the passage already quoted in which he refers to the concomitants of the achievement of the "full complement of riches" that would be the ultimate fate of most economies. An economy might be expected to pass through a characteristic succession of stages, marked by a secular tendency for returns on investment to fall. In the early stages capital would be invested principally in land. Later an increasing proportion of new investment would be attracted toward manufacture; still later into trade and commerce—a development that might also be marked by a tendency to invest increasingly in foreign ventures. As time passed and the focus of investment shifted, the return on investment would decline. Although direct information about returns on investment was not available, Smith pointed to the extremely low level of interest rates in Holland as evidence that the Dutch had largely exhausted local investment opportunities; the Dutch involvement in the carrying trade and investment abroad suggested the same conclusion (1976, i: 98–103, 387–397). England was approaching a similar position, while the substantially higher interest rates obtaining in Scotland and France meant that they were still at some distance from the stationary state (i: 100–103).[4]

Ricardo did not provide a theory of the stages of economic development in the manner of Smith, but the logic of his arguments drove him to a conclusion about the necessary limits to growth and the supervention of the stationary state that has much in common with the views of Smith. The key consideration was the fixed supply of cultivable land; the crucial analytical principle, that of declining marginal returns. Ricardo was well aware of the opportunities for increasing returns in most branches of manufacture, and recognized that even in agriculture improved machinery, finer seed, better selected stock, and more sophisticated methods of organization might produce an increased return to unit inputs of capital and labor, or at least postpone any decline, perhaps for a substantial period. But all such changes are ultimately palliatives rather than cures: eventually the return to capital must decline and real wages must fall (even though money wages would rise). There could be no cheating destiny. Current advance was bought at the price of future retreat. Ricardo expressed his views in the following terms:

> The natural tendency of profits is to fall; for, in the progress of society and wealth, the additional quantity of food required is obtained by the sacrifice of more and more labour. This tendency, this gravitation as it were of profits, is happily checked at repeated intervals by the improvements in machinery, connected with the production of necessaries, as well as by discoveries in the science of agriculture which enable us to relinquish a portion of labour before required, and therefore to lower the price of the prime necessary of the labourer. (1951: 120)

Nevertheless, this process, he explained, pushed up the price of food and with it the cost of labor, which in turn inexorably reduced the return on capital, so that there must be "an end of accumulation; for no capital can then yield any profit whatever, and no additional labour can be demanded, and consequently population will have reached its highest point" (ibid.).

Ricardo was intent upon driving home the universality and inevitability of the tendency he had identified. Later in the same chapter, "On profits," he returned to this theme:

> Whilst the land yields abundantly, wages may temporarily rise, and the producers may consume more than their accustomed proportion; but the stimulus which will thus be given to population, will speedily reduce the labourers to their usual consumption. But when poor lands are taken into cultivation, or when capital and labour are expended on the old land, with a less return of produce, the effect must be permanent. A greater proportion of that part of the produce which remains to be divided, after paying rent, between the owners of stock and the labourers, will be apportioned to the latter. Each man may, and probably will, have a less absolute quantity; but as more labourers are employed in proportion to the whole produce retained by the farmer, the value of a greater proportion of the whole produce will be absorbed by wages, and consequently the value of a smaller proportion will be devoted to profits. This will necessarily be rendered permanent by the laws of nature, which have limited the productive powers of the land.
>
> Thus we again arrive at the same conclusion which we have before attempted to establish:—that in all countries, and all times, profits depend on the quantity of labour requisite to provide necessaries for the labourers, on that land or with that capital which yields no rent. (pp. 125–126)

Ricardo set out his views in a characteristically clear and categorical manner. In spite of the starkly deductive form of the opening chapter of his first *Essay on Population,* Malthus was much more apt to heed the complexity of the historical process, and so less likely to adopt an unqualified stance. He was in general far more inclined to give priority to inductive than to deductive arguments, to "experience, the true source and foundation of all knowledge" (1986a: 10).[5] The question of the limits to growth was one of his prime concerns. The full title of his most famous work in its first edition runs *An Essay on the Principle of Population as It Affects the Future Improvement of Society,*[6] and in the second and subsequent editions, after repeating the first seven words of the earlier title, Malthus added an alternative title, *or, a View of Its Past and Present Effects on Human Happiness; with an Inquiry into Our Prospects Respecting the Future Removal or Mitigation of the Evils Which It Occasions.* While economic growth and real wages were not the only criteria by which success was to be judged, they were of prime importance, an attitude also reflected in the full title of his second great work, *Principles of Political Economy Considered with a View to Their Practical Application.*

In view of his general reputation, and because of the nature of his initial thesis about population behavior, it is perhaps surprising that Malthus's view about the future prospects for mankind should have been less pessimistic than that of either Ricardo or Smith, at least in its mature form. He shared their conviction that the limited supply of land precluded prolonged, exponential growth but developed a less rigid and mechanical view of the link between the slowing and eventual cessation of overall growth and a parallel reduction in the standard of living toward some minimum set by the prevailing conventions of any particular society. He arrived at this view because of his more subtle understanding of the relationship between production and reproduction.

Smith's treatment of the relationship between economic growth and population trends was somewhat simplistic by the standards set by Malthus a generation later. He held an exaggerated view of the fertility of the poor[7] and believed that only the very high level of mortality among the children of the poor prevented rapid population growth. The proportion of children who reached adult years was determined proximately by the available food supply, and more generally by the demand for labor. "Every species of animals naturally multiplies in proportion to the means of their subsistence, and no species can ever multiply beyond it. But in civilized society it is only among the inferior ranks of people that the scantiness of subsistence can set limits to the further multiplication of the human species; and it can do so in no other way than by destroying a great part of the children which their fruitful marriages produce" (1976, i: 89). Then, having explained how increased wages, by ameliorating the lot of the poor, fostered population growth both through lowered mortality and earlier marriage (leading to higher fertility), Smith committed himself to a simple and harsh summation:

> If the reward [the wage level] should at any time be less than what was requisite for this purpose [to meet the demand for labor], the deficiency of hands would soon raise it; and if it should at any time be more, their excessive multiplication would soon lower it to this necessary rate. The market would be so much under-stocked with labour in the one case, and so much over-stocked in the other, as would soon force back its price to that proper rate which the circumstances of the society required. (ibid.)

Even in the first *Essay*, Malthus showed himself to be well aware that Smith's view was closer to a caricature than to a description of the accommodation between population and economy, between reproduction and production (1986a, i: 27–28). Malthus's mature position showed him to have moved well away from the rather mechanical view of the relationship between the two variables adopted by Smith.

Malthus's analysis included both structural and dynamic features that substantially modified and refined the stark simplicity of Smith's treatment of the question. They were agreed that constraints upon population growth were universal and inevitable given the limited scope for expanding the economic base upon which society rested. But whereas Smith assumed that the constraint must operate principally if not exclusively through raising or lowering the level of mortality, Malthus not only appreciated that adjustment might occur through fluctuations in nuptiality (and so fertility) rather than mortality, but also became satisfied, through the empirical researches he conducted between the publication of the first and second editions of the *Essay,*[8] that in western Europe the preventive check greatly outweighed the positive check in preserving the balance between production and reproduction. Further, he understood that if numbers were kept in check principally by heightened mortality, the living conditions of the bulk of the population could scarcely fail to be miserable for most of the time, but that where the preventive check prevailed even those at the base of the economic pyramid might seldom be obliged to face severe deprivation and ultimately starvation. In short, it was Malthus who first appreciated the immense structural importance of what has later been termed the west European marriage system; who first realized the significance of the contrast between a society in which young women began reproduction in response to an economic trigger (when the young couple had acquired sufficient resources to set up an independent household), and a society in which reproduction began in response to a biological trigger (when the girl had become sexually mature and it was thought to be shameful for her to remain unmarried). The former connotes a society capable of reaching a substantially higher level of average real income per head, ceteris paribus, than is likely to be attainable in the latter.[9]

Malthus also differed from his predecessor and mentor Adam Smith in placing considerable emphasis on certain dynamic elements in the relationship between economic and demographic variables. Smith had alluded to brief departures in either direction from the equilibrium position in which demographic behavior served to balance the demand for labor and its supply, but attached no significance to them in reviewing the long-term prospects for real wages. Malthus, in contrast, not only regarded long, slow "oscillations" in the economic–demographic balance as a necessary feature of the relationship between the two variables, but also suggested that such variations periodically presented an opportunity for raising the living standards of the laboring poor. He wrote:

> From high real wages, or the power of commanding a large portion of the necessaries of life, two very different results may follow; one, that of a rapid increase of population, in which case the high wages are chiefly spent in the maintenance of large and frequent families; and the other, that of a decided improvement in the modes of subsistence, and the comforts and conveniences enjoyed, without a proportionate acceleration in the rate of increase. (1986c, v: 183)

Which alternative was followed depended upon the attitudes and habits of the laboring poor, which might either lead them to put present gratification first, or else enable them to "act as beings who 'look before and after' " (1986c: v: 185). At one remove, this possibility of a general amelioration of the condition of the poor pointed to the importance both of the level of education within the community and of the nature of the political regime. Despotism, ignorance, and oppression produced irresponsibility; civil and political liberty and an informed public gave grounds for expecting prudence and restraint.[10]

Malthus's sensitivity to the importance of the cultural and political, as well as to the economic and demographic characteristics of a society in determining its capacity to grow and its ability to afford a decent living to its members led him to a rounded assessment of the circumstances determining the economic attainments and demographic postures of societies. He stressed the frequency with which populations were scanty and living conditions miserable even when the physical environment was richly endowed with the resources needed for the production of wealth. The Turkish empire and the Spanish colonies of South America, for example, were vivid, if depressing illustrations of the way in which men could frustrate the best intentions of providence (1986b, ii: 110–112; 1986c, vi: 269–276). Prosperity was a fragile plant that needed a suitable political and cultural environment even more than a fertile soil; capricious government and arbitrary exactions readily resulted in apathy among the masses and effectively discouraged the foresight and resolution needed to achieve all forms of sustained growth.

Malthus was an advocate of capitalism, though he did not use the term himself,[11] and one reason he advanced in its favor was the institutional support to the maintenance of adequate living standards afforded by a capitalist organization of agriculture. His argument in that connection is a good example of his sensitivity to the importance of social agency in determining economic behavior, in this instance in a manner that tended to enhance rather than damage prosperity. No farmer, he remarked, would consider employing a man unless he was confident that he would produce more than he cost in wages.

> Upon the principle of private property, . . . it could never happen. With a view to the individual interest, either of a landlord or farmer, no labourer can ever be employed on the soil, who does not produce more than the value of his wages; and if these wages be not on an average sufficient to maintain a wife, and rear two children to the age of marriage, it is evident that both the population and produce must come to a stand. Consequently, at the most extreme practical limit of population, the state of the land must be such as to enable the last employed labourers to produce the maintenance of as many, probably, as four persons. (1986b, iii: 405)

Malthus considered, in other words, that the marginal product would never fall lower than the conventional minimum wage, and the average product would therefore be at a higher level. In other economic systems—as, for example, "by the forced direction of the national industry into one channel by public authority" (ibid.)—such safeguards might not exist. Malthus did not refer to systems of peasant agriculture in this context, but he would no doubt have understood the concern of development economists today about the tendency of labor to stay on the land, in conformity with powerful local social conventions, until the average product has fallen to the level of subsistence and the marginal product is well below subsistence.

Malthus, Smith, and Ricardo, therefore, shared the conviction that economic growth must be limited because the land (in a literal and narrow sense) was a necessary factor in almost all forms of material production, and the supply of land was virtually fixed. They might differ about the most convenient way of bringing home the severity of this constraint but not about its nature or its inevitability. They were, however, rather less agreed about the implications of the limits to growth for the level of real wages. Smith and Ricardo recognized that prevailing conventions played a major part in deciding what each community regarded as a minimum acceptable standard of living, and indeed that over time such conventional minima might change.[12] But when treating the prospects for real wages in their own time and in the foreseeable future, they were more inclined to apprehension than optimism and to expect to see exemplified the operation of an "iron law." Malthus was less inflexible, and, without of course suggesting that a progressive and sustained rise in real wages was possible, he explained how a population willing to act with prudence might reasonably hope that all its members could enjoy a secure command of the necessaries of life, and even some of its conveniences.[13]

It is a striking illustration of the power of the arguments concerning the stationary state deployed by the early classical economists to command assent that even in the mid-nineteenth century John Stuart Mill continued to fear that it might supervene, and invested it with the same character as his predecessors so far as the prospects for real wages were concerned. He was more ambivalent about its likelihood than his predecessors, however, as might be expected in view of the intervening economic history. On the one hand, he continued to refer to the same intractable problem affecting future prospects:

> The materials of manufacture being all drawn from the land, and many of them from agriculture, which supplies in particular the entire material of clothing; the general law of production from the land, the law of diminishing return, must in the last resort be applicable to manufacturing as well as to agricultural history. As population increases, and the power of the land to yield increased produce is strained harder and harder, any additional supply of material as well as of food, must be obtained by a more than proportionally increasing expenditure of labour. (1965, i: 182)

On the other hand, because the cost of raw materials was normally only a small part of total factor cost in manufacturing, and labor productivity could be greatly raised by mechanical aids and the division of labor, the general outcome was uncertain:

> It is quite conceivable that the efficiency of agricultural labour might be undergoing, with the increase of produce, a gradual diminution; that the price of food, in consequence, might be progressively rising, and an ever growing proportion of the population might be needed to raise food for the whole; while yet the productive power of labour in all other branches of industry might be so rapidly augmenting, that the required amount of labour could be spared from manufactures, and nevertheless a greater produce be obtained and the aggregate wants of the community be on the whole better supplied, than before. (ibid.)

At all events Mill remained dubious about the secular prospects for the real income per head of the mass of the population, and followed Malthus in urging restraint upon fertility as the surest way of securing a rise in the standard of living of the laboring poor (1965, i: chap. 9, esp. 345–346). The stationary state remained a likely prospect.

Expectations falsified: Production and population

Production

The forebodings of the classical economists about the limits to growth proved to be mistaken, not because of any flaws in the logic of their arguments but because some of their basic assumptions about the nature both of the process of production and of the process of reproduction in society turned out to be ill founded so far as the future, though not the past, was concerned. As long as it was true that food and all important raw materials used in the production process were animal or vegetable in origin; that land was in virtually fixed supply; and that declining marginal returns were sure to afflict production at some stage (at both the intensive and extensive margins of agricultural production), gloom about secular growth trends seemed no more than prudence. A world in which these assumptions held true was also a world whose productive capacity was severely limited by its very modest command of energy for productive purposes. Where mechanical energy is principally obtained from human or animal muscle and heat energy comes mainly from wood, the scale of output per head cannot be raised very high even apart from the other constraints upon individual productivity in a preindustrial economy. Such energy limitations are a secondary handicap inescapable in an organically based economy.

By implication, therefore, one of the most significant changes taking place between the mid-eighteenth and later nineteenth century was the slow transfer of successive sectors of the economy from total dependence upon the products of the land to an increasing freedom from such dependence in favor of mineral raw materials, and above all coal. Major industries were thus freed to develop and grow enormously without provoking the problems that growth had always previously brought in its train. The manufacture of iron, glass, bricks, nonferrous metals, pottery, and many basic chemicals could expand without apparent limit and with declining marginal production costs. A wide range of industries that used the output of these manufactures as input to their production processes were also freed from old limitations—engineering, ship construction, and the building industry, for example. Moreover, the use of coal as a source of heat energy, which had been increasingly common from the sixteenth century onward, was supplemented during the eighteenth century and especially in the nineteenth by its use as a source of mechanical power owing to the development first of the Newcomen and later of the Watt engine. Both changes, but especially the latter, enabled an individual man or woman to raise his or her output by an order of magnitude over earlier times once a suitable method of harnessing the newly abundant power had been found for any particular production process. Such developments meant that all forms of production need no longer be pyramided upon the products of the land, and that therefore one of the assumptions that had caused classical economists to adopt a pessimistic stance was gradually undermined.[14]

Another assumption, that concerning declining marginal returns in agriculture, also slowly lost its force. This came about partly as a result of the changes already briefly surveyed. Mineral-based activities are by definition not subject to any of the problems associated with dependence upon agricultural production. But agriculture itself was slowly transformed by the direct and indirect results of the developments taking place elsewhere in the economy. It had always previously been necessary to ensure that the output of agriculture measured in energy terms should substantially exceed energy inputs. To take a crude example, a field that yielded less grain than was needed to feed the men and beasts employed in its cultivation would not stay long in use. All life depended upon tapping the flow of energy reaching the earth in the form of insolation as it filtered through many life forms—plants, herbivorous animals, carnivores. To expend more energy in securing food than the food was capable of yielding was a recipe for immediate disaster.

The new economic era rendered this form of biological accounting obsolete because *stocks* of energy could be harnessed. The use of coal, and later of oil and natural gas, enabled societies to ignore rules of prudence that had long seemed permanent features of agricultural production. Eventually, by the mid-twentieth century several times as much energy was used to produce food in economically advanced countries as was derived from the food harvested, but the operation as a whole remained viable because of the changed circumstances of production.[15] And it has proved easy to secure increasing rather than decreasing marginal returns in agriculture no less than in other industries under such circumstances. Agriculture has become a form of factory production in the open air using large inputs of energy, chemical fertilizers, and pesticides produced outside the farm to galvanize the local ecological system into yielding far larger outputs than could be had from a locally "closed" system.

In the long run, of course, living off capital stock in the form of mineral endowment involves severe risks not experienced in economies built upon an annual productive flow that can be maintained indefinitely. Modern industrial economies must find a way of reducing their exposure to dependence on diminishing stocks of fossil fuels and of other mineral raw materials or face the problems of accommodating once more to flow-related restrictions. But in the medium term, very large and persistent increases in output were attainable. Production could be induced to rise in an exponential fashion and at a rate that ensured the disappearance of the tension between production and reproduction that had concerned Malthus so greatly. It is a notable irony of intellectual history that Malthus should have framed a singularly successful model of the interplay between economic and demographic variables in the context of a preindustrial economy just when it was about to fail to "save the phenomena" because assumptions that had held true for millennia were ceasing to be valid.

Population

Not only did the circumstances of production change in ways that went against the assumptions of the classical economists, but also their assumptions about reproduction proved fallible. Malthus's views may be taken for the classical economists as a whole for this purpose. Smith's treatment of population was relatively perfunctory, and Ricardo regarded Malthus's work as definitive so far as population was concerned. The first *Essay on Population* had integrated demographic arguments into the main body of economic analysis; in particular it had described a range of possible mechanisms whereby the opportunities for economic advance generally, and for improved living standards especially, were circumscribed by demographic pressures. In common with the other classical economists, Malthus assumed that prosperity would tend to accelerate population growth, and he feared that the powers of reproduction so far exceeded those of production that population pressure would only be eased temporarily even by the briskest of economic advances. Unlike the other classical economists, he did entertain the possibility that some populations might practice prudence with such success that a part of any temporary gain in living standards might be retained. But while this consideration modified it did not infringe upon the fundamental assumption that economic growth rates and population growth rates would be closely and positively correlated.

The reason for making this assumption was twofold. Improved living standards would reduce death rates, and, equally, would raise birth rates, principally by encouraging earlier and more universal marriage. Lower mortality would occur first and foremost because of better nutrition but also owing to a host of related changes: less cramped and drier accommodation; more fuel to permit a more hygienic preparation of food, warmer houses, and more frequent and more effective washing of clothes and of the person; more clothing and of better quality; and so on. In general, experience both before Malthus's day and subsequently supports the belief that higher real incomes meant fewer deaths, though there were countervailing influences. Higher real incomes and economic growth in general tended to increase the proportion of the population living in larger towns and cities, and the urban environment was often unhealthy because the huddled masses were more exposed to infection than widely scattered rural populations, and because a polluted water supply and deficient sewage disposal caused grave health hazards. During the first three-quarters of the nineteenth century, indeed, there was very little improvement in overall mortality in England despite the significant improvement in living standards because more and more people were migrating into the least healthy areas.[16] In each major category along the rural–urban continuum there was a notable improvement in mortality, but the compositional population shifts were so violent as to prevent any major improvement in the national situation (Woods, 1985). Thereafter, however, mortality fell steadily and fairly rapidly. Health and wealth went hand in hand.

Fertility held more surprises. In time fertility behavior came to be better epitomized by inverting the Malthusian assumption than by adhering to it. As with mortality, there was little change in fertility rates in England, whether marital or general, during the first three-quarters of the nineteenth century. Nuptiality declined somewhat from its peak in the opening decades of the century, but the tempo of childbearing in marriage scarcely altered. Illegitimate fertility also fell somewhat, but the overall situation remained largely unchanged (Wrigley and Schofield, 1981: 435–438). In the last decades of the nineteenth century, however, when real wages were rising sharply, marital fertility began its long, unprecedented decline to levels that, by the period between the two world wars, left fertility below the replacement level even though mortality had also declined greatly. The link between intercourse and procreation, which had seemed so natural as to attract very little questioning in earlier times, was broken. Age at marriage and final family size assumed a looser and looser connection. Even more surprising, nuptiality itself actually declined between 1870 and World War I in spite of rising prosperity. By the 1930s it had become the received wisdom that the wealthier a country or social group, the lower its fertility would be. The supplanting of the social control of fertility *by* marriage by the individual control of fertility *within* marriage completely undermined the validity of the assumption that population growth rates would rise in step with prosperity. Mortality conformed to the expectations of the classical economists, but fertility did not do so.[17] The old verities vanished and with them one of the most powerful reasons for pessimism about the future trend of living standards.

Conclusion

The stationary state is not a technical term and it may reasonably be invested with several meanings, or, better perhaps, with a cluster of attributes that may be given different emphases. Its prime meaning for the classical economists derived from their conviction that opportunities for profitable investment would become fewer, causing a progressive loss of the momentum of growth. Once the principle of declining marginal returns on the land had been clearly formulated, and given the dependence of almost all production processes upon animal or vegetable raw materials, the arguments for a gravitation toward a future stationary state appeared irresistible. In human terms, however, it was less the cessation of growth *in se* that appeared so serious than the implications of an economy that had ceased to expand for the well-being of those dependent on it for a livelihood. It was in this connection that Malthus's contribution to the debate was so important, for real income per head represents the ratio between production and population. Numerator (production) and denominator (population) were equally important. An inconvenient tendency for the latter to display livelier powers of growth than the former added a new reason for gloom about the future prospects if the numerator was necessarily subject to progressive deceleration. The fact that Malthus, because he understood how greatly the relationship between the two variables was influenced by contingent circumstances, was inclined to a guarded optimism about the future for societies with "European" marriage characteristics gave an ironic twist to the situation. But no secure grounds for expecting a general, rising prosperity appeared to exist.

Because history has so conclusively demonstrated that the classical economists' views about the limits to growth were misconceived, it might seem perverse to dwell upon their assumptions and the conclusions they drew from them. But their views are not merely of interest because Smith, Malthus, and Ricardo were among the intellectual giants of their time and have remained so influential, but because of the fact that, living in an age which later generations have christened the beginning of the industrial revolution, they should have been so little aware of it. Indeed, the key distinguishing characteristics of the industrial revolution—the exponential growth of output at a much higher rate than any previously achieved, and the substantial and sustained rise in real incomes across the social spectrum—not only were never entertained as a possibility by the classical economists but were explicitly excluded by their analysis of the limits to growth and by their understanding of the relationships between economic and demographic variables.

The paradox is instructive. The industrial revolution was not the culmination of technological, political, legal, or organizational changes long in train. Had it been so, the possibility of such an outcome would not have escaped, say, Adam Smith, whose analysis of the course of change in England and Scotland contains most of the ingredients found in twentieth century expositions of the theory of "modernization."[18] Several of the features that endowed the English economy with an unprecedented capacity for growth were only contingently related to earlier change (Wrigley, 1988: chaps. 3 and 4). To those who see in the classical economists the prophets and apologists of an industrialized world, therefore, and equally to those who would distinguish between an "optimistic" Smith and a "pessimistic" Malthus, it is salutory to heed what the classical economists have to say concerning the limits to growth. In essence, they spoke with one voice, anticipating a future bounded by the same pressures that had afflicted mankind in the past, not one in which the world was to be confronted by unheard of opportunities while having also to face appalling new dangers.

Notes

1 See also the argument of the chapter "Of the different employment of capitals" (i: 381–397).

2 For a brief description of the way in which the level of real wages was affected by the relative strength of the positive and preventive checks, see Wrigley (1985).

3 Ricardo, for example, expected that "both rent and wages will have a tendency to rise with the progress of wealth and population," but that while this would benefit the landlord, "The fate of the labourer will be less happy; he will receive more money wages, it is true, but his corn wages will be reduced; and not only his command of corn, but his general condition will be deteriorated, by his finding it more difficult to maintain the market rate of wages above their natural rate" (1951: 102). He viewed the prospects for profits similarly because the necessity to provide maintenance for the laborer in circumstances where his productivity was declining would leave less and less of the income flow to be directed to profits (pp. 120–121).

4 See also (i: 395–396), where Smith argued that lack of opportunity for domestic investment was forcing more and more Dutch capital into the carrying trade and that England was moving in the same direction.

5 I have discussed the balance between inductive and deductive thinking in Malthus's work in Wrigley (1986).

6 The title page contains an extra clause extending the title, . . . *with remarks on the speculations of Mr Godwin, M. Condorcet, and other writers.*

7 "Poverty, though it no doubt discourages, does not always prevent marriage. It seems even to be favourable to generation. A half-starved Highland woman frequently bears more than twenty children, while a pampered fine lady is often incapable of bearing any, and is generally exhausted by two or three. Barrenness, so frequent among women of fashion, is very rare among those of inferior station. Luxury in the fair sex, while it inflames perhaps the passion for enjoyment, seems always to weaken and frequently to destroy altogether, the powers of generation." And later, "In some places one half the children born die before they are four years of age; in many places before they are seven; and in almost all places before they are nine or ten. This great mortality, however, will every where be found chiefly among the children of the common people, who cannot afford to tend them with the same care as those of better station" (i: 88–89).

8 The first edition was published in 1798; the second in 1803.

9 In the conclusion to his widely influential article on European marriage patterns, John Hajnal remarked, "The main theme of this paper is not new. It is one of the main topics of Malthus's *Essay* and indeed implicit in its very structure (especially in the revised version of the second edition)" (1965: 130).

10 "Of all the causes which tend to generate prudential habits among the lower classes of society, the most essential is unquestionably civil liberty. No people can be much accustomed to form plans for the future who do not feel assured that their industrious exertions, while fair and honourable, will be allowed to have free scope; and that the property which they either possess, or may acquire, will be secured to them by a known code of just laws impartially administered" (1986c, v: 184).

11 Malthus sometimes used the term capitalist but did not habitually refer to capitalism or the capitalist system.

12 "It is not to be understood that the natural price of labour, estimated even in food and necessaries, is absolutely fixed and constant. It varies at different times in the same country, and very materially differs in different countries. It essentially depends on the habits and customs of the people" (Ricardo, 1951: 96–97).

13 It was customary to distinguish between necessaries (food, fuel, clothing, and housing), conveniences (chiefly industrial products of use in the home, such as pottery, furniture, cutlery, or bed linen), and luxuries. Malthus's mature views about the prospects for the laboring poor in a society prepared to behave prudently may be found in a chapter entitled "On the only effectual mode of improving the condition of the poor" (1986b, iii: 482–487).

14 These issues are discussed more fully in Wrigley (1988).

15 Data concerning the relationship between energy inputs and energy outputs in traditional and modern agriculture may be found in Grigg (1982: 78–80).

16 Expectation of life at birth (sexes combined) was 38.1 years on average over the three five-year periods centering on 1806, 1811, and 1816 (i.e., 1804–18); 40.9 years over the comparable periods centering on 1861, 1866, and 1871 (1859–73) (Wrigley and Schofield, 1981: table A3.1, 528–529).

17 Though it has recently been argued that "the preconditions put forward by Malthus for the existence of moral restraint" are "very closely related to the key variables of the modern economic approaches to the study of fertility" (Silber, 1986: 18).

18 For a fuller discussion of this issue see Wrigley (1972).

References

Grigg, David B. 1982. *The Dynamics of Agricultural Change.* London: Hutchinson.

Hajnal, John. 1965. "European marriage patterns in perspective," in *Population in History,* ed. D. V. Glass and D. E. C. Eversley. London: Edward Arnold, pp. 101–143.

Himmelfarb, Gertrude. 1984. *The Idea of Poverty: England in the Early Industrial Age.* London: Faber and Faber.

Malthus, Thomas Robert. 1986a. *An Essay on the Principle of Population* (1798), in *The Works of Thomas Robert Malthus,* vol. 1, ed. E. A. Wrigley and David Souden. London: William Pickering.

———. 1986b. *An Essay on the Principle of Population* (1826), in *The Works of Thomas Robert Malthus,* ibid., vols. 2 and 3.

———. 1986c. *Principles of Political Economy* (1836), in *The Works of Thomas Robert Malthus,* ibid., vols. 5 and 6.

Mill, John Stuart. 1965. *Principles of Political Economy with Some of Their Applications to Social Philosophy,* ed. J. M. Robson. 2 vols. Toronto: Routledge and Kegan Paul.

Ricardo, David. 1951 (3rd ed., 1821). *On the Principles of Political Economy and Taxation,* in *The Works and Correspondence of David Ricardo,* ed. P. Sraffa, vol. 1. Cambridge: Cambridge University Press.

Silber, Jacques. 1986. "Malthus' preconditions to moral restraint and modern population economics," *Genus* 42: 13–21.

Smith, Adam. 1976 (5th ed., 1789). *An Enquiry into the Nature and Causes of the Wealth of Nations,* ed. E. Cannan, 2 vols. in 1. Chicago: University of Chicago Press.

Woods, Robert. 1985. "The effects of population redistribution on the level of mortality in nineteenth-century England and Wales," *Journal of Economic History* 45: 645–651.

Wrigley, Edward Anthony. 1972. "The process of modernization and the industrial revolution in England," *Journal of Interdisciplinary History* 3: 225–259.

———. "The means to marry: Population and economy in pre-industrial England," *Quarterly Journal of Social Affairs* 1: 271–280.

———. 1986. "Elegance and experience: Malthus at the bar of history," in *The State of Population Theory,* ed. D. Coleman and R. S. Schofield. Oxford: Basil Blackwell, pp. 46–64.

———. 1987. *People, Cities and Wealth.* Oxford: Basil Blackwell.

———. 1988. *Continuity, Chance and Change: The Character of the Industrial Revolution in England.* Cambridge: Cambridge University Press.

———, and Roger S. Schofield. 1981. *The Population History of England 1541–1871: A Reconstruction.* London: Edward Arnold.

French Utopian Socialists and the Population Question: "Seeking the Future City"

JACQUELINE HECHT

FOR MORE THAN A CENTURY, the Marxian specter has haunted Europe. It has become the "unpassable horizon" of our time, as Jean-Paul Sartre put it, and, as a body of ideas, it has exerted a kind of "intellectual terrorism," dominating discussion of social questions. But since the 1960s, a reappraisal of Marxist thought has been taking place, leading to a rethinking of fundamental premises. As a result, long-neglected aspects of socialist thought have suddenly received renewed attention. The return to center stage of utopian socialism can be seen as a kind of cultural revolution, occurring in many countries, including France. When this buried set of ideas was uncovered, some aspects had particular appeal—especially utopian notions about population, women, and sexuality. These appeared to offer a middle ground between Malthus and Marx. Concepts of the utopian tradition permitted a new generation to review the old debate and construct a kind of synthesis.

The significance of the utopians' work is wide ranging. Their ideas are imbedded in the language of social analysis. They invented the term "socialism" (coined by Pierre Leroux in 1831) to respond to the "individualism" of Saint-Simon. Later the term "utopian" fell into disfavor as the obverse of "scientific," especially in the language of Marx and Engels, who wanted to reassert the realistic premises of socialist ideas. Utopia was to be avoided as describing what should be; scientific socialism, on the other hand, was supposed to describe what was.

The debate between Godwin and Malthus is better known than those that followed it. Utopian socialists took up the dispute with Malthus, and most saw him as the incarnation of the devil, even though few of them knew his ideas at first hand. Their religious turn of mind informed their optimism about human nature and led them to conclude that social evils—including overpopulation and poverty—arose from purely social causes, not divine or natural ones. Some recognized the strength of Malthus's descriptive writings, but most rejected his explanations and prescriptions.

The utopian tradition

The utopian tradition has an ancient and distinguished pedigree. Those who contributed to it in the nineteenth century were conscious of following in the footsteps of Plato and the Old Testament prophets; of Thomas More, Francis Bacon, Tommaso Campanella, and James Harrington in the sixteenth and seventeenth centuries; and of a series of seventeenth and eighteenth century novelists, including Boisguilbert Fénelon, Jonathan Swift, and the communist utopian Morelly.

Most pre–nineteenth century utopians shared a set of received truths. They considered the present order to be iniquitous and perverse, both morally and socially. The world after the Fall had become a realm of evil. In a remote future, there could be another world, free from original sin, resembling Paradise Lost and forming the outline of Paradise Regained. In this New Jerusalem, there would be neither poor nor rich, Jew nor Hellene, and equality would reign in the most perfect *transparence.*

The utopian scheme was first set forth in a small setting, such as an island isolated from the corruption of the world. Many utopians envisioned areas called "trial boroughs" (*cantons d'esquisse*), from which general policies for the world as a whole would emerge. All these flights of fancy expressed nostalgia for a return to the womb and to a mythical childhood, lost forever. The first descriptions of utopian societies were archaic and ahistorical, with static economic and demographic regimes. Each disturbance of the equilibrium, due to increasing or decreasing growth, undermined the community's harmony, which had to be reasserted by every means. Utopian change was a contradiction in terms.

The nineteenth century utopian socialists are simply incomprehensible outside this specific intellectual tradition. But even after recognizing from whence they came, many questions remain about how they reached their destination. How did utopia grow into socialism? Was the socialist agenda inseparable from the utopian? Was every utopia socialist and were all socialisms utopian? The links between the two ideologies, while not rigorous, are nonetheless substantial.

Both arose out of religious beliefs. Not only under the *Ancien Régime,* but even later, during the industrial revolution, the language of utopians was filled with references to Christ and Christianity. For the revolutionary lawyer Etienne Cabet (1788–1856), for example, Christ was "the most illustrious of all communists" and "no one could be Christian who was not a communist." The social reformer Victor Considérant (1809–1893) juxtaposed the "Social Hell" of the present world with the "Earthly Paradise" that socialism would establish. These writers inherited from the Church and from eighteenth century philosophers a belief in the bounty of God and in the beneficence of Nature.

The utopian vision, however, never ignored the fact that man had to work by the sweat of his brow. Labor was at once hard and painful, and creative of wealth and general benefit. The utopian socialists believed in the sanctity of work. The right to work was inalienable and had to be guaranteed by the state, which was entrusted with its proper organization. The state also had a fundamental role to play in education, a point reiterated by Enlightenment writers, as the central means for the transformation of both the individual and society.

The term "industrial revolution" was first used by the economist Antoine-Eugène Buret (1810–42), in 1840, to describe the then current transformation of the French economy. For utopians, a central feature of this process was the creation of the urban proletariat. The excess mortality of the poor, when compared to the rich, as attested by countless medical and sociological surveys of the new "urban hell," was a perennial concern of socialists. François Raspail (1794–1878), a chemist as well as a revolutionary, stated that proletarians "produced many children, but few survived."

The response of socialists to these problems varied considerably, according to their religious and political outlook. There were Christian, agnostic, or atheistic socialists. Some supported state intervention; others leaned toward a decentralized socialism, a socialism of the people; still others adopted anarchism or similarly libertarian positions. The revolution of 1848 polarized members of this heterogeneous movement: utopian versus scientific; or socialist versus communist. In addition, the events of 1848 buried much of the religious language—but not the religious inspiration—of socialist thought.

Diversity marked utopian socialist views on population as well. Malthus's writings had become a touchstone for all who discussed this problem. But the utopians took several approaches to his argument about population growth outdistancing food growth and the need to exercise prudence in matters of reproduction. The "irreconcilables" rejected Malthus lock, stock, and barrel. Prominent among them were such Christian socialists as Philippe Buchez and Félicité-Robert de Lamennais, and such communists as Cabet and Théodore Dézamy, who attacked Malthus as representing the ideology of the dominant class. Others—we may call them "Malthusians in spite of themselves"—attacked Malthus and his "infamous" remedy, but accepted the validity of his famous geometric and arithmetic progressions for population growth and growth in the means of subsistence, respectively. They differed substantially, though, from Malthus in their causal analysis and in their prescriptions for future action. Among this group, a number of "minor prophets" exerted considerable influence—Constantin Pecqueur, Victor Considérant, and Louis Blanc. They were eclipsed, however, by the "great visionaries" of this period—Pierre Leroux, Pierre-Joseph Proudhon, and Charles Fourier—who castigated Malthus, even as they absorbed some of his ideas.

This essay proceeds chronologically from the two main forerunners of utopian socialism—Saint-Simon and Sismondi—to the early socialists of the first half of the nineteenth century and to the so-called minor prophets of utopian socialism, culminating in the great visionary utopians—Leroux, Proudhon, and Fourier.

Forerunners of socialism: Saint-Simon and Sismondi

The philosopher and social scientist Claude-Henri, comte de Saint-Simon (1760–1825), did not put particular emphasis on the population problem, but it is impossible to exclude him from this discussion, since he was the inspiration for much utopian socialist thought. Like many of the great thinkers of his time, Saint-Simon wanted to be the Messiah of a new religion. He declared that the aim of his *New Christianity* (1825) was to set up a new social organization to assure permanent work to all proletarians, positive instruction to all members of society, and entertainments that would develop their minds (Bruhat, 1982: 343). In his view, all men were brothers and all should aim to increase the well-being of the poorest class. Following Condorcet and other thinkers of the Enlightenment, Saint-Simon held that history was a linear progression toward a defined object: "the golden age is not in the infancy of the human species, it is in front of us" (ibid., p. 338).

For Saint-Simon, politics was the science of production. The government of people must evolve so as to entrust spiritual power to the learned and temporal power to manufacturers. The true producers were, for him, manufacturers, financiers, engineers, and workers. Since in his time "the only men whose work was positively useful to society were answerable to princes or to more or less inefficient retainers," society was really "a world turned upside down" (ibid., p. 340). In industry alone lay the real force in society and the source of all wealth. The future state would distribute the instruments of labor—land and capital—and manage production through a general system of banks.

The Saint-Simonians spoke of "exploiting" and "exploited" classes. They said too that "the capitalists' property right is the right to exact a premium from the work of others" (Leroy, 1974: 47, 89). Saint-Simon hoped that this antagonism would be replaced by solidarity and brotherhood. Happiness, to Saint-Simon, arose from work. "Man must work. The happiest man is he who works" (Saint-Simon, *Works*, 1966, v, 176).

Saint-Simon and, after him, Sismondi were the first to analyze the condition of the proletariat. The proletariat was the supreme agent of production, and the proletarians were the productive class. To the followers of Saint-

Simon, the proletarians were, to a great extent, serfs of their employers. The wage earner was exploited, because he had to accept his master's terms or starve. These exploited people, who camped on the edges of the cities, deserved to be incorporated within them. The Saint-Simonians dreamed of a future of great projects under the direction of engineers, who would be "the officers of the peaceful army of workers" (Bruhat, 1982: 348)—an idea later taken up by Fourier.

Just as for the economists of the eighteenth century, political economy was for Jean-Charles-Léonard Simonde de Sismondi (1773–1842) the science of "happiness" (Sismondi, 1975: 20). This term, along with "pleasure" and "felicity," recurs in his writing. But he refused to reduce happiness to wealth, wealth to production, and production to money. He sought to define a maximum of global well-being, called the "mass of happiness" (Sismondi, 1971: 21).

Sismondi's theory is characterized by the concept of proportions, which should be respected in both economic and social spheres: "in order that wealth will contribute to the happiness of all, it is necessary that its growth conform to the growth of population, that its distribution be spread proportionately . . ." (Sismondi, 1975: 21). Modern society, he wrote, lives on the backs of the downtrodden, that is, the proletariat—a class habituated to having nothing and to living from hand to mouth (ibid., p. 263). The worker, who sells his "labor power" to the capitalist, produces a "better value" that is exploited by the capitalist.

Sismondi tried to refute some of Malthus's "dangerous errors." The Earth could support a growing population by means of intensive cultivation; everything was a question of proportions (ibid., p. 23). Sismondi did not blame machines for making men redundant. On the contrary, the use of machines was favorable to population growth (ibid., pp. 24–25). And he raised the question of the optimum population in his assertion that "the true problem of the statesman is to find the combination of population and wealth which will guarantee the greatest happiness to the human species in a given space" (Sismondi, 1971: 34).

The irreconcilables: From communists to Christian socialists

Since the nineteenth century, there has been a striking similarity between the views of communists and those of some Catholics with respect to population problems. They agreed on rejection of the Malthusian position, and even though their analyses differed and their conclusions diverged, they shared demographic optimism. Catholics saw the solution to the problem of poverty in God and through solidarity and charity; communists saw the solution as lying in man and through a better distribution of wealth. They shared a faith in the development of productive forces and a respect for strict sexual morality.

Communists

The inspiration for the communists was drawn largely from the writings of Gracchus Babeuf (1760–97) in two newly issued texts, *Babeuf's Conspiracy of Equals,* by Filippo Buonarroti (Brussels, 1828) and *The Manifesto of the Equals,* by Sylvain Maréchal (1750–1803). The journalist Albert Laponneraye (1808–49), the lawyer August Richard de La Hautière (1813–82), and the former priest Jean-Jacques Pillot (1808–77) chastized the Malthusians for "errors and popular prejudices," which had to be dispelled (Devance, 1983: 276). These radicals related population to wealth: the more populous a nation, the more industrious its inhabitants. They affirmed that a worker always produced more than he consumed. Poverty arose not from overpopulation but from pernicious forms of social organization.

The desirable form of social organization was elaborated by two early communists: Etienne Cabet and Théodore Dézamy. Etienne Cabet, son of a *sans-culotte* cooper, follower of Thomas More, Fénelon, and Rousseau, influenced by Robespierre, Babeuf, and Buonarroti, was not a great theoretician but he gave voice to many characteristic utopian socialist ideas. In his picaresque novel *Voyages and Adventures of Lord William Carisdall in Icarus,* published in 1839, and republished in 1840 as *Voyage in Icarus,* Cabet described an egalitarian community founded on the following principles: "The first law: to live. The first right: to work. To each according to his needs. From each according to his abilities" (Isou, 1984: 14).

The equality of the members of the community was an "equality of abundance" (Bruhat, 1982: 392), guaranteed by the limitless productivity generated by steam engines, the instruments of happiness. The community furnished to everyone what was needed. There was no longer a proletariat, pauperism, begging, or vagrancy. The working age was set at 18 for boys, 17 for girls. Retirement was at age 65 for men and 50 for women. The work day would be progressively shortened: seven hours in the summer; six in the winter. With new machinery to replace workers, this day would become shorter still. Ultimately "man will be only a creator and director of machines" (Prudhommeaux, 1977: 625).

The community was founded on marriage and the family. Celibacy was forbidden. Everyone able to marry had to do so. Pregnant and nursing women and mothers with children in the home were exempt from work, since "to look after the family and the home is an occupation useful for the Republic" (Cabet, 1848: 103).

Improvements in public health and medicine would bring a doubling of life expectancy. Under the Icarian regime, "female fertility grows progressively, and all women are married, robust, and happy." All women deliver in maternity homes, and public assistance begins with pregnancy. Youth is not decimated by infanticide, war, or suicide. "From 25 million inhabitants in 1782, Icarus [France?] grew almost to 50 million without in-migration." Cabet, like many contemporaries, was both a pronatalist and what one would later call a eugenicist, committed to the improvement of the purity of the race and the perfection of the human species.

Influenced by Robert Owen, in 1848 Cabet led a group to the Midwestern United States to found a utopian community called Icaria. After serving as its president, he withdrew from the community in 1856 as a result of internal dissension.

The former teacher Théodore Dézamy (1808–50), Cabet's secretary, stated in his *Code of the Community* (1842) the central principles of communist society: happiness and liberty, equality and fraternity, unity and community—in short, "all the elements of happiness . . . on earth" (Bruhat, 1982: 394). Dézamy attacked the utilitarian population theorists, Bentham, Malthus, and Smith, and for good measure, Sismondi and Turgot, for trying to deny the proletariat the joys of family life. He believed that famine and poverty were due not to overpopulation but to bad government. A communitarian France would produce in one year five times what it consumed. He defended chastity and temperance, which alone would preserve health and increase pleasure, through what Freud would later call the sublimation of the libido.

Dézamy gave a detailed description of the communal city, where "absolute equality and unity" and "the organization of work" produce an "admirable harmony" (Dézamy, 1842: 37). He estimated that "the most populous cities will perhaps be an impediment to good government, to the proper execution of works," and, following Plato's views on the ideal size of the state, he set the limit of city populations at 10,000.

On a world scale, Dézamy, like Fourier, spoke of millions of men working to "cultivate, reproduce, and decorate the earth" and to transform "as if by enchantment" great works into entertainment (ibid., p. 159). Everything would become possible, from the creation of canals in Panama and Suez, to the draining of the Pontine Marshes, the reforestation of the Alps, and the cultivation of the dryest deserts, like the Sahara.

Christian socialists

The undisputed father of what we now call Left Catholicism, or Social Catholicism, is the physician Philippe Buchez (1791–1865), founder of the Co-operative Association of Producers (1832). "A prophet with a religious vision of social and cosmic progress" (F. Isambert, in Bruhat, 1982: 381), Buchez dreamed of an association of all men under God's law. As a solution to the problem of exploitation, he proposed the organization of labor in workers' associations holding social capital inalienably and indissolvably.

Buchez was convinced that growth of the means of subsistence outstripped population growth. France could feed three times its current population, and Europe's population could double, since the world contained many uninhabited regions. He foresaw the formation of peaceful armies, charged with realizing the sacred task of "peopling and cultivating" the vast territories of the Earth still starved of inhabitants. Consequently he was one of the most ardent adversaries of Malthus. But he came close to Malthus when he rejected "vices" caused by "depraved" sexual appetites. The abuse or premature recourse to the "dark force" of reproduction would lead to illegitimacy and a less healthy race. A eugenic hope appears here, joined to a solid pronatalism.

Malthusians despite themselves: The minor prophets of utopia

Several "minor prophets" of the social state—more reformist than revolutionary—were significantly influenced by Christian messianism. The nickname seems appropriate, for these writers return, with a religious mind, to the great themes of socialist ideology: the exaltation of modernity and of technical progress; the almost mystical belief in the organization of work, made possible by the consensus of interests and by fraternity; and the hope for the establishment of a communitarian city. But none of these prophets, however influential, had the breadth and the wide inspiration of the three geniuses of French socialism, Leroux, Proudhon, and Fourier.

Constantin Pecqueur: The panegyrist of material improvement

For Constantin Pecqueur (1801–87), son of an artisan, dissident Saint-Simonian, labor was the only source of wealth, since in the act of creation it made the instruments of production more productive still. Human energy was complemented, if not replaced, by the new forms of mechanical energy. Pecqueur was wont to praise "material improvements" and machines. "Without machines, man is impotent and society impossible" (Pecqueur, 1839: 1). With them, there will be millions fewer slaves and millions more free men, and the human species could multiply indefinitely (Pecqueur, 1840: 129).

Pecqueur, however, thought it impossible to deny the truth of Malthus's progressions. He tried to synthesize Malthusianism and socialism, but his effort leaned more toward the former than the latter. "Without the limitation of the means of subsistence, . . . population would always grow geometrically" (Pecqueur, 1839: 148). In fact, population growth could only be beneficial for workers if their numbers were limited. Adopting Fourier's notion of "pullulation"—the swarming, teeming of populations—Pecqueur showed that the "foresight of the wage-earning class" was absolutely necessary for wages to rise. The mass of people at the bottom of society—the workers—"teem according to the means of subsistence"; hence, more wealth means a surplus population destined for misery.

Pecqueur wrote that if the "foresight of the masses" did not prevail, then there could be no possible improvement in society, no civilization; poverty would descend on the workers. He insisted on the "ineluctible character" of this "general law of fatal order," which only the responsibility of the individual could countervail (Pecqueur, 1840: 129).

Pecqueur was not opposed to state intervention on population questions. On the one hand, to encourage fathers to moderate their reproduction, one could levy a head tax; on the other hand, to avoid punishing those with children, parents would receive, in addition to their income, a family allowance intended less to stimulate the birth rate than to compensate them for the cost of educating their children (Devance, 1983: 282). The other way to reduce population growth, according to Pecqueur, was to improve the standard of living. The rich had fewer children than the poor.

Pecqueur's optimal level of population growth was characterized by low mortality and increasing fertility. He did not fear excess population in the short term, since much land was still uninhabited (ibid.). Pecqueur hoped not only for the proportional growth of population, but also for its better distribution within France, Europe, and the world, through industrialization and the introduction of railways and canals (Pecqueur, 1839: 122–125, 152).

Louis Blanc: A Malthusian socialist?

While Victor Considérant, the faithful disciple of the Bible and of Fourier, claimed that the earthly destiny of man is the management of the globe (*Destinée sociale,* 1848), the socialist Louis Blanc (1811–82) is best known as the father of national workshops. His starting point was a lively critique of competition, which favored employers' monopolies and depressed wages. The remedy, according to Blanc, was the creation of a state bank that would supply industry by distributing credit to workers grouped in self-governing social workshops (Leroy, 1947: 140). The state, to him, became the chief director of the industrial system. The Saint-Simonian formula, "to each according to his capacity; to each capacity according to its use," was revised by Blanc thus: "to each according to his needs; from each according to his abilities" (Isou, 1984: 15). Like all early socialists, Blanc placed his project of social reform under the patronage of Christianity.

Blanc's discussion of demographic problems resembled that of Malthus. Blanc lamented the unlimited growth of population: "Is this a matter for rejoicing, in the noisy style of short-sighted economists when discussing the French case? . . . Are we not already awaiting the time when we devour each other? Let conquerors tell mothers to be fertile: they need sons to be born, since they need men to kill" (Blanc, 1841: 12–13; 103–104). The theory of human beings as "cannon fodder" can be seen here in an early form.

Blanc, however, emphasized differential fertility and mortality according to social class and income. "It is an incontestable fact that the growth of population is much more rapid in the poor class than in the rich class. . . . It is certainly true that poverty kills" (ibid., p. 35).

Leaving death aside, what remedies existed? The solution advanced by Blanc was to give the poor an income that would increase their foresight. "Would excess population be feared if each worker, assured of an income, would necessarily have adopted the ideas of order and the habits of foresight?" (ibid., p. 88). Blanc demonstrated that a growing population was not always a symptom of prosperity, contrary to what eighteenth century philosophers had thought. Better a happy than a numerous people. The wheel had come full circle, and the socialist Louis Blanc joined Malthus in proposing a stationary state, or at least an equilibrium in the population–resource duality.

The great visionaries

We come then to those who may be counted among the most original and most powerful thinkers of the eighteenth century, writers of the same rank as the visionary poet Victor Hugo and the lyrical historian Jules Michelet.

The Gospel for Leroux, Work for Proudhon, and Love for Fourier are the weapons with which they seek to change the human condition, to solve the social question, and to defeat Malthusianism, even if they end by rejoining this latter through serpentine paths. While at times naive, they incorporate the ideals of Christ, establish the intellectual foundations of Marxist criticism, and anticipate Freud's psychosexual analysis.

Pierre Leroux: The Gospel against capital

The printer Pierre Leroux (1797–1871), former Carbonaro turned Saint-Simonian, believed that humanity was destined to form an immense universal association. He called for the socialization of property and the collectivization of the instruments of labor, alongside wage determination based on ability, work, and need.

He wanted to demonstrate not only the religious origins of socialism, but also the democratic inspiration of Christianity. He emphasized the democratic forms of the early Church councils and saw in them a democratic model. The future city to him was the City of God of which Paul and Augustine wrote. In this new Eden, there would be no private property, only community; no inheritance, no marriage, no family, but a totally new order (Leroux, 1848: 95).

Within this context Leroux launched his attack on Malthus, "the sombre protestant of sad England," and against "the hideousness of Malthusian political economy" (Leroux, 1849: 77, 108). According to Leroux, what Malthusians wanted was in effect an annual massacre of the innocents (ibid., pp. 104, 115, 122, 132, 157).

In a recurrent metaphor in his work, Leroux saw in capitalism not imperialism, but rather a new feudalism; in industry, a new kind of warfare; and in capitalists, a new aristocracy of conquerors and murderers (ibid., pp. 65, 169). Capital is the abuse of property, it is usury, it is a false kind of property. And in effect all resources, all the goods of the world, are human labor or human sweat more or less condensed (ibid., pp. 47, 165, 170). Leroux arrived at an early form of the labor theory of value. The proletarians, deprived by capital of the instruments of labor, are slaves, the property of the capitalists who assert the right by law to determine wages. What Marx would call a reserve army of labor was produced by fewer than 200,000 families. But while capital's need for men was limited, the production of men, or population, was unlimited ("the great seed bed of men is always overflowing") (ibid., pp. 73, 102–103, 132, 146).

For Leroux, capital was an evil force endowed with the capacity for geometric growth (ibid., pp. 68, 82, 176). Capital, accordingly, has an insurmountable advantage over human growth: "It produces, and lives, and produces again, while its products produce again." But Leroux was fascinated with this cold monster, capital: "in itself, capital is a good, an excellent thing, because it is the means whereby humanity takes possession of space and time, the means to increase production." But on account of selfishness, it produces the worst evils (ibid., pp. 178, 195).

For Leroux, poverty was not due to overpopulation; rather the reverse, as the example of Ireland showed. Leroux argued against the view that poverty arose out of the competition of labor for scarce jobs. Surplus populations are destroyed by shortages of resources (ibid., pp. 156–157).

The principles of human reproduction and of the reproduction of capital are antagonists, and the "stronger will destroy the other." True wealth was man, human life, and wealth was made for man, and not the converse (ibid., pp. 153, 175, 222, 230–232).

Against the Malthusian image of Nature's feast, from which many superfluous laborers are excluded, Leroux set the vision of an impartial

Nature, containing nonetheless "infinite treasures." Nature gave to man a domain, that of "inexhaustible fertility." Against the Malthusian school, Leroux set the Gospel, the "true economic science," and against Malthus, Jesus Christ, who was truly "the greatest economist." Religion was truth and life, and economics, only the work of death (ibid., pp. 60, 77, 140, 174–175).

As Marx was to say at a later date, Leroux asserted that Malthus's law of population was true only under the capitalist mode of production and consumption (ibid., p. 173). The law of capital was the outcome of the faulty organization of production and consumption, which ought to be replaced by the return to unity, by communion, and—here is the key word—by association (ibid., p. 159).

Leroux offers as a natural remedy his theory of the "circulus." By his own organization, man produces his own subsistence; all he needs is his own excrement (sic) to respond to Malthus. In effect, nature has established a "circulus" between production and consumption. We create nothing; we destroy nothing; we only change things around. But in the name of what economists, "these great midwives of death," call the "circulation of wealth," men are chased out of this "circulus." To satisfy a minority of the rich, the majority is denied the right to live (ibid., pp. 216–221).

In this dangerous forest where each is busy thieving from his neighbor, many are excluded from the banquet: in France, one out of seven or eight inhabitants is a pauper, that is to say, a million poor people cannot find a place at the feast. The lumpenproletariat accumulated inequalities, risks, and social scourges. The massacre of innocents began at birth, due to a failure of mothers to breastfeed their own offspring: 75–80 percent of deprived infants died before their third birthday; and 95 percent died before they could begin to earn a living (ibid., pp. 100, 101, 109–110, 131).

Leroux refers to the poets and painters of his time, to Byron, Géricault, Delacroix, who had chosen "The Shipwreck of the Medusa" as the "emblem of Malthusian political economy," and as the symbol of the century in which they lived. "Yes, this boat where everyone dies, where one dies of despair, where man eats man, this is the ship of humanity . . . " (ibid., pp. 155–157). Leroux predicted a future apocalypse: the "deluge of evil" will grow with delinquency, failures, madness, criminality. And yet he also professed faith in the future, and his work ends with a dream: "I was yesterday on the summit of a mountain," covered in snow, glacially cold. "I feared that night would come . . . [but] the sun had triumphed" (ibid., pp. 327, 339–340).

P.-J. Proudhon and Homo Faber

Pierre-Joseph Proudhon (1809–65), the "great iconoclast" and one of the founders of the French labor movement, was the son of a domestic servant and a cooper. Like Leroux he became a printer and represented the transition between the older artisan tradition and the new proletariat. Splendidly isolated, full of paranoia and contradictions, Proudhon dominated the highest reaches of socialist thought, being perhaps the only man to argue with Marx as an equal.

Like all romantics, Proudhon was haunted by the idea of death. But he resolved this metaphysical anxiety through an economic allegory of absolute evil and sin. He identified death with the economy and Christ with society put to death by monopoly and by utopia (Proudhon, 1930: 312). Death was the great auditor (*prévôt*) of the economy, charged with reestablishing the balance between population and resources. Political economy announced the death of humanity, and economists were the purveyors of death. "To kill or to prevent birth, this is the destination of Malthus's theory, which is the penal code of political economy," the justification for murder (ibid., pp. 320, 355).

In the socioeconomic sphere, the central questions put by Proudhon were those of property and the organization of work. For Proudhon, property could be justified only when it did not incorporate the paid labor of others. Monopoly, whether labeled rent, annuity, interest, profit, or gain, is the source of "windfall rights," deducted from workers' pay (Bruhat, 1982: 389). Once exposed for what it is, "Property is vanquished; it will never rise again." This rhetoric notwithstanding, Proudhon, like the majority of the socialists of his time, did not want a total suppression of property, just its abuses, and he accorded to property a socially beneficial and determinant role.

Following Saint-Simon, Proudhon made work the basic attribute of man, the creator and poet. Factories would disappear with the rise of workshops: "the workshop would displace the government" was his slogan and that of the workers' tradition. Associations would be set up on the workshop level, just as the federations of sovereign states would be set up on the political level. In his *Organization of Credit and Circulation* (1848a), Proudhon developed the notion of a people's bank, able to provide capital and to organize direct exchanges between producers and consumers. He dreamed of a confederation of autonomous communes established by associations of small producers.

Proudhon's point of departure on the subject of population was poverty, which occurs when the number of mouths to feed exceeds the available resources (Proudhon, 1923: 322, 332). Change the faulty organization of work, which is the basis of wealth and fertility, and an equilibrium could be established between population and the means of subsistence, without recourse to human "prudence," that is, without Malthusian moral restraint (ibid., pp. 322, 332).

Population increase is the inevitable consequence of an increase in the means of subsistence. Production and population are both cause and effect, and riches and mankind can grow together. Proudhon observed that in France, over 50 years, national wealth multiplied fivefold and consumption grew likewise, while the population only doubled (ibid., pp. 326, 334). How, then, to explain the growth of poverty? If the means of subsistence, produced in sufficient quantities, are unavailable to the people, then the fault must lie in political economy.

In order to better destroy them, Proudhon addressed Malthus's ideas with impressive objectivity. This adversary of *l'homme de trop sur la terre* lavished praise on the descriptive part of Malthus's theory, even though he disputed both the interpretation and the remedies Malthus proposed. Malthus's work, "resting on a mass of authentic documentation" (ibid., p. 317), proved that population would double in 18 or 25 years, if no external obstacle stood in the way. "In the end, we do not have to dispute Malthus's theory, since it is something great and elevated, which is superior to everything previously proposed." It was hardly possible to oppose a law that was "irreproachably certain" (ibid., pp. 319, 324, 348, 360).

Having praised Malthus for his greatness and his "sincerity," Proudhon did not hesitate, however, to underline the "Malthusian foolishness" as displayed in the arithmetic progression of the means of subsistence (ibid., p. 342). Malthus simply ignored the fact that in an organized society, the production of wealth would grow more rapidly than population.

In his letter of 10 August 1848 on the Malthusians, Proudhon stepped up his attack. Malthus's theory was one of "political murder, murder by philanthropy, by love of God." The economists had elevated to a providential dogma its "inconceivable blasphemy." At the banquet of Nature, there was not enough room for everyone. Work was a privilege: "in the nation's workshop, there is not a place for everyone." Those who possessed neither savings nor property, and whose labor is not needed, must depart! "You are too numerous on the land, under the sun of the Republic, there is not room for everyone." "Who will tell me that the right to work and to live is not the essence of the Revolution?" "Who will tell me that Malthus's principle is not the counter-revolution?"

Proudhon attacked the Malthusians' advocacy of moral restraint as the sole remedy for the problem of population. "Prudence in love," the deferment of marriage until ages 30–40, this "famine of the heart" set against the famine of the stomach, "this is what Malthus, in his heart of hearts, imagines the most useful, philosophical and moral means of restraining population and its excesses" (ibid., pp. 346–347).

Restraint is an accusation against Providence, an act of distrust of Nature. By logical extension of Malthus's theory, marriage would be reserved for overaged ladies and too-old satyrs. It would lead to useless unions and sterile sex. "The family snuffed out and with it goes property; thus society returns to barbarism." All this for the prevention of poverty (ibid., pp. 348, 350).

Against the Malthusian solution, Proudhon erected an alternative based on liberation through work. He spoke lyrically of the sacred character of work, the outpouring of the human spirit. According to Proudhon, free labor (*travail libre*) would be made attractive by science: each worker would be enthusiastic about work, which would give him a role in the totality of industrial development (ibid., pp. 360, 361).

Proudhon predicted that "without doubt the day will come . . . [when] the population, without [prudential?] restraint and without poverty, will spontaneously cease its upward trajectory" (ibid., p. 335). Population and resources will be balanced through the unceasing growth and intensification of work, brought about, in turn, by the increase in the number of workers and by industrial progress. Proudhon's position rests centrally on this premise of the growth—or, more correctly, the intensification—of work (ibid., p. 363). Given the proper division of labor, mechanization, commerce, credit, and the whole economic infrastructure, the Earth offers infinite resources. Production must quadruple, precisely the square of the growth of the workers' number; thus Malthus's law would be reduced to an absurdity, a theory turned upside down (ibid., pp. 330–331).

Proudhon asserted a natural antagonism between work and love: "the industrial faculty thrives at the expense of the faculty of proliferation." Work is a cause of frigidity and the most powerful of all anti-aphrodisiacs. Chastity is the companion of labor (ibid., pp. 371, 372).

In the long term, this frigidity would have some effect on population growth, not through restraint, but through reason and freedom. Love, in effect, "is the one great, serious, perhaps unique business of mankind." But, for Proudhon, true love—affective and not physical—begins with marriage, and is crowned with procreation. Marital desire, reproduction, and nurturing are phases in human life. Man has the "sovereign woman," successively, as mother, sister, mistress, wife, and daughter. Proudhon was entirely puritanical in condemning the incestuous habits of "concubinage" or simple fornication, that is free or casual unions, which are the worst profanities against women (ibid., pp. 376, 377, 380). Nor should the husband make his wife a "sex machine" (*machine à jouissance*) (ibid., p. 381). Chastity was a crucial duty for married couples, leaving them in time to contemplate each other as pure spirits!

Proudhon believed in marital abstinence, a remedy more Malthusian than the Malthusian, and one that Malthus himself did not recognize. After all his attacks on moral restraint, Proudhon wound up advocating postponement of marriage, celibacy, and virginity in a quasi-religious spirit. Christianity was prophetic in its elevation of virginity.

With a rise in the age of marriage to 28 years for men and 21 for women, and a prolongation of breastfeeding from 15 to 18 months, according to Proudhon, the period of fertility would be reduced to 10 or 15 years, and the number of children would not exceed five. Deducting from this number the shortfall or loss due to sterility and widowhood (1.5 children), death before menarche (2.5 children), and celibacy (0.5 children) would leave only

0.5 children per women to reach the age of procreation. Population would rise by only a tenth every 30 years, and double only after three centuries (ibid., pp. 384–385). Alfred Sauvy (1959) clearly demonstrated the absurdity of this calculation in an article in *Population*.

Proudhon was a true believer in the family—the heart of society and the economy, essential to property, the fundamental element of order, the purpose of which was procreation (Proudhon, 1923: 384–385). Without the family, neither society nor work could exist.

In his *On Justice in the Revolution and in the Church* (1858) and in *Pornocracy* (1875), Proudhon advanced a reactionary view of women. Woman is inferior to man in part because she does not produce the germs of beings or of ideas. Raised from her "bestial state" by man, who serves as her prophet and inspiration, she dedicates herself to her home and her children, who are "gifts of God." More than companion, she becomes the administrator of her husband's work.

Charles Fourier: "Standing among the great visionaries"

Charles Fourier (1772–1837) was in many respects the most original and the most idiosyncratic of all utopian socialists. He shared many of the assumptions of the other thinkers we have discussed, but pushed them into new realms. He shared Proudhon's worship of work, but rejected his patriarchal notions of women and the family.

Fourier's system rests on the theory of Attraction and Universal Harmony, a theory inspired by Newton and applied in the social world. Passionate attraction was "a God-given magic wand," which guides men to act according to their own interest and that of society. The true association was, in his terms, the art of applying to industry all the passions. Just as Kepler described heavenly motion as a divine concert, Fourier saw all passions as "elements in an immense orchestra." Fourier was profoundly theistic, even pantheistic. He saw God working throughout creation. Infinitely wise and provident, God, the "supreme economist," applied his social laws to the whole universe.

According to Fourier, history was divided into different epochs: Eden (the period of monopoly); savagery (the period of individual competition); patriarchy (the period of petty production); barbarism (*moyenne production*); civilization (large-scale industry); "guarantism" (semi-association); "sociantism" (simple association); and Harmony (complex association) (Fourier, 1967: 371; 1973: 111).

The earliest period—paradise—was characterized by free love, scarcity of population, and abundance of animal herds (1967: 104). Monetary wealth was nonexistent. The average man was six feet two and two-thirds inches tall, and lived to 128 years of age. Over time, "excessive reproduction of population" led to poverty, which led to marriage and to division into small family households, which Fourier called "morselization." The golden age had been lost because of population growth. In the future, however, the unity of the Earth would be restored by means of industrial "Attraction" and population equilibrium (ibid., p. 384).

For Fourier, the present, so-called civilized system was one in which deception and "repulsive industry" reigned, "the world turned upside down" (*le monde à rebours*), while the future "societarian" state, based on truth and attractive industry, would be the "world the right way up" (*le monde à droit sens*) (Fourier, 1973: 38, 49–50, 219; 1967: 199).

Fourier identified love as the essential element of existence, the axis of society. Its aim was not merely procreation: it was spiritual as well as material (1973: 251–252). The seed of evil, the state most distant from God, was the family group, the most restricted and the least free of all groups, imprisoned by the exclusive marital bond. This kind of human group was against God's will, which was to form the largest "societarian" combinations and to establish the greatest possible freedom.

In stark contrast to Proudhon, therefore, Fourier denounced marriage and the traditional family and championed unrestricted free love. He advocated a progressive system of households, with marriage coming late in life, solely to comfort the elderly (ibid., p. 275). "What could be more useless," he asked rhetorically, "than perpetual virginity?" (ibid, p. 280).

To Fourier, group love, or orgy, played a fundamental role in "societarian" happiness. It was an erotic and a social ceremony. Men and women could give themselves to others at the same time as they would be committed to each other. Their love might be compared to a divine banquet.

One of the most striking features of Fourier's writing was the high standing he accorded women, in contrast to the mores of his time and the prejudice of many other utopians like Proudhon. "As a general thesis, social progress and periodic change occur due to the progress of female liberation, and the decay of the social order occurs due to the retreat of female liberation" (Barathon, 1980: 24). It was time, he argued, to make room for women in the world of men. Fourier relied on education to emancipate women, and even contemplated quotas in professional recruitment. In the future association, women would rapidly adopt the role designed for them in nature, which was that of rival to men. In their liberated state, women would, Fourier prophesied, surpass men in all functions other than those requiring physical strength (Fourier, 1967: 147, 155; 1973: 186).

Fourier gave an important place in Harmonian society to another oppressed minority—children. In "societarian phalanges," Fourier foresaw a communal method of education, analogous to that of the Israeli kibbutzim. The phalange would support the very old and the very young, nourish the elderly and the infirm, and take care of children until the age of three. Children would be looked after by nurses, or communal mothers, freeing their natural mothers to conduct amorous affairs.

In Harmony, the education of children would follow the first aim of nature, or Attraction—that is to say, the pursuit of luxury. The child would become accustomed by age four to earn his keep, to appreciate good food, and to be trained for work. In the "societarian" order, the father's sole function would be to spoil his children. As for the elderly, the societarian regime would support them and permit them to enjoy free love just as did the younger members of the community (Fourier, 1973: 240, 318).

Like Proudhon and Louis Blanc, Fourier proclaimed the quasi-sacred character of work. His great design was to transform labor into a universal pleasure as attractive as a banquet or a festival. Each would work according to his passions. The most difficult work would be the best paid (Fourier, 1967: 55; 1973: 46).

Like the economies envisioned by other socialists, Fourier's was one of opulence and abundance. But for Fourier, the future economy would rest not only on an abundance of the means of subsistence, but also on money and luxury. On this subject Fourier shared none of the contempt mixed with fascination expressed by other, more puritanical socialists. He praised the new science of political and commercial economy, born in the seventeenth century, which had dared to attack the dogma of Rousseau and Mably that poverty was an admirable state. The poor must enjoy graduated welfare, so that the rich can enjoy happiness (Fourier, 1967: 178–179; 1973: 330).

For Fourier, agriculture was the fundamental sector of the economy. Industry was the second, a complement to the first. The "societarian" worker would devote only one quarter of his working time to manufacture (Fourier, 1973: 197). Industrialization, the most recent and most widely recognized scientific illusion, and commerce, were the real enemies to be defeated (Isou, 1984: 39). All of society followed the lead of the science of "economism," or the worship of commerce, just the way birds are fascinated by a snake (Fourier, 1973: 451). All money was sunk into commerce, a vampire that sucks the blood of the industrial body. This led Fourier to advocate a general monopoly as a safeguard against commerce in the civilized world (Fourier, 1973: 454–455; Leroy, 1947: 96).

The population problem, or, more precisely, the problem of population equilibrium, preoccupied Fourier. He estimated the maximum population of the world under current circumstances as either a "small maximum" (*petit complet*) of 2 billion or a "large maximum" (*grand complet*) of 3 billion; but the optimal number, under his new order, could reach 5 to 5.5 billion (Fourier, 1973: 390). Were the whole world to adopt his regime of universal peace and general abundance, that is, the "societarian state," the population might reach 6 or even 12 billion. To avoid this overpopulation, the new order should provide the most efficient means of maintaining the population at about 5 billion. This figure was Fourier's optimal population total. At this level, the aim would be to assure the happiness of the existing population and not to increase it (ibid., pp. 197, 390).

In a characteristically Malthusian manner, Fourier condemned the high birth rate prevalent among the working class, which lowered salaries and increased competition. The sensible man wanted only a few children, thereby ensuring the prosperity necessary for their happiness (Fourier, 1967: 393; 1973: 198).

The "societarian phalanges" would not produce as many children as were born in "civilization." Nature in the societarian state would set four obstacles to excess population: the physical vigor of women; the "gastrosophic" diet, or refined eating habits; the "phanerogamic" customs, or free love and multiplicity of lovers; and "integral [physical] exercise," or gymnastics. This final obstacle would reduce fertility to such an extent that a Harmonian woman would need to undergo a three-month period of calm and special diet to prepare for childbearing. Instead of surplus population, a deficit might occur, and measures might be needed "to stimulate the fertility that every prudent man fears today." In the future, when the whole world would adopt a unitary government, no barriers would remain to prevent people from swarming all over the globe (Fourier, 1973: 275, 374–375, 391–392; 1967: 163, 179).

Fourier foresaw a kind of green revolution, through the better selection of seeds, irrigation, and so on, that would double or triple the production of cereals. Fruit and cattle output could quintuple. In the future, superabundance would be a periodic scourge, as scarcity was then (Fourier, 1967: 163–164; 1973: 37–44).

The domestic and agricultural association—the phalange—would materialize on the local level in the form of the phalanstère, a settlement dedicated to work, leisure, and residence. Each phalange would contain 300 households, of about 1,500 to 1,600 people. Owing to economies of scale, productivity would rise without impinging on the environment. For example, the need for 300 kitchens and 300 households would be reduced to four or five large dwellings (Fourier, 1973: 41–43).

In the societarian regime, no work session would exceed one and a half or two hours. Profits would be distributed according to the three forms of an individual's contribution to industry: capital, work, and talent. To each according to his abilities and the time he dedicates to work (Fourier, 1973: 213, 284; Barathon, 1980: 71; Leroy, 1947: 98).

Fourier opposed equality. If a scale of inequality did not exist, he said, one would have to invent it (Fourier, 1973: 42). Hierarchies would be maintained in the phalange, where rich and poor would live together. Fourier hoped the poor would receive a share of profits and a minimum income. He believed in class collaboration and did not support the uprising of the proletariat. The "future revolution," in his view, would consist of the creation of a phalanstère, either by government or by a private sponsor.

One of the central functions of association would be to furnish an abundant, refined, and varied diet, which would be prepared and served collectively. For Fourier, the principal pleasures were love and food. In Harmony, gastronomy would evolve into "gastrosophy," or high gastronomical wisdom (ibid., pp. 162, 438).

Harmonian society would maintain immense industrial armies, which, instead of destroying each other, would accomplish prodigious tasks. "The sole pressure of love will gather 120 million legionnaires of both sexes, who will carry out public works whose very idea would freeze with fear our mercenary spirits" (ibid., p. 171). They would cultivate the Sahara desert, build the Panama and Suez canals, and otherwise extend the habitable parts of the world. Fourier described enthusiastically and naively the ardor for work that would seize a progressive sect in its tasks (anticipating accounts of the exploits of Chinese production brigades during the Great Leap Forward). But in describing this epic conquest of nature, Fourier never lost sight of his ecological concerns. He spoke ceaselessly about the restoration of the climate, reforestation, irrigation, and draining of marshes, always from the viewpoint of protecting Nature (Fourier, 1967: 164–165; 1973: 450).

The utopian character of Fourier's approach is fully expressed in his notion of a limited experiment that could be generalized to the whole Earth through a universal association. In his mind the change from the "world turned upside down" to the "world turned right side up" would happen almost overnight, without the least obstacle. "A small experiment on 700 people would be abruptly decisive for the general transformation to follow" (Fourier, 1973: 43, 394).

A new Atlantis: The socialist utopia

Despite the diversity and internal contradictions of utopian socialism, many unifying features bind these thinkers' work together. Most French socialists shared similar social origins, romantic temperaments, an obsession with death (to be overcome by an exaltation of life, work, and love), and often a puritanical attitude toward sexuality. Many of them were marked by pathological phobias, a rich paranoia, and an indignant rejection of the title "utopian."

They shared, too, a socialist agenda, which rested on some common economic grounds. They emphasized the sad facts of proletarian poverty, which they studied from sociological and medical surveys, and which, they agreed, arose out of a pernicious economic system. The early socialists looked to the state to become the future director of industry, organizer of production, and main distributor of credit. They agreed that work was an intrinsic attribute of man; the only problem was how to organize it and make it attractive. Property, capital, and competition were symbols of economic evil, but under a different economic system they could be potentially positive forces. Most socialists were fanatic champions of technological progress, machines, and inventions and looked forward to the mastery (but not the despoiling) of the environment.

They were pioneers in the analysis of class struggle, but their emphasis on fraternity and universal solidarity led most to reject violence as a means for the proletariat to seize power. Some were pioneers, too, in their commitment to the emancipation of women and children and to the protection of the rights of the aged and infirm. The socialists fought for the spread of education and the improvement of the race, and some of their writings were tainted by eugenics, as well as occasional "left anti-Semitism," especially as in the works of Fourier and Leroux.

They parted ways, however, with respect to their attitudes toward sexuality. Some, like Proudhon, treated the subject with puritanical repression and hidden (or not so hidden) fears; others, like Fourier, campaigned for a totally liberated eroticism.

Socialists, population, and Malthus

We have seen that it is impossible to isolate the demographic views of the early socialists from the totality of their social and political thought. Only when we take their ideas as a whole can we understand how and why the population problem was addressed by French socialists between the time of Godwin and Marx.

Their demographic notions arose out of their religious approach to Creation and the universe. The proliferation of mankind was the means whereby God's plan unfolded in the world. Following the Old Testament prophets, utopian socialists believed that multiplication was a sign of Divine benediction, just as nonreligious sociologists in the nineteenth century saw in population growth the most clearcut sign of the progress of civilization. Utopian socialists gave credit to God; sociologists, like Comte and later Durkheim, secularized the process.

The discussion of population was more central to the socialists' work than it was to that of Marx. Marx's key arguments concern the structure and internal contradictions of capitalism. He, too, was a moralist and had a deep acquaintance with religious traditions of thought, but his aim was to arrive at a philosophical and economic synthesis in which the demographic element was but a minor part. In contrast, the religious and moral purpose of the utopian socialists' agenda required them to place population questions at center stage.

Of course, there were substantial variations among utopian socialists: Proudhon had greater affinities with Marx than did Fourier, and Saint-Simon (in contrast to his disciple Comte and his later descendant Durkheim) did not have a particular interest in population questions. Some anticipated Marx's economic analysis; others adopted Malthusian conclusions. In short, we must at all costs avoid considering utopian socialists as a monolithic bloc. On the whole, however, there was more that united their reflections on population (among other matters) than divided them.

Against Malthus and the Malthusians

The influence of Malthus was particularly strong in France in the first half of the nineteenth century, and even orthodox socialists were drawn to the debate surrounding his ideas. We can distinguish between those who accepted and those who rejected his views. Some recognized the validity of his geometric and arithmetic progressions, and feared proletarian "pullulation." They advocated prudence and morality, which they themselves, along with the higher stratum of the working class, certainly adopted. Some even followed Malthus's critique of the Poor Laws, which they saw as contributing to idleness and high fertility.

Others offered two kinds of criticism of Malthus's ideas. The first emphasized the need to liberate the worker from exploitation in order to provide him with the means to support his family (Perrot, 1983: 259). The second violently objected to Malthus's notion of moral restraint as unnatural and immoral, an act of contempt for God and Nature. Nonetheless, some (like Proudhon) subscribed to Malthus's notion of moral restraint, under another name, in their support for late marriage and chastity, or (like Fourier) in their advocacy of fertility control through free love, refined eating habits, and physical exercise.

While they accepted Malthus's progressions, they rejected his causal analysis of poverty and the remedies he proposed. Poverty was not caused by population outstripping resources; nor was it simply inevitable. It was historically grounded in a pernicious form of contemporary social organization, characterized by private property, capital, and competition. Nor was poverty caused by overpopulation per se; on the contrary, overpopulation was caused by poverty and the inability of the working class to exercise a minimum of foresight. Fertility and poverty followed the same path, grew together, and would fall together.

Abstinence and restraint were not solutions to the population problem. They were only palliatives and could even be dangerous for the future of society. The true remedy lay in the total reform of the social and economic system, in the socialization of property, in the intervention of the state, in the organization of credit and work. Finally, the remedy was to be found in the growth of productive forces, notably through the use of machines, which would permit the quadrupling of production and at the least a doubling of the population. A general improvement in the standard of living would provide working people with a minimum guaranteed income, which would enable them to maintain their standard of living by restricting their fertility. Education would also disseminate the ideas of morality and foresight among the masses and would provide the human capital necessary for the new technological society.

Some utopians advocated contraception and expressed in embryonic form the outlines of a population policy. They thought both in terms of family allowances, which had social as well as demographic justifications, and in terms of a graduated taxation system, which would discourage people from having large families.

Far from believing in or advocating unlimited population growth, most utopian socialists recognized that there were physical limits to growth, and that a voluntary check to fertility could reverse the growth trend. Indeed, they foresaw a time when men would have to be compelled to *increase* their fertility. If there were a risk of overpopulation, it was in the remote future. For the present, with the measures they advocated, the likely outcome was a stationary state.

Utopian socialists: Forecasters of our time

Early socialists played a role both in the revolutionary struggles of their time and in the evolution of socialist thought. Marx and Engels recognized how deeply indebted "scientific" socialism was to the utopian tradition. Virtually all of Marx's ideas were prefigured in utopian socialist writing. We see the notion of contradiction and economic antinomies, as in Proudhon; the concept of labor power, as in Sismondi; the idea that industrial concentration was the necessary path from private to social property, as in Pecqueur; the terms feudalism and baronage of manufacture, as in Fourier and Villermé; the concepts of industrial revolution, the mass reserve army of labor, and the floating population, as in Buret; the proletariat, as in Saint-Simon and Sismondi; and the notion that the law is the expression of the interests of the dominant class, as in Lamennais. Marx's genius was to synthesize these ideas in a more powerful if not entirely original contribution.

These visionaries were prophets with a messianic zeal. They went well beyond the crisis of 1848 and announced a future world, in terms considered nonsense at the time, but which now look less irrational. They were the heralds of technological progress. Malthus did not foresee the huge increase in the means of subsistence permitted by this progress, while socialists fervently believed that machines would increase production and relieve human labor. Automation and robotization would not have surprised them, though they did not foresee artificial intelligence. They anticipated the reduction in the working day, the establishment of a retirement age, the provision of family allowances, and a quota system to recruit women to responsible positions.

Fourier spoke of workers' cooperatives. Proudhon speculated on decentralization and federalism. Louis Blanc anticipated workers' control (*autogestion*). On the level of customs and mores, some foresaw women's liberation and sexual freedom, as well as advocating the rights of children and the elderly. The uprisings of May 1968 in France and elsewhere echoed many of the ideas announced more than a century before by utopian socialists.

Certainly their writings contain elements of naivety bordering on the ridiculous. The utopians were the "primitive painters" of socialist ideas. Consider the notion of the natural "circulus" developed by Leroux, the footbath in Icarus related by Cabet, or the conception of future happiness, like a swing suspended in midair, described by Fourier. Engels looked at the French socialists as men of fantasy, but he admitted that their ideas, while strangely expressed, were those of genius (Engels and Marx, 1977: 95).

To understand their writings, we must set them in their own time. The socialist agenda emerged with the proletariat and the workers' movement, but it was born of the French Revolution. The idea of human equality, so important to nineteenth century workers' movements, was developed by the Enlightenment and the disciples of Babeuf, who deduced from it the idea of the suppression of private property. This preindustrial paternity helps account for the at times archaic and backward-looking character of some of French utopian socialist thought.

In addition, the religious imagery and language used by the socialists were undeniably traditional. They looked back in order to describe the future. Consequently, utopian socialists did not create a socioeconomic system of thought as strong as Marx's, but there was more in their ideas than simply anticipations of Marx, whose shadow has prevented until now a full appreciation of their contribution. Toward the end of the twentieth century, the vanished continent of utopian socialism has been glimpsed again. The pre-Marxian French thinkers might be viewed as "master dreamers" (*Maîtres rêveurs*), but they were in fact more modernist than utopian, and perhaps it is time to consider their projects and criticisms in the light of the world we have gained.

References

Barathon, Claude. 1980. *Les Folles idées de Fourier.* Chambray: C.L.D.

Blanc, Louis. 1841. *Organisation du travail. Association universelle. Ouvriers. Chefs d'ateliers. Hommes de lettres.* Paris: Administration de librairie.

Breton, André. 1945. *Ode à Fourier.* L'Archibras.

Bruhat, Jean. 1982. "Le socialisme français de 1815 à 1848," in *Histoire générale du socialisme,* Vol. 1., ed. J. Droz. Paris: P.U.F.

Buonarroti, Filippo (Philippe). 1957 (originally published 1828). *Conspiration pour l'égalité, dite de Babeuf.* Paris: Editions sociales.

Cabet, Etienne. 1840 (originally published 1839). *Voyage et aventures de Lord William Carisdall en Icarie.* Paris: H. Souverain.

———. 1848. *Voyage en Icarie,* 5th ed. Paris: au Bureau du "Populaire."

Considérant, Victor. 1848. *Destinée sociale.* Paris: Librairie phalanstèrienne.

Devance, Louis. 1983. "Malthus and socialist thought in France before 1870," in *Malthus Past and Present,* ed. J. Dupâquier, A. Fauve-Chamoux, and E. Grebenik. London: Academic Press.

Dézamy, Théodore. 1842. *Code de la communauté.* Paris: Prevost et Rouannet.

Engels, Friedrich, and Karl Marx. 1977 (originally published 1880). *Socialisme utopique et socialisme scientifique.* Paris: Editions sociales.

Fourier, Charles. 1967 (originally published 1808). *Théorie des quatre mouvements et des destinées générales.* Paris: J.-J. Pauvert.

———. 1973 (originally published 1829–30). *Le Nouveau Monde industriel et sociétaire ou Invention du procédé d'industrie attrayante et naturelle distribuée en séries passionnées.* Paris: Flammarion.

Isou, Isidore. 1984. *Histoire du socialisme. Du socialisme primitif au socialisme des créateurs.* Paris: Scarabée et Co.

Leroux, Pierre. 1848. *Du Christianisme et de son origine démocratique.* Boussac: Impr. de Pierre Leroux.

———. 1897 (originally published 1849). *Malthus et les économistes ou Y aura-t-il toujours des pauvres?* Paris: Librairie de la Bibliothéque Nationale.

Leroy, Maxime. 1947. *Le Socialisme.* Paris: Les Cours de Droit.

Marechal, Sylvain. 1828. *Manifeste des Egaux,* in Buonarroti, 1957.

Pecqueur, Constantin. 1839. *Economie sociale. Des Intérêts du commerce, de l'industrie, de l'agriculture et de la civilisation en général, sous l'influence des applications de la vapeur. Machines fixes. Chemins de fer. Bateaux à vapeur.* Paris: Desessart.

———. 1840. *Des Améliorations matérielles dans leurs rapports avec la liberté. Introduction à l'étude de l'économie sociale et politique.* Paris: Librairie de Charles Gosselin.

Perrot, Michelle. 1983. "Malthusianism and socialism," in *Malthus Past and Present,* ed. J. Dupâquier, A. Fauve-Chamoux, and E. Grebenik. London: Academic Press.

Proudhon, Pierre-Joseph. 1848. *Les Malthusiens.* Paris.

———. 1848a. *Organisation du crédit et de la circulation.* Paris: Pilhes.

———. 1875. *La Pornocratie ou les Femmes dans les temps modernes.* Paris: A Lacroix.

———. 1923 (originally published 1846). "Système des contradictions économiques ou Philosophie de la Misère," in *Oeuvres complètes de P.-J. Proudhon.* Paris: Librairie de Sciences Politiques et Sociales.

———. 1930 (originally published 1858). "De la Justice dans la Révolution et dans l'Eglise," in *Oeuvres complètes de P.-J. Proudhon.* Paris: Librairie de Sciences Politiques et Sociales.

Prudhommeaux, Jules. 1977 (originally published 1907). *Icarie et son Fondateur Etienne Cabet: Contribution* à l'étude du Socialisme expérimental. Geneva: Statkine.

Saint-Simon, Claude-Henri, comte de. 1966. *Oeuvres de Claude-Henri de Saint-Simon.* Paris: Editions Anthropos.

Sauvy, Alfred. 1959. "A propos d'un calcul démographique de Proudhon," *Population* 13, no. 2: 356–358.

Sismondi, Jean-Charles-Léonard Simonde de. 1971 (originally published 1819). *Nouveaux principes d'économique politique ou De la Richesse dans ses rapports avec la population.* Paris: Calmann-Lévy.

———. 1975 (originally published 1827). *Nouveaux principes d'économie politique. Les trois livres du Second tome. Du Numéraire, de l'impôt, de la population.* Paris: ISMEA.

POPULATION AND IDEOLOGY IN MODERN TIMES

Marxism and the Population Question: Theory and Practice

William Petersen

No review of the debates on population questions during the past several centuries can pass over the various Marxist positions. In spite of the manifest uninterest in the matter of both Marx and most early Marxists, there is a steady flow of exegesis and explication. In 1984, for instance, Parviz Khalatbari, an Iranian-born East German demographer, published a journal paper in German, "The significance of the historical perspective for the development of the Marxist-Leninist theory of population"; in 1985 there appeared a short book in Portuguese by a Brazilian demographer, Francisco de Oliveira, titled *Malthus and Marx: False Enchantment and Radical Difficulty.* Whether of past or more recent vintage, such works are generally embedded in a persistent opposition to the postulates of standard political economy, and their typically polemical tone does not help interpretation.

In this essay I review how major Marxists viewed population both in itself and in relation to economic growth. The essay is largely a recapitulation of fragments or, worse, of silences. In the usually tangential treatment first by Marx and Engels and then by their immediate followers among representatives of the Socialist (or Second) International, population was pictured less as a significant component of the historical process than as an epiphenomenon. This convention was followed, moreover, in the statements of early Soviet leaders on population theory and in their first efforts to apply those formulations; in the Soviet Union demography long remained at the margin of both social analysis and social policy. When today's Marxists try to use past theses as a foundation for their analyses of a related subject, they are seriously hampered by the long indifference to demography in all its aspects.

In a brief essay it will be necessary to omit some relevant matters. During the past decade or so, a few writers who call themselves Marxists have combined their interpretation of the doctrine with standard demographic theories, but to follow them would take us too far afield. Similarly, no mention is made of less developed countries or particularly of China, where the early pronatalism and the subsequent complete reversal of policy were both rationalized with Marxist principles. Even so, it is hoped that this review of the underlying theses of Marx and his most important disciples can form a useful base for elucidating such more peripheral themes.

First formulations on population

The Condition of the Working Class in England (1845), which Engels wrote at the age of 24, can be usefully contrasted with the treatment of population in later Marxist writings. The advent of the machine, Engels wrote, brought unemployment, as well as "want, wretchedness, and crime." Industrial areas witnessed a "gigantic expansion" of population for the reasons specified in the principle of population; Malthus's theory had "a good deal of truth in it under existing circumstances." "The whole of the economy was affected by this expansion" of population. An industrial worker normally received a higher wage than an unskilled or irregular laborer, but in spite of his better pay he was "both legally and in fact a slave of the middle-class capitalists," bought and sold not like slaves of prior eras but "piecemeal by the day, the week, or the year" (in *Das Kapital* of Marx this would become the dictum that the worker is forced to sell his "labor power"). With manufacturers fiercely competing for growing but still limited markets, there was a trade cycle of some five to six years, with each recession deeper than the preceding one. The population surge needed at the height of each boom resulted in unemployment at all other times. "The number of those who are starving increases," and some of those in the "surplus population" may not survive. The "surplus population," usually written between quotation marks, became in *Capital* the "relative surplus population"; the intent of both phrases was to emphasize the allegation that it was only the productive system, not nature, that rendered people surplus (Engels, 1958: 92–191; see also Sherwood, 1985).

In *The German Ideology* (1845–46), Marx and Engels represented population growth as a contributory factor to the basic determinant of historical change in the nature of the productive system.

> [Men] begin to distinguish themselves from animals as soon as they begin to *produce* their means of subsistence, . . . [by which they are] indirectly producing their actual material life. . . . This production only makes its appearance with the *increase of population.* In its turn this presupposes the interaction of individuals with one another. The form of this interaction is again determined by production. (Marx and Engels, 1970: 42–43; emphasis in original)

The last important element in the Marxist theory of population was a "history" of human progress from its beginnings. Working from notes that Marx had left when he died, Engels wrote *The Origin of the Family, Private*

Property, and the State (1884), which in some respects was a notable throwback to the early socialists' fascination with communitarian life (see Feuer, 1966). It was based largely on the work of the American anthropologist Lewis Henry Morgan (1818–81), whose account of primitives' sexual promiscuity and group marriage few prehistorians take seriously today. Engels held that Morgan's theory had "the same importance for anthropology as Darwin's theory of evolution for biology and Marx's theory of surplus value for political economy." A marital type was linked with each of the three main stages in the Marxist schema of history: savagery, group marriage; barbarism, "paired marriage"; and civilization, monogamy supplemented by adultery and prostitution (Engels, 1942).[1]

Population in Marx

According to Marxist economic theory, competition under capitalism drives all entrepreneurs to increase their efficiency to the utmost by installing more and more machinery. "Accumulate, accumulate! This is the Moses and the prophets!" (*Capital,* p. 652). The growing stock of capital goods that results gradually displaces some of the workers who were employed at the earlier, less efficient technological level. "The laboring population therefore produces, along with the accumulation of capital produced by it, the means by which [it] itself is made relatively superfluous, is turned into a relative surplus population; and it does this to an always increasing extent" (ibid., p. 692). Moreover, the composition of the employed force steadily deteriorates; the capitalist "progressively replaces skilled laborers by less skilled, mature labor power by immature, male by female, that of adults by that of younger persons or children" (ibid., p. 697). In the long term no amelioration was possible under capitalism, which depended on this "industrial reserve army" of technologically unemployed: if they were to remain in business, employers had to respond to the state of the market and could not afford to adjust their production also to the supply of laborers (see also Hollander, 1984).

This line of reasoning, a generalization from David Ricardo's statement that mechanization *may* lead to unemployment, can hardly be regarded as a successful prophecy. The effects of technological advance on the size and composition of the work force are considerably more complex than this representation, and the general consequences of the greater efficiency were, in fact, a higher level of living, a shorter work week, and the development of tertiary services. In presently less developed countries, where the surplus agrarian population (what Marx termed the latent industrial reserve army) is often large, the consequent very low wage is ordinarily not the stimulus to capital accumulation that Marx considered it to be but a serious impediment to it.

Even if Marx's main point is granted—that with increasing mechanization there is a long-term trend toward an ever larger number of unemployed—it still does not follow that this trend operates "independently of the limits of the actual increase of population" (*Capital,* p. 693). Given the state of the market, the proportion of the work force able to find employment depends in considerable part on the number of new workers seeking jobs; indeed, in another context Marx noted that "the demand for laborers may exceed the supply and, therefore, wages may rise" (ibid., p. 672). The forecasts of demographers in the 1930s that Western populations would soon decline were proved wrong by the post–World War II baby boom, but in the 1980s downward population projections have again aroused similar concerns. If the number of people were to decline at the same rate as machines displaced workers (taking Marx's theory as valid), then there would be no "industrial reserve army," no "immiseration," no Marxist model at all. He built his system on the unstated and unexamined postulate that the rapid population growth in nineteenth century Europe would continue indefinitely, and the dependence of his model on an increase in numbers exists no matter what the rate of growth.

Marx versus Malthus

According to T. R. Malthus's principle of population, the natural force of sexual attraction tends to raise the population beyond the number that can be supported. Socialists of every denomination—among others, Charles Hall, Robert Owen, P. J. Proudhon, Charles Fourier—unanimously repudiated a theory that nature could be so cruelly unfeeling. Marx rejected Malthus and his theory in language strong even by his standards. "The contemptible Malthus," "a plagiarist," was a "shameless sycophant of the ruling classes" who perpetrated a "sin against science," "this libel on the human race" (quoted in Meek, 1954). In light of his belief in the scientific inevitability of socialism, it is not surprising that Marx rejected Malthus's principle of population. The logic of his argument is revealing:

> If Malthus's theory of population is correct [he wrote], then I can *not* abolish this [iron law of wages[2]] even if I abolish wage labor a hundred times, because this law is not only paramount over the system of wage labor but also over *every* social system. Stepping straight from this, the economists proved fifty years ago or more that socialism cannot abolish poverty, which is based on nature, but only *communalize* it, distribute it equally over the whole surface of society. (Marx, 1933: 40; emphasis in original)

Marx rejected the principle of population also because it was only a biological generalization, valid irrespective of the society's class relations. On the contrary, he wrote:

> Every special historical mode of production has its own special laws of population, historically valid within its limits alone. An abstract law of population exists for plants and animals only, and only in so far as man has not interfered with them. (*Capital*, p. 693)

As with many key assertions in Marx, this one is subject to widely differing interpretations. It may mean that population growth in a capitalist society is no reliable forecast of what the future holds under socialism: material conditions remain in control of the superstructure, but the mode of production shapes the result decisively. Or, alternatively, the contrast between the human species and all other forms of life suggests that Marx was claiming that humans can transgress all biological limitations; and this utopian vista was later adopted by some Soviet spokesmen, as we shall see. From Marx, however, it was a strange dictum. Summing up the essentials of his friend's work at his graveside, Engels held that "Marx discovered the law of evolution in human history: the simple fact, previously hidden under ideological growths, that human beings must first of all eat, drink, shelter and clothe themselves before they can turn their attention to politics, science, art, and religion" (quoted in Mehring, 1935: 555). Marx, of course, was not the first to enunciate materialism; among earlier statements one need look no further than Feuerbach's delightful play on words—"Der Mensch ist, was er isst" (Man is what he eats), and later Communist paraphrases include Bertold Brecht's "Erst kommt das Fressen, dann die Moral" (First comes food, then morality). In the view of Marx and Engels, it was only what they termed utopian socialists who held that with a good social system man could escape the bounds of his physiological limits (and, according to Condorcet and Godwin, perhaps even become immortal in the process).

The later editions of Malthus's *Essay,* one should note, classified the world's societies into what we would call developed and less developed economies, discussing the population pressure typical of each category. Marx, on the contrary, had little or nothing to say about what governed the population growth of primitive, feudal, or socialist societies, the types that he and Engels used to project History into the future. And the remarks about capitalist societies pertained, as we have seen, not to population but to the work force. There was also a fifth type, omitted from the four-stage classification enshrined in Marxist classics by Engels's *Origin of the Family* but elsewhere discussed by both him and Marx as "Oriental despotism," "the Asiatic mode of production," or a synonymous term (Wittfogel, 1957; Lichtheim, 1967; Avineri, 1968). Living and writing in England, Marx examined this fifth class of societies mainly in his articles on India, but as he and Engels defined the type, it also included China, Russia, and some other countries.

The distinctive differences between the main Western types and Oriental despotism were that the latter lacked private ownership of land and that the social progress built into the Western series was totally lacking. According to Marx, "India has no history," but only "successive invaders who founded their empires on the passive basis of that unresisting and unchanging society" (quoted in Avineri, 1968: 9). Because the "Asiatic mode of production" had no internal dynamism of its own, only an external force—that is, European colonial expansion—could establish the capitalist economy that in the Marxist schema was the necessary preparation for socialism.

According to Marx each of the Western types was characterized by a ruling class—the slave-owners in antiquity, the nobility in feudal society, and the bourgeoisie in modern capitalist society—that controlled the means of production and extracted the "surplus" created by workers. Marx ridiculed antagonists who avoided a social-class analysis and "reified" such concepts as "commodity" and the "state." With respect to Oriental despotism, however, he refrained from identifying the bureaucracy as the ruling class and designated only the "state" as in control of the society. Eventually Marx and Engels eliminated Oriental despotism from the classification of societal types, and subsequently other Marxists incorporated examples of it into Western "feudalism" (Wittfogel, 1957: chap. 9).[3]

In other words, Marx's theory of population, thin as it was in general, passed over those portions of the globe that have become a main focus of present-day demographers. If countries like India and China are outside the central Marxist schema (or are returned to it in a way that covers over their distinctive social history), then Marx's theorizing has no direct bearing on population problems of most less developed countries. Neither such direct descendants of Marx as "Maoists" nor such more remote offshoots as "African Socialists" have grappled with the issue of what Oriental despotism implies for, among other questions, the population of their countries.

Socialists on birth control

The Second International was Marxist in only a loose sense (see Wolfe, 1963). Representatives from the 20 countries who attended the inaugural congress at Paris in 1889 ranged from such Marxist pioneers as August Bebel and Wilhelm Liebknecht (of Germany) to such an unconventional designer, craftsman, and poet as William Morris (of England). No control was exercised over diverse or contradictory positions. A permanent body, the International Socialist Bureau, was established only in 1900, and it was no more than a clearinghouse for exchanging information. Even within each of the parties represented, wide and principled differences divided opposed wings, as between the orthodox led by Karl Kautsky and the "revisionists" who followed Eduard Bernstein, or in the French party between those who wanted to support Alfred Dreyfus's fight for justice and those who held that disputes among sectors of the ruling class were no business of a socialist organization (Kolakowski, 1978: vol. 2, 135–136; Bredin, 1986: 294–295). Which of those more or less socialist commentators and organizations one designated as "Marxist" was to some degree a matter of interpretation, as it remains today.

The largest and most influential unit of the Second International, the German Social Democratic Party, was also the most direct descendant of Marx. In Bebel's *Die Frau und der Sozialismus* (1883), that exemplar of German Social Democratic orthodoxy maintained that "socialism is better able to preserve the equilibrium between population and means of subsistence than any other form of community," for in a socialist society man will for the first time "consciously direct his entire development in accordance with natural law." In any event, population control was not urgent, for the world had "a superabundance of land capable of cultivation, awaiting the labor of fresh hundreds of millions" (Bebel, 1897: 169ff).

The principal theorist of the German party, Karl Kautsky, wrote two books on population, of which the first, *The Influence of Population Increase on Social Progress* (1880), represented an all but unique attempt to strike a compromise between Marx and Malthus. Malthus was wrong, Kautsky wrote, in his main thesis, that population always tends to increase faster than the supply of food on which it must subsist. But he was right in his assertion that every improvement in the state of the lower classes is accompanied by an increase in their numbers.[4] Improved methods of production might postpone the danger of overpopulation, but the crucial question for Kautsky would remain how to reduce the number of births.

> The question can no longer be *whether* birth control should be used, but only *when* it should be used. . . . The sterile rejection of population theory, at least on the part of socialism, is definitely out of place, for the two are not in principle incompatible. . . . Only a transformation of society can extirpate the misery and vice that today damn nine-tenths of the world to a lamentable existence; but only a regulation of population growth by the most moral means possible, probably the use of contraceptives, can forestall the recurrence of this evil. (Kautsky, 1880: 166–192; emphasis in original)

Within a few months Engels sent Kautsky an often-quoted letter commenting on his anomalous position. "Professional socialists," he wrote, had persistently demanded that "we proletarian socialists" should solve the problem of possible overpopulation in the future socialist society, but Engels saw no reason to accommodate them. Moreover, it was hardly a burning issue:

> If at some stage communist society finds itself obliged to regulate the production of human beings, . . . it will be precisely this society, and this society alone, which can carry this out without difficulty. . . . It is for the people in the communist society themselves to decide whether, when, and how this is to be done, and what means they wish to employ for the purpose. (quoted in Meek, 1954: 108–109)

This critique followed the standard Marxist position that it was only utopian socialists who attempted to describe the workings of the future ideal society.

Kautsky adjusted his view to Engels's orthodoxy. He wrote in his second book on population that with its superior collectivized agriculture a socialist society would be able to expand food production much faster than any possible population growth "for at least a century." True, mortality would fall "enormously," but fertility would also decline as women took an interest in "the possibility of enjoyment and creativity in nature, art, and science." In fact, with so many distractions from family life, one might suppose that the consequence might be depopulation; but this fear also would be groundless. In short, socialist society would be self-regulating; for whenever population growth varied from the optimum rate, "public opinion and individuals' consciences will make women's duties clear" (Kautsky, 1921: chaps. 15–16).

When some pre-1914 socialists called for *une grève des ventres,* a birth strike, in order to deprive capitalists of the cannon fodder they needed to conduct their wars, it might have seemed that the revisionist thesis of the young Kautsky was widely adopted. However, the slogan soon acquired a somewhat archaic ring. In the United States the Socialist Party, never a significant factor among workers, generally supported the nascent birth control leagues, but in Europe the usual relation between the two movements was antagonistic (Petersen, 1964: 90–102). At its Berlin congress in 1913, such luminaries of the Second International as Rosa Luxemburg and Klara Zetkin opposed propaganda for birth control as a capitulation to reformism.

Why should so many of those committed to establishing a planned society have opposed the planning of families? One reason was a conventional Victorian prudishness. Like the respectable workers and lower middle-class employees who made up their membership, Europe's socialist parties were generally squeamish about any issue related to sex, and in particular they reckoned it politically essential to distinguish themselves sharply from the libertarian or quasi-anarchist advocates of free love.

A second reason for the hostility was the almost accidental association of birth control with Malthus. So far as I know, Marx never commented on the neo-Malthusian movement active in England, particularly from the first Bradlaugh–Besant trial (1876) to his death (1883). According to such Marxist classics as the *Communist Manifesto* and *The Origin of the Family,* in the future socialist society women would be emancipated from household drudgery, but whether also from the bearing of many children was left in abeyance; and Marx's socialist followers were free to transfer to neo-Malthusianism his malevolence toward Malthus. This antagonism was not the doctrinal stand merely of party intellectuals. According to an informed appraisal shortly after World War I, members of the German party were opposed to birth control "almost without exception"; the whole membership was represented, for instance, in a 1913 mass meeting "against the birth strike" (Lewinsohn, 1922).

Nor were such attitudes restricted to German socialists. In any discussion of Western fertility, a principal example is France, whose birth rate began its decline probably before the 1789 revolution and by the 1850s was well below that of the rest of Western Europe and still falling. Particularly after France's defeat in the 1870–71 war with Prussia, French statesmen and scholars devoted much effort to trying to formulate a policy that would halt—or, better, reverse—the trend. The widespread control of births had been effected with no organizational stimulus, mainly, it would seem, by the spread of withdrawal backed up by (illegal) abortions. With the strong pronatalist sentiment prevailing throughout the nation, neo-Malthusian propaganda had little influence. A League for Human Regeneration and an associated periodical, *Régénération*, were founded by Paul Robin, a revolutionary and one-time friend of Marx who was dismissed from his post as a boarding-school director for having espoused the use of contraceptives. Later, Eugène and Jeanne Humbert, who published a series of birth control magazines, were supported mainly by anarchists. The two principal parties of the Left, the Socialists and the Communists, were either indifferent or hostile (Bourgeois-Pichat, 1974). In the 1950s, when Jacques Derogy, a Communist author, wrote *Children in Spite of Ourselves* to oppose the law limiting access to contraceptives (Derogy, 1956), the head of the Communist Party, Maurice Thorez, and his feminist wife, Jeannette Vermeersch, denounced him in the name of Marxist orthodoxy. Their open letter was soon complemented by a book following the party line, *L'épouvantail malthusien*—"The Malthusian scarecrow" (see Sauvy, 1968).

Opposition between the doctrines of socialism and neo-Malthusianism was strongly reinforced also by the hostility to socialism of birth control activists. In England one of the most important figures of the neo-Malthusian movement was George Drysdale, founder of the original Malthusian League and author of *The Elements of Social Science* (1905), a book of some 600 pages that went through 35 English editions and was translated into at least ten other languages. Drysdale's extensive and sympathetic exposition of classical economic theory bound his movement not only to Malthus but to the whole school of thought that socialists opposed. Thus, neo-Malthusianism, "the especial *bête noire* of the socialists, land reformers, and other advocates of redistribution and democratic control," was "disliked by the laboring classes which it was especially intended to help" (Drysdale, 1917: 4). The reason, in the view of the birth control pioneer Marie Stopes, was that "the intense anti-socialism of the Malthusian League antagonized the great mass of the working people" (Stopes, 1923: 28). The two partisan accounts of neo-Malthusians and socialists laid blame on one another, but they agreed that in

England the two movements were adversaries who on both sides conducted a war with intolerant fervor.[5] Class differences in Western fertility, ordinarily explained in part by the greater religious or cultural traditionalism of the lower classes, may well have been the consequence also of the fact that socialism, the main antitraditionalist ideology of the working classes (especially in Germany), opposed contraception either implicitly or in so many words.

Theories of crisis and adjustment

According to Marx, because the "value" of any commodity is based on the human labor expended on it, as the ratio of capital to labor increases in any society, the value of its total social product tends to decrease and the rate of profit tends to fall toward zero. Because all entrepreneurs are driven to accumulate capital goods, which generally result in a higher productivity, there is a long-term tendency for supply to outstrip demand.

The capitalist system would therefore come to an end unless its life was saved by one of the following means, each of which was advocated by economists of various schools.

1 Cartels to restrict production. As Eduard Bernstein, the principal "revisionist" theorist, pointed out, by an "organization of the market" cartels had eliminated waste and cut-throat competition—as well as setting artificially high prices and customs barriers. Although not a permanent solution, such "manufacturers' associations" could long postpone the self-destruction that Marx had decreed as inevitable (Bernstein, 1961: chap. II:d; see also Gay, 1952: 186–187).

2 Malthus's solution of a class of unproductive consumers to match the underconsuming producers. Marx found it politically reprehensible to be "unconcerned with the fate of the agents of production, whether they be capitalists or workers" [!], and troubled only about that of "parasites and self-indulgent drones, in part masters and in part servants, who appropriate gratuitously a considerable quantity of wealth, . . . paying for commodities produced by [the capitalist class] with money they have taken from the capitalists themselves" (Marx, *Theorien über den Mehrwert,* vol. 3, quoted in Meek, 1954: 157–158). In any case the solution is ineffective, he argued, for the first reaction to every crisis is to cut any outlays for such luxuries as servants.

3 The expansion of investment opportunities by the establishment of new industries. This factor was of considerable importance in the early years of capitalism, but according to the exposition of Marxist theory by the American economist Paul Sweezy, its influence has to decline in a mature economy, for the establishment of new industries counteracts the tendency to underconsumption "roughly in proportion to the relative share of total investment for which it is responsible." He found it difficult even to imagine

a series of new industries with "a *relative* importance comparable to that of the textile, mining, metallurgical, and transportation industries in the eighteenth and nineteenth centuries" (Sweezy, 1970: 218–219; emphasis in original; see also Baran, 1960: 34–39). Others might challenge this statement, written originally in 1942, with references to the subsequent exploitation of such fields as electronics, developments from the laser, or space exploration; but in any case all would probably agree that dependence on continuing inventive genius is not a counteracting force that is likely to be effective over the longer run.

4 Improvement of the population's well-being. The process was well under way during the lifetimes of Marx and particularly Engels, both of whom speculated that socialism might be established by peaceful means in England, the United States, and one or two other countries. A more typical comment was Marx's sarcastic remark about the concept of effective demand: "It is sheer tautology to say that crises are caused by the scarcity of effective consumption, or of effective consumers," for under capitalism there is no other kind. The tautology could be given "the semblance of a profounder justification by saying that the working class receives too small a portion of its own product and the evil would be remedied as soon as it receives a larger share of it" (*Capital,* Vol. 2: 410–411). That last phrase—that underconsumption would be "remedied" once the working class got "a larger share" of what it produced—may have been prophetic in a sense Marx did not intend, for that is precisely what happened in Western societies.

5 Increase in population. It is remarkable how little attention Marxists have paid to this factor, for any increase in numbers would mitigate the effects of overproduction—at least until the children were old enough to enter the work force. In a paper on a related topic, one of a series he wrote on "Problems of Socialism," Eduard Bernstein noted that a rise in population size and density would result in a greater division of labor, "leading to greater responsibilities of the state administration as it takes over more kinds of enterprise and converts them into public services" (Bernstein, 1897). In other words, population increase would reinforce the trend toward socialism rather than the reverse. In Rosa Luxemburg's main work, *The Accumulation of Capital* (1913), she remarked that the supposition that more consumers would solve the capitalist dilemma of underconsumption was not well founded. For according to Marx's schema, any increase in the number of persons would mean either more capitalists or more workers—or, by extension, more unproductive consumers; and for the reasons both Marx and Luxemburg had already noted, none of these social classes could remedy the overproduction (Luxemburg, 1951: 133–135).

An extended exposition of the matter appeared—so far as I know for the first time in Marxist writings—in Sweezy's book, which was written after the publication of Keynes's *General Theory* had stimulated an active exchange of views in a non-Marxist context. From a distantly related passage in Marx's *Theorien über den Mehrwert,* Sweezy wrote, a "general principle may be deduced":

> The strength of the tendency to underconsumption stands in inverse relation to the rapidity of population growth. . . . Over the last four centuries, the population factor has been extremely favorable to rapid and uninhibited expansion of capitalism, . . . a most important factor in counteracting the tendency to underconsumption. . . . [However,] the well known downward trend in the rate of population growth, which is characteristic of all highly developed capitalist countries, . . . is in no sense accidental. . . . Resistance to underconsumption is steadily diminishing. (Sweezy, 1970: 222–225)

6 Imperialism. If the population of the home country did not grow enough to counter underconsumption, the same remedy could be sought by expanding the market to other countries. First expounded in 1902 by the English radical liberal J. A. Hobson, this thesis was developed by a whole series of Marxists—Otto Bauer (1907), Rudolf Hilferding (1910), Rosa Luxemburg (1913), Nikolai I. Bukharin (1918), Fritz Sternberg (1926), and Henryk Grossman (1929) (see Daalder, 1968). In particular, the version by Lenin (1916) had a massive political impact, as great as any of his writings. For revolutionaries, it became axiomatic that capitalism would inevitably lead not only to its own destruction but in the process to wars of novel intensity.

Lenin and the early Bolsheviks

The loose and diverse movement that Peter Struve, the economist and theorist of legal Marxism, labeled *Narodniki* or Populists was for the several decades ending the nineteenth century the dominant element in Russia's radical politics. Their unifying theme was a veneration of the *obshchina,* or village commune; and in a famous letter that Marx wrote to the Russian revolutionary Vera Zasulich in 1881 (first published in Russia in 1924), he asserted that if it was cleansed of its deleterious characteristics and allowed to develop spontaneously, the commune would be "the pivot of Russia's social regeneration" (Carew Hunt, 1954: 68–72).[6] What we now know as Russian Marxism evolved in a running debate with Populism, a debate concerned largely with the relevance to national politics of local agrarian communes.

Lenin's first works, in part analyses of agriculture, were in greater part political tracts to demonstrate that the *obshchina* could not serve as the nucleus of a larger cooperative society. Both inside and outside the village commune, Lenin argued, agriculture was developing in a capitalist framework. Instead of the unitary communes that Populists wrote about, Lenin saw the peasantry being split into three subclasses, "rich," "middle," and "poor," that were parallel to the class structure of the industrial population.[7] Migration from agriculture, mainly of middle peasants, gave "an enormous impetus to the disintegration of the peasantry." The Narodnik program to impede such movements would not only deny the individual migrant the advantages he was seeking but also retard a progressive social phenomenon. Proper policy, Lenin contended, would be to remove all obstacles to migration and facilitate it "in every way possible" (Lenin, "The development of capitalism in Russia").[8] This analysis was correctly Marxist. In the *Communist Manifesto* Marx and Engels had ridiculed those who would preserve the "hard-won, self-acquired, self-earned" property of the small peasant, which "the development of industry has to a great extent destroyed and is still destroying daily." By increasing the proportion of the population living in cities, the bourgeoisie had rescued many agriculturists from "the idiocy of rural life."[9]

Although Lenin wrote prodigiously on many subjects—the fifth Russian edition of his works appeared in 55 volumes—he had little to say specifically on population theory. Indeed, as one scholar has remarked, his writings on population are generally "merely a few pedestrian details of economic and social statistics" (Besemeres, 1980: 328).[10] Like Marx before him, Lenin opposed what he represented as Malthusianism. In the best known statement on the issue, an article in *Pravda* (16 June 1913) titled "The working class and neo-Malthusianism," he attacked those who would justify legalized abortion in order to avoid the suffering of future offspring. Such a petty bourgeois pessimism he contrasted with the life-affirming vigor of the proletariat.

> Why not have children so that they may fight better . . . than we against the living conditions which are deforming and destroying our generation? . . . We are already laying the foundation of the new building and our children will finish its construction. That is why—and that is the *only* reason—we are unconditional enemies of neo-Malthusianism, which is a trend proper to the petty bourgeois couple, hardened and egotistical. . . . It stands to reason that such an approach does not in any way prevent us from demanding repeal of all laws prosecuting abortion or laws against the distribution of medical works on contraceptive measures and so on. . . . These laws do not cure the ills of capitalism but simply turn them into especially malignant and cruel diseases for the oppressed masses. (quoted in Besemeres, 1980: 19)

The notion that excess fertility can be the cause of working-class misery was in Lenin's view "reactionary and impoverished." Moreover, if the use of birth control were limited to members of the moribund classes, the restriction of their reproduction would hasten their defeat.

Somewhat related to Lenin's ambiguous stand on contraception was his position on "free love," a topic much discussed in revolutionary circles during the first years of the Soviet regime. His most detailed statement was a comment on a pamphlet that Inessa Armand was proposing to publish on "the woman question." The demand for free love, he wrote her, is "really not a proletarian but a bourgeois demand," for the public will understand the term to mean freedom from serious relations and from childbirth, the freedom to commit adultery. It was particularly the last point that one would suppose Armand might have resented—and no wonder, for she was (or would soon become) Lenin's mistress who for many years lived with him and his wife in a *ménage à trois* (Wolfe, 1981: chap. 6). Most of the early Bolsheviks were a bit puritanical in their judgment of sexual transgressions, but in this as in other matters Lenin was the exception.

Joseph Stalin, who succeeded Lenin as leader of the Communist Party of the Soviet Union and of world Communism, professed an expertise in all fields. Concerning the relation between population and the economy, he followed the standard Marxist line that the organization of society is decisive, but in fact he commented only incidentally on the growth of numbers as a factor in social progress. In demography his interest centered on ethnic composition. *Marxism and the National Question,* a work he had written in 1912, became after his accession to full power the definitive text on that subject.[11]

Since neither Lenin nor Stalin—nor, indeed, any of the other early Bolsheviks—evinced much interest in population theory, the few writings that appeared were essentially paraphrases of Marx's thin dicta. Whatever influence there may have been on population policies was overwhelmed by the effect of World War I and the overlapping civil war, of famines and epidemics, and of terror on a new scale. One can understand Soviet demographic theories only against a background of the facts about Soviet population.

The relation of population to resources

The development of the Soviet economy and society since the revolution has been erratic, with a counterpart of the business cycle setting alternating stages of greater repression and relative relaxation. During each upswing the Party drove the country at breakneck speed toward its planned future; then the clogged economy and resistant population forced the leaders to slacken the pace during an ensuing downswing. When this looser control encouraged a threat to its power, the Party enforced its full domination again and renewed its forward thrust. Generally, the abrupt turns in policies took place through factional disputes within the Party, with recurrent purges of the losing side. Dramatic shifts have occurred in every element of the society from the family to the arts, from central–provincial relations to the pace of industrialization. In this context it is appropriate to stress how the relation of the state to the peasantry has affected agricultural production, for that has been both a significant trend in itself and the one most relevant to the balance between resources and population.

In pre-1917 debates within the Party, it was axiomatic that the key to taking and holding power in an overwhelmingly agricultural country was a so-called *smychka*, or union of the urban proletariat with the peasantry. Thus, the Bolsheviks borrowed some key elements of the Populists' program, especially their demand that large estates be divided among those who worked the land. For Lenin and his comrades, however, the rural-urban coalition never evolved from its theoretical statements. After the Bolsheviks took power in the main cities, and while they were still fighting to establish control over the rest of the country, they tried to institute immediate full communism. The sale or purchase of commodities was prohibited, but no alternative system was established. Cities could be fed only by sending armies into the countryside to confiscate peasants' food, including often their seed grain. Thousands were killed by terror and counterterror, hundreds of thousands in civil strife. Epidemics spread with the constant movement of hungry hordes; typhus alone killed more than 1.5 million in 1919–20. According to official figures of the Soviet Central Statistical Bureau, 5,053,000 lives were lost in the famine of 1921–22 (Heller and Nekrich, 1986: 120). One informed estimate of total losses from World War I, the civil war, and the attempt to establish a communist economy makes sober reading. By comparing figures from the censuses of 1897 and 1928, Lorimer calculated 2 million military deaths and 14 million civilian, a net emigration of 2 million, and 10 million fewer births than would have occurred had fertility continued at its prior level. The total deficit of 28 million, he thought, is probably correct to the nearest million. "During the years 1915–23 the Russian people underwent the most cataclysmic changes since the Mongol invasion in the early thirteenth century" (Lorimer, 1946: 42).

Under the New Economic Policy proclaimed by Lenin in March 1921, the two principal goals were to reinstate the *smychka* and, in Lenin's words, "to increase at all cost the quantity of output." Both goals were sought by granting peasants a relatively free use of their land and whatever they produced on it. Private enterprise was authorized not only in agriculture but in trade and petty industry, while the Party retained control of the "commanding heights" of large-scale industry, banking, and foreign trade. A remarkable economic revival resulted, but many Communists opposed the establishment of a mixed economy that Lenin himself termed "state capitalism."

With the high cost of manufactured goods, peasants found it uneconomic to produce for the market and gradually shifted to subsistence farming. But the industrialization beginning in the mid-1920s needed both food for the urban work force and raw materials. Stalin sought a solution to this so-called scissors in an all-out forced collectivization of agriculture. The Party tried to exacerbate antagonisms between "rich" and "poor" peasants; and the most efficient among the former, the "kulaks," were ousted from the land in spite of opposition to this risky course from Nikolai Bukharin and other leading Communists. As Stalin put it, expropriation of the kulaks "is an integral part of the formation and development of the collective farms. That is why it is ridiculous and fatuous to expatiate today on the expropriation of the kulaks. You do not lament the loss of the hair of one who has been beheaded" (Stalin, 1942: 145–164).

Nor were these "rich" peasants permitted to join the collective farms being established out of their land. In the words of an American Communist, Anna Louise Strong, who was in the Soviet countryside during the process, "a million families suddenly found themselves pariahs, without any rights which need be respected, and without any knowledge as to what they might do to be saved" (Strong, 1931: 81). Deprived of their means of subsistence, they lost also their ration cards and the right to purchase in the cooperative stores; their children were expelled from school, and their sick were excluded from medical treatment. Whole groups of villages were starved out (Monkhouse, 1934: 207). The remaining resistance of Ukrainian peasants was broken by a deliberately planned famine that killed millions (Conquest, 1986). In this and the more general famine brought about by the chaos in agriculture, the number of deaths was greater than 12 years earlier, but the regime not only sought no aid from abroad but refused to accept it when it was offered. Since it could not be admitted that a socialist society might be short of food, the head of an international relief organization was permitted to send in only a few food parcels (Ammende, 1936). The ousted peasants formed one principal element of developing forced-labor camps, which furnished the industrialization programs with timber and minerals as well as fish from the northern seas.

The brutality of the forced collectivization of agriculture broke opposition to it, but it also destroyed Soviet agriculture. Every Soviet leader since the First Five-year Plan has tried to repair the damage, and none has succeeded. Still in the mid-1980s, the crux of Mikhail Gorbachev's proposed reforms was in agriculture. Tiny private plots have been permitted, now totaling some 3 percent of the country's farmland. Yet at least a quarter of the total farm output, varying in proportion from one commodity to another, is produced on those private plots, which symbolize the gross inefficiency of the socialized system. As measured by its food production, the Soviet Union, one of the two superpowers, is a member of the Third World.

Soviet views on the control of fertility

Orthodox doctrine holds that in a country with a socialist economy no control of fertility is appropriate. According to two of today's best known Soviet demographers, B. TS. Urlanis and D. I. Valentei, in capitalist countries private ownership resulted in an excessive decline in fertility, but the Soviet Union was immune from that social disease and the consequent economic disorganization.[12] In some expressions of this dogma, however, unlimited human reproduction was advocated even in other types of society. In 1947, when for the first time representatives of opposed ideologies formally met in the United Nations Population Commission to debate the problems of world population, the Ukrainian delegate (supported by the other Soviet delegate) recited the canon with breathtaking abandon: "I would consider it barbaric for the Commission to contemplate a limitation of marriages or of legitimate births, and this for any country whatsoever, at any period whatsoever. With an adequate social organization it is possible to face any increase in population" (quoted in Sauvy, 1969: 525). And the Yugoslav delegate added, "Cruelly, you [Western demographers] intend to adjust the population to the economy, while we Communists want to adjust the economy to the population" (quoted in Sauvy, 1968).

The contrast in views became a standard element of Soviet propaganda. As the principal Soviet delegate to the 1954 World Population Conference in Rome, T. V. Riabushkin concentrated his report on birth control, which he termed the dominant issue that divided the East from the West—"the struggle between two trends in the underlying questions of theory and practice of population statistics: the reactionary one, connected with neo-Malthusian ideas, and the progressive one, led by the delegates of the Soviet Union and the People's Democracies." In 1959, when the UN Population Commission was listing words to be included in a projected demographic dictionary, Riabushkin objected to "Malthusianism" and "birth control" on the ground that "such mistaken concepts should not find a place in an official dictionary" (quoted in Sauvy, 1969: 525*n.*). In international bodies like the United Nations, there was a strange cooperation between Communist and Catholic spokesmen, uncomfortable for both and, for proponents of planned parenthood, a constant source of hilarity (see McQuillan, 1979).

As earlier in the dispute between socialists and neo-Malthusians, whatever rational substance existed on either side of the argument was often buried under extremist rhetoric. Even one familiar with the language of Bolshevik polemics must find the distortions and bizarre associations of the Stalinist period something of a new departure. According to these effusions, Bertrand Russell, because he supported birth control, called for "immediate atomic bombing of the peace-loving peoples and advise[d] the rulers to see to it that 'the death rate is high.' " He preached "the raving fascist idea of breeding a special stock of people especially adapted to atomic warfare." "The American racist Margaret Sanger" argued that there should be compulsory reduction of Japan's population. "Masquerading as scientists and philanthropists, lackeys of American monopolies openly advocate cannibalism and try to justify the demoniacal plans for the mass extermination of peoples." The "progressive forces" struggling against this "Malthusian obscurantism" were also a curious array, including Friedrich Burgdörfer, a leading population official of Nazi Germany; Josué Castro, a Brazilian physician who had revived August Bebel's theory on the relation between food and fecundity; Lucas, "a British ichthyologist"; such Communist scientists as J. D. Bernal and R. Palme Dutt; and Maurice Thorez, head of the French Communist Party (see Petersen, 1964: 114–118). A. IA. Popov, a philosopher and journalist, wrote such longer works as *Modern-day Malthusianism: A Misanthropic Ideology for the Imperialists* (1953). Like Popov, most of those in the front line against family planning advocates had little or no training in demography. Exceptions were likely to be such professional demographers or statisticians as B. IA. Smulevich, who was German-trained and prominent abroad and therefore suspect. He was under arrest or in internal exile from 1937 to 1946, and after his rehabilitation he became one of the crudest exponents of the orthodox Marxist theory of population. At the 1965 World Population Conference in Belgrade, for example, he held that "the main factors affecting population replacement are the manner in which material wealth is produced, the form of the state as determined by the social and economic structure of society, and the policy of the state in population and health matters."[13]

It took about ten years from Stalin's death in 1953 for the Stalinist line in population theory and policy to begin to erode (see Brackett, 1968; Desfosses, 1976). Very low birth rates in Eastern Europe, particularly in Hungary, suggested that in spite of the contrary expectation from Marxism, a socialist economy provides no guarantee against eventual depopulation. When the small-family system spread to portions of the Soviet population, V. I. Perevedentsev, a sociologist-economist who had begun his career with analyses of internal migration, became a prolific advocate of pronatalist policies, and his exhortations to raise Soviet fertility were usually interpreted abroad as expressions of official views. V. P. Piskunov of the Ukrainian Academy of Sciences wrote papers on the same theme—frequently with his wife, V. S. Steshenko—as well as a book on the general theory of population reproduction. For several years, however, the revised orientation that such intimations in the mid-1960s seemed to presage did not develop fully. Rather, differences continued not only among those writing on population policy but also, one can presume, among top members of the Party. Even the use of the opprobrious term "birth control" (*kontrol' nad rozhdaemost'iu*) could be indicative, for in Russian the word *kontrol'* "suggests bureaucrats or indeed policemen stationed by the bedroom door" (Besemeres, 1980: 102). Genady Gesarimov, a prominent journalist, suggested that the term "birth control" be supplanted by "guidance of the birth rate" or the avoidance of "deliberate motherhood."

As Soviet demographers repeatedly pointed out, the work of females outside the home has been a prime factor in the country's low fertility, for it is especially difficult in the Soviet Union for a woman to combine the roles of mother and worker/employee. The state's concentration on accumulating capital goods and weaponry has made it impossible to improve housing conditions significantly or to provide many of the consumer goods that would make a homemaker's tasks less burdensome (e.g., Perevedentsev, 1979). Yet the contributions of female workers cannot easily be forgone, for the sex ratio was badly skewed by massive losses of adult males in the successive Stalinist purges and World War II, and then aggravated by increased conscription into the armed forces.

The sizable differences in fertility by nationality, which have remained and in some cases widened, also pose a dilemma to policymakers (Bernstam, 1986). Russians (including those with other forebears who chose to declare themselves Russian), who according to the 1979 census constituted only slightly over half of the population, have small families and a population structure with relatively few in the peak reproductive ages. The same is true of the two other major Slavic nationalities, Ukrainians and Belorussians, and of the three Baltic peoples, the Georgians, and the Moldavians. The Muslim nationalities, on the contrary, grew by a quarter or even a third over the prior intercensal period (see Feshbach, 1982), and if the trend continues they may be able to express their demographic weight in political decisions. This contrast, disastrous in the Russians' view, has been repeatedly analyzed with public opinion polls, census data, and vital statistics (Andorka, 1978: 328–332).

A significant development came with recurrent proposals to vary family allowances regionally in order to stimulate the fertility of Slavs, but not of Muslims. As director of the Center for the Study of Population at Moscow University, Dmitri Valentei was perhaps the most prominent demographer to propose this solution. But as P. G. Podiachikh, a statistician at the Central Statistical Administration, pointed out, a differentiated policy would give more aid to the relatively well-to-do families in the Baltic states than to the poorer ones in Central Asia (the examples avoided any mention of either Russians or other Slavic peoples), and such an allocation would contradict the "policy of raising the welfare of all members of socialist society" (quoted in Besemeres, 1980: 100). At the 26th Party Congress in 1981, the delegates endorsed a "step-by-step" differentiation that eventually would encourage fertility only in populations with small average families (Weber and Goodman, 1981; Riabushkin, 1982). Whether it will be possible to restore the Russian sector to its full dominance is doubtful, for to offer modernist couples enough to really compensate for the losses they incur (or perceive) in having children would entail a complete reworking of Soviet society (Heer, 1977, 1980).

A gradual revision also occurred in attitudes toward population growth in less developed countries. Hints in Soviet journals in the late 1960s, with some abatement of the shrill denunciations of the birth control movement and its operations, expressed a nascent concern about world population pressure. In 1965 two articles on world population appeared in *Literaturnaia Gazeta:* the first, by one Cheprakov, continued to prescribe social and economic reforms that would bring into play the "unlimited" capacity of science; in the second, the demographer Boris Urlanis in effect responded to Cheprakov and, without yet calling for a program to limit births, spelled out how serious the problem was becoming (Besemeres, 1980: 99).

A most remarkable fact about the sharp reversal in both domestic and international population policy, in sum, is how little discussion there was on the tacit turnabout also in population theory. It is no longer axiomatic that a socialist economy would protect a society against the small families that are supposedly endemic under capitalism. And to date, Soviet demographers have continued to exercise prudence in challenging too openly the older doctrines that, in their empirical work or policy recommendations, they implicitly reject. Still, there has been a very limited "glasnost" in recent demographic discussions, the ultimate outcome and implications of which are matters beyond the scope of this essay.

Conclusion

Karl Marx died just over 100 years ago, and one might have expected him to have receded into a comfortable chapter in histories of Western thought, the counterpart of, say, Adam Smith or John Locke. Why have movements more or less based on his writings continued to flourish? In his book *The Unfinished Revolution,* the American political scientist Adam Ulam traced radical schools of thought of the nineteenth century against a background of the attitudes generated by industrialization and its social and political concomitants (Ulam, 1960). One wing—anarchists, guild socialists, Russian Populists—sought its utopia in the preservation or reconstitution of a preindustrial *Gemeinschaft;* another wing—Saint-Simon or the Fabians—projected the rise of industry and science by a quite different route to a remarkably similar ideal world. Only the Marxists squared the circle and successfully combined the appeals of the revolutionary élan of a Mikhail Bakunin with the rational practicality of a Sidney Webb. The Bolshevik victory in Russia contradicted fundamentally the Marxist timetable, but it also produced a bureaucracy that tended to label any rebellious movement as Marxist or, if that term had to be stretched even beyond the wide expanse of Marx's interests, as neo-Marxist.

For both author and reader, an essay on Marxist theories of population is a frustrating experience. This is a drama in which most of the characters have but a few lines, speak them haltingly, and hurriedly leave the stage to seek roles more to their taste. In Marx's few relevant passages he either denied the importance of population growth in human affairs or, more frequently, denounced Malthus for his contrary view. Even such deviants from orthodoxy as Eduard Bernstein offered no striking or original observations on the interdependence of population and resources. The one major exception, the young Kautsky, reversed himself as a mature theorist. In this large desert one might have anticipated at least one oasis, for the question of how population growth affects underconsumption is closely tied to the Marxist interpretation of the capitalist system. The only Marxist scholar to address this question at length, Paul Sweezy, could do no better than to suppose that if Marx had lived to develop fully the thesis that he found implicit in *Capital,* then Marx would have written as Sweezy himself did.

Non-Marxist infidels, for whom population is a necessary and central component of any rounded analysis of how a society or an economy operates, must find it puzzling that Marx and virtually all who deemed themselves Marxists more or less passed over this factor in their theoretical and practical work. As some in the Western Marxist tradition indicated, they did not overlook the topic so much as willfully bypass it, and on occasion they said why. Within capitalism, they believed, the resources on which a population depends, the food that people need to live, set limits; wherever it was established, the socialist world would flourish unimpeded by these encumbrances. Engels criticized Saint-Simon, Fourier, Owen, and others as utopians. But does it evade utopianism to adopt this Marxist position and in one's analyses to ignore crucial demographic factors that impede the transformation to socialism? Without an appreciation of the population factor, Marxism is the most utopian of all the denominations.

Notes

1 Following Morgan's lead, Engels held that the matriarchal gens existed everywhere prior to its patriarchal counterpart and, moreover, that "the overthrow of mother right was the world historical defeat of the female sex." The status of women had declined disastrously with the establishment of capitalism, and a fully free marriage could come only with the advent of socialism. Recently some feminists have based their radical proposals on a revival of this Marxist reconstruction of human history.

2 The tendency of population always to increase up to the limit set by the subsistence available to it means that a virtually unlimited supply of labor can always be hired at a fixed wage. The relation, dubbed "the iron law of wages" by the German socialist Ferdinand Lassalle, was analyzed most fully by David Ricardo, Malthus's contemporary and friendly antagonist. For Ricardo, as for Marx, the rigidity of wages was a consequence of Malthus's principle of population, but Malthus himself rejected the link. As he wrote repeatedly in both the *Essay on the Principle of Population* and *Principles of Political Economy,* a rise in wages tends to generate a taste for a higher level of living, which the worker will endeavor to preserve, among other ways, by reducing the size of his family. Virtually alone among socialists who have written on the matter, two English Fabians had a correct appreciation of Malthus's social philosophy. "The ordinary middle-class view," Sidney and Beatrice Webb wrote, "that the 'principle of population' renders nugatory all attempts to raise wages otherwise than in the slow course of generations was, in fact, based on sheer ignorance not only of the facts of working-class life, but even of the opinions of the very economists from whom it was supposed to be derived" (Webb and Webb, 1919: 632–635).

3 During the past two decades Marxists in several Western countries have developed theories of the state more elaborate than those in Marxist classics. Polemics started with *The State in Capitalist Society* by Ralph Miliband (1969) and two papers by Nicos Poulantzas in the *New Left Review* (1969, 1976). The confrontation between "instrumentalist" and "structural" approaches was, according to John Holloway and Sol Picciotto (1978), "a false polarity which has done much to delimit and impoverish discussion." Holloway and Picciotto edited a collection of translations from German expounding various versions of the "state derivation" school, which has tried to show specifically how the state develops out of a capitalist economy. More generally, these works and others like them have used Marxist categories to forge a link between political science and economics as these disciplines are conventionally viewed by either Marxists or non-Marxists (cf. Jessop, 1977). However, as far as I have perused these writings, none of them includes even a parenthetical commentary on Oriental despotism, the Marxist category in which the state controls all of society.

4 Although this remains a common interpretation of Malthus's theory, his final stand was precisely the opposite: workers who raised themselves into middle-class circumstances generally have adopted the smaller families typical of the middle class (see Petersen, 1979: chap. 9).

5 As late as 1925 the British Labour Party took an ambivalent stand toward planned parenthood. When the Department of Health banned birth control information from its clinics, a Party Conference refused to protest, declaring: "The subject of birth control is in its nature not one which should be made a political party issue, but should remain a matter upon which members of the Party should be free to hold and promote their individual convictions" (Cole, 1948: 200–201). One reason for this neutral position, of course, was that the leaders did not want to affront the many Catholic members, but another was that nothing in the socialist tradition denoted this policy as one that demanded a principled stand.

6 Some Populists could reasonably be designated "Marxists"; one of them, N. F. Danielson, was sympathetic enough to translate the first volume of *Capital* into Russian. Populists despised political democracy, and they invoked Marx's authority to denigrate the formal liberties of the bourgeois state. In their view capitalism would crush the peasantry into an amorphous proletariat, and they cited Marx on the spiritual degradation that capitalist accumulation would effect. According to Populist analyses, Russian entrepreneurs, too weak to compete abroad, were destroying even their home market; this variation on the theme of capitalist overproduction was adopted by all the major Russian Marxists from Struve to Lenin (Kolakowski, 1978: chap. 13). However, the hope of the principal Populists that they could skip the capitalist stage and move directly to a socialist society, a goal ultimately realized under Lenin's direction, flatly contradicted Marxist doctrine. G. V. Plekhanov, as orthodox a Marxist as could be found anywhere, wrote in *Our Differences* that if a handful of revolutionaries succeeded in taking power, the consequence would be the reconstitution of Oriental despotism, "a political abortion after the manner of the ancient Chinese or Persian empires—a renewal of tsarist despotism on a communist basis" (quoted in Kolakowski, 1978: 335).

7 In judging Lenin's analyses we should note that the statistics available to him were fragmentary and that he used them to delineate a stratification still in process. Although in the 1890s he probably overestimated the extent and speed of the peasantry's transformation, over the longer run he was probably correct (see Nove, 1967; Willetts, 1967).

8 He developed this argument also in a number of subsequent works; see Lenin, *Selected Works,* vol. 12; Pokshishevskii, 1970.

9 The future socialist society, however, would witness a "combination of agricultural with manufacturing industries, a gradual abolition of the distinction between town and country by a more equitable distribution of the population over the country." The agricultural plan that Stalin eventually carried out in the Soviet Union was also set in the *Manifesto:* first, "expropriation of the land and use of the rent for state needs," then "armies of laborers" cultivating the land according to a

"common plan" (see also Mitrany, 1961: chap. 3).

10 "For a vain struggle to find something to say about Lenin's contribution to demographic theory (a struggle sustained over several pages)," the passage continues, "see D. I. Valentei, ed., *Marxist-Leninist Population Theory* (in Russian; Moscow, 1974), pp. 5ff." (Besemeres, 1980: 328).

11 An interesting extension of Stalin's thesis on how the ethnic units of the Soviet Union should be coordinated is found in a 1920 letter to Lenin (later expunged from Stalin's collected works). Stalin noted with remarkable prescience that a transitional form of annexation must be provided for states that had never been in the tsarist empire and, like the later People's Democracies, were not yet part of the USSR (see Wolfe, 1969: 276–277).

12 An interesting exchange in English took place between A. IA. Kvasha (1966), a demographer at the Central Statistical Administration and at Moscow University, and the American anthropologist Stephen Dunn (1967).

13 Smulevich's thesis was countered in a paper by Wilhelm Billig, a Polish physicist and demographer who several years later retired, or was forced to retire, possibly because of his Jewish origin. He concluded from an analysis particularly of the agricultural population that the faster growth identified with the so-called law of population has no basis in fact (see Schubnell, 1972, vol. 2: 340–371).

References

Ammende, Ewald. 1936. *Human Life in Russia.* London: Allen & Unwin.

Andorka, Rudolf. 1978. *Determinants of Fertility in Advanced Societies.* New York: Free Press.

Avineri, Shlomo (ed.). 1968. *Karl Marx on Colonialism and Modernization.* Garden City, N.Y.: Doubleday.

Baran, Paul A. 1960. *The Political Economy of Growth.* New York: Prometheus Paperback.

Bebel, August. 1897. *Woman in the Past, Present, and Future.* San Francisco: Benham.

Bernstam, Mikhail S. 1986. "The demography of Soviet ethnic groups in world perspective," in *The Last Empire: Nationality and the Soviet Future,* ed. Robert Conquest. Stanford, Calif.: Hoover Institution Press.

Bernstein, Eduard. 1897. "Die sozialpolitische Bedeutung von Raum und Zahl," *Neue Zeit* 15, no. 2: 100–107.

———. 1961. *Evolutionary Socialism* (1909). New York: Schocken.

Besemeres, John P. 1980. *Soviet Population Politics.* White Plains, N.Y.: M. E. Sharpe.

Bourgeois-Pichat, Jean. 1974. "France," in *Population Policy in Developed Countries,* ed. Bernard Berelson. New York: McGraw-Hill.

Brackett, James W. 1968. "The evolution of Marxist theories of population: Marxism recognizes the population problem," *Demography* 5: 158–173.

Bredin, J.-D. 1986. *The Affair.* New York: Braziller.

Carew Hunt, R. N. 1954. *Marxism Past and Present.* New York: Macmillan.

Cole, G. D. H. 1948. *A History of the Labour Party from 1914.* London: Routledge & Kegan Paul.

Conquest, Robert. 1986. *The Harvest of Sorrow: Soviet Collectivization and the Terror-Famine.* New York: Oxford University Press.

Daalder, Hans. 1968. "Imperialism," *International Encyclopedia of the Social Sciences* 7: 101–109.

Derogy, Jacques. 1956. *Des enfants malgré nous.* Paris: Éditions de Minuit.

Desfosses, Helen. 1976. "Demography, ideology, and politics in the USSR," *Soviet Studies* 28: 244–256.

Drysdale, C. V. 1917. *The Malthusian Doctrine in its Modern Aspects.* London: Malthusian League.

Dunn, Stephen P. 1967. "Comments on demography and population policy in the developing countries," with a "Reply" by A. IA. Kvasha, *Soviet Sociology* 6: 47–51.

Engels, Frederick. 1942. *The Origin of the Family, Private Property, and the State* (1884). New York: International Publishers.

———. 1958. *The Condition of the Working Class in England* (1845), ed. W. O. Henderson and W. H. Chaloner. Stanford, Calif.: Stanford University Press.

Feshbach, Murray. 1982. "The Soviet Union: Population trends and dilemmas," *Population Bulletin* 37, no. 3 (August).

Feuer, Lewis S. 1966. "The influence of the American communist colonies on Engels and Marx," *Western Political Quarterly* 19: 456–474.

Gay, Peter. 1952. *The Dilemma of Democratic Socialism.* New York: Columbia University Press.

Heer, David M. 1977. "Three issues in Soviet population policy," *Population and Development Review* 3, no. 3 (June): 229–252.

———. 1980. "Population policy," in *Contemporary Soviet Society,* ed. J. G. Pankhurst and N. S. Sacks. New York: Praeger.

Heller, Mikhail, and Aleksandr Nekrich. 1986. *Utopian Power: The History of the Soviet Union from 1917 to the Present.* New York: Summit Books.

Hollander, Samuel. 1984. "Marx and Malthusianism," *American Economic Review* 74: 139–151.

Holloway, John, and Sol Picciotto (eds.). 1978. *State and Capital: A Marxist Debate.* London: Edward Arnold.

Jessop, Bob. 1977. "Recent theories of the capitalist state," *Cambridge Journal of Economics* 1: 353–373.

Kautsky, Karl. 1880. *Der Einfluss der Volksvermehrung auf den Fortschritt der Gesellschaft.* Vienna: Boch und Hasbach.

———. 1921. *Vermehrung und Entwicklung in Natur und Gesellschaft,* 3rd ed. Stuttgart: Dietz Nachfolger (first edition 1910).

Kolakowski, Leszek. 1978. *Main Currents of Marxism,* 2 vols. Oxford: Clarendon Press.

Kvasha, A. IA. 1966. "Some problems of the demography of the developing countries," *Soviet Sociology* 41: 3–11.

Lenin, V. I. n.d. "The development of capitalism in Russia," *Selected Works,* Vol. 1, pp. 236–237, 292–294. New York: International Publishers.

Lewinsohn, Richard. 1922. "Die Stellung der deutschen Sozialdemokratie zur Bevölkerungsfrage," *Schmollers Jahrbuch* 46: 813–859.

Lichtheim, George. 1967. "Oriental despotism," in *The Concept of Ideology and Other Essays.* New York: Random House.

Lorimer, Frank. 1946. *The Population of the Soviet Union: History and Prospects.* League of Nations. Princeton, N.J.: Princeton University Press.

Luxemburg, Rosa. 1951. *The Accumulation of Capital* (1913). New Haven, Conn.: Yale University Press.

Malthus, T. R. 1986a. *An Essay on the Principle of Population,* 6th ed. (1826), in *The Works of Thomas Robert Malthus,* ed. E. A. Wrigley and David Souden. Vols. 3–4. London: William Pickering.

———. 1986b. *The Principles of Political Economy,* 2nd ed. (1836), in *The Works of Thomas Robert Malthus,* ed. E. A. Wrigley and David Souden. Vols. 5–6. London: William Pickering.

Marx, Karl. 1906. *Capital,* vol. 1 (1867). Chicago: Kerr.

———. 1933. *Critique of the Gotha Program* (1875). New York: International Publishers.

———. 1967. *Capital,* vol. 2 (1885). New York: International Publishers.

———, and Friedrich Engels. 1962. "Manifesto of the Communist Party" (1848), in *The Communist Blueprint for the Future,* ed. Thomas P. Whitney. New York: Dutton.

———, and Friedrich Engels. 1970. *The German Ideology* (1845–46), Part 1, with Selections from Parts 2 and 3, ed. C. J. Arthur. New York: International Publishers.

McQuillan, Kevin. 1979. "Common themes in Catholic and Marxist thought on population and development," *Population and Development Review* 5, no. 4 (December): 689–698.

Meek, R. L. (ed.). 1954. *Marx and Engels on Malthus.* New York: International Publishers.

Mehring, Franz. 1935. *Karl Marx: The Story of His Life.* New York: Covici-Friede.

Miliband, Ralph. 1969. *The State in Capitalist Society.* New York: Basic Books.

Mitrany, David. 1961. *Marx against the Peasant.* New York: Collier.

Monkhouse, Allan. 1934. *Moscow, 1911–1933.* Boston: Little Brown.
Nove, Alec. 1967. "Lenin as economist," in *Lenin: The Man, the Theorist, the Leader,* ed. Leonard Schapiro and Peter Reddaway. New York: Praeger.
Perevedentsev, V. I. 1979. "We are growing from year to year, . . ." *Literaturnaia Gazeta* (no. 40, 3 October), translated in *Population and Development Review* 6, no. 1 (March): 169–174.
Petersen, William. 1956. "Marx versus Malthus," *Population Review* 1: 21–32.
———. 1964. *The Politics of Population.* New York: Doubleday-Anchor.
———. 1979. *Malthus.* Cambridge, Mass.: Harvard University Press.
Pokshishevskii, V. V. 1970. "Population migration and its evaluation in Lenin's works," *Soviet Education* 12, nos. 3–5: 86–100.
Poulantzas, Nicos. 1969. "The problem of the capitalist state," *New Left Review* 58: 67–78.
———. 1976. "The capitalist state: A reply to Miliband and Laclau," *New Left Review* 95: 63–83.
Riabushkin, T. V. 1982. "Demographic policy in light of the decisions of the Twenty-sixth Congress of the CPSU," *Soviet Law and Government* 21 (Fall): 21–30.
Sauvy, Alfred. 1968. "Marx et les problèmes contemporains de la population," *Social Science Information* 7: 27–38.
———. 1969. *General Theory of Population.* New York: Basic Books.
Schubnell, Hermann. 1972. "Demography," in *Marxism, Communism, and Western Society,* ed. C. D. Kernig. New York: Herder and Herder.
Seccombe, Wally. 1983. "Marxism and demography," *New Left Review* 137: 22–47.
Sherwood, J. M. 1985. "Engels, Marx, Malthus and the machine," *American Historical Review* 90: 837–865.
Stalin, Joseph. 1942. *Leninism: Selected Writings.* New York: International Publishers.
Stopes, Marie. 1923. *Early Days of Birth Control.* London: Putnam.
Strong, Anna Louise. 1931. *The Soviets Conquer Wheat: The Drama of Collective Farming.* New York: Holt.
Sweezy, Paul M. 1970. *The Theory of Capitalist Development.* New York: Modern Reader Paperbacks.
Ulam, Adam B. 1960. *The Unfinished Revolution: An Essay on the Sources of Influence of Marxism and Communism.* New York: Random House.
Webb, Sidney, and Beatrice Webb. 1919. *Industrial Democracy.* London: Longmans, Green.
Weber, Cynthia, and Ann Goodman. 1981. "The demographic policy debate in the USSR," *Population and Development Review* 7, no. 2 (June): 279–295.
Willetts, Harry. 1967. "Lenin and the peasants," in *Lenin: The Man, the Theorist, the Leader,* ed. Leonard Schapiro and Peter Reddaway. New York: Praeger.
Wittfogel, Karl A. 1957. *Oriental Despotism.* New Haven, Conn.: Yale University Press.
Wolfe, Bertram D. 1963. "French socialism, German theory, and the flaw in the formation of the socialist internationals," in *Essays in Russian and Soviet History,* ed. J. S. Curtis. New York: Columbia University Press.
———. 1969. *An Ideology in Power.* New York: Stein and Day.
———. 1981. *Revolution and Reality.* Chapel Hill: University of North Carolina Press.

Fascism and Population in Comparative European Perspective

Paul Weindling

European fascism between 1918 and 1945 coincided with a period of economic depression, declining birth rates, and political turmoil. In the sphere of population, fascism is notorious for racism and genocide supported by such ideologies as "blood and soil" and of racial purity of select groups of Nordic or Aryan extraction. Eugenics has often been denounced as fascist. Yet fascism is a problematic concept. While not denying the importance of political subordination, war-mongering, and the racial persecution of such groups as Jews, gypsies, and homosexuals, this essay takes as its starting point the fact that fascism occurred in a number of authoritarian social systems and was supported by diverse social interests—including those of certain social scientists and demographers. There were consequently varied racial and population policies both within such regimes as Nazi Germany, and between such fascist states as Italy and Germany. The rise of movements for social planning, based on social science and applied by armies of newly professionalized social workers, permitted the formulation and application of state-supported population policies. Fascist regimes could appropriate these for racial ends. Before considering population policies under fascism, some preliminary definitions are required.

Concepts and definitions

The Nazi model

Adolf Hitler's *Mein Kampf* (*My Struggle*), first published in 1925, contained dire warnings as to the result of interbreeding between human "races." Degeneration of the higher race, and physical and intellectual regression would be the inevitable results. Violation of these "iron laws of Nature" would bring about national and racial ruin with "distress, misfortune and diseases." All human culture, art, and civilization were proclaimed as achievements of the "culture-bearing" Aryan race. Hitler believed that obedience to racial laws as natural laws would lead to rebirth of the German nation and race. Only "Jewish effrontery" denied that modern civil and moral society had overcome Nature (Hitler, 1925).

Hitler's manifesto gives important insights into Nazi ideology as it relates to population, resources, and the environment. Yet it is primarily a call for political mobilization, providing little more than a sketch of a new racial order or of the mechanisms by which this could be obtained. Political analysts have long recognized that national socialism cannot be simply explained by the ideas of *Mein Kampf*. There is far more to national socialism, and certainly to fascism as an international phenomenon between 1918 and 1945. Leading ideological diatribes such as *Mein Kampf* do not explain the full range of population policies, whether implemented or proposed. The historical sociology of ideas suggests an approach that takes into account such social processes as professionalization, bureaucratization, and the differences between scientific expertise and popularization; distinctive national cultures, political opportunism, and changing socioeconomic conditions were also factors. Fascism is still an intellectually divisive and highly emotive concept. Much ink has been spilled in intellectual brawls between analysts of fascism, such as those wishing to subsume fascism under totalitarianism and those emphasizing distinctions between Italian fascism and German national socialism (Laqueur, 1979). There has been only limited analysis of the administrative structures, of social policies, and of the balance between natural resources, population, and the economy. Texts such as *Mein Kampf* have to be located within their social context in order to establish their significance and influence.

Fascist science

At the same time as *Mein Kampf* enjoyed mass distribution (for example, it was presented by registrars to newlywed couples), German demographers developed techniques for analyzing population movements. Their calculated rigor (as in the measurement of fertility of birth cohorts) contrasted to the tone of racial ideologues. Yet both the ideological and technocratic approaches claimed to be scientific and to mutually reinforce each other. Whether fascism produced demographic and biological thought worthy of being discussed as scientific is a moot point. It raises the question of whether fascist demography was as rigorous and systematic as its counterparts in the democratic societies of the same era. A number of conceptual barriers have to be surmounted before one can analyze a type of thinking as scientific without being an unintended apologist for ideas and measures associated with some of the worst instances of brutality and genocide in human history. For many years the problem of fascist science was ignored, because fascism was understood mainly as mass ideology rather than as having an appeal to educated elites, as having rational coherence, and as an essential element in the planning and implementation of social policies. If, following Georg Lukacs, one sees fascism as the culmination of the destruction of the values of reason, science, and intellect, then fascist science and intellectual thought become impossibilities. At most one can cite examples of scientists seeking to preserve the values of truth and objectivity from the regime's encroachments, or scientists sacrificing their identity to the dictates of the regime. There has been virtually no discussion as to whether an overarching medical and demographic model was shared by fascist and other authoritarian regimes; whether health and welfare policies indicate a pluralism inherent in fascist ideology and social structures; or whether fascists were parasitic in appropriating demographic and scientific thought first developed under less authoritarian social systems (Mehrtens and Richter, 1980; Lukacs, 1954).

A plurality of regimes

Debates on fascism have been dominated by political sociologists engaged in a taxonomy of party political organization. Until recently, social historians have concentrated on activist party cadres. They have tended to exclude movements organized "from above" from being classified as fascist. Thus there is less interest in the social and demographic policies and conditions in the kindred dictatorships of Hungary, Romania, Spain under Primo de Rivera and Franco, in Portugal, Austria before the Anschluss, and Poland. Such regimes are excluded because of their ideological syncretism and because they recruited higher civil servants, technologically minded military officers, and successful professionals to their national social movements. The political taxonomists have ignored areas of scientific administration classified as "de-politicized." Yet during the 1930s, regimes such as those in Hungary and Poland developed institutions for analysis of demographic statistics. For reasons of national strategy demographers became obsessed with explaining and measuring trends in fertility (de Konkoly, 1937; Szulc, 1934). The emergence of a new breed of technocrat in authoritarian and fascist social systems is as worthy of analysis as are the new crop of charismatic dictators who dominated the political scene between 1918 and 1945.

Professional and technocratic elites offer a means of evaluating Jürgen Habermas's contention that processes of rationalization embody specific forms of political authority. While scientific and technological progress might have been expected to increase personal freedom and rational decisionmaking, they in fact have authoritarian implications (Habermas, 1968). These issues are apparent in the role of such technocrats as demographers, welfare workers, and medical officers in the "policing of families," as agents of social control, and as mediators of the social value of the "family state" (Donzelot, 1980). Under Nazism were merged the two strands of professional and party political control of minds and bodies. Professional experts regarded an authoritarian political structure as an opportunity to rationalize and plan from a collective point of view by invoking such priorities as national efficiency and the welfare of future generations. Demographers and health officials exerted immense influence in social policy affecting every aspect of family life, as well as in the construction of agencies to monitor and influence the quantity, quality, and mentality of the population.

A narrowly economic interpretation of fascism suggests that population and welfare policies were intended to produce an adequate labor force for the military-industrial machinery of the fascist state. A broader interpretation is needed, however, to allow for social diversity. One can turn for help to the general contention that fascism was an ideology of modernization: a way of integrating peasants, landowners, and craftsmen with mass industrial and urban society (Turner, 1975). Fascist social policies did assist rural and other selected population groups. But the concept of a welfare state supporting the poor and infirm was irreconcilable with the fascist hostility to socialism and to liberal humanitarianism, and with the cult of power. There was a craving for a new type of social order that would be neither socialist nor capitalist. Fascist welfare was an important element in a vision of a corporatist economy that integrated labor, employers, and the state.

Yet "integration" is too mild a term to express the high degree of authoritarian control, and it is intellectually too neutral. It obscures the duality between individual leadership cults and the consolidation of power in state bureaucracies. On the ideological side of the problem, it is worth considering how dictators liked to see themselves as the "iron surgeon"—a term popularized in Spain—to cure national ills. Hitler's *Mein Kampf* was written in this vein. The national leader would renew and regenerate a decaying and disintegrating nation, conceptualized as a social organism. A medical mystique, drawing on the traditional mythology of the supernatural powers of healers, boosted leadership cults and sanctioned the blood-letting associated with political violence.

Expertise and authority

The conceptualization of moral and political issues in terms of social and medical science helped rulers to modernize social structures while avoiding politicization. Concepts of a social pathology were helpful in transposing economic and political problems into naturalistic terms. Just as dictators created elaborate police systems, so they relied on a new breed of technocrat to solve social problems. Their regimes had special powers to mobilize large-scale resources suited for Big science and monitoring of population movements, even if they expelled scientists of Jewish origins as inherently incapable of "properly" national research. There was common ground between fascist politics and technocrats in the striving for an alternative ideology to capitalism and socialism, and in the efforts to construct an integrated, organic, and harmonious society. Modern technologies—including the demographic—were to be harnessed to reinforce traditional values.

The strategies of ruling elites need to be assessed in the light of social conditions. The social historian Tim Mason cautioned that "a well-founded interpretation of national socialist Germany is premature without analyses of topics like the social and geographical mobility of the population, family structure, position of women, health and housing conditions, as well as of welfare institutions and policies" (Mason, 1975). National socialists wished to mobilize the nation's economic reserves and population. In a study of the attempt to create a one-class society, or *Volksgemeinschaft,* Mason focused on "reproducers of wealth"—the working class. He uncovered conflicting population policies under national socialism. Fluctuations in economic and military priorities produced conflicts between the need to recruit women into the labor force and the role of women as reproducers of the race. Subsequent work has attempted to reassess how racial policies were determined by biologistic concepts of gender, and by the priority of producing a fit and healthy race. Despite the attention given to professional interests, population policies have continued to be interpreted as instruments of Hitler's racial priorities (Bock, 1986; Klee, 1983; Lilienthal, 1985). This is fundamentally correct when it comes to the mass extermination of the Jews, but far more problematic regarding compulsory sterilization, and pronatalism. Nazi racism encompassed different völkisch and anti-Semitic, as opposed to technocratic forms. They were to be ultimately synthesized by the SS. I would prefer to follow a line that allows for a diversity of racial policies. Interpretations of Germany under national socialism have shifted from "totalitarianism" to "polyocracy" with rival interest groups and power blocs (Kershaw, 1985). Reappraisal of racial and population policies is also necessary in this light.

Acknowledging a plurality of racial policies within national socialism removes obstacles to recognizing plurality between social systems. Fascism can thus be used as a generic term for the anti-democratic, anti-socialist, ultra-nationalist movements in this period, while in no way implying that these movements have a single socioeconomic explanation or organizational structure. Although whether there is a single demographic model that can be labeled fascist is problematic, it does seem that the family, nation, race, and nature were central values. Fascists stood for ideas of master races, for male dominance in the family and in the economy, party, and state, and for restoring a natural order to society. Their views on the relation between population, the economy, and the environment were distinctive. Fascists imposed new forms of restraints on reproduction from a national and racial point of view. They abhorred neo-Malthusian advocacy of contraception as a decadent form of individualism. They also opposed liberal ideas of free movement of populations (hence losing migration as a safety valve for social problems) and of racial equality. While accepting that natural resources were limited, fascists considered that racially superior populations could be sustained by social or artificial selection and by the conquest of foreign territories. In a natural environment, the struggle for existence would result in a fit and healthy population. But urban and industrial society shielded populations from natural selection, and degenerate groups distorted the natural balance: as Jews were in the vanguard of capitalism and urban culture, they had too few children; the chronically poor had too many. Resources would be increased by the removal of inferior races and of degenerative social influences. Economic and demographic considerations provided a rationale for foreign conquests. Although the concepts of "Geopolitik" and "Lebensraum" predate fascism, they came to underpin the expansive militarism of the German and Italian regimes.

The only aspect of racial policy to have received substantial attention is anti-Semitism and the Holocaust. Historians have compared differing levels of anti-Semitism in Italy and Spain with the more virulent forms existing in Central and Eastern Europe. Yet few attempts have been made to analyze the specific components of fascist racial ideologies, to consider policies toward other ethnic minorities, or to grasp how measures were part of coordinated population policies. Far more is known about the organization of Himmler's security police, the SS, and the National Socialist Party (NSDAP) than about the demographic, biological, or ecological thought that provided a rationale for their policies. Fascist ability to organize censuses and build up data banks on populations was impressive. Registration of the population was a preliminary to extermination (Roth, 1984). Demography and racial surveys of populations were preconditions for the Holocaust.

By a shift of emphasis to the issue of expertise, resources, and scientific racism, new problems of diversity come to light. Nazi Germany saw the most fully developed programs for compulsory sterilization and extermination of the sick and of ethnic minorities, whereas Italy and Spain rejected such policies. By contrast, Scandinavia, Britain, Estonia, and the United States saw either vociferous lobbies for eugenic sterilization, or implementation of legislation. Between the two World Wars, racial and corporatist terminology was rife among technocrats and planners within democratic societies. This raises additional problems regarding comparison of fascist and other contemporary social systems. A conceptual distinction between party ideologues and professional technocrats might seem a line of inquiry worth pursuing. At least it is necessary to determine when and to what extent demographers and eugenicists espoused such fascist ideals as the notion of

Führer and party as vital national forces. An alternative view would be to see the authoritarian regimes as entering into an alliance of convenience with social scientists and demographers, allowing them to pursue distinctive aims that conceded authority within limited spheres. Here, too, problems of authoritarianism within scientific concepts and institutional structures are confronted.

The intellectual and historical location of fascism

Fascism was clearly a product of the political dislocation resulting from World War I and its aftermath. However, underlying social trends were important. Although the demographic transition has been accepted as a normal feature of industrialization, many nationalist-minded groups regarded such signs of modernization as the declining birth rate and urbanization to be pathological: the "two-child system" was stigmatized as a disease of the social organism (Marschalck, 1984). World War I compounded the trends of a sharp decline in births with a rise in mortality rates so that in Germany, for example, the birth rate sank below the death rate. During the war many countries planned legislation to raise the birth rate and promoted popular campaigns to instill in women a sense of motherhood as a national duty. Germany saw a movement to support "child-rich" families with four or more children. In part this was derived from French support for *familles nombreux,* and in part it arose from the concept of the human economy, or *Menschenoekonomie,* postulated by the Austrian economist Rudolf Goldscheid. He urged that the aim of any social system ought to be maintaining the population, rather than production for profit. The economic and social crises following the war gave rise to a sense that the German race was on the brink of extinction (Weindling, 1988). While the Freikorps (anticommunist militias) idealized the German family and racial purity, bureaucrats and statisticians launched ambitious eugenic population policies.

During the 1920s fascists faced new threats of Soviet communism and American-inspired consumerism. Bolshevism posed a threat to the social system as well as to the family because of the Soviet Union's initial permissive legislation with regard to abortion and women's rights. Conservatives in Germany abhorred the growing demand for consumer goods as diverting women and family income away from children. Moral-purity campaigners were increasingly associated with the ultra-Right. They attacked the twin enemies of sexual bolshevism and unbridled consumerism. While there are innumerable analyses of political activists, only one—that by Klaus Theweleit (1980) on male fantasies—has asked what were the self-perceptions, the family loyalties, and ideals of womanhood and of the family that these marauding males sought to defend.

Although eugenics and the ideas of the ultra-Right derive from non-Marxist critiques of bourgeois society, eugenics was not necessarily proto-fascist (Teitelbaum and Winter, 1985). Rather than demanding a single strong leader, eugenicists advocated expert panels to prevent or arrest degenerative social processes. In this sense eugenics represented an extreme form of professional power rather than völkisch racism. Many eugenicists or racial hygienists were critical of unscientific racial mythologizing such as Joseph de Gobineau's theory of a superior Aryan race, first expounded in the 1850s and representing an ideological root of *Mein Kampf.* Gobineau opposed biological and medical anthropology, which in the mid–nineteenth century had many liberal traits. Although racial anthropology became increasingly drawn into support for imperialism, tensions persisted between scientists and racial ideologues. Many eugenicists, however right-wing, saw Hitler as a psychopath with a degenerate physique.

It was in Italy, the cradle of fascism, that a fusion of eugenics, demography, and fascism first occurred. The demographer Corrado Gini was a member of the state constitutional council from 1924. In 1923 Edmondo Rossoni launched a fascist journal with the Galtonian title *La Stirpe* (the race). Following the Matteoti crisis of 1925, Benito Mussolini eliminated the vestiges of liberal rights and set about implementing a planned fascist social system. At the same time as the state apparatus was extended, Mussolini established a Central Statistical Institute in 1926. An ambitious pronatalist population policy was inaugurated (Pogliano, 1984; von Delhaes-Guenther, 1979; Livi-Bacci, 1974 and 1977).

Differences between Italian and German ideologies evened out during the 1930s. The Nazis became concerned with implementing a comprehensive population policy to raise the birth rate of groups of presumed high racial quality. Mussolini became increasingly anti-Semitic and imposed racial laws, which were moderated by their unpopularity as well as by Italian corruption and inefficiency (Michaelis, 1978; Pommerin, 1979). While the Nazi leaders and the SS sought to impose their remedies of mass extermination of the Jews, other fascist regimes differed in their responses. But it is worth considering whether there were distinctive common ends to fascism, even though the means might differ. Such aims included buoyant birth rates, racial homogeneity, and a military style of social regimentation that invaded the domain of the family.

Spain illustrates the political divide over eugenics. Some eugenicists stood firmly on the side of Republicans and modernizers. Doctors urged biological strategies of social reform, and eugenicists founded institutions for social medicine in the early 1920s. But most doctors, especially gynecologists and pediatricians, supported the Church in the campaign to raise the birth rate. Tracts appeared correlating racial vitality with a high birth rate. More extreme than such pronatalism were demands for "higiene racial" by such Falange ideologues as Eugenio Montos. The conflicts in terms of policy can be illustrated by the dictatorship of Miguel Primo de Rivera, which in 1926 instituted the concept of "familia numeroso," entitled to special benefits. These benefits were suspended in 1932 by the Republicans, but were reinstituted by Francisco Franco in 1944 (Alvarez-Peláez, 1984a and 1984b, 1985; de Miguel et al., 1977).

The 1930s saw a number of regimes ban abortion and birth control, while promoting the health of selected rural groups. An example of a non-fascist state adopting pro-rural measures was the Republic of Ireland with its subsidies for "Gaeltaecht," the pure Gaelic-speaking rural communities. In 1935 the sale and distribution of contraceptives were banned in Ireland. The Papal Encyclical *Casti Conubii* of 1930, condemning contraception, reinforced the Catholic Church's pronatalism. Population and social policies of the 1930s tended to be generally more interventionist whatever the social system. Concepts of national vitality as measured by buoyant birth rates permeated demographic thought and social policies.

Modes of analysis of scientists and ideologues

New techniques of demographic analysis such as Hollerith (punch) cards and automatic sorting created possibilities for analysis of birth cohorts and for more effective census procedures. In 1931 the first Italian census of fertility was carried out. In Germany registration of the total population took place in 1938, a national card index or Volkskartei was introduced in 1939, and identity numbers were issued in 1944. Analysis of birth cohorts was made possible by the census of 1939. Numerous analyses were made of the fertility and health of small population groups over many centuries in order to determine long-term demographic trends. Hopes were expressed that tighter social controls and the analysis of data on heredity could provide solutions to such social problems as poverty and crime. Biological data banks and racial surveys were compiled of groups selected for their racial value, using such new medical techniques as human genetics and blood group typing. Medical innovations like sterilization, and demographic schemes for comprehensive registration of the population and for reclassification on a racial basis offered techniques of social control.

The ideological variant of fascism combined adulation for a charismatic dictator with a mystic emphasis on racial psyche and physique. Racial qualities were an explanation for long-term demographic trends. A postwar species of völkisch (although not fascist) ideology provided inspiration for fascist ideologues. An example was Oswald Spengler's prophecies of racial senescence accompanied by infertility (1921). Among American racial ideologists, Madison Grant predicted the end of the "Great [i.e., white] Race," and Lothrop Stoddard feared a rising "colored flood" that would drown white civilization (von zur Mühlen, 1977). They were the intellectual counterpart of ultra-nationalist groups like the Freikorps and Fascisti. These were initially hostile to academic, professionalized, and bureaucratized ideas of population policy. But there was an increasing tendency toward synthesis. For example, the medical statistician and demographer Richard Korherr took Spengler as the inspiration for his 1927 study of the declining birth rate; in 1928 it appeared with a preface by Mussolini, and in 1935 with a preface by Heinrich Himmler. Thus one can trace the changing ideological orientation of a demographer, who came to head the Statistical Department of the SS (Korherr, 1927, 1928, and 1935; Aly and Roth, 1984). Ambitious schemes were launched to impose demographic controls and to promote corporate unity by propaganda campaigns supported by public health, church, and economic interests. Yet there remained a conflict between the modes of analysis of the ultra-Right's intuitive and violent authoritarianism and the scientific discourse of the professional experts, analyzing birth cohorts and initiating racial surveys of populations.

Racial/biological models of fascism

Fascist population policies were characterized by a belief in natural and hereditary inequalities. Special privileges were extended to selected political, racial, and national elites. Gender roles were stressed, with women encouraged to devote their lives to producing healthy and numerous children, while men took leading social and economic roles. Personal freedom in marriage and migration was restricted. In Germany an antinatalist campaign of unparalleled severity, with compulsory eugenic abortion, sterilization, and castration, was implemented as a result of attempts to screen the genetic health of the total population (Book, 1986). A basis for fascism lay in selective controls on and incentives for reproduction of selective population groups (Stephenson, 1979). The state and party were akin to natural forces, capable of extreme forms of intervention into the spheres of the family and the individual.

Allan Chase has suggested that the historic functions of fascism, scientific racism, and Malthusianism have been the same: to keep what Malthus had called "the lower class of people" from ever rising above their spheres at birth. He sees Malthusianism and fascism as identical in their concern to eliminate chronic pauper stocks (Chase, 1977). His interpretation should be set against the writings of Gini, who was critical of the Malthusian assumption that the reproductive powers of populations remain constant over generations. Gini subscribed to a theory of the cyclical rise and fall of populations. There were young and old races, the latter being more liable to decay. Population size developed as a parabolic curve, which Galton had also assumed as describing the structure and development of populations. Gini considered that Malthus had ignored the evolution of the reproductive tendency, as well as heredity, as a factor. Moreover, favorable conditions of life among the prosperous elite seemed to diminish individual reproductive powers (Gini, 1930, 1931, and 1942). Gini and the leading German demographer, Friedrich Burgdörfer, argued that natural societies would maintain a high birth rate. But industrialization and urbanization had sterilizing effects, sapping natural vitality. Demographic investigations revealed growing urban–rural and regional differentials in fertility. This distressed fascists, who were obsessed with forging national unity.

Prior to World War I, German demographers emphasized how urban culture and democratic values were causing a decline in the birth rate. The problems of the two-child system and of the "rationalization of sexual life" became increasingly urgent to fascist demographers, whose predictions of race suicide were more dire and their solutions all the more authoritarian. They were especially concerned with differential birth rates. Analyzing the age structure of populations, they were distressed by the lower fertility of elite social groups, or Führerschichten. Echoing the ideology of a "Volk ohne Raum," Burgdörfer declared Germany a "Volk ohne Jugend" (Eversley, 1959; Glass, 1953; Knodel, 1974; Burgdörfer, 1932). Gloomy forecasts were made of an aging population and of national decay, in the absence of a radical change of lifestyle and a shift away from individualism. Demographers thus contributed to the political climate that precipitated a shift toward the extreme Right.

Such demographic predictions led to a search for new policies of national rejuvenation to restore fertility and national strength. The declining birth rate could be countered by engendering a new will to have large families as well as by constructing a new national-social order. Theories of evolutionary recapitulation (of ontogeny and phylogeny) suggested that a racial consciousness of the period when a race was still in its young and vigorous stage of development could conjure up this will. Such ideas appealed to youth—and, indeed, fascist movements were often youth movements. Enthusiasm abounded for historical and anthropological studies of the early Nordic and Teutonic heroes. Himmler dreamt of reviving a Germanic Reich. History thus served a demographic and biological purpose of rejuvenation. The will was embodied in the national leader and party. Force was justified in civil matters because it was considered equivalent to natural processes. The idea of a welfare state was attacked on grounds that it prevented natural selection. Welfare was to be provided on a selective basis for groups of high racial quality. Doctors and social workers were required to serve the interests of the race rather than of the sick individual.

Problems arose over the scientific basis for ideas of a German or Aryan race. Racial concepts in biology caused similar divisions. Attempts were made to introduce a specifically fascist type of biology. Its emphasis on environmentalism and dynamic behavior of animal populations in the wild (as opposed to domestic populations) was useful to underpin the fascist belief in natural aggression and the need to reverse industrialization and return to an Aryan arcadia of peasant farmers. One problem was who constituted the master race. Italians were outraged by Nazi insistence on Nordic superiority and Latin inferiority. Some Italian fascists were hostile to the "Nordic barbarians," while others developed a theory of a Latin branch of the Aryan race. The Spanish favored the idea of an Ibero-American race (Preti, 1974). Conflicts arose as to the possibilities of producing a master race given the constancy of Mendelian inheritance. However, Mendelism also condemned those races deemed degenerate and those traits deemed pathological to extermination, in that it would be impossible to eradicate bad genes. These views affected policy vis-à-vis half- and quarter-Jews, toward whom the Italians were far more liberal than the Germans. Mendelism also affected the idea of degeneration as producing the congenitally deviant (but highly fertile) antisocial. Correlations were posited between social deviancy, disease (e.g., tuberculosis, venereal disease, and alcoholism as "racial poisons"), and mental deficiency. Whether the illegitimate carried degenerate traits was a matter of controversy among eugenicists, as some objected to the SS's promoting of special welfare benefits for the illegitimate (Lilienthal, 1985).

In line with the rejection of Malthusian assumptions of limited natural resources, fascists argued that larger populations could be sustained. They urged conservation of natural resources, internal colonization, and improvement of wastelands. Overseas emigration was regarded as the loss of a valuable natural resource. Positive measures to sustain rural communities of increased size were a common feature of fascist regimes. An aim was self-sufficiency in food production. Mussolini embarked on an ambitious program of land reclamation that went as far afield as Libya. Other projects to prevent depopulation were concerned with forestry and with new transport and water systems. In Spain the traditionalist-minded Right was agrarian in sympathies: Primo de Rivera declared "Non-industrial Spain is the true Spain" (Ben-Ami, 1983). Walther Darré, the Nazi agriculturalist, developed a comprehensive strategy to sustain the German peasantry, with the allocation of small holdings and subsidies for the racially suitable (Bramwell, 1985). This was the basis of the infamous "Blood and Soil" propaganda. Conquest and resettlement were favored. While the German policies were extreme in involving large-scale population movements and extermination, one must also bear in mind the colonial ventures of Spain and Italy in North Africa.

Predictions and prescriptions

Declining birth rates were feared as causing strategic weakness and internal divisions, along with the loss of power by the intellectual and propertied elites. Vigorous attempts ensued to raise the birth rate and improve the quality of the population by "positive" and "negative" means. To promote selected racial elites, governments adopted marriage loans, health examinations prior to marriage, and child allowances. Variations between state policies can, in part, be correlated with differing demographic conditions. Where birth rates were relatively high, measures were less drastic. Because Italy had a relatively high fertility rate, the modest aims were to check the decline (Glass, 1940). Social conditions also played a part: policies were more interventionist when there was a higher level of engagement in war.

Ideology shaped policies, just as it influenced perceptions of demographic trends. In 1927 Mussolini set the goal of 60 million Italians by 1950. The Falange demanded 40 million Spaniards (de Miguel, 1976; de Miguel et al., 1977). Italians and Germans felt threatened by 200 million Slavs. David Glass remarked that the highly developed Italian population policy was "specifically a product of the fascist era." From 1927 Italy carried out a comprehensive population policy. Negative controls included restrictions on emigration and the imposition of economic penalties on bachelors and childless couples. It became more difficult to obtain contraceptives (although condoms remained legal as barriers against infection) and to arrange abortions. Positive measures included exhortations to marry and legislation for the protection of maternal and child health. Marriage and birth premiums were paid (although, as Glass observes, these were set at meager levels).

The revenue from the bachelor tax subsidized an organization for maternal and child welfare, the Opera nazionale per la protezione della maternità e dell' infancia (abbreviated to ONMI). Founded in 1925 to coordinate family welfare organizations, ONMI extended pre- and postnatal care (Caldwell, 1986; Meldini, 1975). The second source of care was the National Fascist Institute for Social Insurance, which provided family income subsidies. Only in 1940 was medical assistance extended to family dependents, as hitherto only the insured worker had a right to medical care. Under fascism there continued to be a plurality of social welfare institutions, even though there was a high degree of politicization of welfare organizations.

Since marriage and birth rates in Italy were found not to be rising, the Fascist Grand Council passed new resolutions in 1937. The resulting policy included family allowances and preferential employment for fathers of large families. Family allowances were financed as part of the social insurance scheme, and a marriage or family loans scheme was initiated, with cancellation of a part of the debt at the birth of each live and viable child. A Fascist Union of Large Families was promulgated on the model of the German League for Child-Rich Families. The measures were accompanied by nationalist propaganda against neo-Malthusians.

Measures of the Vichy regime in France had many similarities to those of the Italians in their favoring of rural and traditional values. Family allowances may have helped in the marked upturn in the birth rate. Extra rations were supplied to expectant mothers, and fathers of large families were exempted from compulsory labor service (Dyer, 1978). Of special interest was the elitist sociobiology of Alexis Carrel developed at a new institute for eugenic and demographic research in German-occupied Paris.

Voluntarist and Church-controlled forms of welfare were important to more agrarian social systems. In Spain between 1923 and 1930, Primo de Rivera supported the idea of a national Catholic Church that controlled education and family welfare. Public morality was supervised by juntas of the mayor, the government, and the Church. The Italian state also looked to the Church in family matters. The concept of "clerico-fascism" has been invoked to describe Church support for authoritarian regimes as a means of social integration. The Church supported corporatism in the economic sphere, and was often ready to ally itself with positive eugenic forms of medicine and welfare to sustain its position. Indeed, attempts were made in Germany between 1930 and 1933 to synthesize Roman Catholicism with eugenics, although after July 1933 certain groups of Catholics were the most vociferous opponents of eugenics (del Campo, 1974; Díez Nicolás and de Miguel, 1981; de Miguel and Díez Nicolás, 1985; Pérez Puchal, 1980).

The importance of the Church or of the surrogate religious tone of pronatalist propaganda derived from recognition that ideological approaches to population problems were as important as fiscal and other inducements. It was necessary to reinculcate the "will to have children." Catholic states drew on the Madonna cult, exploiting the religious susceptibilities of women, to enforce the idea of the family as sacrosanct. In Spain women were venerated as the soul of the home and family. In Italy a Mothers' Day was instituted in 1933. In Germany the Protestant Church's medical and demographic expert, Hans Harmsen, campaigned on behalf of the Union for Health for a state-supported Mothers' Day. Certain German towns had had a Mothers' Day since 1924, and it was popular among the Southern Germans of the South Tirol. Support came from churchmen, doctors, demographers, and such commercial interests as the Association of German Flower Sellers. The inclusion of commercial interests indicated the attempt to exploit the rampant consumerism for pronatalist ends. The campaign relied on a chain of command: from specialists educating doctors, from doctors to voluntary first-aid workers, and from these to the population at large (Hausen, 1980). Fascists endeavored to politicize marriage and family life. For example, in Italy special bonuses were awarded to couples marrying on dates like 28 October 1937, the anniversary of the 1922 March on Rome. Techniques of mass psychology were meant to induce "psychic rebirth" of the nation.

Nazi policies were remarkable in their attempt to supplant the Church and traditional elites. Whereas the Italians merely wished to retain existing demographic characteristics, the Germans sought to attain a higher level of racial vitality. From 1933 a combined race and population policy was implemented that differed markedly from the more voluntaristic Weimar eugenics (Weindling, 1984 and in press). For example, marriage loans depended on satisfying racial and political requirements, as well as those of good health, appropriate ancestry, and that the woman not be in paid employment. Such loans were intended to remove women from the labor market and stimulate consumer demand for household goods (Stephenson, 1981; Glass, 1940; Pfeil, 1940). Racial, strategic, and political aims were combined in Himmler's vision of a belt of peasant farmers as the bulwark against bolshevism. The SS represented a highly technocratic approach to demographic and racial matters. Darré and Himmler were devotees of racial biology and racial demography, and they drew on the advice of leading scientists. From 1931 on, SS officers were subject to a eugenic marriage code, and they were schooled in racial biology. The SS pushed the polarity between positive and negative measures to an extreme. Positive measures included combating infertility: in 1936 female infertility was declared an illness for insurance purposes, and in 1942 infertility clinics were established. Improving the quality of the German race was to be achieved by elimination of unfit genes—by compulsory sterilization—and of the carriers of these genes—by killing patients in mental hospitals, and by measures to register and segregate such antisocial groups as gypsies, vagabonds, the work-shy, juvenile delinquents, and criminals (Mosse, 1985). World War II provided the opportunity for abandoning legal and Christian traditions sanctioning reproduction only in the family. Racial measures culminated in the policies of the SS for obtaining Lebensraum. Ethnic Germans were repatriated from Eastern Europe for "Germanification," whereas German peasant stocks were resettled in the East. Inferior races were subject to forced labor, to ghettoization, and to extermination (Broszat, 1961; Koehl, 1957; Schechtman, 1946). National socialism was singular in its ruthless racism and genocide, reflecting the greater degree of social conflicts and contrasts in Germany than in other fascist social systems. But the ideals of an authoritarian social structure and a demographic and social backbone of rural smallholders with fertile wives were shared by the other fascist regimes.

Lessons from fascist demography

As a mass ideology, fascism is virtually extinct in contemporary Western Europe. Nazi racism has become legendary for the dangers of the political exploitation of ethnic differences and for the abuses of science. Apartheid in South Africa, however, has similarities to such fascist measures as the 1935 Nuremberg Laws to segregate the Jews and the Italian Laws of 1937 preventing cohabitation of blacks and whites in African colonies. Genocide remains an option employed by authoritarian regimes in maintaining power. Fascist policies must be considered as combining negative with positive measures. Fascist regimes recognized how positive social benefits could stabilize their position. Franco introduced social insurance; Nazi welfare and social insurance measures were beneficial—in theory at least—for the industrial work force. Social forms of fascism were often transmuted into Christian Democracy, as in Italy and Germany in the 1950s and 1960s. This made explicit the continuing social role of the Church, although the tone was now more voluntaristic and market-oriented, in line with British and US conservatism.

In Western Europe migration of labor from the south and from former colonial territories has resulted in new problems of social integration and racism. State immigration controls persist. The post-1945 baby boom meant that there was less incentive for interventionist demographic policies. Less conspicuous but perhaps more enduring than the racial ideological forms of fascism have been the professionalized and technocratic interests. This again poses the problem as to whether professional power under fascist regimes should be classified as a variant of fascism. Demographers who had complied with Nazi policies, such as Harmsen and Burgdörfer, remained influential in postwar Germany. For example, Harmsen presided over the German family planning association, Pro Familia, from its establishment in 1952 until 1984 (Kaupen-Haas, 1984). Organizations like ONMI persisted in Italy until 1975, and legislation regarding contraception continued until 1971. In Germany, the national socialist structure of public health, as well as the laws on contraception and abortion (David et al., 1988), remained in force until the mid-1960s. The compulsory sterilization law was not repealed; because this has been regarded as a medical rather than a national socialist measure, victims have been refused compensation (Bock, 1986). Only gradually has the scientific reification of social concepts and conditions been reversed. The rise of the social sciences, feminism, and the Green movements represent a belated attempt to uproot fascist and corporatist/eugenic attitudes.

With the rise of women's demands for reproductive autonomy, control over contraception has passed from the state to the individual (Aitken-Swan, 1977). Professional controls remain (as for abortion and sterilization), although fascist coercion is supplanted by professional persuasion. Developments in pharmaceutical products have meant that antibiotics now cure venereal disease and tuberculosis when once eugenic methods of prevention would have been used against these so-called racial poisons. New technologies continue to be politically problematic. Genetic engineering, artificial insemination, and screening for diseases have revived alarming specters of authoritarianism and eugenics (Kevles, 1985).

The question of the type of authority and power exercised by professionals during and after the fascist period remains problematic. Bernhard Schreiber formulated a powerful indictment of professional authority, arguing that the associations which dominated the areas of abortion, family planning, euthanasia, sterilization, and mental hygiene have been controlled by a single overlapping elite (as in Great Britain). These organizations promoted on an international level scientific, medical, and demographic policies that—if recklessly applied—could be as potentially lethal as those applied under Nazism (Schreiber, 1975). Certainly, the medical profession thrived under national socialism and gained greatly in public esteem. The collectivist power wielded by experts in the formulation of social policies raises the question whether the professional expertise of technocrats amounts to a new form of authoritarianism (Hogben, 1963). Followers of the French philosopher Foucault, who analyzed the power relations in such institutions as hospitals, suggested the coercive function not only of the institutions but also of the forms of knowledge. This can be exemplified in demography by problems of collecting, storage, and use of aggregate data. National aggregates may serve the interests of elites in political control, and one must remain aware that, if misapplied, they tend to distort and obscure rather than represent the real processes as encountered and experienced by individuals, minorities, and underprivileged groups. The power of demographers, planners, and health officials is so great that, potentially at least, society could be transformed into a total institution.

Finally, I should mention the gap between noble scientific rhetoric and actual brutality in the implementation of fascist policies. Coercion and killing were sanitized by such rhetoric as "the alleviation of suffering" or care for the interests of future generations. In practice, racial and demographic surveys and medical diagnoses were often based on flimsy evidence. For example, victims of compulsory sterilization objected that they were being sterilized because they were poor and had not enjoyed educational and economic opportunities. Concepts of disease and subnormality offered the opportunity for deprivation of political rights and for dehumanization. At its most radical, fascism sought to eliminate poverty, unemployment, the sick, and the infirm by exterminating afflicted persons. We are only beginning to uncover the depth of authoritarianism and coercion inherent in science and scientized spheres. For these reasons the continuing assessment of fascist demography teaches salutary lessons.

Note

I acknowledge the help of Esteban Rodriguez Ocana in collecting the Spanish-language literature on this topic.

References

Aitken-Swan, Jean. 1977. *Fertility Control and the Medical Profession*. London: Croom Helm.

Alvarez-Peláez, R. 1984a. "El Instituto de Medicina Social: primeros intentos de institucionalizar la Eugenesia (en España)," *Actas III Congreso Sociedad Española de Historia de las Ciencias. San Sebastián, Octubre 1984.*

———. 1984b. "Eugenesia e Ideología," in *La Ciencia moderna y el Nuevo mundo. Actas de la I Reunión de Historia de la Ciencia y de la Técnica de los Páises Ibéricos e Iberoamericanos. Madrid, Septiembre 1984,* ed. J. L. Peset. Madrid: Consejo Superior de Investigaciones Científicas, pp. 349–358.

———. 1985. "Introducción al estudio de la Eugenesia española (1900–1936)," *Quipu* 2: 95–122.

Aly, Götz, and Karl Heinz Roth. 1984. *Die restlose Erfassung: Volkszählen, Identifizieren, Aussondern im Nationalsocialismus.* Berlin: Rotbuch Verlag.

Ben-Ami, Schlomo. 1983. *Fascism from Above: The Dictatorship of Primo de Rivera in Spain 1923–1930.* Oxford: Oxford University Press.

Bock, Gisela. 1986. *Zwangssterilisation im Nationalsozialismus.* Opladen: Westdeutscher Verlag.

Bramwell, Anna. 1985. *Blood and Soil: Walther Darré and Hitler's Green Party.* Abbotsbrook: Kensal Press.

Broszat, Martin. 1961. *Nationalsozialistische Polenpolitik 1939–1945.* Stuttgart: Deutsche Verlags-anstalt.

Burgdörfer, Friedrich. 1932. *Volk ohne Jugend: Geburtenschwund und Überalterung des deutschen Volkskörpers.* Berlin.

Caldwell, Lesley. 1986. "Reproducers of the nation: Women and the family in Fascist policy," in *Rethinking Italian Fascism,* ed. David Forgacs. London: Lawrence and Wishart, pp. 110–141.

Chase, Allan. 1977. *The Legacy of Malthus.* New York: Knopf.

David, Henry P., Jochen Fleischhacker, and Charlotte Höhn. 1988. "Abortion and eugenics in Nazi Germany," *Population and Development Review* 14, no. 1: 81–112.

de Konkoly, Jules. 1937. "The population movement of Hungary and the reforms in the Hungarian population statistics," *Population* 2: 40–46.

de Miguel, A. 1976. *40 millones de españoles 40 años después.* Barcelona: Ed. Grijalbo.

———, et al. 1977. *La pirámide Social española.* Barcelona: Ed. Ariel.

de Miguel, J. M., and J. Díez Nicolás. 1985. *Políticas de Población.* Madrid: Espasa Calpe.

del Campo, S. 1974. *La politica demografica en España.* Madrid: Edicusa.

Díez Nicolás, J., and J. M. de Miguel. 1981. *Control de natalidad en España.* Barcelona: Fontanella.

Donzelot, Jacques. 1980. *The Policing of Families: Welfare versus the State.* London: Hutchinson.

Dyer, Colin. 1978. *Population and Society in Twentieth Century France.* London: Hodder and Stoughton.

Eversley, D. E. C. 1959. *Social Theories of Fertility and the Malthusian Debate.* Oxford: Oxford University Press.

Gini, Corrado. 1930. "The cyclical rise and fall of population," in *Population,* ed. Corrado Gini et al. Chicago: University of Chicago Press, pp. 1–140.

———. 1931. *Le basi scientifiche della politica della popolazione.* Catania: Moderno.

———. 1942. "Über die differenzierte Fruchtbarkeit und einige verwandte Frage," *Archiv für Rassen- und Gesellschaftsbiologie* 35: 177–208.

Glass, D. V. 1940. *Population Policies in Europe.* London: Oxford University Press, esp. pp. 260–268.

———. 1953. "Malthus and the limitation of population growth," in *Introduction to Malthus,* ed. D. V. Glass. London: Watts.

Habermas, Jürgen. 1968. *Technik und Wissenschaft als 'Ideologie.'* Frankfurt: Suhrkamp.

Hausen, Karin. 1980. "Mütter zwischen Geschäftsinteressen und kultischer Verehrung: Der 'Deutsche Muttertag' in der Weimarer Republik," in *Sozialgeschichte der Freizeit,* ed. G. Huck. Wuppertal: Peter Hammer, pp. 249–280.

Hitler, Adolf. 1925. *Mein Kampf.* Munich: Max Amann.

Hogben, Lancelot. 1963. *Science in Authority.* London: Unwin University Books.

Kaupen-Haas, Heidrun. 1984. "Eine deutsche Biographie—der Bevölkerungspolitiker Hans Harmsen," in A. Ebbinghaus, Heidrun Kaupen-Haas, and Karl Heinz Roth, *Heilen und Vernichten im Mustergau Hamburg.* Hamburg: Konkret Verlag.

Kershaw, Ian. 1985. *The Nazi Dictatorship*. London: Edward Arnold.
Kevles, Daniel J. 1985. *In the Name of Eugenics: Genetics and the Uses of Human Heredity*. New York: Knopf.
Klee, Ernst. 1983. *''Euthanasie'' im N.S.-Staat*. Frankfurt am Main: S. Fischer.
Knodel, John E. 1974. *The Decline of Fertility in Germany, 1871–1939*. Princeton: Princeton University Press.
Koehl, Robert L. 1957. *RKVDV: German Resettlement and Population Policy 1939–1945*. Cambridge, Mass.: Harvard University Press.
Korherr, Richard. 1927. *Geburtenrückgang*. Munich: Süddeutscher Verlag.
———. 1928. *Regresso delle Nascite: Morte dei Popoli*, with a preface by Benito Mussolini. Rome: Libreria del Littorio.
———. 1935. *Geburtenrückgang, Mahnruf an das deutsche Volk mit einem Geleitwort des Reichsführers SS Heinrich Himmler*. Munich: Süddeutsche Monatshefte.
Laqueur, Walter (ed.). 1979. *Fascism: A Reader's Guide*. Harmondsworth: Penguin.
Lilienthal, Georg. 1985. *Der ''Lebensborn e.V'': Ein Instrument nationalsozialistischer Rassenpolitik*. Stuttgart: Gustav Fischer.
Livi-Bacci, Massimo. 1974. "Italy," in *Population Policy in Developed Countries*, ed. Bernard Berelson. New York: McGraw-Hill.
———. 1977. *A History of Italian Fertility During the Last Two Centuries*. Princeton: Princeton University Press.
Lukacs, Georg. 1954. *Die Zerstörung der Vernunft*. Berlin: Aufbau Verlag.
Marschalck, Peter. 1984. *Bevölkerungsgeschichte Deutschlands im 19. und 20. Jahrhundert*. Frankfurt am Main: Suhrkamp.
Mason, Tim. 1975. "Women in Germany, 1925–1940: Family, welfare and work," *History Workshop*, no. 1: 5–32.
Mehrtens, Herbert, and Steffen Richter. 1980. *Naturwissenschaft, Technik und NS-Ideologie*. Frankfurt am Main: Suhrkamp.
Meldini, Piero. 1975. *Sposa e madre esemplare: Ideologia e politica della donna e della famiglia durante il fascismo*. Rimini and Florence: Guaraldi.
Michaelis, Meir. 1978. *Mussolini and the Jews: German–Italian Relations and the Jewish Question in Italy, 1922–1945*. Oxford: Clarendon Press.
Mosse, George L. 1985. *Nationalism and Sexuality: Respectability and Abnormal Sexuality in Modern Europe*. New York: Fertig, pp. 153–180.
Pérez Puchal, P. 1980. *La natalidad en España: discurso leido en la solemne apertura del curso 1980/81*. Valencia: Secretariado de Publicaciones de la Universidad de Valencia.
Pfeil, Elisabeth. 1940. "Wandlungen in der deutschen Bevölkerung seit 1933," *Der Erbarzt* 8: 275–276.
Pogliano, Claudio. 1984. "Scienza e stirpe: eugenica in Italia (1912–1939)," *Passato e presente:* 61–97.
Pommerin, Reiner. 1979. "Rassenpolitische Differenzen im Verhältnis der Achse Berlin–Rom 1938–1943," *Vierteljahreshefte für Zeitgeschichte* 27: 646–660.
Preti, Luigi. 1974. "Fascist imperialism and racism," in *The Ax Within: Italian Fascism in Action*, ed. Roland Sarti. New York: New Viewpoints, pp. 187–207.
Roth, Karl Heinz (ed.). 1984. *Erfassung zur Vernichtung*. Berlin: Verlagsgesellschaft Gesundheit.
Schechtman, Joseph B. 1946. *European Population Transfers 1939–1945*. New York: Oxford University Press.
Schreiber, Bernhard. 1975. *The Men Behind Hitler: A German Warning to the World*. London: Tadeusz.
Spengler, Oswald. 1921. *Der Untergang des Abendlandes*. Munich: Beck.
Stephenson, Jill. 1979. " 'Reichsbund der Kinderreichen': The League of Large Families in the population policy of Nazi Germany," *European Studies Review:* 350–375.
———. 1981. *The Nazi Organisation of Women*. London and Totowa, N.J.: Croom Helm and Barnes & Noble.

Szulc, Stefan. 1934. "The Polish Institute for the Scientific Investigation of Population Problems," *Population:* 14–35.

Teitelbaum, Michael S., and Jay M. Winter. 1985. *The Fear of Population Decline.* Orlando: Academic Press.

Theweleit, Klaus. 1980. *Männerphantasien.* Reinbek bei Hamburg: Rowohlt.

Turner, Henry A. 1975. "Fascism and modernization," in *Reappraisals of Fascism.* New York: New Viewpoints, pp. 117–139.

von Delhaes-Guenther, Dietrich. 1979. "Die Bevölkerungspolitik des Faschismus," *Quellen und Forschungen aus italienischen Archiven und Bibliotheken* 59: 392–419.

von zur Mühlen, Patrik. 1977. *Rassenideologien, Geschichte und Hintergründe.* Bonn: Dietz.

Weindling, Paul. 1984. "Die Preussische Medizinalverwaltung und die 'Rassenhygiene,' " *Zeitschrift für Sozialreform:* 675–687.

———. 1988. "The medical profession, social hygiene and the birth rate in Germany, 1914–1918," in *The Upheaval of War: Family, Work and Welfare in Europe 1914–1918,* ed. J. Winter and R. Wall. Cambridge: Cambridge University Press.

———. In press. *Health, Race and German Politics from National Unification to Nazism.* Cambridge: Cambridge University Press.

Woolf, S. J. 1968. *European Fascism.* London: Weidenfeld and Nicolson.

Socialism, Social Democracy, and Population Questions in Western Europe: 1870–1950

JAY M. WINTER

CONSERVATIVE GROUPS AND PARTIES IN EUROPE in the twentieth century have strongly supported measures to raise the birth rate and protect the family, as is both well known and unsurprising. What is puzzling is the convergence of conservative and socialist views on these matters. This essay explores the gradual adoption of a similar language and similar proposals linking the socialist, the center-left, and the nonsocialist discourse on population questions in Western Europe. The outcome was a consensus that, by the late 1930s and following World War II, made population policy largely a matter of family policy, on whose broad outlines most political factions could agree. This evolution of ideas and attitudes did not occur simultaneously throughout Europe, but the process of political accommodation was the same.

This essay explores some of the reasons why most Western European socialists who addressed population questions in this century have wound up in the pronatalist camp. All responded to an unprecedented demographic trend: the secular decline in fertility in all European countries starting in the 1870s and continuing up to and following World War II. Some welcomed this trend; most did not and adopted arguments and policies aimed at reversing it. The explanation for the strength of left-wing pronatalism must be sought in three areas: in socialist theory, in socialist esthetics, and in socialist politics.

Many of the people whose work we shall discuss were socialists, committed to transforming capitalist society into what they took to be a more just social order, based on the common ownership of the means of production. Others were social democrats, who shared the view that a collectivist state was the ideal, but who were prepared to accept as a viable compromise a mixed economy under conditions of parliamentary democracy. Still others were left-wing liberals, interested more in freedom than in equality, but willing to support the use of state power to improve the lot of the masses. This collectivist community cannot be defined with precision in any European country, but it was (and is) a group of activists and writers committed to democracy and opposed to the untrammeled workings of the free market economy.

Social democracy and the population question

Anyone interested in the population question in the late nineteenth century would have been aware of Marx's polemics against Malthus, Engels's exploration of the origins of the family, and Karl Kautsky's varied and at times contradictory discussion of demographic questions (for examples, see William Petersen's essay in this volume). These works were widely known, but in and of themselves they did not provide the basis for a socialist discourse on contemporary problems related to population and the family. Of much greater importance in this respect were the writings of one of the towering figures of the European labor movement, August Bebel. A founder of the German Social Democratic Party, Bebel exercised a moral authority second to none in his leadership of the socialist movement, both in Germany and, through the socialist Second International (a federation of workers' organizations), elsewhere in Europe (Maehl, 1980).

Bebel and women under socialism

Bebel's most important essay on population and the family was *Women under Socialism*. Bebel's *Frau*, as it was affectionately known, became one of the most widely read and influential books in the socialist literature. It went through 55 editions between 1880 and 1930, and was translated into 20 languages.

Women under Socialism provides irrefutable evidence that a commitment to women's rights was an integral part of the socialist agenda in the period of the Second International and thereafter. But the link between aspirations and action in the history of socialism has always been problematic, and this case is no exception. It is apparent that, as moving and powerful as it was, the position Bebel advanced was inspirational rather than operational. As we shall argue below, his feminism was well in advance of working-class attitudes to women and, under the inauspicious political conditions of the period 1880–1914, unlikely to lead to any practicable political program.

Bebel's impassioned voice gave *Women under Socialism* its extraordinary appeal. For Ottilie Baader, a seamstress who became a prominent German feminist, reading Bebel was tantamount to a "religious rebirth":

> Life's bitter needs, overwork, and bourgeois family morality had destroyed all joy in me. I lived resigned and without hope. . . . News came of a wonderful

> book that . . . Bebel . . . had written. Although I was not a Social Democrat, I had friends who belonged to the Party. Through them, I got the precious work. I read it nights through. It was my own fate and that of thousands of my sisters. Neither in the family, nor in public life, had I ever heard of all the pain the woman must endure. One ignored her life. Bebel's work courageously broke with the old secretiveness. . . . I read the book not once, but ten times. Because everything was so new, it took considerable effort to come to terms with Bebel's views. (quoted in Quataert, 1979: 60)

The Italian socialist Anna Kuliscioff similarly claimed that whereas Marx had provided the method, Bebel provided the message that made sense of the lives of ordinary men and women. He had shown the way to convert Marxism into a tool to unravel the miseries and contradictions of daily life. By pointing to the family as a locus of oppression under capitalism, Bebel had successfully "called into battle and [thrown] into the struggle the proletarian woman, three times the slave—in the workshop, in the family, and in society" (ibid., p. 162).

The secret of the success of Bebel's book was indeed that it dealt with ordinary workers' daily lives, which after all were largely spent within the confines of the family. It was thus the first major work to imbricate socialist ideas about population, women, and the family within working-class culture.

An understanding of the moral morass of capitalism was impossible, Bebel argued, without a close analysis of the nature of the family under capitalism. And it was to disabuse his readers of the bourgeois illusions surrounding the holy sacrament of matrimony that Bebel directed his most scathing remarks. He chose one paean to patriarchy as his text, that of Professor L. von Stein. In it, the professor remarked that

> Man deserves a being that not only loves, but also understands him. He deserves a person with whom not only the heart beats for him, but whose hand may also smooth his forehead, and whose presence radiates peace, rest, order, a quiet command over herself and the thousand and one things upon which he daily reverts: he wants someone who spreads over all these things that indescribable aroma of womanhood, one who is the life-giving warmth to the life of the house.

To Bebel this "song of praise" concealed the base facts both of woman's own degradation and of the "low egotism of man," who benefited from the bondage known as marriage under capitalism. Countless unhappy marriages testified to the fact that "hard, raw reality wipes off the poetic coloring more easily than does the hand the colored dust of the wings of the butterfly" (Bebel, 1904: 90–91).

This is the essence of Bebel's achievement: he located the difficulties of marital and sexual life within a social framework, and thereby pointed out to many working men and women that their unhappiness and personal problems were, to a large degree, socially determined. Whatever the truth of this argument, it had obvious popular appeal.

To Bebel, one of the most devastating consequences of capitalism was its deformation of normal elective affinities by forcing them into the mold of property relations. "With the large majority of women, matrimony is looked upon as a species of institution for support, which they must enter into at any price." Similarly many men approached the decision to marry as an exercise in cost–benefit analysis. And even when real feelings were predominant, before long "raw reality brings along so much that disturbs and dissolves, that only in rare instances are the expectations verified which, in their youthful enthusiasm and ardor, the couple had looked forward to" (ibid., p. 87). Among working people, the necessary and wearying labor of women to keep the family above the level of subsistence meant that "the family life of the working class goes ever more to pieces, the dissolution of marriage and the family is a natural result, and immorality, demoralization, degeneration, diseases of all natures and child mortality increase at a shocking pace" (ibid., p. 180). Indeed, according to Bebel, the miserable state of the majority of working women—both psychological and physical—constituted a "social calamity . . . urging the race towards its destruction" (ibid., pp. 122–123).

The political implications of this argument were evident. First, socialists must convince people of the corrosive effects of capitalism on the most intimate aspects of everyday life. Second, male workers must accept that they are co-exploiters of women within the family. In the short run, men benefited from the subordinate position of women, but in the long run it crippled men both spiritually and politically. Third, the irresistible logic of women's entry into the labor force must lead to an alliance of women workers and their male comrades in a class struggle at the point of production. Fourth, only when women succeeded in asserting their equal rights alongside men would the natural function of marriage and reproduction be freed from the constraints of an inhuman system of property relations.

It should be clear from the foregoing examples that the assertion of women's rights to a full productive life was on the agenda of socialist thought by the end of the nineteenth century. As we shall note below, not all socialists shared Bebel's feminism, but few were prepared to ostracize half the human race from the struggle for liberation from the yoke of capitalism.

It is apparent, though, that other contemporary and later socialist writing on this cluster of questions departed from Bebel's position in fundamental ways. While these writings had important things to say, they suffered from some of the same difficulties as did Bebel's work, without having the compensating virtues of his indignation and his anger. They tended to examine the family and women's rights primarily or exclusively within the context of national fertility trends and of the need to balance population and resources either by increasing the birth rate or by stabilizing it at a moderately high level.

Let us consider three excursions into socialist and social democratic demography that gave pride of place to the question of optimal fertility. They are the work of very different scholars: Arsène Dumont, Francesco Nitti, and Gunnar and Alva Myrdal.

Dumont and social capillarity

Arsène Dumont was a fiercely polemical French demographer who wrote in the 1890s and who in 1902 died by his own hand at a relatively early age. He is chiefly known for his theory of social capillarity, which held that the desire to enhance one's social and economic position was hampered by large family size, rendering the most ambitious members of society the least fertile.

Dumont approached demography with the unbridled passion of a secular moral crusader. His major works were *Dépopulation et civilisation: étude démographique*, published in 1890, and *Natalité et démocratie*, which appeared eight years later. Dumont also wrote a number of pioneering studies on regional fertility trends in France and elsewhere (Sutter, 1953: 79–92). He was one of an array of French social critics, on both the left and the right, who were deeply troubled by the problem of *dénatalité* (depopulation). Shortly before his death, he was appointed to serve on an extra-parliamentary commission on dénatalité, whose membership demonstrated the wide political appeal of a commitment to reversing France's fertility decline (Teitelbaum and Winter, 1985: ch. 3; Becchia, 1986: 201–246).

Dumont's Republican zealotry had as its major target what he took to be the disease of liberal individualism. This disease had, as its necessary outcome, the dissolution of social solidarity in all aspects of life. The most salient instance of the individual's preference for his own advancement was, to Dumont, the secular decline in fertility. But the rot of individualism corroded all other "socially indispensable functions" as well. Among Dumont's catalogue of the ills of individualism were the waning of French patriotism and military prowess (so patently evident in the disasters of the 1870–71 war with Prussia), the flight from the land, and "the progressive diminution of marital and paternal authority" as reflected in rising divorce rates. Indeed, to Dumont, these four social diseases were inextricably related:

> In effect, the decline of natality is nothing other than the denial of social solidarity over time between generations; the decline of patriotism is the denial of social solidarity among citizens of a particular area; the flight from the land of the richest inhabitants is the denial of village solidarity; finally the decline in paternal and marital authority is the denial of familial solidarity, more or less in its prescribed and necessary form. (Dumont, 1898: 165–166)

Demography had an essential part to play in reversing this trend, by exposing the depth of the crisis and by destroying the domination of individualism over the moral and political life of the nation. Socialism would lead to a revival of fertility, just as surely as individualism had undermined it. To this end, Dumont was prepared to back concrete reforms, including enfranchising the smallholder on his land and decentralizing the political, economic, and social life of the country (Dumont, 1890: 404).

Of equal importance was the struggle against the clergy and against religion in general, the source in his eyes (and in the eyes of many on the Republican left) of much that was wrong with France (ibid., p. 444). How could it be otherwise, when the Church venerated both a Virgin (thus denigrating fertility) and a Man who "had neither country, nor property, nor profession, nor family, nor wife, nor children" (ibid., p. 351)?

Given the power of the Church and the logic of individual social advancement, the French Republic remained a republic in name alone. In effect, the task of demography was to disclose and thereby to loosen the hold of contemporary French society in which social mobility is legally permitted and great inequalities of wealth prevail.

Nitti and social solidarity

Some of Dumont's ideas were idiosyncratic, but the core of his contribution to demography was the concept of social capillarity, the filtering-down of forms of behavior from one social stratum to another. This notion was accepted and developed by many more temperate and influential writers. One such was the Italian economist Francesco Nitti, professor of political economy at the University of Naples, a liberal in politics who held collectivist views on economic and social issues. He became Prime Minister of Italy at the head of a center-left coalition after World War I. Nitti wrote extensively in the 1890s on population questions and in 1923 received the Nobel Peace Prize for work on behalf of the League of Nations.

In his most important scholarly study, *Population and the Social System*, published in 1894, Nitti followed much of Dumont's argument as to the depressing effects of individualism on fertility (Nitti, 1894: 115). Nitti even accepted the notion that Catholicism, in some forms, led to a veneration of celibacy, but he refused to be persuaded by Dumont's obsessive hatred of the Church (ibid., p. 123).

Above all, Nitti followed the logic of Dumont's claim that in contemporary society, "the law of social capillarity acts with most intensity" (ibid., p. 128). But he departed from Dumont's view that socialism would substantially increase fertility by equalizing opportunities for all. Instead, he opted for the more moderate view—shared by his teacher, Achille Loria—that under a more egalitarian society with a much wider distribution of landed property, the birth rate would attain a rough equilibrium with the means of subsistence. This provided a demographic justification for land reform in Italy, a central tenet of radical politics in the late nineteenth and early twentieth century (ibid., p. 191; Eversley, 1959: 134–135).

The most striking contrast between Nitti and Bebel exists with respect to their discussion of women. For Bebel, women's predicament was central to the socialist agenda; for Nitti and most other social reformers, women's rights were at best marginal concerns. Indeed, Nitti raised the subject only twice in his book, once with respect to factory labor, once in connection with contraception.

Nitti firmly opposed both. In his view, "the working classes would gain very much from the moral point of view, and would lose very little from the economic point of view, if the work of women in manufactories were suppressed." Male wages would then rise, the birth rate of the poorest would fall, and the cause of family unity would be advanced (Nitti, 1894: 148, 116). This was to be preferred in every respect to the "moral aberration" of contraception, which "simply leads to the degeneration of the senses, and the decadence of the race" and thereby only serves "to kill the family ideal, the sentiment of social duty; to shake the very foundations of civilisation and progress" (ibid., p. 165). Contraception is the ultimate form of individualism, to be firmly resisted.

Perhaps it was inevitable that a Catholic Liberal like Nitti would harbor some of the antifeminist sentiments of his culture (Nitti, 1895). In this, he was probably no different from the bulk of those who supported the left in the workshops and in voting behavior.

The Myrdals: Pronatalism and feminism

Let us now consider the work of Gunnar and Alva Myrdal, two remarkable Swedish scholars and political activists, whose demographic work dates from the 1930s. Both were Nobel laureates, Gunnar in economics (in 1964) and Alva for peace (in 1968). Their work on Swedish population policy was, we argue, a fusion of the two facets of socialist demography: Bebel's feminism and the pronatalism of many French and other European socialists.

In effect, the Myrdals tried to combine the best of both worlds. They accepted pronatalism, but refused to sacrifice women's rights on the altar of higher birth rates. Instead, they transferred to the very different demographic, political, and economic conditions of the 1930s the same primary concern with women's rights that inspired Bebel's book 50 years before.

The main contrast between Bebel's position and the Myrdals', though, is the latter's acceptance of the defense of the family as a primary socialist objective. This reflects the very different political terrain in which they operated. Bebel led a successor party, the center of an alternative culture, that awaited the moment when the collapse of the old order would present socialists with the chance to remake the world. The Myrdals spoke to and for a Social Democratic Party already in power in a country disfigured by few of the profound divisions that marred German society. In a way, the Swedish labor movement represented what the German Social Democratic Party never had the opportunity to become: the hegemonic power of an advanced industrial state.

To maintain the vitality and international standing of that state, the Myrdals argued, required a revival of fertility. Parenthood had to be freely chosen and relieved by the state of some of the economic impediments to family formation. This is the form in which their approach to population policy as family policy emerged in the 1930s, at a time when the total fertility rate in Sweden had dropped to the then all-time low of 1.67 births per woman, a full 20 percent below replacement level (Teitelbaum and Winter, 1985: Appendix A). The result was a major review of population questions, in which the Myrdals played a decisive part.

Their first intervention in the debate was a book entitled *Crisis in the Population Question.* Its originality lay in the blending of socialist egalitarianism, pronatalism, and feminist arguments about the right to contraception and abortion. The Myrdals accepted that fertility levels well below replacement reflected a crisis in family life. Not only were most families unable to command an income or find housing suitable for raising children, but it appeared that perhaps 50 percent of the dwindling number of Swedish births were unwanted. The future was gloomy indeed: a stagnant economy, an aging and conservative society, an increasing number and proportion of immigrants in Swedish society, even the possible dissolution of Swedish culture itself.

To help produce an estimated 40 percent increase in native births, the Myrdals presented a bold program of social reform, incorporating many measures that, as socialists, they supported on grounds of natural justice. They advocated tax relief for large families, rent and housing allowances, free health care and schooling for all children, and maternity benefits. In effect, it was difficult to see where their socialist principles ended and their pronatalist zeal began.

Perhaps this was the source of their success: they found a way to use demography as "the most effective argument for a . . . radical socialist remodeling of society" (Myrdal and Myrdal, 1934: 117, quoted in Carlson, 1983: 75). This ambitious project could mobilize support precisely because it appeared to be a necessary precondition for the demographic revival of Sweden. The country was, Gunnar Myrdal believed, on the "threshold of a new epoch in social policy . . . which will most naturally and necessarily be directed at the family and at the children who are the people of the future." Population policy was thus a form of investment in human capital, by far the most important kind of investment, for "the principal wealth of a nation always lies in the quality of its population" (Myrdal, 1940: 100). Here we find the Myrdals' approach encapsulated: to link population, family, and the nation together in an inextricable (and socialist) embrace.

The chief vehicle for this political program was the Royal Commission on Population, established in 1935 with the backing of the ruling Social Democratic government and of all other major political factions (Gille, 1948: 3–70). Gunnar Myrdal, its dominant intellectual figure, succeeded in bringing like-minded people on to the Commission's staff; he managed to handle the complex business of a wide range of subcommittees; and he had a central voice in drafting most of the 16 major reports produced by the Commission between 1935 and 1938.

The Myrdals maintained public interest in the Commission's work—and that of the similarly pronatalist Social Housing Commission, on which Gunnar Myrdal also sat—through their newspaper articles and radio broadcasts. Alva Myrdal even appeared on newsreels that preceded feature films in Swedish cinemas. They were engaging in what Lenin termed all-sided political agitation.

The result was first and foremost to rally support for their ideas both from the radical camp and from some of the more cautious elements within the Social Democratic Party. But the Myrdals also succeeded in demonstrating that socialist family policy had true political appeal. The latter should not be ignored. In 1936, the ruling Social Democratic–led coalition resigned and appealed to the voters on a reform platform. Its central theme was the need to return to power a government dedicated to restoring the Swedish family and thereby the Swedish nation. The Myrdals campaigned actively for the pronatalist reforms on the agenda of the Population Commission.

The result was a sweeping success for the Social Democratic Party and a mandate for legislation in the area of family policy. This body of measures dominated the 1937 parliamentary session, familiarly known as the "mothers and babies" session. The range of reforms was impressive, encompassing family allowances, prenatal financial assistance, marriage loans at low interest, and measures to improve midwifery and hospital delivery services (Carlson, 1983: 86).

The Myrdals' pronatalism was not an argument to return women to the home and to restrict their right to control their reproductive lives. On the contrary, time and again they asserted that only by helping women to combine extra-domestic paid work with childbearing would the birth rate rise. They reaffirmed women's right to work and pointed to the need for "a large number of social reforms, adjusting housing, supervision of children, and working conditions, et cetera, in such a way as to allow women to have both work and a family." Herein lay the most salient "radical possibilities" disclosed by the debate over the population problem. These were issues that enabled feminists—perhaps for the first time, in Gunnar Myrdal's opinion—to find a common language with other radicals in the development of family policy (Myrdal, 1940: 102ff.).

Alva Myrdal's detailed study of these matters—aptly entitled *Nation and Family*—written during World War II but reviewing their prewar work, dealt with other aspects of the politics of reproduction. She started with the premise that "marrying must be encouraged" in order to revive the nation's fertility, and pointed out that the best way to ensure an increase in marital fertility was to defend the married woman's right to work and to equalize the burden of child support throughout the population. But the climate in which an increase in the birth rate would occur had to be created as much through education as through transfer payments and statutory regulations. To this end she advocated mandatory sex education in schools, free access to contraceptive information and methods, and (as a last resort and only under certain conditions) the right to abortion (Myrdal, 1941: 117ff.).

In 1937, some of the Myrdals' ideas on liberalizing the law relating to contraception were translated into new legislation. Parliament passed a series of measures on contraception and abortion that substantially followed their arguments. The 1910 anticontraceptive statutes were repealed, and abortion was legalized on certain medical and social grounds.

Further measures were advanced by the Population Commission in 1938, but by then the clouds of war had gathered, and population questions were no longer at the center of political debate (Carlson, 1983: 87–88). A second population commission was set up in 1941, without the Myrdals' participation. Basically it consolidated the gains made in the previous decade (Gille, 1948: 7).

The political achievements of the Myrdals' work as socialist demographers should not be underestimated. They translated demographic analysis into a sound political strategy and showed that in framing and enacting family policy, social democrats could demonstrate their patriotism and concern for the future welfare of the nation as a whole. In effect they showed that socialist demography made good political sense.

The sexual politics of socialist esthetics

Any analysis of socialist population policy (or for that matter, any other aspect of the socialist agenda) that remains in the rarefied atmosphere of theory is bound to be unsatisfactory. In all discussions of social policy, we must resist the tendency to see its evolution as the product of a dialogue among politicians, advisors, and bureaucrats, whose deliberations exclude the objects of their enterprise—namely, the population at large.

This is especially true with respect to the socialist and social democratic discourse on population, certain facets of which we have already surveyed. Socialists were all too conscious of working against the backdrop of a given social and political situation. In other words, whatever theoretical commitments the labor movement made, its leaders recognized the explosive nature of any attempt to introduce measures that affected the family and sexual behavior.

A glance at the iconography of the labor movement will suffice to show how sensitive socialists were to the need to cultivate traditional images of women and the family in their didactic art. Indeed this absolute traditionalism of gender roles and images is the most striking feature of the symbolism through which European labor expressed its hopes and aspirations.

There is a vast body of visual evidence about images of women in the art of European labor movements in the period under review. As Eric Hobsbawm has said, all political movements require a language of symbolic statement in which to announce their ideals (Hobsbawm, 1978: 121–140). In late nineteenth century Europe, the political allegories of Labor frequently took the form of painting, sculpture, and other decorative arts, some of the best known of which adorn trade union banners. The one feature these banners have in common is their traditional treatment of women as sources of inspiration, not action. For instance, the banner of the Workers' Union is decorated with a delicate young woman in sandals and a white dress, pointing to a rising sun representing "The Better Life." The woman is "Faith." The Tottenham Branch of the National Union of General Workers proudly displayed a banner on which another young woman pointed to a better world in the shape of a children's playground. On her dress is inscribed the motto: "Light, Education, Industrial Organization, Political Action, and Real International."

Other artists with links to labor movements presented woman as consolation, or as symbol of suffering and endurance. The paintings of Constantin Meunier and the etchings of Käthe Kollwitz are some of the better known examples of a genre of artistic work that can be found throughout Europe. In light of the millions of corpses deposited on European battlefields in this century, it is not surprising that the visual arts should portray the grieving wife or mother as a universal symbol. Kollwitz was one of millions of women whose loss of loved ones in wartime marred their lives. Her art speaks profoundly of her personal grief and that of her generation, who did not have the privilege of dying one at a time.

Hobsbawm's central point is to distinguish these artistic motifs from an earlier plebeian tradition of Republican art, in which women were presented at the barricades, or as political actors in the class struggle. The most celebrated example of this genre that he cites in support of his argument is Delacroix's portrait of Marie Deschamps at the Parisian barricades of 1830.

But, as Maurice Agulhon has pointed out, this line of argument does not stand up to careful scrutiny. First, feminine images of revolt faded in France in the late nineteenth century, partly because the Third Republic needed to construct its own armory of images. In doing so, it co-opted femininity as its ideal in the various forms of "Marianne." A labor movement dedicated to transforming or overthrowing a bourgeois republic increasingly chose other, more masculine forms to represent its ideals and its self-proclaimed muscular integrity (Agulhon, 1979: 162–173).

Second, Hobsbawm's view of a "heroic" phase of the popular iconography of women is flawed because it does not take account of the degree to which the allegorical preoccupations of the artist led inevitably to an idealization of all women, which presented them in imaginary poses. Such is the case with the painting of Marie Deschamps, disrobed by Delacroix precisely as Classical convention required.

Socialist art abounded with allegorical women in Classical poses. The iconoclastic Parisian journal *L'Assiette au Beurre,* which appeared from 1901 to 1913, specialized in drawings of women, who were invariably either symbolic figures or prostitutes. What was much more difficult to design were images of ordinary women, at work, at home, or in any other mundane attitude (Dixmier, 1974: 161).

Even feminist artists tended to follow convention in their graphic representations of women. As part of a pre-1914 woman's campaign against drink, for example, a poster depicted angry womanhood, in appropriately Classical garb, expelling with whips an army of bottles of alcohol. Another pre-1914 poster, drawn to coincide with an international convention for women's suffrage in Budapest, shows a Classically clad woman helping Atlas to shoulder the burdens of the world.

There were attempts to break away from these conventional, restricted images of women. The rich collection of feminist posters at the Bibliothèque Marguerite Durand in Paris includes many representations of women that attempt to bypass stereotypical forms. The main techniques of doing so were to draw groups of women, rather than individual figures, and to concentrate on faces and heads only, not on the female body. But prior to the 1960s, the iconographic world of feminist art was not very remote from that of the mainstream labor movement.[1]

Feminist art tried to challenge convention, but it did so hesitantly and incompletely. Artistic stereotyping was the rule, not the exception. We must conclude, therefore, that throughout the period 1870–1950, the imagery of women in socialist iconography has been idealized, passive, and maternal, rather than realistic, active, and liberated from traditional conventions of the nature of womanhood.

There is little doubt as well that socialist art reiterated a view to be found elsewhere in working-class culture as to the virtues of a strict sexual division of labor. Partly because women's wages were lower than men's, partly because women's extra-domestic labor threatened male authority and (so men thought) women's virtue, substantial opposition was voiced in several European labor movements to women's work in general and to women's participation in the trade union movement in particular (Sowerwine, 1983). Whatever Bebel had to say, it was clearly not possible to present women figuratively in socialist art as workers who shared the same fate as their male comrades. Instead, women rarely took a form other than as creatures who were delicate, soothing, maternal, ethereal, indeed eternal, and therefore apolitical.

Within the body of writing discussed above are several instances of this kind of sexual stereotyping spilling over into demographic analysis. Consider the following remark of Arsène Dumont, which forms part of his fulmination against the Church's attitude toward childbearing. Images of the Virgin and her beatified successors, according to Dumont, denigrated fertility. For instance,

> The virgins of Lourdes, which are produced today by the hundreds of thousands, not only are without a child, but are patently incapable of having one. Perched on legs much too long, having neither hips, nor breasts, they wouldn't have milk to give a child, and their pelves are so narrow that the head of a child of the superior race simply couldn't get out. (Dumont, 1890: 351)

Such is one example of the sexual (and racial) stereotyping that was endemic in the labor movement, as it was elsewhere in European culture in the late nineteenth and early twentieth century.

Socialism, the nation, and the family

The socialist esthetics of gender was the first of two substantial obstacles to the emergence of a socialist family policy committed both to women's rights and to the strengthening of the family. The second was the need to build coalitions with middle-class groups emphasizing the nation and family as key social values. Of equal importance in establishing the case for a socialist family policy was its clear electoral appeal.

Most European socialist parties in the period 1870–1914 were electorally weak. In the interwar years, some—as in the case of Sweden—were able to become parties of government. Most others were in perpetual opposition, only intermittently managing to mobilize mass working-class electoral support. In Italy and Germany, the situation was to become desperate with the rise of fascism, but even in the relatively more stable countries of Europe, socialist politics remained minority politics. The only road to power was necessarily through coalition. What better way to describe the community of interests of center-left groups than in terms of the common cause of defending the family?

The problem remained, though, that most of these potential allies of socialists had no commitment whatsoever to women's rights, and some were explicitly opposed to women's extra-domestic political or economic activity. Hence, the politics of coalition-building frequently forced socialists to choose between defending the family and defending women's rights. Given the perceptual myopia about gender roles that most socialists shared with their contemporaries, the outcome was a foregone conclusion.

In the period before World War II, therefore, both the cultural proclivities and the political weakness of socialists helped turn family policy into a rallying point for the popular front. After 1945, socialists and social democrats were in a more favorable political position, partly due to the embarrassment of many right-wing groups about their ideological proximity to or active collaboration with the Nazis. The upsurge of popular support for the left gave socialists a chance not only to nationalize key sectors of the economy but also to bind the wounds of European nations. What better means to do so than to give family policy a high political priority?

The emergence of such policies must also be set against the backdrop of the profound disturbances to family life during and immediately following the 1939–45 war. Twice in this century, the upheaval of total war tore families apart and increased political and social pressures leading to a revival of domesticity (Winter, 1986: 81–109). The politics of the family thus symbolized and gave practical force to a broad body of opinion, which, both during and after World War II, shared the view that strengthening hearth and home was at the heart of social reconstruction.

Socialist patriotism and the birth rate

One of the obstacles to an unequivocal socialist commitment to increasing the birth rate was the hysterical nature of reactionary appeals to fertility as the salvation of the nation. The outcry from patriots of the old school at the work of French neo-Malthusians is a case in point. Paul Robin and other advocates of birth control in the late 1800s and early 1900s were vilified for daring to suggest that women ought to have the right to avoid "the frightening fate of being mothers against [their] will" (Robin, quoted in McLaren, 1983: 104). Hence by a kind of negative reference, many labor militants advocated birth control out of a repulsion for pronatalist arguments that, whatever their merits, were dear to their political enemies. Thus one reason why some trade unionists in France supported birth control was simply to antagonize the bourgeoisie. Others shared the view that more people meant more cannon fodder and lower wages.

To the left of the collectivist community that is the central subject of this essay were the anarchists. Hostile to the state and to the bourgeois family, many were drawn to birth control as an act of defiance. French trade unionists who espoused anarcho-syndicalism—an ideology of workers' control emphasizing industrial militancy and rejecting political reform—were sympathetic to the work of Robin and occasionally passed resolutions in favor of *la grève des ventres,* or "the belly strike." But the link between anarchism and birth control ironically may help to explain why more moderate and patriotic trade unionists, proud of their "respectability," insisted on drawing a veil of discreet silence around the subject (Ronsin, 1979: 85–117).

The same was true with respect to socialist parties, which chose to avoid taking a clear stand on the issue of birth control before 1914. The war crisis and the experience of war itself changed the situation entirely. Pronatalism swept all before it. The best illustration of the *volte face* of those previously hesitant or hostile to birth control is the case of Gustave Hervé, the antimilitarist and militant editor of the socialist newspaper *La Guerre Sociale.* Before 1914, its editorials had tended to support birth control. But by that year, Hervé had adopted the view that increased fertility was essential for "la patrie révolutionnaire." How, he asked, could birth-controllers ignore the disparity between German and French birth rates? "The metaphysics of rubber [condoms] has placed such a blindfold over their eyes that it makes it impossible for them to understand the immediate dangers that this loss of equilibrium between France and the other nations poses to all of us" (quoted in McLaren, 1983: 133–134).

During World War I, the pronatalist campaign grew enormously, finding a receptive audience among socialists dedicated to "union sacrée." Pronatalist rhetoric reverberated on both sides of the trenches during the war, and found in the picture postcard a new and effective means of dissemination. Soldiers wrote millions of postcards to their families during the war. Many featured illustrated messages on the reverse side depicting the virtues of patriotic procreation (Huss, 1989: 329–368).

After the armistice, some socialists returned to the adage of the prominent French socialist leader, Marcel Sembat: "the more people, the more revolutionaries" (quoted in Armengaud, 1966: 16). This argument took the form of claiming that the revival of the birth rate might shore up the political fortunes of the labor movement. With the Communist challenge on the left and a growing counter-revolutionary force on the right, social democracy in Europe needed all the help it could get.

There was some force to the argument that the European labor movement needed a replenishment of numbers following World War I, although it is difficult to see how an increase in the birth rate would do much good in the short term. Still, socialists were used to living with long-term hopes. This may have been in the mind of one prominent socialist pronatalist in Germany, Alfred Grotjahn. In 1923, he wrote in the socialist newspaper *Die Neue Zeit:*

> It must be emphasized, first of all, that the political and economic power of the working class is very largely a question of numbers. . . . If the birth rate continues to decline, it will, in the long run, have a very definite effect on the political posture of the entire population. If the politically active and alert

> working class in the big cities and the industrial regions cannot replenish itself from among its own children, who have already grown up as socialists, then it will be a question of starting fresh with the former agricultural workers who recently migrated from the countryside to the city. (Grotjahn, 1923, quoted in Crew, 1986: 237)

In the 1930s, despite chronic mass unemployment, other socialists discovered the virtues of pronatalism. Some, like Gunnar Myrdal, followed an embryonic Keynesian approach, arguing that a falling birth rate could not sustain effective demand at the level of full employment (Myrdal, 1940: ch. 2). Later in the decade, some Western socialists pointed to Soviet population policy as a model of what the West should do to increase fertility. After the appalling losses due to forced industrialization and the early purges, Stalin suddenly discovered motherhood. Soviet sympathizers in the West—both within and outside the Communist movement—saw in this pronatalist posture a way to demonstrate their own patriotism as well as a new-found commitment to strengthening the family (Delpla, 1975: 151). French leftists were thus able to join the consensus that led to the enactment of the family code of 1939 (Prost, 1984: 7–28).

In Britain, the theme of patriotic pronatalism was reiterated time and again by social democrats in the 1930s and 1940s. One forceful exponent was Richard Titmuss, who later became a prominent theoretician of the welfare state. His patriotism was an inherent part of his call for public action both to decrease infant mortality rates and to increase the birth rate. The first was a long-standing socialist commitment, and formed part of the traditional social message of the left. In 1942, Titmuss published a study of *Birth, Poverty and Wealth*. Here he argued that while in aggregate terms infant mortality had fallen precipitously since the turn of the century, in relative terms the poorest infants were worse off in the 1930s than at the beginning of the century. Hence the demographic disadvantages of social class for manual workers had actually worsened, despite improvements in the health of the nation as a whole (Titmuss, 1942: ch. 2).

Titmuss's book was widely reviewed, and its reception must be understood as part of the ferment of wartime opinion leading to the Labour Party victory of 1945 and the construction of a new welfare system between 1945 and 1951. In order to defeat the Nazis, the argument went, much that was wrong with prewar Britain had to be swept away. In this context, the appalling waste of infant life, as revealed in infant mortality statistics, was clearly indefensible. Consider the view of one syndicated columnist who reviewed Titmuss's book. Writing in the *South Wales Argus*, Alexander Thompson ruminated on Titmuss's statement that, had the children of the poor the same advantages as those of the rich, approximately 24,000 lives would be saved each year. This waste of young life was one reason,

Thompson argued, why women were restricting their fertility: they simply refused to bring up children under "normal" conditions of prewar poverty. But note the link to the political realm. "We are alarmed," Thompson maintained, "by any prospect of a fall in the birth-rate which, if unchecked, would lower Britain's rank and influence among World Powers, and her value to great countries like the United States of Russia and America in the maintenance of peace" (Thompson, 1943).

Titmuss had explored the link between population and international politics in his earliest writings.[2] In an unpublished polemic on the arms race (written in the late 1930s under the pseudonym Richard Castin), he followed without much originality the well-trodden path of denouncing the "merchants of death," or the armaments makers of the prewar decade (Titmuss, n.d.). But in the last chapter of the manuscript, his argument assumed a much more creative and evocative tone, warning of population decline. Titmuss argued that Conservative advocates of the arms race missed the real threat to the nation—that of a dwindling birth rate. "Can a declining population," he asked, "maintain our position as a great Power? Will it, as it declines, deteriorate in quality, and as it grows older, maintain the unity of the Empire?" (ibid., p. 109). To Titmuss the declining birth rate was "a far more vital problem" than defense expenditure; the former stripped the nation of the resources needed for demographic revival. Furthermore, if Britain's population were to decline to the (mistakenly) projected level of 5 million inhabitants over the next several generations, the country would be entirely indefensible anyway. "So the dying remnants of England's greatness will, in the fullness of time, disappear from 'this seat of Mars' " (ibid.).

This was, for Titmuss, the first of a number of forays into left pronatalism. His writings elaborate his discovery that to speak of the population problem was to gain a political voice that was both progressive and patriotic. These are the unifying themes of his essay *Poverty and Population,* published in 1938, and of *Parents Revolt,* jointly written with Kathleen Titmuss in 1942.

Just as the Myrdals argued at roughly the same time, the Titmusses claimed that low fertility meant rule by the aged, which was not an auspicious situation for those who believed in reform (Titmuss and Titmuss, 1942: 42). If the fertility decline continued, they held, then "everything will point to national suicide" (ibid., p. 56). To reverse this trend, both economic reforms and a change in social values were essential. Here again, the Titmusses were largely following the lead set by Gunnar Myrdal a few years before (ibid., pp. 73, 102, 113–115). But they put Myrdal's arguments in a characteristically English Christian-socialist framework, in which "class thinking" and the "virus of acquisitiveness" were deemed to be the enemies of high fertility. For the Titmusses, demography showed that "Capitalism is a biological failure" precisely because it "sets man against man, private greed above public interest" (ibid., pp. 116, 122).

Such appeals for equality and a higher birth rate were commonplace during World War II. In England, the Labour Home Secretary Herbert Morrison frequently spoke on this theme, as did the Independent Member of Parliament Eleanor Rathbone, a central figure in the political campaign in favor of family allowances. They were joined by liberals like Maynard Keynes and William Beveridge and even by some enlightened conservatives who were seeking a way to avoid political oblivion under the new circumstances of the war (Morrison, 1942; Rathbone, 1942; Teitelbaum and Winter, 1985; Smith, 1986, passim).

We have already noted the tendency of some socialists to idealize Soviet population policy in the 1930s. The reiteration of this theme during World War II was, perhaps, inevitable. The Communist newspaper *Daily Worker* applauded Titmuss's effort to draw attention to the "murder" of England's children, who were deprived of adequate material and social support. On the previous page of the same issue, in early March 1944, the paper reported the other struggle: "6 Miles from Pskov: New Battle in Bend." The message was obvious: when so much blood was being shed to defeat the enemy, saving children's lives was an urgent national mission.

Once again the Soviet "ideal" entered British political debate on the issue of maternal and child health. In her preface to the Titmusses' book, *Parents Revolt,* Beatrice Webb pointed to the Soviet Union as a model of what England should do in this area (Titmuss and Titmuss, 1942: 10). The Royal Commission on Population, established in March 1944, took evidence on Soviet population policy and circulated the decree of the Presidium of the Supreme Soviet on "the strengthening and protection of motherhood and childhood" (Royal Commission papers, n.d.). *The Economist*—hardly a socialist weekly, but staffed by journalists sympathetic to the Soviet Union—published an encomium to "Mother Russia" in 1944, celebrating Soviet pronatalism, translated into policies that were "perhaps the most radical and comprehensive programme . . . that any Government has yet formulated" ("Mother Russia," 1944).

Of course, these comments arose in the unusual atmosphere of wartime, and little of the enthusiasm for Soviet policy heard before 1945 survived the onset of the Cold War. But in a sense, their content is less important than the frame of mind they describe: one in which socialism and pronatalism took on an unmistakably patriotic appeal.

Socialism and the family

In his celebrated wartime essay "The Lion and the Unicorn," George Orwell described England in terms that epitomize a central theme in socialist demography: the tendency of social analysis to emphasize common culture rather than adversarial material interests. In a nutshell, it is the rhetoric of the family rather than the rhetoric of class. In Orwell's words, England

> resembles a family, a rather stuffy Victorian family, with not many black sheep in it but with all its cupboards bursting with skeletons. . . . It is a family in which the young are generally thwarted and most of the power is in the hands of irresponsible uncles and bed-ridden aunts. Still it is a family. It has its private language and its common memories, and at the approach of an enemy it closes its ranks. A family with the wrong members in control—that, perhaps, is as near as one can come to describing England in a phrase. (Orwell, 1968: 88)

Many of those who adopted socialist pronatalism were, in this sense, Orwellian. In other words, their deep-seated patriotism predisposed them to develop a political discourse about the national family and its problems. Their language was a clear alternative to that of class antagonism and class struggle. This is not to imply that those who used it were unaware of the injustices of the class structure; rather they believed that social inequality could be reduced, if not eliminated, by appealing to the national sentiments of disparate political groups, and to their sense of common loyalty and mutual responsibility for the nation's children and their future.

Again, we can find antecedents of this familial discourse in earlier forays in socialist demography. The French anthropologist Robert Hertz was unequivocally devoted to the proposition that an increase in France's birth rate was essential for the future of socialism. In a book entitled *Socialisme et Dépopulation,* published in 1910 and warmly commended by *La Revue Socialiste,* Hertz asserted that "a powerful stream of French culture is indispensable for the socialist civilization of tomorrow." This in part depended on the size of the population of France itself. Furthermore, Europe was the home of liberal and democratic ideas that were threatened by autocracies, which generally followed the rule: "the more enslaved, the more fertile." Domestically, dénatalité led to economic decay and an influx of poor immigrants, prepared to accept low wages and impervious to socialist propaganda. The solution was to invest in the country's human capital, in ways socialists had supported for years. In essence what was required was the dissemination of the view that "the nation must be seen as a huge family, responsible for the well being and the health of all her children" (Hertz, 1910: 10, 11, 15, 23; Armengaud, 1966: 16–18).

Hertz did not survive the 1914–18 war, but his ideas did, both in France and elsewhere in Europe. Perhaps the fullest elaboration of this position was that of the Myrdals. The central theme of Gunnar Myrdal's book *Population: A Problem for Democracy* was the need for social democrats to work for a deepening of the "psychological identification of the individual with the people. . . . Psychologically, it is a question of expanded family sentiment, and thus a mild form of nationalism" (Myrdal, 1940: 84, 85).

The primary aim of this appeal was to increase the birth rate, but Myrdal did not ignore its likely effects on socialists themselves. While "the population problem turns political opinions away from conservatism and toward radicalism," and thereby disarms reactionary opposition to social reform, its effect on socialists was to make them more majoritarian and less oppositional in their political outlook. Precisely because of their position on the population question, socialists could no longer "very well be depicted as a destructive force" working for the "denial of national and family values" (ibid., pp. 96, 98, 99). Socialist demography thus enables "the radicalism in radicalism" to be strengthened. The likely outcome, Myrdal believed, was "a transfer of interest from social aid to social investment, and an emphasis on family before social class" (ibid., pp. 99–100).

Family policy or women's rights?

Family before social class: this is the dominant motif in the evolution of European socialist and social democratic ideas about population over the last century. But a second theme recurs throughout these discussions: it may be summarized under the heading of family before women's rights.

We have argued that a central feature of European socialist demography is its recurrent reference to images of nation and family. Most often, this discourse led away from feminism and toward support for the family, maternity, and childbearing in its traditional forms. The case of Sweden suggests that the commitments to feminism and to the family are not necessarily mutually exclusive, although usually the one has canceled out the other.

Why? Part of the reason is ideological, both with respect to the terms of the argument as set out by socialist writers and with respect to cultural barriers to sexual equality visible throughout European society. But part of the reason as well is that the implementation of family policy has frequently exposed its conservative assumptions about gender roles and family structure.

In effect, family policy has meant shoring up the nuclear family, with a father at work and a mother at home. The fact that this ideal never fully existed in working-class communities (Niethammer and Bruggemeier, 1976, quoted in Wickham, 1983: 315–341; Evans, 1981: 256–288), and that in recent years it has become even more remote from reality, is of little consequence. The intention has been to use state power to give workers the chance to enjoy family life, conceived of in very traditional ways.

Family policy offered three kinds of assistance: cash or other subsidies in the form of transfer payments; statutory regulation of women's work; and social work. Each set of measures grew out of a particular notion of what family life ought to be. Let us briefly consider each in turn.

Family allowances have been a pillar of family policy. The origins of these measures have been varied, but a number grew out of the exigencies of wartime experience. For instance, the provision of separation allowances for soldiers' wives and families during World War I was explicitly framed as a measure to fill the gap in both income and male authority left by mobilized men (Pedersen, 1986). The same problems yielded similar, though more comprehensive, solutions during and after World War II. Here military necessity required the temporary breakup of the family; the state acted to ensure that women and children would not suffer materially or morally as a consequence.

Regarding the second set of measures, socialists have mobilized the state to help protect "the family" by limiting the damage to domesticity and maternity that they attributed to women's work. The ambivalence of some socialists and trade unionists toward women's work is well known. Many trade unionists had fought long and hard for a "family wage," which entitled a man to sufficient pay to support an entirely dependent wife and children (Sowerwine, 1983). But after the major contribution women made to the efforts of all the combatant powers in World War I, this argument lost much of its force.

Given the inevitability of high rates of female extra-domestic employment, the question became how to prevent women's work from interfering with what was deemed to be the normal life cycle of the family. There were real problems to which this campaign was addressed: unequal pay rates, sweated labor, sexual exploitation, and so on. But on occasion the efforts of socialists to correct the evils of women's labor had the underlying intention of preserving for men the domestic services to which they had become accustomed.

There is no denying the altruism of socialist efforts to protect women at the workplace. Much of their activity was coordinated by the International Labour Office, established in 1919 as an adjunct of the League of Nations. The ILO established conventions on job protection and on paid leave for women, both during pregnancy and after childbirth, and on restrictions on women's work in dangerous trades and in night work. An impressive number of countries, both in Europe and elsewhere, ratified these conventions in the interwar years (ILO, 1930, 1932).

These measures restricting, if not eliminating, the exploitation of women at work brought material benefits to women workers and their families. But the other dimension of family policy has never been far from the surface. It established means by which state action could limit the extent to which women's work disturbed the gender roles of the family, particularly women's maternal role. Of course, if male wages had been high enough, many women would not have had to work. But given the recurrent phenomenon of mass unemployment and the chronic persistence of low-paid employment, male workers could not afford to maintain their families without a second wage. Working-class women simply had to work, a situation whose negative features the state could mitigate by the three means we have cited: cash grants, statutory controls, or social work.

Let us briefly consider the third form of family assistance, that of social work. In Weimar Germany, local authorities established family care offices to enable social workers to help families in difficulty. Most of their efforts were directed toward restoring traditional family values, or, in the words of one social democrat, toward bringing "the family back on to the path of order and peace" (cited in Crew, 1986: 259). There was little doubt as to the kind of family structure they—and social workers in many other countries—had in mind.

Other forces also helped to reinforce the ideal of the nuclear family as the model on which all social policy was based. After 1945, the traditional family in Europe experienced a kind of renaissance. The reasons for this are obvious. It is not difficult to appreciate the extent to which people turned to family life as a source of sustenance in a period of violent, and at times catastrophic, political upheaval. This phenomenon, which underlay the postwar baby boom (Winter, 1986), was not directed from above; it grew out of the experience of millions of ordinary men and women.

The profound disturbances to family life in Europe in the 1940s gave a particular urgency to family policy and, owing to the increased labor force participation of single and married women, was bound to affect the discussion of its bearing on women's rights. In certain German cities following the war, the sex ratio reached 172 females to 100 males. Millions of men had been killed or had vanished during the war, and in its aftermath women had to keep their families together by dint of their own resources. A survey conducted in 1950, after most prisoners-of-war had returned home, concluded that perhaps one-third of the 15 million families in West Germany were headed by women (Moeller, 1988).

What happened to the family structure in Germany was an extreme case, but to a lesser degree the pattern was repeated elsewhere. The mass graves, the displaced-persons camps, the hospitals and orphanages bursting with charges, all spoke eloquently of the cruelty and bereavement that were the stark realities of the postwar world. To reconstruct the family in this context was a human, rather than primarily a political, necessity.

This is the context in which to place the flowering of family policy in the post-1945 period. In France, as Antoine Prost and others have shown, this led to the creation of political agencies to oversee both family policy and demographic research (Prost, 1984; Laroque, 1983; Doublet, 1948; Watson, 1952; Sauvy, 1977; Mauco, 1977). In Britain, it led to the report of the Royal Commission on Population and to subsequent legislation intended to ease the economic burdens of parenthood (Notestein, 1949). In Germany, the *Grundgesetz,* or fundamental law, adopted by the Parliamentary Council of the Western occupying powers sought both to recognize the equality of women and to restore the family to its centrality in the nation's social life (Moeller, 1988: 4–5). Here we return to one of the key dilemmas of population policy, socialist or otherwise. The postwar celebration of the family as the fundamental social unit was unavoidable. But—with the possible exception of the Swedish case—the enactment of family policy in the wake of the war led to the postponement, dilution, or obliteration of socialist commitments to women's rights. These commitments were neither hypocritical nor hollow; they were made by men and women who genuinely believed in sexual equality and in a woman's right to personal fulfillment outside the home. Hence it is possible to suggest that the dilemma of family policy or feminism was (and remains) unresolved. More than a century after Bebel wrote *Women under Socialism,* the question can still be posed: What is the price women pay for the strengthening of the family?

This question raises a final point of wider relevance to our discussion. After the baby boom of the late 1940s and the 1950s, the prewar fertility decline resumed throughout the developed world. Today total fertility rates are at or below levels reached in the 1930s. Could it be that the subordination of the goal of women's rights to that of increasing the birth rate—a process we have tried to describe above—provides a clue to the failure of family policy to raise fertility to replacement rates or above? A policy that placed women's rights in a secondary position and nurturing the family in a primary position may simply have bypassed the key actors in the story and their aspirations. Since women stand between demographic rhetoric and demographic reality, any analysis of family policy—current or historical—that subordinates the question of women's attitudes and aspirations is bound to have a hollow ring.

Notes

1 Thanks are due to the staff of the Bibliothèque Marguerite Durand in Paris for helping me consult their unusual collection of feminist art.

2 I am grateful to Dr. Ann Oakley for permission to consult the Titmuss Papers, which are in her possession.

References

Agulhon, M. 1979. "On political allegory: A reply to Eric Hobsbawm," *History Workshop Journal,* no. 8: 167–173.

Armengaud, A. 1966. "Mouvement ouvrier et néo-malthusianisme au début du xxe siècle," *Annales de Démographie Historique,* 3.

Bebel, A. 1904. *Women under Socialism.* New York: New York Labor News Press, 33rd ed.

Becchia, A. 1986. "Les milieux parlémentaires et la dépopulation de 1900 à 1914," *Communications,* no. 47: 201–246.

Boxer, M. J., and J. H. Quataert (eds.). 1978. *Socialist Women: European Socialist Feminism in the Nineteenth and Early Twentieth Centuries.* New York: Oxford University Press.

Carlson, A. C. 1983. "The Myrdals, pro-natalism and Swedish social democracy," *Continuity,* no. 6.

Crew, D. 1986. "German socialism, the state and family policy, 1918–33," *Continuity and Change* 1.

Delpla, F. 1975. "Les communistes français et la sexualité (1932–1938)," *Mouvement Social,* no. 91.

Dixmier, E., and M. Dixmier. 1974. *L'Assiette au Beurre.* Paris: Maspéro.

Doublet, J. 1948. "Family allowances in France," *Population Studies* 2: 219–239.

Dumont, A. 1890. *Dépopulation et civilisation: Etude démographique.* Paris: Lecrosnier & Babé.

———. 1898. *Natalité et démocratie.* Paris: Lecrosnier & Babé.

Evans, R. J. 1981. "Politics and the family: Social democracy and the working-class family in theory and practice before 1914," in Evans and Lee (1981), pp. 256–288.

———, and R. W. Lee (eds.). 1981. *The German Family.* London: Croom Helm.

Eversley, D. 1959. *Social Theories of Fertility and the Malthusian Debate.* Oxford: Oxford University Press.

Gille, H. 1948. "Recent developments in Swedish population policy," *Population Studies* 2.

Grotjahn, A. 1923. "Proletariat und Geburtenruckgang," *Die Neue Zeit* 41: 164–172.

Hertz, R. 1910. *Socialisme et dépopulation.* Paris: La guerre sociale.

Hobsbawm, E. J. 1978. "Man and woman in socialist iconography," *History Workshop Journal,* no. 6: 121–140.

Huss, M. M. 1989. "Pronatalism and the popular ideology of the child in wartime France: The evidence of the picture postcard," in Wall and Winter (1989).

International Labour Organization (ILO). 1930. *Report of the Governing Body of the International Labour Office upon the Working of the Convention concerning the Employment of Women before and after Childbirth.* Geneva: League of Nations.

———. 1932. *Women's Work under Labour Law: A Survey of Protective Legislation,* Studies and Reports, Series I (Employment of Women and Children) No. 2. Geneva: League of Nations.

La Vigna, C. 1978. "The Marxist ambivalence toward women: Between socialism and feminism in the Italian Socialist Party," in Boxer and Quataert (1978).

Laroque, P. (ed.). 1983. *The Social Institutions of France,* trans. R. Evans. New York: Gordon and Breach.

Maehl, W. H. 1980. *August Bebel: Shadow Emperor of the German Workers.* Philadelphia: American Philosophical Society.

Mauco, G. 1977. "Le Général de Gaulle et le 'Haut Comité de la Population et de la Famille,' " *Espoir,* no. 21: 21–27.

McLaren, A. 1983. *Sexuality and Social Order: The Debate over the Fertility of Women and Workers in France, 1770–1920.* New York: Holmes & Meier.

Moeller, R. 1988. "Women and the state in the *Wirtschaftswunder:* Protecting mothers and the family in post–World War II West Germany," *Feminist Studies.*

Morrison, Herbert. 1942. "We need charter of motherhood," *News Chronicle,* 15 February.

"Mother Russia," *The Economist,* 15 July 1944.

"The murder of 90,000 babies," *Daily Worker,* 2 March 1944.

Myrdal, A. 1941. *Nation and Family: The Swedish Experiment in Democratic Family and Population Policy.* New York: Harper & Bros.

Myrdal, G. 1940. *Population: A Problem for Democracy.* Cambridge, Mass.: Harvard University Press.

———, and A. Myrdal. 1934. *Kris i Befolkningsfragan.* Stockholm: A. Bonnier.

Niethammer, L., and F. Bruggemeier. 1976. "Wie wohnten die Arbeiter im Kaiserreich?" *Archiv für Sozialgeschichte* 16: 61–134.

Nitti, F. 1894. *Population and the Social System,* trans. M. Mackintosh. London: Sonnenschein.

———. 1895. *Catholic Socialism,* trans. M. Mackintosh. London: Sonnenschein.

Notestein, F. 1949. "The report of the Royal Commission on Population: A review," *Population Studies* 3: 232–240.

Orwell, George. 1968. *The Collected Essays: Journalism and Letters of George Orwell.* Volume 2: *My Country Right or Left 1940–1943.* Harmondsworth: Penguin Press.

Pedersen, S. 1986. "Separation allowances in Britain during the Great War," unpublished manuscript.

Prost, A. 1984. "L'évolution de la politique familiale en France de 1938 à 1981," *Mouvement Social,* no. 129: 7–28.

Quataert, J. H. 1979. *Reluctant Feminists in German Social Democracy, 1885–1917.* Princeton, N.J.: Princeton University Press.

Rathbone, Eleanor. 1942. "Family allowances," *The Times,* 24 June.

Ronsin, F. 1979. "La classe ouvrière et le néo-malthusianisme: l'example français avant 1914," *Mouvement Social,* no. 106: 85–117.

Royal Commission on Population. n.d. "The USSR," R.C. 16, in Titmuss Papers.

Sauvy, A. 1977. "La création de l'Institut National d'Études Démographiques," *Espoir. Revue de l'Institut Charles de Gaulle,* no. 21: 18–20.

Smith, H. (ed.). 1986. *War and Social Change.* Manchester: Manchester University Press.

Sowerwine, C. 1983. "Workers and women in France before 1914: The debate over the Couriau affair," *Journal of Modern History* 55: 411–441.

Sutter, J. 1953. "Un démographe engagé: Arsène Dumont," *Population* 8: 79–92.

Teitelbaum, M. S., and J. M. Winter. 1985. *The Fear of Population Decline.* New York: Academic Press.

Thompson, A. M. 1943. "Children of the war," *South Wales Argus,* 30 October.

Titmuss, R. M. (Richard Castin). n.d. "Crime and tragedy," in Titmuss Papers.

———. *Poverty and Population.* London: Macmillan.

———. 1942. *Birth, Poverty and Wealth.* London: Secker & Warburg.

———, and K. Titmuss. 1942. *Parents Revolt: A Study in the Declining Birth-rate in Acquisitive Societies.* London: Secker & Warburg.

Wall, R., and J. M. Winter (eds.). 1989. *The Upheaval of War, Family, Work and Welfare in Europe, 1914–1918.* Cambridge: Cambridge University Press.

Watson, C. 1952. "Birth control and abortion in France since 1939," *Population Studies* 5: 261–286.

Wickham, J. 1983. "Working-class movement and working-class life: Frankfurt am Main during the Weimar Republic," *Social History* 8: 315–341.

Winter, J. M. 1986. "The demographic consequences of the Second World War," in Smith (1986).

Catholic Conservatives, Population, and the Family in Twentieth Century France

ANTOINE PROST

IT IS IMPOSSIBLE TO STUDY the Catholic approach to population problems without locating it in a specific social context. Philosophers and theologians study ideas and beliefs in and of themselves; social historians insist on the inextricable link between ideas and the people who hold them. Ideas exist *hic et nunc,* and their meaning varies with time and place. From this perspective, it is particularly interesting to look at the case of twentieth century France, since Catholics have played an important part in the adoption of French pronatalist and family policies.

This is so despite the fact that in political terms, Catholics constitute a minority in France. Although France is said to be a Catholic country, the political scene during much of the Third Republic (1870–1940) was dominated by anticlerical Republicans. Indeed the very success of the Republic has been perceived as a defeat of Catholic politics. Consequently, in the political sphere at the end of the nineteenth century, the weakness of French Catholics was more evident than their strength.

How, then, did Catholics in the twentieth century manage to realize a family policy that embodied most of their aims? We must make some preliminary distinctions before beginning to answer this question. The first point to make is that it is impossible to speak of French Catholics at the turn of the century as a unity. They were profoundly divided not only on political issues, but even on religious matters. Actually, their conflicting political views were the consequence of conflicting conceptions of life and religion. As seen from abroad, or as seen from the point of view of French Republicans or Protestants, French Catholicism might have appeared to be homogeneous. It certainly was not. One faction obstinately opposed the Republic as a form of government and, indeed, as the embodiment of a set of principles, a philosophy, a way of life counter to Catholic values. Another faction opposed Republican anticlerical policies, but progressively accepted the principles of equality and individual freedom as a Christian inheritance. These Catholics thought it would be better to work with Republican politicians to change the laws and align them more closely with their ideals than to defend unsuccessfully an anachronistic version of Christianity. Hence the history of French Catholicism, demography, and the family is the history both of a divided religious community and of the successful engagement of some Catholics in the sphere of policymaking.

Catholicism, population, and sexuality

In and of itself, Catholicism does not contain any particular demographic theory. One can find in it diverse views, starting from *Genesis* I:28: "Be fruitful and multiply and replenish the earth," and running the gamut to the ascetic counsel of chastity within marriage, based on Pauline doctrine along the lines of *I Corinthians* VII:29: "But this I say, brethren, the time is short: it remaineth, that . . . they that have wives be as though they had none. . . ." In any event, rather than adopt a specific economic or demographic position, the Church took a moral stance that had demographic consequences. The population problem was never considered on its own terms. At the end of the nineteenth century, though, the French Catholic Church had a longstanding tradition of teaching through the catechism and imposing—or trying to impose—by confession an explicit sexual morality that rested on three premises.

The first is that sexuality is an evil. The Cartesian division between body and soul recapitulated the Pauline opposition between the flesh and the spirit: "the spirit is willing, but the flesh is weak." The body, identified with the flesh, is also suspect: it is evil, or at least subject to the temptation of evil; one ought not to look at it or display it. Contempt for the body was considered virtuous, and among the exemplary merits that led to the canonization of St. Benoit Labre was the fact that he neither bathed nor shaved until his death. The ideal was still chastity and restraint within marriage. Republicans scoffed at the Catholic clergy and its chastity: if they rejected the world, how could they pretend to educate the future fathers of this world? Together with poverty and obedience, chastity was one of the three vows required of priests and nuns. Evangelical perfection is not the large family; rather, it is union solely with Christ, the sacrifice of physical affection and the preservation of chastity.

However—and this is the second premise—this ideal is very difficult to realize. Sexuality is a powerful force. To resist it totally requires an extraordinary act of will. In general, it is better for simple Catholics not to aim so high. As Pascal said, "Whoever tries to be an angel turns into a beast." The Catholic Church harked back to Paul: "Nevertheless, to avoid fornication, let every man have his own wife, and let every woman have her own husband" (*I Corinthians* VII:1–2). Marriage is a concession to human weakness, or rather to masculine weakness, since in this period sexual desire was considered to be normal among men, but not among women. Sexuality outside of marriage is therefore condemned forcefully, and the clergy ceaselessly railed against situations—such as dancing—that might lead to it. Within marriage, by contrast, sexuality is acceptable. Better still, it constitutes a conjugal duty: a wife must not refuse her husband, nor a husband refuse his wife, though this symmetry was largely notional since sexuality was considered above all masculine.

This is not to say that sexual behavior of all kinds was legitimate within marriage. The third premise of the Catholic Church is that procreation is the aim of sexuality within marriage: the first purpose of marriage is the perpetuation of the species. Herein lies the legitimacy of sexuality. The Church therefore forbids couples to practice contraception, with the exception of abstinence. The catechism, sermons, and above all confession were mobilized in the struggle against masturbation, withdrawal, and other nefarious practices. When they heard confession, priests had to ask specific questions on this point.[1] Women were treated more leniently, since they had to obey their husbands; men, by contrast, were without excuse. This indiscretion on the part of the priests in confession is one of the sources of popular anticlericalism, and helps explain the evolution of religious practice by age: among men, it collapsed after puberty, and did not return until the latter years of life, whereas religious practice was much more regular among women throughout life.[2]

This sexual morality was insufficient, however, as a basis for a politics of procreation and the family. Superimposed on it, with respect to the political and social questions of the period, was a doctrine of the family explicitly presented as counter-revolutionary and therefore conservative.

For Catholics, the family does not rest on a contract between spouses. This was the notion of the jurists of the Revolution and it entailed divorce by mutual consent: all contracts can be broken. For Catholics, the family arises out of the sacrament of marriage. God himself unites the spouses, hence divorce is excluded: "Whom God unites let no man put asunder" (*Matthew* XIX:6).

To the indissolubility of marriage—a constant doctrine from the beginning—French Catholics in the nineteenth century added a new dimension, following papal teaching. The family is the cellular base of society: it is a natural reality, existing prior to the state and superior to it. Revolutionary individualism, the source of universal suffrage, is therefore condemned: the abstract man of the Declaration of the Rights of Men does not exist. The real man is first the man in his family, then in his natural community, his profession, and his region. Two related implications follow.

First, the family is the locus wherein social discipline is inculcated: the individual learns there to submit to collective constraints. This is well demonstrated in the debate over the law of 1884 on divorce. The argument that in forbidding divorce one does not create a united home, but only two unhappy people locked in marriage, carried no weight among Catholics: individual happiness to them is suspect; the search for happiness lies only in the escape from self and in giving oneself to others. The family is precisely the school of renunciation. This idea led even the legitimist Charles Chesnelong to resist free education: "The family is the school of sacrifice: give to it what enhances it and strengthens it, what gives it its moral grandeur and what assures its social efficiency. . . . For the father of a poor family, sacrifice is there all the time. . . . When he sends his son to school, he gives up the fruit of his labor, and the sacrifice continues."[3]

If the family is for all its members the school of devotion and sacrifice, it is not a school of equals. The second implication of this counter-revolutionary conception is to define the family in terms of the natural authority of the father. The declaration of the rights of the family, solemnly adopted by a conference of the main family associations at Lille on 3 December 1920, begins with these words: "The family, founded on marriage, hierarchically constituted under paternal authority. . . ."[4] In 1938 Senator Georges Pernot, president of the National Federation of Associations of Large Families, succeeded in inserting in a new law on the status of married women these words: "the husband, head of the family. . . ."[5]

The privileged status of the family in conservative thought arises also from what is understood as the sacrosanct nature of obedience to natural authorities. The relation of the father to his children is the matrix and the model of all social relations: the relation of the landlord to the farmer, of the factory owner to the worker, of the vicar to the parishioner, of the mayor or leading citizen to ordinary people, of the officer to the soldier.[6] Conservatives defend the family as the cornerstone of a society that rests on a pyramid of natural authorities, not on a social contract.[7]

More than a notion of the family is needed to establish a pronatalist and family policy. It is necessary also to admit the legitimacy of a policy in this domain. French Catholics at the end of the nineteenth century did not accept the intervention of the state in questions concerning the family. Founded by God through marriage, the family possessed, according to Catholic thought, indefeasible rights both prior to and superior to those of the state. With respect to schooling, for example, Catholics opposed not only nondenominational education but the obligation to provide any education at all; for them, to send children to school was the responsibility of parents alone, not of the state. In 1913, l'abbé Lemire, deputy from the North, was taken to task by conservative Catholics for having said, in the Chamber of Deputies, that "society did not have the right to leave children to the mercy of antipatriots and apaches [sic]. They cannot do what they want to these poor children," he added. "The child is not the property of the father" (quoted in Mayeur, 1968: 410). The majority of Catholics in this period rejected any state intervention in education.

More generally, Catholics did not accept that the state had, as l'abbé Lemire had said, "a social duty toward the collective." Their attitude was dictated first by their distrust of the Republic. Catholics thought that nothing good could come from a state that rested on the French Revolution and the individualism of the rights of man. This hostility toward the Republic and its principles was condemned in 1892 by the papal encyclical *Inter Sollicitudines,* which urged French Catholics to accept the institutions of the state, that is, of the Republic, in order to play a role in the legislative process. But the rallying of Catholics to the Republic was far from universal. At the beginning of the twentieth century, radical anticlericalism and the opposition to religious congregations reinforced the idea among Catholics that the Republic was fundamentally evil. They strove therefore to prevent its intervention in social affairs.

Catholics had a second reason for rejecting state intervention: their emerging liberalism. The liberalism that characterized this period and particularly the bourgeoisie was not specifically Catholic. On the contrary, it had been regularly condemned by the Catholic Church in the nineteenth century, precisely because it grew out of revolutionary individualism.[8] French Catholics applauded the condemnation of political liberalism. On the other hand, economic liberalism appeared to them to be in the nature of things. For the great majority of Catholics, there was no "social question." Poverty and misery were as inevitable as the cold of winter; the only remedy was charity. A minority admitted the existence of a social question, but only Albert de Mun, Patrice de La Tour du Pin, and their followers envisaged state intervention in labor legislation.

The encyclical *Rerum Novarum* (1891) spawned much controversy. Admitting the "unjust misery" of the workers, born of the denial of religious principles, the encyclical affirmed the necessity of a "just wage," which would give the worker a "proper" part of the common wealth of which his work is the unique source. Above all, it accepted for the first time the intervention of the state in the determination of wages and hours of labor. This social doctrine had many reverberations and provoked conflicting views. The highly influential Catholic employers of the North continued to reject all social legislation and to consider that wage questions were their sole responsibility. In 1924, the textile consortium of Lille, Roubaix, and Tourcoing, a strong organization of Catholic textile employers, denounced Christian trade unions to the Vatican and accused them of "state socialism" because the unions wanted the state to intervene in setting the level of family allowances.

In this ideological context, the only Catholics ready to propose a family policy before World War I were the so-called social Catholics who had come to terms with the Republic. These included the Christian Democrats of *Sillon,* specifically condemned by Pope Pius X (pope from 1903 to 1914) in 1910. (Sillon was a kind of movement, association, or league, headed by Marc Saugnier, that published a review entitled *Le Sillon.* Sillon, the seed of the

Christian Democratic Party, was very attractive to young Catholics eager to act in the social and political field.) According to l'abbé Lemire, who tirelessly pressed in the Chamber of Deputies for family allowances for civil servants, the state ought to fulfill its duty as an employer according to the ideas of social Catholicism; but he was totally isolated. On one side, Catholics scorned him for his republicanism; on the other, to *laiques* Republicans, who valued him, his defense of the family was a clerical policy.

The first Catholic family movements

World War I profoundly changed the French political situation: the sacred union *(union sacrée)* of all parties in support of the government reconciled Catholics to the Republic. In addition, the scale of human loss (1,450,000 killed, or 3.5 percent of the population) highlighted the demographic problem and furnished indisputable arguments to pronatalists. Three broad types of movements consequently developed.

The first and oldest was not originally Catholic, but rather radical, that is to say, *laique Républicain.* This group exerted a decisive influence on the politics of the family through the National Alliance for the Growth of the French Population. Founded in 1896 by Jacques Bertillon, the Alliance brought together demographers, well-known physicians, such as Charles Richet, and political figures, such as André Honnorat and Adolphe Landry, a demographer who became minister of health at the time of the vote on the law on family allowances in 1932, and who was spokesman for the parliamentary report that led to another important law on the subject in 1946. Alfred Sauvy, principal author of the Family Code of 1939, was also part of this current of thought.

In this context, it is more appropriate to speak of a pronatalist than a family policy. Before 1914, the National Alliance analyzed the demographic deficit of France in purely economic terms: families were not having fewer children because morality had declined nor because they were estranged from religion, but rather because the cost of raising children was too high. It was necessary, therefore, to reduce the cost of children by providing families with fiscal relief, such as the Alliance had successfully introduced in 1914 in the income tax, and by family allowances. Catholics supported this program, but they deemed it too materialistic and inadequate. "It is not a question," declared one of their leaders, Auguste Isaac, in opening the first congress on natality in Nancy in 1920, "of appealing for births no matter where and no matter how" (quoted in Talmy, 1962, vol. 1: 209). Nonetheless, many influential Catholics rallied to the cause of the Alliance.

The two other currents, which gained force after the war, were both Catholic in origin: one, while comprised largely of Catholics, avoided overt religious affiliation; the second embraced it. Proponents of the former approach departed from the National Alliance in their analysis of the decline in the birth rate and in their priorities. They saw in the disintegration of the family and the progress of secularization the fundamental causes of the decline in the birth rate. They therefore set as their priority restoring the family and family values rather than increasing the birth rate. Since only a large family, they believed, could be truly moral and Catholic, they were simultaneously profamily and pronatalist. Their differences with adherents of the Alliance were political and ideological, but none the less important for that.

The National Federation of Associations of Large Families, an association without religious affiliation, was run by practicing Catholics. It was formed in September 1920 in order to unite several rapidly growing associations created mostly during the war. Its president, Auguste Isaac, was 71 years old. An industrialist and former president of the Chamber of Commerce of Lyon, he was elected to the Chamber of Deputies in 1919 and was appointed Minister of Commerce. A practicing Catholic and father of 11 children, Isaac played an important role in 1916 in the foundation of the Catholic family movement. In 1920, he presided over the first congress on natality and became head of the new National Federation.

The Federation espoused Catholic family doctrine: it praised large families for accepting the will of God and practicing the sexual morality taught by the Church. Couples without many children were suspected of indulging in "deadly" practices. Morality and virtue were measured by the number of children, with the Federation admitting families having at least three children. The decline in the birth rate was viewed as the consequence of immorality, and it was deemed necessary to defend public morality if one wanted to increase the birth rate. Religious groups naturally were able to work in cooperation with this effort.

The originality of the National Federation was not in its doctrine, but in the projection of this doctrine. The Federation was not a confessional organization, and it did not claim to be officially Catholic. The reasons for this neutrality were twofold. First, political prudence: if one wanted to create a family policy, far better not to make aggressive declarations of faith that would be perceived as clerical and that would offend those political circles in which anticlericals were numerous before the war. In the "blue horizon"[9] Chamber of Deputies (1919–24), Isaac and his colleagues carefully avoided anything that could revive the anticlericalism of the early years of the century. First and foremost, they wanted domestic peace on this issue, which they believed was in line with the interests of the Church.[10] Georges Pernot, professor of public law and a Christian Democratic senator, succeeded Isaac at the head of the organization in 1930 and followed the same line as his predecessor.

This political prudence in family politics incorporated a new progressive notion of religious action. For the Catholics who directed the Federation, the ultimate objective was certainly the re-Christianization of France: the complete restoration of the family required it. But re-Christianization was impossible without a detour. The process had to begin with the moralization of the country, and the best means to this end was to develop family virtues. In sum, one could say that the restoration of the family was a first and neutral stage in the campaign for the restoration of religion.

Those Catholics in the third current of thought in support of the family objected to the neutral position on religion taken by the National Federation. In order to study the diverse questions raised by demography, the first two congresses on natality convened by the Federation had set up sections, of which one was a religious section, itself subdivided into three subcommissions, Catholic, Protestant, and Jewish. But in 1921, the Episcopacy, with the approval of the Vatican, decided that the views of Catholics on such questions of morality as divorce and the restriction of births should not be submitted to the third congress on natality. To enable Catholics to participate, the Catholic religious section had to be made independent of the plenary session of the congress. It was more important for Church authorities to protect Catholics from doctrinal contamination than to increase their influence through the intervening medium of a large familial movement, doctrinally neutral but headed by Catholics.

This dispute over the structure of the family movement grew out of a doctrinal disagreement. Catholic intransigents believed that morality meant nothing without religion: outside of Catholicism, there was no true family. In not proclaiming this, the National Federation showed not only a shameful timidity; it also wandered into a dead end. If one wanted to restore familial virtues, one had to have the courage to locate them within an explicitly Catholic perspective. This third current, familial and pronatalist like the other two, parted from them in being confessional. It was represented, for example, by the Committee for Family Studies.

Formed in 1919 by Catholic employers from the North, around Achille Glorieux, this committee registered from the outset its disapproval of the timidity of familial associations that hesitated to denounce the true causes of depopulation—in their view, religious causes. In Rouen in 1923, they organized an *Etats généraux* of the family at which they asserted a counter-revolutionary purpose. Allowances and fiscal measures faded from the agenda, and four working groups studied respectively housing, morality, regionalism, and the familial vote. Since the fundamental vice was revolutionary individualism, which brought to France laws to protect the rights of individuals, the individual vote was also seen as the way of evil. Hence the insistence on the familial vote.[11] With respect to regionalism, the committee expressed nostalgia for the "old regime," which was partly a figment of their imagination. The French Right condemned centralized government as Jacobin and therefore revolutionary.[12] One had to see the nation as an organism: just as the cells form organs, which in turn form a living body, so does the family, the cellular base of society, form communities, then regions, and finally nations. Both the familial vote and regionalism were part of the effort to substitute a constitution based on the family for one based on the individual. The family is no longer an objective part of Republican state politics, but the foundation of a new non-Republican political order. Cardinal Charrost[13] wrote to the Congress of Fathers of Breton Families organized in Lannion in 1924 by the Committee for Family Studies: "I want to salute you for having stated boldly that your objective is the reconstruction of a political system for the family. It is the only effective reaction against the revolution" (quoted in Talmy, 1962, vol. 1: 217).

In this debate, we see that, unlike the National Alliance, the two Catholic factions did not really address the population question per se. They were profamily and pronatalist; but of equal importance, they saw in the large family a sign of morality and social order. Depopulation and demographic growth were conflicting symptoms of the moral state of a society. But while proponents of the National Federation held that family policy could unite Catholics and non-Catholics in the effort to create a nondenominational social order favorable to religion, proponents of the Committee for Family Studies saw in the politics of the family the means of constructing a counter-revolutionary and properly Catholic social and political order. For Isaac as for Glorieux, the politics of the family was a response to the anticlericalism of the early part of the century. But for Isaac, what mattered was to overcome antagonisms by finding an area of agreement with Republicans: a society in which familial values were honored and in which Catholics could feel at home, even if it were not an officially Catholic society. For Glorieux, on the other hand, the politics of the family was an arena in which to fight Republicans. In this arena the nineteenth century debate, for or against the Republic, lingered on. French Catholics in this period approached population problems not only from a moral but also a political standpoint: one group accepted the religious neutrality of the state, the others dreamed at all times of Christendom.

The influence of these three currents was unequal. The third was too reactionary, in the proper sense, for its influence to extend beyond limited regional circles (Brittany, the North, Normandy) and social circles (the comfortable bourgeoisie). But it did exert a continuing check on the Right, by outbidding in its ardor Catholics of the second current. The influence of the third group diminished with the new lead given the Church by Pius XI (pope from 1922 to 1939).

In contrast, the agreement between the second (Catholic and familial) and the first (radical, pronatalist) currents accounts for the development of family policy in France between the World Wars. In the blue horizon Chamber of Deputies, in which Catholic Republicans like Isaac predominated, many steps were taken of a moral nature: repression of abortion, outlawing of information on contraception, creation of a national mothers' day for mothers of large families, reductions in railway fares for families. Family allowances were left to the initiative of employers. In 1932, the union of these two currents brought about a law obliging employers to subscribe to family allowance funds. Submitted by Minister of Health Landry, this law was sponsored by Jean Lerolle, a Catholic member of the Popular Democratic Party, who advocated a theory of wages arising directly from the encyclical *Rerum novarum.*[14] In contrast, although it was prepared by the High Commission on Population, dominated by Christian Democrats like Pernot, the Family Code of 1939 reflected the more purely pronatalist preoccupations of the first current.

After World War II, a policy of giving preferential treatment to families of at least three children and in which the mother did not work outside the home was pursued with the support of the National Alliance. Landry also sponsored a law of 1946 that substantially increased family allowances, to the point that, for an unskilled worker who was the father of three children, allowances reached half the average salary, and, for a father of five children, exceeded the average salary. But family policy was above all the work of the Popular Republican Movement, a new Christian Democratic party born in the Resistance. The second current of Catholic opinion, together with that party, brought it about. But this second current had been profoundly transformed, it is true, by the events of 1940–44.

The second era of family movements

The early Catholic family movements did not enroll childless families, or those with one or two children. A family cannot, however, become large immediately: between marriage and the birth of the third child, are families to be held in low esteem? Small families were not yet of interest to the pronatalists, but they were for the defenders of the family, or in any event, for the Catholics among them. The Catholic religion speaks to all couples, including the youngest, and even sterile couples are not ipso facto guilty, as long as their sterility does not arise from contraceptive practice. The sanctity of marriage does not require large families. The exclusion of families with fewer than three children was therefore difficult to justify from a strictly Catholic point of view.

In practice, certain groups did address all families, large and small. Between the World Wars, these groups joined forces in the General Confederation of Families, founded by a priest, l'abbé Viollet. The objectives of this Confederation were different from those of the National Federation. The Confederation was a society for mutual aid and education and had no political views. The groups forming the Confederation were neutral, nonconfessional.

Alongside them, l'abbé Viollet also founded a second organization for Catholics, the Association for Christian Marriage, to address family questions from a purely religious point of view, to prepare young people for marriage, and to sustain married couples in their spiritual life. These groups, the duality of which was explicitly stated, constituted in fact a fourth current of thought. This new movement strictly separated the two levels, civic and spiritual, and thereby stood at the opposite pole from the Committee for Family Studies.

Albeit without direct influence on the politics of the family, this fourth current profoundly modified the Catholic conception of marriage and the family. The majority of Catholic discourse on the family was moral or dogmatic; it fixed individual and collective norms. The Association for Christian Marriage posed a different problem: the deepening of faith within marriage. The encyclical *Casti connubii* (1930), while reiterating the Church's traditional teachings (the indissolubility of marriage; the condemnation of divorce, abortion, and contraceptive practice), paved the way for these new concerns. Procreation remained the primary aim of marriage, but it was not the only aim: love between husband and wife, a love "of charity," was taken into account. In the use of the celebrated Pauline text (*Ephesians* IV:22–23), the encyclical emphasized not only the principle of the husband's authority, but also the statement that the union of a couple is symbolic of the union of Christ and the Church. Marriage is not only the foundation of the family and society, it is a mystery, a sign of the love of God—in sum a sacrament in the proper religious sense of the word.[15]

Espousal of this credo widened at the end of the 1930s. Between 1927 and 1933 the Church had created organizations for particular social groups, notably the Working Christian Youth (*jeunesse ouvrière chrétienne*) and Agricultural Christian Youth (*jeunesse agricole chrétienne*). Although each group was divided in two branches—one for men, the other for women—the members began to marry one another. Trained to discuss in small groups the conformity of their lives with the Gospels, members naturally adopted this practice in their marriages; they created groups of young families and founded the Working Christians' League (*ligue ouvrière chrétienne*) in 1934 and the Christian Farmers' League (*ligue agricole chrétienne*) in 1938. These groups organized study days on the sanctity of marriage, marital relations, the education of children, and the like. With the purpose of Christianizing their milieux, a purpose that led them to change their names respectively to the Popular Family Movement in 1942 and the Rural Family Movement in 1940, these groups formed a new type of Catholic family movement: no longer of large families, but of young families. The period of World War II and the Occupation—in effect an inner migration into domestic life—accelerated this development. There soon appeared Catholic movements of young families without reference to specific social milieux, such as the Golden Ring.[16]

The teaching of the Church was displaced. Henceforth one spoke of "conjugal spirituality" and no longer of "familial morality." The accent was placed on the mutual support that spouses must provide each other, materially, psychologically, and spiritually. The sign of a successful Christian marriage was no longer the number of children, but the profound understanding of couples, the strength of the unit that they formed. Expressed in books like those of Herbert Doms, *On the Meaning and the Aims of Marriage,* and of A. Christian (pseudonym of Georges Gallichet), *This Sacrament is Great,* both appearing in 1938, this new doctrine had many reverberations. Indeed the Holy Office reacted in 1944, reaffirming that the primary aim of marriage is the procreation and education of children, with the mutual development of the couple only a secondary aim (Lestapis, 1954). But this was the last time that the Vatican reiterated the traditional doctrine: this way of posing the purpose of marriage had become incomprehensible and irrelevant.

In this new focus on the sanctity of marriage, the most sensitive change undoubtedly concerned sexuality. On the one hand, it gained a new dignity and beauty: it was no longer a shameful instinct that had to be controlled; it was a sign and the very language of love. Pleasure was not culpable among spouses as long as they loved each other and did not use contraceptive methods other than abstinence. On the other hand, pleasure was to be shared: female sexuality was thus recognized. One can see the influence, on Catholics and on the rest of society, of the diffusion of psychology and of Freudianism.

For our theme, this was an important step. Previously Catholics had posed the population problem through that of the family; here they posed the problem of the family through that of the couple. They advocated as always the large family, but as an extension of conjugal love. The notion of the large family therefore changed in meaning: four or five children, not eight, ten, or more. The ideal was no longer to reach the limit of natural fertility.

This doctrinal revision was accompanied by a change in the relationship between the various family movements and the government. Family associations were purely private organizations; the state consulted them when it judged useful, but when it wanted an authoritative opinion it created a superior council or a high committee,[17] or it invited for consultation the presidents of the most important family associations, without giving them any particular powers or rights. The Republican state did not consider extending to these associations the responsibility for public order; that was the duty of the administration.

The Vichy government undertook to create a kind of "familial corporation." By the Gounot Law of 29 December 1942, it created in each commune an "association of families," representing all local families. These associations were grouped in family unions by département, and then again in a national federation. The committee chairmen of these diverse groups were elected by the families, through a family vote. This did not mean "familial syndicalism": families were not obligated to join communal associations, and existing organizations could join these new groups or remain independent. But the law gave to the associations it created a monopoly to represent families before public authorities, which charged them with administering family services in the public interest. The associations were a semi-official structure (Coutrot, 1972).

The Gounot Law was approved by the existing familial associations. The familial philosophy of the new order underpinned them and the law did them no harm. Under Vichy, the politics of the family continued along the same lines as under the Third Republic. What the Gounot Law added was an organic representation of family groups: given the anti-individualism of Catholic familial movements, they could only approve. After Liberation, some of the organizations set up under the Gounot Law were maintained. The ordinance of 3 March 1945 reaffirmed this pluralism by creating departmental unions of local family associations (UDAF) coordinated at the national level by one union (UNAF). These federations of voluntary family associations were given a monopoly on representing family interests before public authorities. UNAF nominated certain of its members to the Economic and Social Council, and the UDAFs acted in their respective *départements* as guardians of public order concerning assisted families.

It is surprising that the Left, predominant in 1945, did not simply suppress the family organization set up by the Vichy government. The first reason for the maintenance of an organic representation of families was the influence of the Communist Party at this time. The Minister of Health and the Family was then the Communist François Billoux. On family issues the Communists were closer to the Catholics than were the Socialists. A second reason was the influence of Catholics like Robert Prigent, responsible for family policy in Billoux's ministry. A worker and an active member of the Resistance, Prigent belonged to the left wing of the Popular Republican Movement (MRP) and later became Minister of Population and the Family. He supported the maintenance of the UNAF and UDAFs, because he thought left-minded Catholics could dominate and give a radical content to these organizations created by eminent conservatives and bourgeois leaders.

He was wrong. Christian Democrats of the left-wing and working-class side of the MRP were rapidly marginalized. As early as 1947, the UNAF was in the hands of family men of mature years, well-known provincial notables: highly regarded, moral, generous, and open to social questions. Undoubtedly, they were Republicans and no longer denounced the Rights of Man. The counter-revolutionaries of Glorieux's kind had practically disappeared. But the non-Christian Left, and even Catholics of the Left, had lost their influence. The UNAF had come to resemble the largely Catholic but not overly religious National Federation of Isaac and Pernot.

Under the Fourth Republic (1946–58), family policy as defined in 1938–39 had the support of a substantial consensus: prime importance was placed on the birth of the first child within two years of marriage; a monthly family allowance for the second child, with larger allowances for the third and later children; a monetary grant for mothers who do not work outside the home and whose husbands are wage earners (Prost, 1984). After the war, the Popular Republican Movement oversaw these policies and added collateral measures: the closure of brothels (1948) and the extension to the non–wage-earning population of the housewives' monthly grant (1955–56).

The MRP was not a confessional party; it was not entitled "Christian," as were its Italian and German counterparts. It was, however, supported by the Catholic Church; its activists were often former members of the movements for Catholic action; its ideas arose directly out of social Catholicism. It united the diverse currents of the Catholic familial movement. As long as the focus was on maintaining and developing existing policies, the various factions could agree: the family did not have the same emotional, ideological, or religious connotations for different groups, but everyone favored a relatively large family in which the mother did not work outside the home.

From 1960, and more clearly, from 1970, this political alignment of various profamily groups disintegrated. The shrinkage of the Popular Republican Movement is not itself a sufficient explanation, since this party's decline must be accounted for. The central point here is the crisis of Catholic youth movements, which in the 1950s ceased to furnish the MRP with militants and supporters. The colonial policy of the MRP was one of the reasons for this disaffection. A conflict between generations was a second reason: the young people of Catholic social action movements demanded a degree of independence from the Church that the latter was not prepared to provide, and furthermore, these young activists engaged in a critique of class society that the Church deemed dangerous. Some joined the United Socialist Party (PSU) on the left of the Socialist Party; others worked within the mainstream Trade Union Movement close to the Communists, or within the Christian Trade Union Movement, which became through their efforts nondenominational in 1964. Class relations emerged as the central issue. Family policy was examined as an element in the policy of social transfer payments: it was criticized for giving more to the rich than to the poor and thereby losing its initial purpose, which had been to establish a relative equality of living standards between childless people and those with children.

Another force in the disintegration of the politics of the family was the beginning of female emancipation, among Catholics as well as other groups. Young men and women educated in the movements for Catholic action began to develop a much more egalitarian view of the couple than had older families. It seemed to the new generation that husbands and wives should share everything, rather than wives simply obeying husbands. On such issues, they did not stand apart from the rest of French society. They approved new laws giving the wife rights equal to those of her husband with respect to money and finance (1965), and giving equal parental authority to fathers and mothers (1970). They accepted the new valuation of women's work in terms of the autonomy it confers and not in terms of economic need. Although some extreme conservative Catholics have opposed divorce by mutual consent (as enacted in 1975), legal and unfettered access to contraception (enacted in 1967), and legalized abortion (under the Veil law, 1975), the overwhelming majority of French Catholics believe that these are private matters over which the state ought to give individuals the freedom to act according to their own conscience. Herein lies the ultimate logic of the existence of a state neutral on religious matters and of the demise of what once was called Christendom. Most Catholics accept both as facts.

With respect to family policy, these new ideas are hardly compatible with the set of measures promulgated in 1938–39 and extended under the Fourth Republic. The special allowance to mothers without paid work had not been adjusted for inflation since 1958. In 1972, the allowance was eliminated except for lower income families, which were eligible for payments on condition that they were bringing up more than three children of any age or had children under the age of three.

Other measures reflected the new environment. Mothers raising children in single-parent families were given special consideration: a special allowance was created in 1970 to help them raise their children. Mothers working outside the home who faced substantial costs for child care protested that they were more severely treated than mothers staying at home, who were given a monthly grant to mind their own children. It was deemed simple justice in 1972 to give mothers working outside the home a subsidy for child care, in order that they not lose too much income.

The aim of these policies is not to favor large families and to discourage mothers from working outside the home, but rather to assist poor families with special needs. It is a social policy rather than a family policy. Its thrust is not to encourage a particular kind of family life, or even to equalize the financial burdens of persons with and without children, but rather to reduce levels of inequality between wealthy and deprived families, and between women who work outside the home and those who do not. The switch is effectively from family policy to social assistance.

The reasons for the decline in the politics of the family in France are to be found not only in such general trends as the spread of individualism throughout society, though these may be decisive. Inasmuch as French family policy was promoted mainly by Catholics, its decline must be ascribed in part to the internal history of French Catholicism.

Two points may be stressed here. First, the weakening of Catholicism itself explains why there is no longer in contemporary France either a true politics of the family or a commonly accepted family model. Today, only 16 percent of French men and women attend Mass at least once a month; only 14 percent of Catholics go to Mass every Sunday. The influence of the Church on the faithful is weak: 80 percent of those who call themselves Catholic consult their own conscience, rather than the position of the Church, on the major questions in their lives. Among regular church-goers, the figure is 53 percent. Among these, 25 percent accept the principle of legal induced abortion, 49 percent accept sexual relations before marriage, and 34 percent believe in the class struggle.[18] Not only has the Christian population been reduced, but what remains today is not what it used to be.

As our second point, it remains to account for the importance that French Catholics attached to the politics of the family during most of the twentieth century. Why, with the exception of forerunners like l'abbé Lemire, did they wait until World War I to mobilize their efforts for this cause?

The politics of the family was not a necessary consequence of the moral posture of the Catholic Church, since this hardly varied from the beginning of the nineteenth century. The Catholic family movement was born of the conjunction of the particular situation of Catholics in French political culture and of the opening of Catholicism to social questions. Catholic family policy is the child of Republican anticlericalism and of *Rerum novarum*. Radicalism triumphant drove French Catholics into a corner, to the point of secluding them from political life, or of restricting them to denunciations of the very basis on which Republican politics rested. The defense of the family gave Catholics a favorable terrain for political intervention: in this domain, they could promote measures in conformity with their values without being reviled a priori by Republicans, since they defended these measures as simple citizens of their time.

They could not have done it, however, had the Church of Leo XIII (pope from 1878 to 1903) and then Pius XI not discerned the depths of the social question and asked the faithful to resolve it, and had this social doctrine not been made amenable to state intervention. Social Catholicism and the politics of the family enabled French Catholics to escape from the impasse in which they had been trapped by the anticlerical quarrel of the early twentieth century. In this sense, the steady extinction of the politics of the family expressed both the weakening of Catholicism and the integration of French Catholics into French political life.

Notes

1 Whether priests would have to ask questions on such points had been discussed in the early nineteenth century. The issue was submitted to the Vatican Holy Office in 1849; the answer was yes. See Zeldin (1971), McLaren (1983), and, for a regional study of actual practice, Hilaire (1964).

2 Christiane Marcilhacy (1963) presents statistics of religious practice by age and sex for selected cities and rural settlements.

3 Debates of the French Senate, session of 4 April 1884, *Journal officiel* (1884): 587.

4 Robert Talmy (1962, vol. 1: 236–237) gives the entire "charte de la famille." Talmy's book deserves special consideration, since he had access to the archives of several family associations.

5 Debates of the French Senate, session of 8 December 1938, *Journal officiel* (1938): 1564.

6 This pattern of social relations still exists in some conservative rural areas, such as the Mauges, near the Vendée, as described in Laurence Wylie, *Chanzeaux, village d'Anjou* (Paris: Gallimard, 1970).

7 Right-wing conservatives supported the authority of fathers over children more strictly and firmly than did the Catholic Church. For instance, they opposed marriage without the father's consent, while the Church accepted and consecrated such marriages if the partners were not minors.

8 One could cite the well-known encyclicals *Mirari vos* (1832) and *Quanta cura* (1864). The latter ended with a large list of errors, the *Syllabus*, in which the major liberties, and liberalism itself, were anathematized on principle.

9 This Chamber of Deputies was known as *bleu horizon* because of the large number of deputies who were war veterans. The color of French soldiers' uniforms in World War I was blue.

10 A clear sign of this commitment to domestic peace on the religious issue was given by Isaac and his colleagues in December 1921. The extreme Right and *Action française* had placed on the parliamentary agenda a bill providing subsidies for private Catholic education to pupils whose fathers had been killed in the war. Although he was a practicing Catholic, Isaac successfully blocked this proposal. See Debates of the Chamber of Deputies, 11 December 1921, *Journal officiel* (1921): 4917. It is worth noting that the so-called Marie and Baranger Laws, which were passed in 1951 with the votes of the Popular Republican Movement, the "Rassemblement" of French People, and the conservatives, had exactly the same purpose.

11 Isaac, too, supported the familial vote; in his view, however, it was not a key issue.

12 Interestingly, Charles Maurras's well-known characterization of the Vichy regime as a "divine surprise" was inspired by a statement from Marshal Pétain supporting decentralization.

13 Cardinal Charrost was then the Archbishop of Rennes. As Bishop of Lille, on the eve of World War I, he had publicly forbidden l'abbé Lemire to say Mass, to hear confession, and to receive the Eucharist because this Catholic priest, returned to the Chamber of Deputies by Republican voters, supported measures Charrost thought to be erroneous and dangerous. In addition, Lemire had stood as a candidate in the 1914 general election, despite the fact that Charrost had advised him not to do so (Mayeur, 1968: 393ff).

14 In his parliamentary report on the family allowances bill, Lerolle commented: "Labor is not a good on the market; it is a human attribute, inseparable from the laborer's being. Hence one has to consider the needs of the human being not only as an individual, but as the person responsible for a family, if one is to consider what fair wages are." See Debates of the Chamber of Deputies, *Journal officiel*, no. 3827 (1932): 1392.

15 The definition of a sacrament in Catholic theology is an "efficient sign." After the Council of Trent, the Catholic Church placed great emphasis on the "efficiency" of sacraments. New Catholic movements in the 1930s underlined the other term of the formula—the meaning of the sign—asking whether signs were efficient for people who did not perceive them as such and hence did not understand their meaning. The Council of Trent had used the Latin words *significando causunt*, in which the efficiency is inseparable from the meaning of the sign.

16 The first issue of *L'anneau d'or*, or the *Golden Ring* (which dealt with "conjugal spirituality"), was published in January 1945. On the subject of Catholic groups of young *foyers*, see Chenu (1949).

17 The *Conseil supérieur de la natalité*, instituted in 1920, and the *Haut comité de la population*, instituted in 1939, are good examples of such committees.

18 These figures come from a public opinion poll published in *Le Monde*, 1 October 1986.

References

Chenu, R. P. Marie-Dominique. 1949. "Communautés de jeunes foyers," *Economie et Humanisme* (July): 22–27.

Coutrot, Aline. 1972. "La politique familiale," in *Le gouvernement de Vichy, 1940–1942,* ed. R. Remond and J. Bourdin. Paris: Presses de la Fondation Nationale des Sciences Politiques.

Hilaire, Yves-Marie. 1964. "Les missions intérieures face à la déchristianisation pendant la seconde moitié du xixe siècle dans la région du Nord," *Revue du Nord* (January–March): 51–68.

Lestapis, R. P. Stanislas de. 1954. "Evolution de la pensée exprimée par l'Eglise catholique," in *Renouveau des idées sur la famille,* ed. R. Prigent. Paris: Presses Universitaires de France.

Marcilhacy, Christiane. 1963. *Le diocèse d'Orléans sous l'épiscopat de Mgr. Dupanloup, 1849–1878.* Paris: Plon.

Mayeur, Jean-Marie. 1968. *Un prêtre démocrate, l'abbé Lemire, 1853–1928.* Tournai: Casterman.

McLaren, Angus. 1983. *Sexuality and Social Order.* New York: Holmes and Meier.

Prost, Antoine. 1984. "L'évolution de la politique familiale en France de 1938 à 1981," *Le Mouvement social* 129: 7–28.

Talmy, Robert. 1962. *Histoire du mouvement familial en France (1896–1939),* 2 vols. Paris: Union Nationale des Caisses d'Allocations Familiales.

Zeldin, Theodore. 1971. "The conflicts of moralities: Confession, sin and pleasure in the nineteenth century," in *Conflicts in French Society,* ed. T. Zeldin. Oxford University Press.

POPULATION AND NATURAL SCIENCE

Evolution and Debates over Human Progress from Darwin to Sociobiology

SHARON KINGSLAND

IS SOCIAL PROGRESS A BIOLOGICAL PROBLEM? Or, to pose the question more concretely, must the demographer and social planner also have the insights of an evolutionary biologist? The modern advocate of sociobiology, the study of the evolution of social behavior, would answer with an unequivocal "yes." Debates over human progress have been conducted in an evolutionary context since the theories of Jean-Baptiste Lamarck and Charles Darwin were proposed in the nineteenth century. These debates, which have continued unabated to the present time, began with the controversial claim that man was subject to the same laws as the rest of creation.

Darwin's theory made use of Malthus's argument, advanced in the *Essay on Population,* that a struggle for existence would follow from the tendency of populations to increase beyond their food supply. Malthus's point was that this law applied throughout nature and that the human species could not be an exception. Malthus concluded that the law of population growth set definite limits to the future improvement of society. Darwin used Malthus's argument to show that the universal laws of nature were evolutionary, thereby brilliantly reversing, at least in the biological sphere, the Malthusian conclusions about the limits to change. But as we shall see, when considering social improvements Darwin's conclusions remained very close to those of Malthus.

Taking his evolutionary perspective to its logical limits, Darwin argued that every aspect of the human species could be made the object of biological, evolutionary scrutiny. What this meant for ideas of human nature and for the possibility of making fundamental changes in social organization has been the subject of continuous debate ever since Darwin. In his time it was felt that the very idea of our simian ancestry would shake the foundations of society by encouraging turbulent behavior among the lower classes. Indeed, evolutionary ideas imported from the Continent to Britain were used as ideological weapons by radical reformers in the 1830s and 1840s to challenge aristocratic and Church privilege. To combat such radical uses of evolutionary theories, the establishment depicted transmutation theories as degradations of man because they sought to derive mind from matter. Recently Robert Richards (1987) has challenged this view of Darwinism as a materialist degradation of human nature, arguing that the Darwinian image of man was that of an innately moral being. Evolutionary thinkers in the nineteenth century were very concerned that evolution not threaten the image of the human as elevated above the animal world by a moral sense and superior intellectual capacity, even if the roots of that capacity could be traced to our animal ancestors.

The first section of this essay discusses the intellectual background to *On the Origin of Species,* focusing on Darwin's transformation of the concept of the struggle for existence brought about by his reading of Malthus. Darwin's essentially historical method of analysis and his destruction of the teleological framework of natural history raised the problem of how progress, especially the moral progress of man, could be explained as the outcome of natural selection. The second section discusses two alternative views of human evolution proposed by Herbert Spencer, an influential English philosopher, and Alfred Russel Wallace, co-discoverer of the principle of natural selection. The third section discusses Darwin's own ideas of human evolution in *The Descent of Man.* The fourth section surveys the emergence of the engineering mentality characteristic of the twentieth century, exemplified in the eugenics movement, which interpreted human progress as a problem of biological engineering. This movement stimulated a great deal of research on heredity, evolutionary biology, and population growth. The fifth section discusses the neo-Darwinian viewpoint of sociobiology, which addresses the biological origins of social behavior and carries controversial implications for population policy and social planning.

Darwinism through the decades has represented an invasion by the biologist of the terrain of theology, philosophy, and, in the twentieth century, the social sciences. Darwinian biology suggests that any social planning must take into account the fact that basic social structures have evolved and therefore are adaptive in a biological sense, and that human populations are still evolving. This essay draws on recent scholarship dealing with Darwinism, the eugenics movement, and sociobiology, to chart the main currents of this evolving debate over evolution and human progress. For a more thorough analysis the reader is referred to Jones (1980) on Social Darwinism in Britain, and especially to Richards's (1987) provocative revision of Darwin scholarship and theories of mind and behavior.

The origin of species: Science and ideology

Early nineteenth century naturalists worked within the context of natural theology, believing that the study of nature revealed the power, wisdom, and goodness of the divine creator (Gillispie, 1951). Natural theology was especially important in British natural history: the viewpoint sustained a belief in a static social structure in which aristocratic, Anglican privilege was secure. Nature was seen to be perfectly balanced and all species performed their parts, in accordance with God's plan, to ensure the harmony of the whole. The idea that each species existed not just for its own sake, but for the benefit of other species in the system, was captured in the phrase "economy of nature." The concept of the economy of nature derives from antiquity, but was given canonical form by the Swedish naturalist Carl Linnaeus in the eighteenth century (Linné, 1972; Linnaeus, 1977). According to this view, reproduction was adjusted to the species' role in nature's economy. Poultry produced more eggs than did hawks, for instance, because they were a more important food source (Linné, 1972). In all species, propagation balanced mortality, so that the entire economy was stable.

The idea that pain and death acted for the benefit of the economy as a whole recurs in much of the naturalist literature with which Darwin was familiar. In the economy of nature, predation was a way of preventing overpopulation among prey—overpopulation that would lead to famine and suffering far worse than the total suffering of those killed in the hunt. Moreover, predators removed any prey that were sick, aged, or enfeebled, or any that strayed outside their proper locality (Buckland, 1837; Eiseley, 1959). Since these deviants had failed to perform "the office for which Providence designed them," their removal was thought to be part of the divine plan. The selective elimination of deviant individuals by predators served to maintain the species' "pristine characters without blemish or decay" (Eiseley, 1959, p. 142).

The natural theologian had no trouble accommodating Malthus's argument that a struggle for existence would result from the tendency of the population to outstrip its food supply. Malthus himself concluded the first edition of the *Essay on Population* (1798) with two chapters showing the compatibility of his views with natural theology; he argued for the beneficial results of the struggle for existence, despite its many evil effects. Malthus saw the struggle as a stimulus to progress, where progress was understood to be the achievement of a higher material standard of living. Without such a struggle, man would lack the desire to improve himself and would sink into indolence. Although Malthus believed that the structure of society as a whole would likely not change in the future, there was room for improvement in the human condition through efforts to mitigate the evil effects of the struggle that followed population increase. God had made us struggle, not for punishment, but to spur us to action (Malthus, 1926).

The Reverend William Paley, whose works on natural theology and moral philosophy had formed a large part of Darwin's intellectual diet at Cambridge, concurred with Malthus that the struggle for existence was inevitable. Like Malthus, Paley saw in this conclusion no reason for despair. The law of population increase and the attendant evils of poverty might set limits to human happiness in the realm of material goods. But those limits had not yet been reached in any part of the world, so that material progress was still possible. Moreover, spiritual happiness—the happiness of a religious life of moderation—was not limited in the same way by population pressure. Paley considered Malthus's conclusion about the limits of perfectibility to apply only to "animal wants" (Young, 1985, pp. 28–29).

Darwin read the sixth edition of the *Essay on Population* in 1838 and drew a radically different conclusion from Malthus's discussion of the various checks to population increase, a conclusion that enabled him to overturn the teleological view of the natural theologians. He saw how the struggle for existence in nature might lead to gradual change in the species itself. Already, before reading Malthus, Darwin had concluded from his biological studies that species were capable of change. Now he grasped the mechanism of change: variations favorable to survival would be preserved and handed down to the next generation, while those injurious to survival would perish. Those individuals having favorable traits would compete with and drive out any forms lacking the beneficial variation. Over a long enough period of time new species would be created in place of the old. To this process of differential survival and reproduction of individuals possessing different inheritable traits, Darwin gave the metaphorical name "natural selection." As he stressed in the *Origin of Species*, published in 1859, the biological struggle for existence was "the doctrine of Malthus applied with manifold force to the whole animal and vegetable kingdoms" (Darwin, 1964, p. 63).

The extent to which Darwin's theory was derived from Malthus has been a topic of controversy (Bowler, 1984; Gale, 1972; La Vergata, 1985). It seems clear that although Malthus crystallized Darwin's ideas about natural selection, many puzzles as to how natural selection could explain complicated adaptations remained to be solved before Darwin felt confident enough to publish his theory. To these details Darwin devoted two decades of intensive study, finally publishing in 1859 because he feared that Alfred Russel Wallace had discovered the same principle of selection and would publish before him.

To explain the catalytic effect of Malthus on Darwin, Ernst Mayr (1982) has argued convincingly that Darwin's reading of Malthus was crucial because it made him realize that the struggle for existence mainly occurred *within* the species—in other words, that the members of a population were in competition with one another. According to the viewpoint of natural theology, struggle was usually described *between* different species, as between predator and prey, and its result was to regulate populations and preserve the "pristine character" of the species. The kind of selective elimination that the naturalist described in this context was conservative in function; it ensured that the species' characters did not change. But once Darwin saw that in addition to this kind of struggle there was also competition for resources between individuals within a population, he could appreciate why the outcome might lead to major changes in the species itself. Competition within a species had a totally different significance from that between species. It was Darwin's recognition that the metaphor of the struggle for existence included the competition for limited resources among equals or near equals, and that this competition would be most severe because the needs of these individuals were alike, that allowed him to see natural selection as a genuine creative force, not just a means of weeding out deviants.

Darwin's emphasis on competition as a mechanism of progress and his use of economic metaphors in describing the economy of nature has led many people from Darwin's time on to reflect that his theory merely extended current economic theory to the animal and plant worlds (Bowler, 1984). As William Irvine observed, several economic ideas have parallels in the *Origin of Species*, including the concepts of utility, pressure of population, marginal fertility, barriers in restraint of trade, the division of labor, progress and adjustment by competition, and the spread of technological improvements (Irvine, 1959, p. 98). One historian, focusing on the idea of the "division of labor" which Darwin cited as a principle of species divergence, has argued that Darwin's writing about natural selection reflected the economic theories of the Scottish Enlightenment, especially the theories of Adam Smith, which he translated into biological terms (Schweber, 1985). Darwin's use of these ideas is cited as one example of the "uniquely British character" of his thought (La Vergata, 1985, pp. 945–946).

The connections between Darwin's biological theory and British political economy were not straightforward, however. For instance, in the *Origin of Species* Darwin cited not Adam Smith on the division of labor, but the French physiologist Henri Milne-Edwards, who had developed the concept of the "physiological division of labor" in the 1820s. Milne-Edwards was explicitly translating the economic concept, derived from Smith and common in French economic literature at the time, into zoological terms. It appears to have been Milne-Edwards's use of the concept, rather than Smith's, that directly stimulated Darwin to extend the idea to explain species divergence in the natural economy. Therefore Darwin's use of economic ideas that were "in the air" does not illustrate the "uniquely British" character of his thought. Nevertheless, these efforts to unravel the many strands that were woven into

Darwin's biology do serve to draw attention to his extraordinarily wide reading and his familiarity not only with all branches of science but also with moral philosophy and political economy. Darwin did address this literature directly in *The Descent of Man,* as will be discussed in a later section.

To understand the influence of Darwin's milieu on his science, it is especially useful to look to his studies of animal breeding, or artificial selection, which made him realize that an analogous process of selective pressure might operate in nature (Secord, 1985). Darwin's use of examples from animal breeding and horticulture, and the coining of the central metaphor of "natural selection" itself, point to the importance of agricultural research as both a source of ideas and the main testing ground for his theory. Darwin was a product of his social background in the sense that his theory was the "natural and inevitable outcome of a culture of agrarian capitalists, who had spent decades in empirical horticulture and stock-breeding" (Thompson, 1978, p. 61). As we shall see, these same influences were reflected indirectly in the ideas of Darwin's younger cousin Francis Galton, who upon reading the *Origin of Species* conceived a utopian plan for the breeding of a better race of humans.

Apart from animal and plant breeding, Darwin's theory was greatly influenced by the ideology of "uniformitarianism," as it was awkwardly dubbed by the philosopher William Whewell. The principle of uniformitarianism asserted that the processes of nature were uniform and that one could understand the past by understanding the present and extrapolating backward in time. Charles Lyell, a geologist and mentor to Darwin, most fully enunciated this principle in the 1830s in his explanations of the Earth's geology. There was no need, in Lyell's view, to suppose that unusually severe cataclysms of the past had created the mountains and other geological features of the globe. On the contrary, he asserted, the features of the crust represented the slowly accumulated effects of the various processes that we could see operating in the world today (Lyell, 1830–33; Rudwick, 1976; Ruse, 1979).

Uniformitarianism enabled Darwin to bring the puzzle of the origin of species into the domain of science. Lyell himself was not an evolutionist: the world to him was in a steady state, and he was at pains to discount the appearance of progression in the fossil record. But Darwin saw that uniformitarianism could be used to show not only how progressive change could occur, but also how we could understand the mechanisms of change by observing what was going on in front of us. The slow and continuous process of speciation was not the result of some unusual event whose cause was forever hidden from our view, but was fully explicable by the "laws acting around us" (Darwin, 1964, p. 489). These laws were the principles governing growth, reproduction, inheritance, and variability, as well as the law of population increase, which led to a struggle for existence and natural selection.

The actions of these laws were uniform throughout nature. The same laws that produced new varieties, and that animal breeders tried to manipulate to their advantage in artificial selection, also operated in nature, more subtly, to create new species. For Darwin it was strangely inconsistent to argue that the mechanisms of producing varieties in the greenhouse or stockyard should be different in kind from those producing species in nature.

Darwin's theory was mainly an argument against "special creation," the doctrine that species originated suddenly and by divine intervention. The theory of special creation removed the origin of species from scientific study. By Darwin's time, however, a more refined concept of special creation was current: that species were formed by natural causes, but the laws of progress which guided creation toward greater perfection, culminating in man, were established by God. Richard Owen, Britain's foremost comparative anatomist and opponent to Darwin, believed that such causes might yet be uncovered, though he refused to speculate publicly about them before the *Origin of Species* appeared. In Owen's view of creation, science and theology were still closely intertwined (Desmond, 1984).

An alternative evolutionary theory, one Owen regarded as dangerously atheistic, had been advanced by the French naturalist Jean-Baptiste Lamarck in 1809. It was widely debated in the early nineteenth century; Charles Lyell devoted considerable space to refuting this materialistic doctrine in the 1830s. Lamarck's theory, which was couched as a philosophical exercise because it was speculative, postulated two mechanisms for evolutionary change (Burkhardt, 1977). One was an inner force that caused the organism to become more complex, pushing it along an evolutionary path toward the crowning human form. The second mechanism was the ability of the organism to respond unconsciously to its environment, developing adaptations that then became hereditary. These adaptive responses would cause divergence from the strictly linear course charted by the inner force, thereby accounting for the fact that species did not form a linear chain of being. Darwin dismissed the idea of an inner force directing evolution, but accepted the possibility that some characteristics acquired during an organism's lifetime might become hereditary. In his later writings in particular, he acknowledged several instances of the inheritance of acquired characteristics in cases where natural selection alone did not fully explain an adaptation. Darwin believed, with Lamarck, that the inherited effects of habit could produce permanent evolutionary change, although his carefully reasoned arguments were far removed from the speculations of Lamarck.

From the point of view of natural theologians like Owen, the theories of Lamarck and Darwin degraded man by deriving mind out of matter and making no reference to God's guidance of evolutionary progress. Darwin did believe in progress: natural selection worked only for the good of each being, so that "all corporeal and mental endowments will tend to progress towards perfection'' (Darwin, 1964, p. 489). Evolutionary progress meant two things: perfection of adaptation by natural selection's constant scrutiny of individual variations; and (on a broader time scale) the progress from lower to higher forms of life, and finally to man, that could be seen in the fossil record. Darwin believed his mechanism explained progressive evolution (Ospovat, 1981). But his progress was the uncertain outcome of daily struggle, not the predetermined unfolding of a progressive ''tendency.'' Darwin's theory was not teleological, for the historical process of the survival of variations arising by chance did not specify any fixed goal or show nature to be striving to fulfill a divine plan. It was precisely this historical analysis that so impressed Karl Marx when he read the *Origin of Species* in 1860 and saw that Darwin's argument contained the basis in natural history for the class struggle in history. He explained the significance of Darwin's work in a letter to Ferdinand Lassalle: ''Despite all deficiencies, not only is the death-blow dealt here for the first time to 'teleology' in the natural sciences but their rational meaning is empirically explained'' (quoted in Thompson, 1978, p. 256).

This essentially historical way of thinking was difficult for contemporaries to grasp. Even those who accepted evolution had trouble understanding how natural selection could explain evolutionary progress, in particular the progress toward the advanced mind of the human species. Darwin convinced his contemporaries that evolution occurred; he did not convince them that natural selection, incorporating the ''law of higgledy-piggledy'' as physicist John Herschel dismissively remarked, was its main mechanism (Hull, 1983). Natural selection strained the imagination of Darwin's friends and opponents alike. Alternatives to Darwin's mechanism, in the form of Lamarckian ideas of an inner directing force or of directed response to environmental change, were invoked as necessary to account for the appearance of new adaptations. Evolutionists toyed with a cluster of different mechanisms working in combination, as did Darwin himself, though he gave greatest weight to natural selection. Others played down natural selection: their choice of alternative mechanisms sometimes reinstated the teleological view of nature that Darwin ostensibly had overturned, allowing naturalists to see evolution as a linear, goal-directed process (Bowler, 1983, 1986). It is important to keep this point in mind when speaking of ''Social Darwinism,'' a term pertaining to the application of evolutionary theories to social problems and to the consideration of human progress. ''Social Darwinians'' were not necessarily adhering to Darwin's own explanations; they merely believed that human progress could be understood in an evolutionary context.

When considering the human species, progress meant the development of man's intellectual and moral nature and the advanced level of civilization that accompanied this development. Much of the difficulty of understanding Darwin's theory revolved around this question of whether natural selection could account for man's mind and spirit. Ideas about human progress were bound up with views of human nature: what were our essential qualities, how did they arise, and how did they determine our social behavior and civilized institutions? If mind had been drawn from matter, how could we act as moral beings? Another complaint, voiced both in Darwin's time and our own, was that his emphasis on competition implied a view of society as composed of selfish individuals, ruthlcssly engaged in struggle against their fellow men and lacking any motive for altruistic behavior. In fact Darwin's own ideas about natural selection implied a far more benign view of human nature. His theory as applied to humans, though not utopian in intent, was anything but a degradation of the human spirit: it was a celebration of human potential.

Darwin did not discuss human evolution in the *Origin of Species,* but tackled the problem in *The Descent of Man,* published in 1871. His discussion was in part a response to a number of criticisms questioning the role of natural selection in human evolution. The debate over human origins had been raging in the 12 years between the publication of the *Origin* and the *Descent,* leaving a copious literature upon which Darwin drew. In the next section I shall consider only two alternative views of human evolution that preceded the publication of the *Descent:* that of Herbert Spencer, an influential philosopher and social theorist, and that of Alfred Russel Wallace, co-discoverer of the principle of evolution by survival of the fittest. Then I shall discuss Darwin's own views about human evolution and their implications for his concept of man as a moral being.

Evolution and human progress: Two alternatives

Herbert Spencer's philosophical system embraced physics, biology, ethics, sociology, and psychology (Peel, 1971). Although he is neglected today, his works were widely read and his contemporaries found his ideas stimulating, even when they were not wholly convinced by his deductive style of argument. Spencer was interested in creating a social theory based on the laws of nature. In an essay published in 1857 on "Progress: Its law and cause," he argued that the modern concept of progress, which considered any change—material, intellectual, or social—to be progressive if it increased human happiness, was unsatisfactory because it judged progress in reference to human interests (Spencer, 1891). It should be possible, he thought, to arrive at a more objective definition of the nature of these changes without reference to our interests. What was required was a concise statement of the laws of progress that would apply to any kind of progressive change.

These laws, Spencer believed, were evolutionary; that is, the evolutionary law of organic progress was the law of all progress. At all levels, wherever change occurred, "whether it be in the development of the Earth, in the development of Life upon its surface, in the development of Society, or Government, of Manufactures, of Commerce, of Language, Literature, Science, Art," one could see a gradual change from a homogeneous state to a more specialized heterogeneous state (ibid., p. 10). When Spencer spoke of "evolution" he referred to an increase in complexity that could be seen on all levels, from geological change to cultural advance. In this general definition of evolution, Spencer believed he had discovered the law governing all change. The statement of this "law" formed the basis for his discussion of progress and gave him a way to see human social progress as a natural process.

Although Spencer is often depicted as a "Social Darwinian," his mechanism of evolutionary change was in fact Lamarckian. He had become acquainted with Lamarck's theory in the 1840s through reading Lyell's geological works. Lyell had argued against Lamarckian mechanisms of progress, but Spencer found his refutation of Lamarck unconvincing given the fossil evidence of progress. Spencer's evolutionary theory emphasized the idea that species were transformed through interaction with the environment and through the inheritance of characteristics acquired during an organism's lifetime. After the publication of the *Origin of Species,* Spencer accepted Darwin's theory that natural selection also operated in the evolutionary process, but he never abandoned the Lamarckian perspective of his earliest essays.

Spencer came close to anticipating Darwin's theory in an essay on the theory of population published in 1852. He argued that population pressure had been the cause of progress because crowding forced people to develop social relationships. In the course of this social development, those with the greatest power of self-preservation would advance; they would be the select of their generation. The struggle for existence therefore gave rise to the "survival of the fittest," a phrase Spencer coined. But Spencer did not appreciate, as Darwin did, how this process would select for certain variations and produce a change in the species. He saw the process as creating only higher forms of the same type; moreover, the basic mechanism of change was Lamarckian, for the individual and society as a whole were directly adjusting to external conditions in an adaptive way.

In addition to his Lamarckian perspective, Spencer also saw nature as a dynamic equilibrium, a point of view that reflected his early interests in mechanical engineering. What we observe is the product of antagonistic forces that approximately balanced each other; as the evolutionary process unfolded, these forces came into perfect balance. Spencer's notion of "force" was broad and not clearly defined: he meant the term to apply not only to physical forces, but also to social and economic "forces," which might be measured, for instance, by changes in population. The biological applications of his equilibrium viewpoint were developed in *The Principles of Biology,* published in 1864. The final section of this work, entitled "Laws of multiplication," bore particular relevance to human evolution.

Spencer began by reasoning that the preservation of races implied a stable equilibrium between destructive forces (those causing death) and preservative forces (those contributing to individual life and reproduction). These forces of population increase and decrease were not exactly balanced, so that the population level fluctuated. In addition, there was on the individual level a balance between the energy used for individual survival and for reproduction: the more energy required for survival, the lower the fertility. The processes of life could be analyzed in economic terms, as balances between the costs of living and of reproducing. In this respect Spencer was creating literally an "economy of nature." He believed that indirectly the antagonism between these forces was molded by natural selection and the survival of the fittest, for any species unable to maintain an economic balance would die out. But natural selection could not work against the economic principles themselves: it could not, all else equal, produce an increase both of fertility and of individual maintenance cost at the same time (Spencer, 1896, sec. 363).

These principles of economy applied equally to humans. Although the pressure of population growth was the original stimulus of human evolution, the development of human intelligence necessitated a decline in fertility. The evolution of higher civilization occurred at the expense of reproduction. Gradually as evolution progressed, Spencer imagined, a stable equilibrium would be reached between man's inner nature and his outer relations with society; the individual would gradually adjust his needs to those of his fellow men. The goal of this continuous development was a classless society in which the individual's genuinely developed social sense would yield the greatest happiness for the greatest number (Richards, 1987). This equilibrium between individual and society would coincide with equilibrium between births and deaths in the population. The Malthusian law of population increase would no longer apply at this stage. Evolution by natural selection, from Spencer's point of view, was merely a phase in the general Lamarckian evolutionary trend, and the Malthusian principle would apply only to this phase of development (Peel, 1971). All evolution moved toward a harmonious state where antagonistic forces were balanced. Spencer's theory transposed the balanced world of political economy (and, in a secular context, of natural theology) into a framework that allowed for some developmental change. But his evolution was not open-ended, like Darwin's concept of change: the implication of Spencer's theory was that evolution, and human progress, would at some stage come to a halt in a perfectly equilibrated world, a conclusion with which he was not entirely comfortable.

For Spencer, therefore, evolution was a universal law that led to the moral perfection of man, mainly through the Lamarckian mechanism of adaptive change in response to the environment. He concluded that society should not be interfered with, so that the adaptive process could operate unchecked. Any welfare measures would remove the pressure on the individual to adapt himself to the social state. Spencer also imagined that society formed an organic whole, whose character depended on the character of the parts taken together. Artificial preservation of the unfit would lower the quality of society as a whole and merely store up miseries for a future generation to cope with. The idea that society was an organic whole also suggested that the individual, in exercising his freedom and fulfilling his own nature, would at the same time perform a function for the social unit. In so doing, he fulfilled a basic law of nature. Spencer also believed that the individual's continual adjustment to the social state, through the Lamarckian mechanism of inherited habit, would create an innate tendency to act altruistically (Richards, 1987, p. 310). A society of moral individuals, acting selflessly, was the outcome of the evolutionary process.

As Robert Young has pointed out, Spencer's theory was anti-Malthusian; his optimistic laissez-faire liberalism was closer to Rousseau, Condorcet, and Godwin than to Malthus (Young, 1985, p. 51). Moreover, his early writings promoted socialism, for he envisioned as the end product of evolution a classless society where land was held in common, government had withered away, and each citizen (including women and children) was perfectly free. These ideas appealed to a number of socialist thinkers, such as the Russian anarchist Prince Peter Kropotkin, the Italian socialist Enrico Ferri, and Spencer's close friend Beatrice Webb (Richards, 1987, p. 327). But Spencer's thought also evolved: by the 1890s, with the growth of Marxism, he gave up the argument for common land ownership, suggested that perfect adaptation could be reached only in "infinite time," and erased from his writings all hints of the utopian socialism of his younger days (Richards, 1987, pp. 260–267).

Spencer's idea of the natural evolution of civilized society influenced Alfred Russel Wallace, who believed that the theory of natural selection would support Spencer's view that human moral character was a goal of evolution. But Wallace refined his idea of how natural selection acted in order to accommodate this conclusion. As early as 1864 he saw the need to exempt man from the principle of the survival of the fittest as far as physical change was concerned (Kottler, 1974; Richards, 1987). He first suggested that the human mind had shielded the body from the action of natural selection, putting an end to structural change in humans starting from the time at which the brain had fully evolved. At that point selection had been raised to the cultural plane and the struggle for existence operated mainly between races. The more intellectually and morally advanced races would displace the less advanced ones. Although our intellectual and moral nature had originated in our animal ancestors, therefore, it had developed to its present level by cultural selection in the struggle between races. Darwin accepted Wallace's thesis, which did not contradict his own views.

Darwin was astonished to find that by 1869 Wallace's argument had altered radically. Wallace now doubted whether man's unique physical features, as well as his intellectual capacities, could have been developed by natural selection, because these features and capacities were not adaptive in the primitive life of early man. Certain features such as hairlessness might even have been disadvantageous to early man; others, such as a large brain (with the accompanying capacity for speech and thought) or the delicacy of facial expressions and the esthetic sense, were not required for the rude life of the prehistoric savage. These seemed to be pre-adaptations to a higher civilized state. As pre-adaptations, they could not have been produced by natural selection, which only produced features of direct, immediate benefit to the possessor.

Wallace's argument, with its strict interpretation of the utility of human features, was taken from Spencer. It was an unsatisfactory refutation of Darwin's theory, for the needs of primitive man were unknown: how could one be sure that the power of speech and abstract thought were not needed in early human life? But Wallace was influenced by factors other than the utility of adaptation in his abrupt denial of natural selection. His change of mind was partly a consequence of his conversion to spiritualism, that is, to a belief that spiritual forces acted throughout nature (Kottler, 1974). He was not alone among the eminent scientists of his time who took an interest in the "evidence" offered by such fads as spiritual photography and the seance, but he was exceptionally credulous in taking these results at their face value. His conversion led him to propose an alternative to natural selection, which he finally revealed in 1889, when he argued that a spiritual force must have acted twice in history, once at the origin of life and again at the origin of man's intellectual and moral nature. Just as man had guided the development of many animal and vegetable forms, so a superior intelligence had guided man in a definite direction (Richards, 1987, p. 184). Wallace rejected natural selection because he had faith in the inherent progressiveness of human nature.

Wallace was also impressed by the argument, advanced by the Scottish moralist William Rathbone Greg, that in modern times the poor and the reckless were breeding faster than the frugal and virtuous members of society. Darwin also drew attention to this paradox: natural selection, if given free rein, might lead to the degradation of society. Although Wallace remained a strict selectionist in explaining animal adaptation, he could not see how the Malthusian principle of struggle and the selection to which it gave rise could account for human social progress. His solution was to argue that progress could not be achieved without a basic restructuring of society along socialist lines (Wallace, 1900).

With the improved living conditions in a socialist state, Wallace believed, natural selection would operate differently and society would not degenerate. War, pestilence, and famine would be eliminated, but since the removal of these checks would cause the population to increase, as Malthus had warned, new checks would be needed. Wallace rejected the idea of socially enforced sterility and counted instead on late marriage and the natural decrease in fertility that he thought would follow from intellectual development, as Spencer had argued. These benign checks would control the population. Further improvement in society would be achieved by a new system of selection that would come spontaneously into action and "steadily tend to eliminate the lower and more degraded types of man, and thus continuously raise the average standard of the race" (Wallace, 1900, p. 517). This new form of selection was the prudent choice of mates by educated women. Progress in a socialist state depended on a rational approach to reproduction, which in turn depended crucially on the advancement of women. Wallace felt certain that, given intelligent female choice, the idle, selfish, weak, and deformed would be rejected. The progress of human civilization depended not only on the "cultivated minds and pure instinct" of men, but especially on the minds and instincts of the "Women of the Future" (ibid., p. 526). The human species was not entirely exempt from the Malthusian law, but the organization of society would determine which checks were most important in limiting growth and whether progress was possible.

Both Spencer and Wallace believed that natural selection alone could not account for man's superior intellect and moral nature, but each also felt that human progress was a consequence of natural law. Spencer's ideas about Lamarckian evolution supported a philosophy of laissez-faire individualism, but his early ideas about the kind of society to which the evolutionary process led were compatible with the socialism Wallace espoused. Darwin, on the other hand, was convinced that natural selection could indeed explain complex human mental and moral faculties. He firmly resisted the visions of utopia conjured up by Wallace and the early Spencer, for Darwin was a natural historian, not a social engineer. But he did see his theory as having a direct bearing on moral philosophy. The argument in *The Descent of Man*, written in the context of Spencer's and Wallace's ideas and following decades of debate on human progress, was a refutation of the Utilitarians' hedonistic view of human nature.

Darwin and human progress: The seeds of sociobiology

What is most remarkable about *The Descent of Man* is its thoroughgoing biological approach to the problem of human behavior. Where Darwin might have limited himself to a discussion of the anatomical and physiological affinities between humans and animals, he ranged much further and subjected every aspect of human life to scrutiny from the standpoint of natural history. The most important obstacle to the acceptance of Darwin's theory was the belief that man's moral sense could not have originated by natural selection. Darwin made no exceptions in his efforts to find a connection between humans and their animal origins, down to the last psychological detail: esthetic sense, religious feeling, and conscience were all to be found, in rudimentary form, in the lower world. In this respect Darwin's approach pushed the biological view of man to its limit; here we have the origin of what is now called sociobiology.

One of the most difficult problems was to account for altruism in humans, which Darwin considered to be the basis of the moral sense. He connected altruism to the social instincts, including parental and filial affections, which were found in the animal world, but which in humans had been perfected under the influence of natural selection. To explain how selection could create altruism, which after all did not benefit the altruistic individual, Darwin introduced the idea of community selection (Richards, 1987). Natural selection, he suggested, could act at the level of the community, preserving characteristics that would give the community as a whole an advantage over another community, even though they did not seem to benefit the individual directly. Darwin had used this idea in the *Origin* to explain the evolution of sterile worker castes in insect societies: their sterility did not benefit the workers directly, but they were specialized to help their queen produce more workers efficiently, and the community flourished under their tireless efforts. In the *Descent* he turned the idea to the human community, arguing that altruistic traits would be crucial advantages in competition between different tribes: "There can be no doubt that a tribe including many members who, from possessing in a high degree the spirit of patriotism, fidelity, obedience, courage, and sympathy, were always ready to give aid to each other and to sacrifice themselves for the common good, would be victorious over most other tribes; and this would be natural selection" (quoted in Richards, 1987, p. 215).

Darwin's idea that moral advance would give one tribe a competitive advantage over another was similar to Wallace's original argument for natural selection on the cultural level, but Wallace had dropped this argument in his later turn to spiritual causes. The main problem with the theory of community selection is that the human community is not as closely related as the insect society, so that it is not clear how altruistic behavior would become established within the population. Darwin was aware of this problem, but thought that in early societies members of tribes would be fairly closely related. He believed strongly that the basic social instinct, the feeling of sympathy that served as a social bond, was inheritable like any other instinct and had developed through natural selection. Human nature was, at its roots, altruistic. His explanation differed from Spencer's, but both concluded that morality was innate, a product of evolution.

Darwin's interpretation was a biological version of the moral philosophy of James Mackintosh, a leading Whig politician in the two decades before his death in 1832. He was also connected to the Darwin family, being the brother-in-law of Darwin's uncle Josiah Wedgwood. Mackintosh argued that humans had an instinctive sense of right and wrong, a kind of moral impulse that guided behavior, quite apart from any rational motive such as the anticipation of pleasure, with which such behavior might be associated. Darwin gave this innate moral sense a biological history. Like Mackintosh, he intended the argument that altruism was innate to be a response to the British Utilitarian theorists of the time, who argued that human actions were guided by a search for pleasure and avoidance of pain, in other words by selfish motives. To the contrary, Darwin thought that humans often seemed to act unconsciously, as if from instinct or long habit. Far from being guided by a search for happiness or pleasure, people seemed to be impelled by a deeply planted social instinct. Morality was founded not on selfishness, but on an altruistic impulse, which had a biological basis and could be seen in undeveloped form in the lower animals. The goal of altruistic behavior was not the general happiness, but the general good of the community, defined as the maximum production of healthy, vigorous offspring having all their faculties intact (Darwin, 1896; Richards, 1987, pp. 115–116).

Darwin did make one small concession in response to the criticism that natural selection could not account for the adaptive value of every human characteristic. This exception was developed in his theory of "sexual selection," which had been introduced in the *Origin* and was greatly expanded in the *Descent*. Sexual selection was based on the observation that some characteristics did not directly affect an individual's own survival, but did improve its chances of reproducing by helping it to attract a suitable mate or ward off rivals. Such animal features as colorful ornamentation, spurs, or antlers, or the power of song, appeared to evolve as a result of the direct competition of males for the available females. Darwin referred to this process as sexual selection, which he considered to be different from natural selection because the organism's survival did not hinge on the possession of the trait. Wallace disagreed with Darwin that sexual selection was different in kind from natural selection, for both types of selection involved competition within the population and both affected reproductive success. The fact that Darwin thought of sexual selection as different indicates that he interpreted natural selection as meaning mainly differential survival, whereas sexual selection meant only differential reproduction. His discussion of sexual selection reflected his awareness that success in leaving progeny was a crucial part of the struggle for existence.

Sexual selection implied that females had the power to discriminate among males and to select the more desirable ones for mating. As we have seen, Wallace used this idea in arguing for a socialist utopia, although otherwise he disagreed with many of Darwin's specific uses of sexual selection to explain adaptations. Darwin himself used sexual selection to explain differences between the races of man and the differences between the sexes, for instance the perceived greater tenderness of women and the greater inventiveness and aggressiveness of men. As with his explanation of the moral sense, these adaptations were considered to be based on innate differences; they were parts of human nature. They projected onto nature Darwin's image of Victorian men and women; the intellectual differences between the sexes were not seen to be products of differential learning or opportunity, but to be biologically evolved and adaptive differences.

Darwin was mainly interested in past evolution, but in the *Descent* he allowed himself a brief speculation about the future. He noted with regret that the struggle for existence did not always lead to progress, for the reckless often reproduced faster than the virtuous. The Scottish moralist Greg, as noted above, had already developed the argument that selection could have a deleterious effect on society, and Darwin quoted Greg's example in the *Descent*: "The careless, squalid, unaspiring Irishman multiplies like rabbits: the frugal, foreseeing self-respecting, ambitious Scot, stern in his morality, spiritual in his faith, sagacious and disciplined in his intelligence, passes his best years in struggle and in celibacy, marries late, and leaves few behind him" (Darwin, 1896, p. 138). In such a society, the "less favoured" race would prevail.

But Darwin did not despair. He believed that the checks to population increase, such as disease or famine, operated more harshly on the inferior classes of society, so that in the long run their growth would be checked more than the growth of the middle class. Moreover, he felt that continued struggle was a prerequisite for future advance, for otherwise men would sink into indolence. "Hence our natural rate of increase, though leading to many and obvious evils, must not be greatly diminished by any means," he concluded (ibid., p. 618). Malthus, one might imagine, would have nodded vigorous agreement. But Darwin added that natural selection was not the sole means toward progress, even though it had produced the basic social instincts from which civilization grew. Learning and reasoning were even more important for the development of man's moral nature and would continue to be important for man's future progress, far outweighing the struggle for existence.

This verdict on human progress was echoed by Thomas Henry Huxley, who in two essays on evolution and ethics written in the 1890s developed the idea that the cosmic process (which was governed by natural selection) and human civilization were destined to oppose each other (Huxley, 1894). Like Darwin, he saw that the moral sense was built on our natural capacity to feel sympathy. Although humans had been at one time subject to natural selection, their evolution from the primitive feeling of sympathy to the fully developed moral sense entailed a repudiation of the struggle for existence—of man's aggressive and competitive nature—in favor of cooperation. The gradual strengthening of the social bond arrested the struggle and put an end to the kind of evolution that occurred in nature.

Cultural advance happened only under the protection of the artificial environment of society, just as the beauty of the garden compared with raw nature was the product of a protected, cultivated enclave. But this Garden of Eden had its serpent, in the form of the Malthusian law of population increase. Huxley rejected the idea of planned selection within society as impractical; but, if population increase could not be limited, and if selection could not be controlled, then the perfectibility of society was always limited. Huxley and Darwin agreed that the Malthusian law could not be evaded, and like Malthus both spurned utopian visions, while allowing for some progress in the future. Huxley, however, went further than Darwin in depicting the struggle for existence as fundamentally opposed to civilized progress. His target was not Darwin but Spencer, in particular what he saw as Spencer's "fanatical individualism," which tried to apply the analogy of cosmic nature to society (Richards, 1987, p. 316).

All of these discussions of human progress and natural selection were inevitably bound to arguments about moral advancement. Darwin and his contemporaries could not avoid the habit of equating human fitness with advanced intellectual ability and moral superiority. The questions being debated were whether natural selection had had any role in creating these qualities, and whether it could account for further progress in this direction. It might seem as though these evolutionists muddled the issue by not adopting a value-free definition of fitness as survival and reproductive success. Were they not simply projecting onto nature their ideas of the superior moral qualities of the middle-class Victorian by arguing that these qualities were innate? They were indeed defining human nature by looking in a mirror, yet as Richards (1987, p. 175) points out, their discussions show them to have been aware that survival was merely a criterion of fitness, not a definition of fitness in itself. It was important to recognize that there should be a criterion of fitness independent of survival, for otherwise one fell into a circular definition of natural selection, namely: "natural selection means that organisms that cannot live, die." To avoid the tautology, one must be able to judge what traits give the "fit" individuals an advantage in the struggle for life, apart from their mere survival. For the Victorians, these traits in humans included a well-developed moral sense.

Yet the problem of defining fitness was an important one, and it became even more so when social engineers in the twentieth century started to argue that human breeding should be controlled in order to perfect society. The danger in this interventionist approach to progress was that any form of social deviance could be targeted as "unfit." The engineering mentality, satirized by Aldous Huxley in *Brave New World*, which did not greatly exaggerate the ideas of the 1920s (Haldane, 1924), was a dominant ideology by the turn of the century. In combination with the ideals of Social Darwinism and with advances in the science of genetics, it produced a scientific and political movement devoted to human breeding. The movement was spearheaded by Darwin's cousin Francis Galton.

Engineering human progress

Darwin was aware of the possibility that natural selection might have a deleterious effect in modern society, but he believed that in the long run selection had the power to limit reproduction among the criminal classes and among those with weak constitutions. Others were not so optimistic; they felt that harmful though the rapid reproduction of the lower classes might be in any culture, it would be suicidal in a democratic society. Francis Galton responded to this perceived threat to British society with the suggestion that progress required scientific control over human reproduction. He imagined a perfect society in which human breeding would be taken as seriously as the breeding of domestic animals, a society in which the ideal of "race improvement" would become the basis for a new ethics that would supplant Christianity. He conceived the idea for a program of selective breeding in 1865 and in 1883 coined the word "eugenics" to describe it (Kevles, 1985). Galton dismissed the common idea, argued by Spencer, of an inverse relation between intelligence and fertility (Cowan, 1977). Instead, he believed, the "fittest" members of society could be encouraged to marry and reproduce if given the right incentives.

Galton's entire program rested on his conviction that intelligence and other mental qualities were determined by heredity, that nature was supreme over nurture. This conclusion was opposed to the scientific orthodoxy of the 1860s; nor did Galton have the scientific evidence to back up his claims at first. Most scientists and educators asserted that environmental effects were decisive in shaping character and intelligence. To this belief they added the idea that some characteristics acquired during a person's lifetime, in response to the environment, could become hereditary. Darwin himself believed that the continued effects of habit could form the basis for instincts that became hereditary. Spencer's theory of evolution was even more completely based on the Lamarckian mechanism of adjustment between individual and environment. Proposals for social reform in the environmentalist tradition naturally stressed improvement of the environment. Galton's theory, in contrast, denied the possibility of the inheritance of acquired characteristics. Reform could only be achieved by changing human nature itself through selection of the fittest.

After 1865 Galton continued to promote his ideas assiduously in private discussions. Publicly he set about creating a scientific foundation for his political program. His research took the form of statistical studies of human variation, buttressed by some experimental and mathematical work on the mechanisms of inheritance. Galton's interest in statistics was a near-obsession, one that paid off at a time when few biologists had any mathematical training and when the science of heredity was in a state of confusion arising from a mountain of observations, collected over decades of breeding experiments, but unordered by any coherent theory. The mathematical method pioneered by Galton succeeded in bringing some order to the subject, chiefly by allowing for more precise definition of such concepts as "heredity," "variation," and "reversion to type" (the tendency of individuals to resemble the average type of the population). Darwin himself drew on Galton's findings to show that many mental traits were indeed inherited. In short, his research helped to turn the study of heredity into "positivist science," where positivism meant the ideal of a science of exact measurement and mathematical law, following the trends in the physical sciences in the nineteenth century. But all of these achievements, which secured Galton a place in history as a founder of biometry and population genetics, sprang directly from his enthusiasm for eugenics and his need to provide eugenics with a scientific basis.

The founder of eugenics had no children, but he did live to see his intellectual child flourish in the first decade of the twentieth century. He publicly reintroduced the concept of eugenics in 1901, this time to enthusiastic acclaim. By the turn of the century the hereditarian outlook and its implications for social reform had become the new orthodoxy among biologists as well as social scientists (Cravens, 1978). In this new climate Galton's vision of a eugenic society seized the public imagination. In 1904 a Eugenics Record Office was established in London; in 1906 it was renamed the Francis Galton Eugenics Laboratory. Eugenics was forming the basis for movements of social reform that differed in their political affiliations but made a common appeal to the scientific principles of heredity. In Europe and America parallel eugenics movements began to have political impact.

The history of the eugenics movement, and the dominance of hereditarian attitudes in the biological and social sciences, have been described in recent books by Cravens (1978), Kevles (1985), Ludmerer (1972), and Weiss (1987). Leaders of the eugenics movement tended to be middle-class professionals—biologists and social scientists, clerics, professors, physicians, and politicians—and the movement reflected the biases of that class. Belief in the superiority of the Caucasian race was widespread, although there was no agreement as to the superiority of the Nordic type within that race. The intelligence tests introduced in the early twentieth century as educational diagnostic tools quickly became one of the "scientific" weapons of those who argued for the inherent inferiority of certain populations (Gould, 1981). The heritability of several kinds of defects, as well as of alcoholism, certain diseases such as tuberculosis, and various sorts of moral degeneracy, formed a large part of the eugenics literature. In the United States, geneticists embraced eugenics along with the new Mendelism and set about collecting data on the hereditary traits of various populations. Much of the data was stored at the Eugenics Record Office at Cold Spring Harbor, New York, set up in 1910 to provide "a sort of inventory of the blood of the community" (Kevles, 1985, p. 55).

Debates about prostitution, sex education, and birth control were tied to eugenic discussions. Some eugenicists opposed birth control, on the grounds that it would be used only by middle-class women, while birth control advocates such as Margaret Sanger tried to forge an alliance with the eugenics movement as a way to gain credibility for the birth control movement (Borell, 1987; Reed, 1984). Sanger also solicited the support of biologists to organize the first World Population Conference, held in Geneva in 1927, which was intended to stimulate interest in population issues. Although the conference tried to uphold a dispassionate scientific image, avoiding controversial questions involving birth control, Sanger did hope to increase scientific support specifically for contraceptive research (Borell, 1987).

Advocates of eugenics came from the educated middle class, but they represented no single political outlook. Just as Darwinism had been bent to serve many political views, both conservative and liberal (Jones, 1980), so the eugenics ideal found supporters from the entire political spectrum. What eugenicists had in common was a definition of "fitness" in terms of social and cultural achievement, reflecting the values of their class. The same was true of the racial hygiene movement in Germany, which prior to Hitler's rise to power was no different from many other eugenics movements in its aims and political diversity (Weiss, 1987). The main areas of legislation influenced by the eugenics movement concerned the passage of restrictive immigration laws and sterilization laws applied to poor people and the institutionalized population. In Britain the move to legalize voluntary sterilization failed, but in the United States several states passed compulsory sterilization laws, though not all were enforced (Kevles, 1985; Ludmerer, 1972).

If Galton had only conceived and promoted the idea of a eugenic utopia, he would merit a small place in history as a contributor to a relatively short-lived reform movement. His significance extends beyond this role because he saw that eugenics needed a solid scientific basis if its program of social engineering was to be accepted. Many of the leaders of eugenics were motivated to turn the study of heredity, population growth, and evolution into an experimental and mathematical science, whose goals were the discovery of scientific laws and whose methods were seen to be as objective as any part of human inquiry could be. When some biologists criticized the eugenics movement in the 1920s, it was not because they disagreed with the principle of planned breeding per se, but because the movement had been wrested from the hands of scientists by laymen whose ignorant pronouncements were destroying the movement's credibility. Eugenics was not just a call to political action; it was also a springboard to a great deal of research on human heredity.

The connection between eugenics and the positivist ideology in science is best seen in the work of Karl Pearson, Galton's protégé and successor as the leading British authority in mathematical biology and eugenics. Pearson's *The Grammar of Science*, published in 1892 with a second edition in 1900, was an influential statement of the positivist philosophy of science and at the same time a justification for the analysis of social problems using scientific methods. He argued that the methods of science, based on the logical derivation of laws from hard facts, freed the mind of individual prejudice and could therefore be applied to social problems in a rigorous, objective manner. The extension of the scientific method to the social sphere was seen as a means of promoting sound citizenship and social stability. And because the results of the scientific method would be universally valid, science could have a direct bearing on the practical treatment of social problems (Pearson, 1900).

As a young socialist, Pearson was especially interested in the application of the law of natural selection to society (Pearson, 1897). He argued that natural selection did not apply within the single society, but rather operated between different societies. This idea was not new, for Wallace had raised and later abandoned it, and Darwin had used the idea in his concept of community selection. Pearson elevated the action of natural selection to the level of whole nations. In his view the modern struggle for existence consisted of the economic competition between nations, a competition that could be won only if a society suppressed the struggle between its individual members and reorganized to maximize its efficiency. This regulation of society would necessarily proceed from the state, making the individual subservient to the state.

Eugenics became an important component of Pearson's scheme for the creation of an efficient modern state. Like Galton, he believed that if human evolution were to be controlled scientifically, the central concepts of natural selection and heredity had to be defined objectively, that is, quantitatively. He considered his research into human variation and heredity to be thoroughly objective because its method was mathematical, even though the results of the research clearly supported his eugenic agenda. Pearson invoked the ideology of positivism, of the objective scientific method extended into the realm of social problems and human reproduction, to support a proto-fascist ideology of national socialism.

A similar link between scientific theory and eugenics can be seen in the research of Pearson's successor, Ronald A. Fisher, whose work was important in effecting a synthesis between Darwinian theory and Mendelian genetics in the 1920s. As an undergraduate, Fisher helped to establish a eugenics society at Cambridge University in 1911; this interest in eugenics led him to the mathematical study of evolution (Norton, 1983). Even as an undergraduate Fisher saw the importance of reconciling the two sides of the controversy raging in Britain between the advocates of a statistical approach to evolution, led by Pearson, and the followers of the new Mendelian genetics, led by William Bateson. Fisher believed that a resolution of this conflict would enable a stronger argument to be made for the importance of nature over nurture, thereby aiding the eugenic cause.

Moreover, Fisher's later work in the mathematical theory of evolution owed its very shape and emphasis to his eugenic goals. He was not interested in speciation, diversification of species, or extinction, although these issues would be expected to serve as central questions to the student of evolution in the wild. Instead he was concerned predominantly with the rate of change of existing species and with whether progress could be achieved through selection. His mathematical style was also unusual in drawing heavily on demographic techniques, reflecting his interest in the human species. His classic treatise, *The Genetical Theory of Natural Selection* (1930), contained five chapters on human society and eugenics. Just as for Galton and Pearson, the character of Fisher's biology was determined by his desire to set eugenics on a scientific foundation.

The biological analysis of population growth was also stimulated by an interest in eugenics. The question of whether populations were actually behaving in a Malthusian fashion was highly relevant to debates about the eugenic implications of differential growth rates in the population. Raymond Pearl, an American statistician, geneticist, and eugenicist, noted that Western population growth rates did not tend to follow the Malthusian exponential curve. He proposed instead that they would eventually level off and follow an *S*-shaped curve, which he called the "logistic curve" (Pearl and Reed, 1920; Pearl, 1924). Pearl's habit of treating the population as a discrete entity led him to suggest that the logistic curve describing population growth was actually a law of growth, comparable to Kepler's laws and Boyle's law. He saw his law as being universally valid and dependent on an underlying biological mechanism, namely an inhibition of fertility caused by increased population density. The modern decrease in the growth rate was seen to be an automatic response of populations that had attained a certain density (Kingsland, 1985).

In suggesting that the population obeyed a biologically grounded law of growth, Pearl felt himself to be following the lead of Galton and Pearson in developing a branch of mathematical biology. In this case he was trying to create a new biological science, the "biology of groups," based on the population as the unit of analysis. The underlying motive of this research was relevant to eugenics: to find out whether environmental or biological factors were more important in determining how populations grew. Pearl's answer came out squarely on the side of biological determinism, but his argument was flawed by circular reasoning. In fact he had merely assumed that his "density effect" was the main factor determining the growth rate, but he had not proved it. His biological explanation of population growth and the enunciation of his "law" raised an immediate controversy among economists, sociologists, demographers, and biologists, who felt that, in view of his cavalier disregard of environmental and social variables acting on the population, he had not actually explained anything (Kingsland, 1985).

Pearl was trying to bring the science of populations into the domain of biology, as opposed to sociology or demography, and the logical errors in his reasoning stemmed from his adherence to this disciplinary perspective. His unwillingness to see population growth as the product of a unique historical context, rather than the unfolding of a biological "law," inevitably drew critical responses from social scientists and demographers, who preferred to interpret population changes as the consequence of multiple economic, cultural, and psychological causes. This debate over the logistic curve lasted well over a decade from the mid-1920s through the 1930s.

Pearl's theory, by suggesting that a decrease in the growth rate was an automatic biological response to increasing density, implied that birth control had no effect on the modern population decline. The "contraceptive hypothesis" was therefore advanced as an alternative to Pearl's logistic hypothesis. One of Pearl's strongest critics along these lines was the British physiologist and social biologist Lancelot Hogben, who was interested in the implications of birth control for the organization of society (Hogben, 1931). He envisioned that control of the birth rate would become the focus of major social changes in the future, just as the control of mortality had become the focus of social change in the nineteenth century (Hogben, 1932). Pearl actually was an advocate of birth control and had worked directly with Margaret Sanger to promote contraceptive research among biologists. He regarded birth control as an adaptive biological response to population pressure and, therefore, one of the reasons the population did follow the logistic curve.

The debate over the logistic hypothesis was further complicated by the feeling that adherence to it implied a degree of complacency with respect to population growth. One eugenicist and demographer, George Knibbs, argued that Malthusian growth would lead to dire consequences unless checked by immediate social measures, meaning in this case a eugenics program designed to raise the level of human intelligence, for the ultimate purpose of controlling the rate of increase (Kingsland, 1985, pp. 78–79).

Indeed, Pearl did begin to relax his views on eugenics as he pursued his population studies. Previously he had been a strong advocate of eugenics, following the lead of Pearson. In the late 1920s he softened his position and began to argue against the class bias that pervaded the eugenics movement (Pearl, 1927). He still believed that heredity rather than environment played the main role in producing intellectual superiority, but he suggested that the lower classes often produced superior individuals, who, given the opportunity for social mobility, would become valuable members of society. The higher reproduction rate of the lower classes need not be feared. These views prompted further attacks from eugenicists.

The eugenics movement was coming under attack from other quarters as well. The Catholic Church was opposed in principle to human tampering with the germ plasm, while civil libertarians were growing concerned about the application of sterilization laws (Kevles, 1985). By the 1920s many biologists and social scientists like Pearl began to distance themselves from the more exaggerated claims of eugenicists. As Hogben remarked in 1932, "The term 'eugenics' has become identified with ancestor worship, anti-semitism, colour prejudice, anti-feminism, snobbery, and obstruction to educational progress" (p. 209). Too many eugenicists continued to make simple-minded assumptions that mental and moral traits, including those associated with poverty, were controlled by the genes.

Not only did new genetic research indicate that gene interactions were far more complex than those assumed by the early Mendelians, but the social sciences were emphasizing in the 1930s the importance of the environment as a determinant of human behavior. The opposition of biologists to eugenics was not so much to the principle of planned breeding or to the idea that truly deleterious genes should be eliminated from the population, as to the fact that the movement exhibited none of the caution associated with application of the scientific method (Jennings, 1930). Pearl, for instance, argued that it was time to replace eugenics with a more scientific approach aimed at human genetics. Partly with that goal in mind, he helped to found the International Union for the Scientific Investigation of Population Problems (later the International Union for the Scientific Study of Population) following the World Population Conference in 1927. The union was meant to act as a coordinating body for population research conducted in a "strictly scientific spirit" (Pearl, 1928). Similarly, the eugenic ideal that underlay contraceptive research was eroded as scientists recognized the limitations of using biology to justify political decisions. As F. A. E. Crew, a geneticist at the University of Edinburgh, observed, "In the past the biologist has justified feudalism, Manchester Liberalism, socialism and every other type of social organization and political programme by reference to selected biological phenomena" (quoted in Borell, 1987, p. 84).

Although eugenics texts continued to spread the gospel throughout the 1930s, the movement was thoroughly discredited by the 1940s as a result of Hitler's use of eugenic laws to enforce mass sterilizations and, starting in 1939, euthanasia. The term "eugenics" disappeared by the 1940s and gave way to scientific research into human genetics, which culminated finally in programs of genetic testing of human populations in an attempt to eliminate certain hereditary defects (Kevles, 1985). The naive enthusiasm for the eugenics movement as a panacea for all social ills had disappeared, but the ideal of engineering human reproduction continued to guide society. The questions of what criteria to use to judge the "fitness" of a human being and how to respond to the presence of "unfit" individuals are still problematic.

Sociobiology and progress

While the eugenics movement revealed the dangers of applying biology to politics and showed the errors of naive genetic determinism, it by no means dispelled the belief that human social behavior was a legitimate subject for biological analysis. Darwin's theory of natural selection, after a period of eclipse around the turn of the century, gained support from the 1920s on, with advances in the science of population genetics and the final demise of the Lamarckian theory of the inheritance of acquired characteristics. Interest in the biological study of social behavior increased especially after World War I and culminated in the creation of a new field called sociobiology, inaugurated by the publication in 1975 of *Sociobiology: The New Synthesis,* by the Harvard zoologist Edward O. Wilson. Wilson defined sociobiology as "the systematic study of the biological basis of all forms of social behavior, including sexual and parental behavior, in all kinds of organisms, including man" (Wilson, 1978, p. 10). The new field synthesized several decades of research in the fields of population genetics, population ecology, and ethology (or, in the case of human studies, anthropology). The characteristic perspective of sociobiology was evolutionary: social behaviors are seen as adaptive traits molded by natural selection. Sociobiology was advanced as a logical extension of Darwin's theory, differing from past research on behavior in that it was methodologically more sound, relying not on anecdote and analogy, but on rigorous testing of hypotheses.

The central precept of sociobiology was that the evolution of social behavior in animals could be understood through an understanding of demography and of the genetic structure of populations (Wilson, 1980). The goal of the theory ultimately was to predict the features of social organization from a knowledge of these population parameters and of the way the genes set constraints on behavior. In the 1950s and 1960s, evolutionary biologists had come to understand that the demographic parameters of animal populations, for example the intrinsic rate of increase of a population, were determined by the genetic composition of the population. Therefore they were subject to evolution by natural selection. Thus one could speak of species as having evolved reproductive strategies to suit different environments. Selection in unstable environments, for instance, might favor rapid rates of population increase, whereas selection in a stable environment would favor a different reproductive strategy (MacArthur and Wilson, 1967). The demographic features of a population, such as survivorship or mortality schedules, were thought to represent close to the optimal (or most productive) schedules that members of the population could achieve in the environment in which the species lived (Wilson, 1975). The significance for sociobiology of the idea that reproductive strategies had evolved lay in the connection between a species' method of reproduction and its social evolution, for some reproductive strategies entailed extended parental care and fairly complex social behavior.

The use of natural selection to explain social, and especially altruistic, behavior required extending the concept of fitness to include not just the individual but also groups of related individuals within the population. Darwin had developed a broader idea of fitness to account for the evolution of sterile insect castes and of altruistic behavior in humans. Twentieth century biologists reinvented the same idea and gave it more rigorous genetic analysis. In 1962 the Scottish biologist V. C. Wynne-Edwards developed a wide-ranging theory of behavioral evolution, postulating that selection could operate on a group to promote survival of a population at the expense of individual reproduction. Some forms of behavior, such as dominance hierarchies in birds and mammals, might lower the fitness of certain individuals by preventing them from breeding, but they benefited the group as a whole by ensuring that the population did not increase beyond the limits of available resources. Group selection was seen to be an evolutionary mechanism for population regulation. This theory of group selection, which was intended to explain the evolution of certain forms of behavior among the higher animals, set off intense controversies in the 1960s (Williams, 1966). The final verdict was that although group selection was logically possible in certain special circumstances, it was not a significant cause of behavioral evolution.

A restricted form of group selection, called kin selection, was proposed as a more plausible form of selection above the level of the individual. In kin selection the concept of fitness was extended to include the close relatives of an individual. Kin-selected behavior therefore benefited not the individual alone, but the wider family group. This concept was used to explain certain kinds of altruistic behavior, of which the purest form was the evolution of sterile female castes in social insects. Darwin's ideas were precursors to the theory of kin selection.

The sociobiologist, adopting a modern genetically based Darwinism, interpreted behavior from the point of view of the gene. The gene became the basic unit of selection, for the whole purpose of life was to help the gene to replicate. The gene was also the basic unit of selfishness. Any behavior that appeared to be altruistic would have arisen by natural selection only if the behavior helped the survival of a gene that was shared by the relatives of the altruist. In other words, altruism was really selfish from the gene's point of view, because its purpose was to help the gene to survive. Kin selection, or natural selection of the family group, was the mechanism by which altruism evolved.

This view of behavior from the point of view of the "selfish gene" meant that the sociobiologist, while claiming to be extending Darwin's insights, actually interpreted human nature quite differently from Darwin himself. The sociobiologist did not deny that a capacity for genuine, disinterested altruism might be a unique human quality, but the argument for the selfish gene did not imply that we are innately altruistic, as Darwin believed. This was not to suggest that we are totally at the mercy of our selfish genes. The sociobiologist's view of our future was not necessarily pessimistic, for it was suggested that we had the intellectual capacity to defy our selfish genes and deliberately cultivate altruism, which would serve our long-term rather than our short-term selfish interests. In this way of thinking, the human being as a genuinely altruistic animal would be one who had rebelled against "the tyranny of the selfish replicators" (Dawkins, 1976, p. 215). This perspective, which pitted man-the-genuine-altruist against man-the-repository-of-the-selfish-gene, was not the image of man that Darwin himself had cultivated. Darwin's belief that our morality had roots in our animal past and had evolved by natural selection was a celebration of the human as a genuinely altruistic being. The biological explanation was not meant to demean our humanity.

Sociobiology was controversial in part because it assumed that selection could act at the family or group level, although these claims were widely disputed and the importance of group selection in the higher animals had not been demonstrated. But the most controversial aspect of sociobiology was its extension of the concepts of selection to human behavior. Sociobiologists and the anthropologists who adopted this perspective postulated that differences between cultures might be genetic, implying that cultural details were in part adaptive in the Darwinian sense.

The sociobiological perspective met with strong resistance from social scientists for this claim. Wilson's response was to argue that the kinds of variations the social scientist studied were undoubtedly due to cultural and environmental circumstances, but that the sociobiologist chose only the most general features of human behavior—those common to all cultures—which were most likely to reflect some underlying genetic control. These general features were compared with those of primate species in order to reconstruct the evolutionary history of social organization and discover its genetic residues in modern culture (Wilson, 1978).

The basic categories for such behavior were sex, aggression, altruism, communication, and religious ritual. These were also categories of behavior discussed by Darwin and were the main forms of behavior studied by anthropologists and ethologists. The forms of behavior and the social structures that arose from them could, according to the sociobiologist, be studied almost as "organs": they were extensions of the genes that existed because of their superior adaptive value. Wilson made it clear that because biology (including sociobiology and neurobiology) provided the most basic level of analysis possible, it would take precedence over philosophical and sociological approaches to human society and ethics. Where Darwin, in analyzing man from the viewpoint of natural history, had invaded the territory of religion and moral philosophy, the modern sociobiologist proposed to invade the territory of moral philosophy and the social sciences. This invasion created nearly as much controversy for Wilson as it had for Darwin (Albury, 1980, 1983).

The difficulty with interpreting social behavior as biologically adaptive was the same difficulty Darwin had faced. It was not clear how one made an objective decision about the adaptive value of a given trait or form of social interaction. It was easy to make up a story to account for the adaptive significance of every trait, but, the critics argued, these were hardly more convincing than Rudyard Kipling's "just-so stories," which offered whimsical explanations of "how the leopard got its spots" and similar tales. The philosopher of science Philip Kitcher (1985) has made a thorough analysis of sociobiological claims about human behavior, with several examples of the extreme lengths to which sociobiologists went to uncover supposed adaptations, and has found the logical and observational basis of many such claims to be very weak. The sociobiologist might respond by pointing out that these examples merely reflected bad reasoning, not that the methods of sociobiology were inherently flawed, and Kitcher has admitted as much in referring to his examples as "popular" sociobiology.

Darwin, in trying to account for the differences between men and women as evolutionary adaptations, transformed his Victorian middle-class biases into biological justifications for the differences he observed. Critics of sociobiology have pointed out that the same dangers lurked in this latest theory. The sharpest criticism along these lines came from Marxists, who saw sociobiology as the latest form of biological determinism, not substantially different from the ideology responsible for the worst excesses of Social Darwinism and eugenics (Lewontin, Rose, and Kamin, 1982).

Sociobiology, unlike Social Darwinism and eugenics, but like Darwin's own theory, is not a reform ideology; its goal is not to change society. Its ideas are nevertheless relevant for social planners. Sociobiology suggests that many of the differences we observe within and between societies are the products of evolution, adaptations to a past environment. In trying to change them, the sociobiologist argues, we risk tampering with human nature in a way that may have untoward consequences. Sociobiology does not argue against social planning explicitly, but it does issue some caveats for the planners: "If the planned society—the creation of which seems inevitable in the coming century—were to deliberately steer its members past those stresses and conflicts that once gave the destructive phenotypes their Darwinian edge, the other phenotypes might dwindle with them. In this, the ultimate genetic sense, social control would rob man of his humanity" (Wilson, 1980, p. 300).

This statement has prompted criticism that sociobiology is merely a biological justification for the status quo; that, like all theories of biological determinism, it locates the cause of inequality in the nature of individuals, rather than in the structure of society. Under the guise of scientific rigor, sociobiologists are really arguing that social institutions might not be alterable because they reflect something deeply rooted in human nature. Wilson denied that he was a biological determinist, although he saw nothing objectionable in adopting a reductionist approach to these biological problems for its heuristic value. This debate cannot be resolved on ideological grounds; the fate of sociobiology will be decided on the basis of its scientific merits as an explanation for the evolution of social behavior.

The debates over sociobiology, like the earlier debates over Malthus's theory and Darwinian theory, show that any discussion of population issues entails discussion of human "nature" and of whether our social behavior, including reproductive behavior, is part and parcel of our evolved natures. Where Darwinian biology, in its modern dress as sociobiology, becomes important for social engineering and population policy is in its assertion that any social plan must be based on an understanding of the adaptive significance of social behavior and the implications of the genetic shifts that are still occurring in our populations. The sociobiologist, like his Darwinian predecessor, wishes to remind us that we are still evolving. But science has not yet told us how to identify social adaptations without projecting our cultural biases onto nature, nor how to build a social policy on a surer foundation than a set of "just-so stories."

References

Albury, William R. 1980. "Politics and rhetoric in the sociobiology debate," *Social Studies of Science* 10: 519–536.

———. 1983. "The politics of truth: A social interpretation of scientific knowledge, with an application to the case of sociobiology," in *Nature Animated*, ed. Michael Ruse. Dordrecht: Reidel, pp. 115–129.

Borell, Merriley, 1987. "Biologists and the promotion of birth control research, 1918–1938," *Journal of the History of Biology* 20: 51–87.

Bowler, Peter J. 1983. *The Eclipse of Darwinism: Anti-Darwinian Evolution Theories in the Decades around 1900.* Baltimore: Johns Hopkins University Press.

———. 1984. *Evolution: The History of an Idea.* Berkeley and Los Angeles: University of California Press.

———. 1986. *Theories of Human Evolution: A Century of Debate, 1844–1944.* Baltimore and London: Johns Hopkins University Press.

Buckland, William. 1837. *Geology and Mineralogy Considered with Reference to Natural Theology,* 2 vols. Philadelphia: Carey, Lea and Blanchard.

Burkhardt, Richard W. 1977. *The Spirit of System: Lamarck and Evolutionary Biology.* Cambridge, Mass. and London: Harvard University Press.

Cowan, Ruth S. 1977. "Nature and nurture: The interplay of biology and politics in the work of Francis Galton," *Studies in History of Biology* 1: 133–208.

Cravens, Hamilton. 1978. *The Triumph of Evolution: American Scientists and the Heredity–Environment Controversy, 1900–1941.* Philadelphia: University of Pennsylvania Press.

Darwin, Charles. 1896. *The Descent of Man and Selection in Relation to Sex,* Revised edition. New York: D. Appleton.

———. 1964. *On the Origin of Species: A Facsimile of the First Edition.* Cambridge, Mass. and London: Harvard University Press.

Dawkins, Richard. 1976. *The Selfish Gene.* Oxford: Oxford University Press.

Desmond, Adrian. 1984. *Archetypes and Ancestors: Palaeontology in Victorian London, 1850–1875.* Chicago: University of Chicago Press.

Eiseley, L. C. 1959. "Charles Darwin, Edward Blyth, and the theory of natural selection," *Proceedings of the American Philosophical Society* 103: 94–158.

Fisher, Ronald A. 1930. *The Genetical Theory of Natural Selection.* Oxford: Oxford University Press.

Gale, Barry G. 1972. "Darwin and the concept of the struggle for existence: A study in the extra-scientific origins of scientific ideas," *Isis* 63: 321–344.

Gillispie, Charles C. 1951. *Genesis and Geology: A Study in the Relations of Scientific Thought, Natural Theology and Social Opinions in Great Britain, 1790–1850.* Cambridge, Mass.: Harvard University Press.

Gould, Stephen Jay. 1981. *The Mismeasure of Man.* New York: W. W. Norton.

Haldane, John B. S. 1924. *Daedalus, or Science and the Future.* New York: Dutton.

Hogben, Lancelot. 1931. "Some biological aspects of the population problem," *Biological Reviews* 6: 163–180.

———. 1932. *Genetic Principles in Medicine and Social Science.* New York: Alfred A. Knopf.

Hull, David L. 1983. *Darwin and His Critics: The Reception of Darwin's Theory of Evolution by the Scientific Community.* Chicago and London: University of Chicago Press.

Huxley, Thomas H. 1894. *Evolution and Ethics and Other Essays.* London: Macmillan.

Irvine, William. 1959. *Apes, Angels, and Victorians: Darwin, Huxley, and Evolution.* Cleveland and New York: Meridian.

Jennings, Herbert S. 1930. *The Biological Basis of Human Nature.* New York: W. W. Norton.

Jones, Greta. 1980. *Social Darwinism and English Thought: The Interaction between Biological and Social Theory.* Brighton: Harvester.

Kevles, Daniel J. 1985. *In the Name of Eugenics: Genetics and the Uses of Human Heredity.* Berkeley and Los Angeles: University of California Press.

Kingsland, Sharon E. 1985. *Modeling Nature: Episodes in the History of Population Ecology.* Chicago and London: University of Chicago Press.

Kitcher, Philip. 1985. *Vaulting Ambition: Sociobiology and the Quest for Human Nature.* Cambridge, Mass.: MIT Press.

Kottler, Malcolm. 1974. "Alfred Russel Wallace, the origin of man, and spiritualism," *Isis* 65: 145–192.

La Vergata, Antonello. 1985. "Images of Darwin: A historiographic overview," in *The Darwinian Heritage,* ed. David Kohn. Princeton, N.J.: Princeton University Press, pp. 901–972.

Lewontin, Richard, Steven Rose, and Leo Kamin. 1982. "Bourgeois ideology and the origins of biological determinism," *Race and Class* 24: 1–16.

Linnaeus, Carl. 1977. "The oeconomy of nature," in *Miscellaneous Tracts Relating to Natural History, Husbandry, and Physik,* trans. B. Stillingfleet. New York: Arno.

Linné, Carl von. 1972. *L'Equilibre de la nature.* Paris: Vrin.

Ludmerer, Kenneth. 1972. *Genetics and American Society: A Historical Appraisal.* Baltimore and London: Johns Hopkins University Press.

Lyell, Charles. 1830–33. *The Principles of Geology, Being an Attempt to Explain the Former Changes of the Earth's Surface, by Reference to Causes Now in Operation,* 3 vols. London: John Murray.

MacArthur, Robert H., and Edward O. Wilson. 1967. *The Theory of Island Biogeography.* Princeton, N.J.: Princeton University Press.

Malthus, Thomas Robert. 1926. *First Essay on Population, 1798.* Reprint. London: Macmillan.

Mayr, Ernst. 1982. *The Growth of Biological Thought: Diversity, Evolution, and Inheritance.* Cambridge, Mass. and London: Harvard University Press.

Norton, Bernard. 1983. "Fisher's entrance into evolutionary science: The role of eugenics," in *Dimensions of Darwinism: Themes and Counterthemes in Twentieth-Century Evolutionary Theory,* ed. Marjorie Grene. Cambridge: Cambridge University Press, pp. 19–29.

Ospovat, Dov. 1981. *The Development of Darwin's Theory: Natural History, Natural Theology, and Natural Selection, 1838–1859.* Cambridge: Cambridge University Press.

Pearl, Raymond. 1924. *Studies in Human Biology.* Baltimore: Williams and Wilkins.

———. 1927. "The biology of superiority," *American Mercury* 12: 257–266.

———. 1928. "Interim report of the first general assembly of the International Union for the Scientific Investigation of Population Problems," *Journal of the American Statistical Association* 23: 306–317.

———, and L. J. Reed. 1920. "On the rate of growth of the population of the United States since 1790 and its mathematical representation," *Proceedings of the National Academy of Sciences U.S.A.* 6: 275–288.

Pearson, Karl. 1897. *The Chances of Death and Other Studies in Evolution*, 2 vols. London: Edward Arnold.

———. 1900. *The Grammar of Science*, 2nd ed. London: Adam & Charles Black.

Peel, John D. Y. 1971. *Herbert Spencer: The Evolution of a Sociologist*. London: Heinemann Educational.

Reed, James. 1984. *The Birth Control Movement and American Society: From Private Vice to Public Virtue*. Princeton, N.J.: Princeton University Press.

Richards, Robert J. 1987. *Darwin and the Emergence of Evolutionary Theories of Mind and Behavior.* Chicago and London: University of Chicago Press.

Rudwick, M. J. S. 1976. *The Meaning of Fossils: Episodes in the History of Palaeontology*, 2nd ed. New York: Neale Watson.

Ruse, Michael. 1979. *The Darwinian Revolution: Science Red in Tooth and Claw.* Chicago and London: University of Chicago Press.

Schweber, Silvan S. 1985. "The wider context in Darwin's theorizing," in *The Darwinian Heritage*, ed. David Kohn. Princeton, N.J.: Princeton University Press, pp. 35–69.

Secord, James A. 1985. "Darwin and the breeders: A social history," in *The Darwinian Heritage*, ed. David Kohn. Princeton, N.J.: Princeton University Press, pp. 519–542.

Spencer, Herbert. 1852. "A theory of population, deduced from the general law of animal fertility," *Westminster Review* 57: 468–501.

———. 1880. *First Principles*, 4th ed. New York: Thomas Y. Crowell.

———. 1891. "Progress, its law and cause," in *Essays, Scientific, Political and Speculative*, Vol. I. New York: D. Appleton.

———. 1896. *The Principles of Biology*, 2 vols., Revised edition. New York: D. Appleton.

Thompson, Edward P. 1978. *The Poverty of Theory and Other Essays*. London: Merlin Press.

Wallace, Alfred R. 1900. "Human selection," in *Studies Scientific and Social*, Vol. I. London: Macmillan, pp. 509–526.

Weiss, Sheila F. 1987. *Race Hygiene and National Efficiency: The Eugenics of Wilhelm Schallmayer.* Berkeley: University of California Press.

Williams, George C. 1966. *Adaptation and Natural Selection: A Critique of Some Current Evolutionary Thought*. Princeton, N.J.: Princeton University Press.

Wilson, Edward O. 1975. "Some central problems of sociobiology," *Social Science Information* 14: 5–18.

———. 1978. "What is sociobiology?," *Society* 15: 10–14.

———. 1980. *Sociobiology: The New Synthesis*, Abridged version. Cambridge, Mass.: Harvard University Press.

Wynne-Edwards, Vero C. 1962. *Animal Dispersion in Relation to Social Behaviour.* New York: Hafner.

Young, Robert M. 1985. "Malthus and the evolutionists: The common context of biological and social theory," in *Darwin's Metaphor: Nature's Place in Victorian Culture*. Cambridge: Cambridge University Press, pp. 23–55.

Human Population from an Ecological Perspective

FRANK B. GOLLEY

THE OBJECTIVE OF THIS ESSAY is to examine human populations from the perspective of ecological science. Ecology is concerned with the interactions of living organisms and their environment. The German zoologist Ernst Haeckel (1866) coined the term ecology in the latter part of the 1860s. His definition, translated from an 1870 article in the textbook *Principles of Animal Ecology,* states:

> By ecology we mean the body of knowledge concerning the economy of nature—the investigation of the total relations of the animal both to its inorganic and to its organic environment; including, above all, its friendly and inimical relations with those animals and plants with which it comes directly and indirectly into contact—in a word, ecology is the study of all those complex interrelations referred to by Darwin as the conditions of the struggle for existence. This science of ecology, often inaccurately referred to as "biology" in a narrow sense, has thus far formed the principal component of what is commonly referred to as "Natural History" (Allee et al., 1949: v).

The science of ecology can provide insight into the study of human populations for at least four reasons. First, ecologists, unlike demographers, can experiment with their subjects in the field and laboratory. Experimental population ecology has had a distinguished history, providing much of the convincing evidence for a theory of populations.[1] An example of the approach is the work of Thomas Park on the flour beetle, *Tribolium confusum,* which passes its entire life cycle in flour in a container on the laboratory shelf. By experimentally establishing populations with different numbers of beetles and altering the population size or the habitat, Park was able to develop and test ideas concerning population structure and dynamics. For example, he demonstrated that increase in population size is a function of the number of original stock in the containers. If there are too few animals, population increase was retarded because the animals meet infrequently and reproductive performance is reduced. A slightly larger initiating population permits maximum increase, but too large an originating population depresses growth. Thus, Park demonstrated that there was an optimum size of the original population for maximum increase. The concept of optimal population was elaborated for other organisms, including humans, in the classic textbook on animal ecology of which Park was a coauthor (Allee et al., 1949).

In contrast to the laboratory ecologist, fisheries ecologists observe experimentally manipulated populations. Studies of fish populations (Everhart and Youngs, 1981) have demonstrated that taxonomic categories such as species, subspecies, and even races may not be fine enough divisions of the genetic character for the manager who must manipulate these populations in nature. Individual populations of fish may discriminate between the streams flowing from different watersheds, and they may have different feeding characteristics and different electrophoretic patterns of serum proteins that correlate with physiological differences. Transplantation of fish from one site to another, or from a hatchery to a lake, may fail because the innate behavior of the donor population is not matched to the requirements of their new environment. For example, stream populations of trout are not usually successfully transplanted to lakes, and vice versa. These field studies show how varied population response to environment can be and how diverse are the genetic characteristics underlying these responses.

Experimental laboratory and field ecologists have shown how expanding populations fit the sigmoid or logistic growth curve; how populations oscillate after reaching the asymptote of this curve; how populations interacting with their environment reach a point—termed the carrying capacity—at which the available resources will not support further growth; how they alter or condition their environment; and so on.

Second, ecologists have tended to ignore distinctions between animal and human populations. The assumption that humans are a biological species that performs according to ecological rules is fundamental and unquestioned. Thus, ecologists reason by analogy from their experimental and field studies of animal populations to humans. A particularly eloquent example of this reasoning is given by Aldo Leopold in the first textbook on game management in America:

> Man thinks of himself as not subject to any density limit. Industrialism, imperialism, and that whole array of population behaviors associated with the "bigger and better" ideology are direct ramifications of the Mosaic injunction for the species to go the limit of its potential, i.e., to go and replenish the earth. But slums, wars, birth-controls, and depressions may be construed as ecological symptoms that our assumption about human density limits is unwarranted; that we may yet learn a lesson in sociology from the lowly bobwhite, which . . . "refuses" to live in slums, and concentrates his racial effort on quality, not ciphers. Where his racial exuberance gets the upper hand and causes him to

> depart occasionally from the rule, he suffers economic cycles and social unrest, and his civilization relapses to near-zero for a new start. (Leopold, 1933: 49)

If one can accept the assumption that human populations follow rules similar to those governing animal and plant species—and we shall see that many do not—then the evidence from field and laboratory studies very convincingly leads some ecologists to be strong advocates for human population control.

Third, ecologists experienced a sudden rise in popularity in the 1960s and 1970s, with the worldwide recognition of the environmental crisis. Ecologists were identified as scientists who had extensive experience on environmental topics, had applied this experience in managing populations and ecosystems, and were willing to extrapolate from their experience to problem solving. Some ecologists became celebrities,[2] and many were willing to develop new policy options, to become politically active, and to venture into such fields as economics, political science, and history. Indeed, the distinction between ecological scientists and environmentalists has become blurred as ecologists have become involved with practical problems. Beginning in the 1960s, ecological science has become relevant to many aspects of public concern, including human population growth. Thus, while the study of the dynamics of human populations falls in the domain of demography, and the study of the causes and implications of human population change falls in the realm of the social sciences, some biological ecologists have not been reluctant to take sides in population debates and to extrapolate from their work to human population consequences.[3] Usually these activists among the ecological community have been opposed to population growth.[4]

Fourth, ecology employs a variety of metaphors that can be usefully adapted to the study of human populations. In one such metaphor, living systems are viewed as complex machines, in which components interact through exchange of energy, materials, and information. Reductionist analysis reveals the nature of these interactions. In theory the parts could be put together to reconstruct the living system, in the same way as an engine is built up from its parts. In another view, living systems are organisms in complex ecological environments. It is asserted that the organism has special properties not revealed by reductionist analysis,[5] and that these holistic properties are a result of interactions between the components and the functions. Another view considers the organism as a dynamic, evolving entity that has been selected as the one most fit for the particular circumstances of its environment. In these cases the metaphors simplify reality, permitting us to interpret poorly known complex natural systems in terms of familiar concepts of machines or organisms. The metaphors are important in providing support for the idea that man is part of a mechanical or organic system and that human populations follow the general rules characteristic of such systems.

Implications of ecological concepts for population problems

Ecological science has delineated a variety of patterns of plant and animal population growth and of the development and relationships of populations with the environment.[6] In my opinion, three ecological issues are directly relevant to the study of human populations, and I will restrict my attention to these. The three issues are resource limitation, excessive population growth, and the impact of human population growth on the environment.

Resources as a limitation on growth

In ecology the environment is defined as all phenomena external to the subject of interest that directly affect its structure or function. Thus, the environment includes climate, soils, other organisms, pathogens, artifacts of civilization, and culture and institutions. Since no living system is either closed or isolated, the environment provides both a source from which the organism obtains all its needs and a sink into which the organism loses its products and wastes. The environment controls or regulates the well-being, survival, and reproduction of the organism through its action as both source and sink.

A human population at the most basic level requires from its environment food, space, oxygen, water, and absorption of wastes. Humans, following the discovery of fire, also require fuel. In each instance the amount of the resource in the environment is limited, and the demand from a population can exhaust the resource. For example, in some unsophisticated human populations defecation near the living compounds eventually renders the area unlivable. The traditional solution for these humans is to move to a new location. Where the density of villages is high, diseases associated with fecal matter, such as diarrhea, increase, especially among infants, for it is no longer possible to find uncontaminated locations outside the territories of other groups. These diseases may control the population size until a technological advance, such as latrines, is discovered and introduced.

Since naturally regulated populations are limited at each point in time by some environmental factor, provision of more of this resource allows the population to grow until another limitation comes into effect. Justus Liebig in 1840 recognized this idea and applied it to the interaction of crop yield and the nutrients required for plant growth. Eugene Odum integrated Liebig's concept with those of other writers into a "combined concept of limiting factors." The combined concept states that "the presence and success of an organism or a group of organisms depends on a complex of conditions. Any condition which approaches or exceeds the limits of tolerance is said to be a limiting condition or a limiting factor" (Odum, 1953: 28).

Populations require innumerable resources, any of which might be in short supply and limit the population's growth. In addition, resources interact and it may be the interaction that causes limitations, not the quantity or quality of the resources per se. The human situation is further complicated both because of the complex nature of resources needed for modern civilization and because man can conceptualize resources. In other words, humans are capable of endowing the environment with properties it does not have and then acting as if the resources existed in fact. For example, humans designate certain places as wilderness, set aside for a specific kind of human use. Wilderness is a cultural, esthetic concept applied by a specific civilization, whether designated for recreation or conservation. For this civilization, wilderness becomes an essential resource. Under these circumstances, wilderness can be subjected to cost–benefit analysis.

Thus, humans are capable of declaring that absolutely necessary resources (such as pure air) are not resources and are uninteresting from an economic point of view whereas other elements of the environment that are not directly needed for human biological reasons are of great value and must be conserved. Humans also have the capability of devising ways to overcome resource limitations. Indeed, success in overcoming one such limitation after another leads some to conclude that no resources are limiting to human population growth or survival.[7] These particular characteristics of humans make the evaluation of population and resource issues especially difficult.

Let us move from the ecological idea that resources can be limiting to populations to consider the specific interaction of population growth and resources. Ecologists have observed in laboratory and field studies that when a key resource, such as food, is available in abundance the population increases in number.[8] The increase in numbers if plotted against time in equal increments has an *S* shape; this is called a sigmoid growth curve or logistic curve (Kingsland, 1985). Increase begins slowly, speeds up to a maximum, and as the limit in the resource is neared, the rate of increase slows. Then growth decreases and becomes zero at the point where the resource is limiting. This point, termed the asymptote, defines the carrying capacity of the resource.[9]

After the population reaches the carrying capacity of the environment, it may equilibrate with the resource and maintain a steady state at that level; it may continue to increase, destroy the resource, and then plummet; or it may alter the resource so that the capacity to sustain the population size is slowly reduced. This simple model points up two features of resource limitation that are useful to our discussion. First, it reflects capacities of the environment to support a population. The population is linked to the environment and resources through its input sources and its outputs to other populations and the physical environment. Limitation of inputs or outputs may negatively affect any property of the population. Second, resource limitation often prevents further population growth at the point called carrying capacity. The input–output model derived from economics and the logistic growth model derived from population studies have been combined to produce a limits-to-growth model in which the capacities of source and sink resource pools, rates of resource use by populations, and population response to carrying capacity are specified for various population growth scenarios. Such a model predicts when a population will stop growing for given resource and use states. Limits-to-growth models were popular in the 1970s, as typified by the US government's study of human population and resources under the administration of President Carter.[10] A limitation of such models was that they could not anticipate human invention to overcome resource scarcity.

Adverse effects of high population growth rates

There is a section of the *S*-shaped population growth curve where resources are not limiting and the rate of growth is maximum, that is, exponential. This section of the growth curve precedes the point at which the carrying capacity comes into play and the population numbers become limited. When ecologists examine the curve describing human population growth for the entire Earth, they conclude that the human population is at the stage of maximum increase. For most of recorded history, the human population numbered less than 500 million. Increase in numbers was slow and steady; however, in the modern period the growth rate abruptly increased. In 1850 there were about one billion humans; in 1930, 2 billion; and in 1975, 4 billion (Ehrlich et al., 1977). Now there are over 5 billion. Some human populations are declining, others have reached an asymptote of growth, others continue to increase. Our concern here is with the growth of the total human population.

These data on human population growth raise several questions. How long will growth continue? What will happen after the asymptote is reached? Will numbers decline precipitously, remain at a high level, or oscillate somewhere in between? What would be the conditions of life under these different population states?

By and large, ecologists view the human growth curve with concern. Exponential increase cannot continue indefinitely. The point at which resource limitation will begin to control the population cannot be predicted, but if this mechanism comes into play it will involve decreased natality and/or increased mortality. In confined mammal populations overpopulation has been shown to result in social disorder, violence, aggression, stress disorders, and disease. Those who would extrapolate from this experience trace the rise in crime rates and similar phenomena as portents of population regulation.

Further, we cannot predict whether uncontrolled human population growth will exceed carrying capacity, destroying the Earth's environment.

The sheer increase in human populations places pressure on natural resources; gradually the biosphere is transformed, species are lost, and the overall environment deteriorates. However, human populations also alter their environment and available resources through changes in per capita demand and through changes in the relationship between man and nature. As humans convert the natural world into a human-designed environment, they alter their relationship with the natural world in a fundamental way.

The impact of human populations on the environment

Ecologists have attributed a decline in resources and a deterioration of the environment to excessive human population growth and improper management of the environment. Of course, these concerns are not new. Plato attributed the decline in the fertility of the soils to the loss of the forests in Attica, cut to build ships for the Greek wars. It was not until the eighteenth and nineteenth centuries, however, that evidence of undesirable changes in nature caused by humans began to accumulate in volume. This concern reached its culmination in George Perkins Marsh's *Man and Nature* (1864), which in its time was the most extensive discussion of land management in the English language.[11]

In the United States mounting concern over the destruction of forests and the loss of open spaces led, at the turn of the century, to the formation of the US Forest Service and the National Parks. Widespread soil erosion in the Midwest and the Southeast led in the 1930s to the organization of the Soil Conservation Service. Rachel Carson's 1962 book on chemical pollution, *Silent Spring,* ushered in the contemporary debate on environmental issues. This sequence of environmental concerns had parallels in other countries.

The characteristic approach to management of the environment was direct control of use. For example, Leopold (1933) described the temporal sequence of management of wild game, as: (1) restriction of hunting, followed by (2) predator control, (3) reservation of game lands in parks and refuges, (4) artificial replenishment through restocking and game ranching, and eventually, (5) control of the environment through management. Not until after World War II did the juxtaposition of ecological knowledge, environmental concern, and available resources lead to a broader, more effective environmental management approach, in which human populations were considered part of the problem.

Garrett Hardin (1968), in his classic essay "The tragedy of the commons," called attention to the potential for abuse of essential resources that exist outside of private ownership and for which no controls over use exist. Excessive use of the commons by an individual benefits that individual exclusively, but the cost of injury to the commons is borne by all users equally. Thus, there is no motivation for an individual to curtail use. The problem is how to regulate a commons so that its use by all parties is preserved and the resource is not destroyed. Hardin called for mutual coercion, mutually agreed upon.

"The tragedy of the commons" combined ecological and economic thinking in terms the average person could understand. Hardin's concept was flawed in certain aspects, yet the essay is still cited and applied. It focuses attention on such important issues as inventory and monitoring resource use, as well as development of a forum in which resource use can be discussed and mutually agreed-upon rates of use can be assigned to each user. Since such commons as ocean fisheries, clean air, and water in rivers cross national boundaries, mutual agreement is an international issue.

Ecologists have amassed persuasive evidence of environmental deterioration. Carbon dioxide levels in the global atmosphere have been rising for decades.[12] Global rates of soil erosion are increasing. Forests in several parts of the world are declining in growth or are dying. Living organisms, in even the remotest parts of the world, have accumulated radioactive fallout elements and chemical pesticides. Such environmental changes can cause disruption throughout the global ecological system. For example, carbon dioxide increase in the atmosphere could raise the temperature at the Earth's surface, leading to changes in climate, in the rate of build up or melt of glaciers and ice caps, and in the level of the oceans. These changes could have an impact on vegetation distribution, plant production, and human life.

While environmental change can be demonstrated, understanding causation is much more difficult, in part because it is difficult to carry out experiments, but also because in complex ecological systems multiple causation and feedback between causal elements are the rule. Even so, it is probable to most ecologists that rapid human population growth contributes to environmental degradation. The demands on the resources and environment of these added numbers of people exaggerate problems of meeting human needs. The inability to recognize the relationship between numbers and environment is deeply rooted in culture and political systems.

Technologist versus ecologist

The argument that man's biological nature is not relevant in the modern world hinges largely on faith in the capacity of technology to overcome problems created by human numbers. Humans have created a technology that has provided a rising standard of living, with greater material benefits, for more humans as the population has increased.[13] As prosperity has mounted, human culture has changed: populations are increasingly urban and interact less with nature.

Related to the notion of technology as panacea is the idea that high—or at least moderate—population growth is beneficial to the human condition: with each mouth comes a pair of hands; the more people, the more geniuses; the more people, the more likely that ways will be found to use resources more effectively. If problems of resource use materialize, human creativity can devise ways to overcome the problem, and if the political and economic conditions are favorable, the solutions may be put into place.

This perspective, illustrated by the writing of Julian Simon (1977), emerges from a progressive, utopian view of modern society. The constraints to human well-being are thought to lie mainly within the human population itself, not within the external environment. This view asserts that mankind can solve environmental problems, if humans can be organized politically and economically to use available resources in an efficient way. It would argue that resources are wasted in a variety of ways, especially in construction of weapons, but that if society could be organized effectively, then many more humans could be supported without deterioration of the Earth's life-support system. For example, the distinguished Soviet geographer Innokenty Gerasimov, reviewing the theoretical aspects of geography, quotes Leonid Brezhnev at the 25th Congress of the Communist Party of the Soviet Union:

> Soviet scientists should not lose sight of the problems of environment and population growth which have recently assumed such a serious aspect. Improvement of the socialist use of natural resources and the formulation of an effective demographic policy are an important task facing a whole complex of natural and social sciences.

To do this, Gerasimov calls for the following:

— the comprehensive study of all diverse forms of developed socialist societies' impact on the environment; research into the main direction of that impact and the intensity of changes in the environment; the elaboration of properly substantiated forecasts of the most probable ecological consequences of production activity, and also of scientifically substantiated methods for the recording of direct and indirect consequences of societies' impact on the natural environment;

— the continued surveying for and assessment of natural resources and their regional distribution, necessary for the development of socialist society; outlining of methods for their effective exploitation;

— the rational development, deployment and regional organization of production and the deployment of the population to ensure not only economic efficiency but also the regeneration of natural resources and the improved quality of the environment;

— elaboration of ways in which purposefully to transform the environment using present day technology and that of the future, and to improve the population's living conditions, a goal made possible first and foremost by

> the planned nature of the economy in developed socialist society. (Gerasimov, 1981: 39–40)

These words would represent the thinking of capitalist technologists as well, if the references to the planned economy were changed to free market processes. The statement lays out a dominant technological imperative characteristic of modern society.

Paul Shepard and Daniel McKinley (1969) called ecology the subversive science because it describes a future fundamentally different from that of the technologist. Some elements of its subversiveness arise from the education and character of ecologists, while others come from the social and political context of modern ecology. As I have pointed out above, ecologists' concern about human population growth and the rapid deterioration of the Earth's environment derives largely from their experience with diverse plant and animal populations. I think many ecologists are deeply frustrated by their inability to convince decisionmakers and the general public that further progress on the current path will lead to tragic consequences for humankind and the Earth.

Ecologists as the inheritors of the tradition of natural history, as students of nature in the field, and frequently as advocates for a new philosophical and cultural view of the postindustrial age often hold a rather pessimistic view of further human development along the lines of the past several hundred years.[14] Technologists, on the other hand, profess faith in human rationality and creativity, and have confidence in mankind's ability to solve problems no matter how large or how serious. These two themes have an ancient heritage, at least dating back to the Greek roots of Western civilization. They form one of the unresolved debates of human history, with fundamental and uncertain consequences for human well-being and survival.

Notes

1 David Mertz and David McCauley (1980) point out that between 1930 and 1950 population studies were in the forefront of laboratory ecology, and the foundations of modern population theory were laid at this time (p. 230).

2 For example, Barry Commoner, author of *The Closing Circle* (1971), graced the cover of *Time* magazine on 2 February 1970.

3 An example of the ecologist's extrapolation from experience with nature to explanation of human history is Paul Colinvaux's *The Fates of Nations* (1980).

4 Paul Ehrlich represents one of the most consistent and active proponents of zero population growth. Ehrlich is especially well known for the text, coauthored with Anne Ehrlich, *Population, Resources, Environment* (1970).

5 Properties are said to "emerge" from the organic system, the whole being more than the sum of its parts.

6 It is not my intention in this essay to review the field of population ecology. The reader is referred to the excellent textbooks of Pianka (1983) and Krebs (1978).

7 I have purposely omitted discussion of the Malthusian argument here because it is covered in other essays in this volume. Malthus argued that resources increase at an arithmetic rate, while population increases geometrically. Julian Simon (1977) attempts to refute the Malthusian conclusion: "Though paradoxical, supplies of natural resources may be expected to *increase* indefinitely, and the long-run resource outlook is good. The ultimate constraint upon resource availability is human imagination, and hence population growth can augment resources in the long run by increasing knowledge" (p. 107; emphasis in original). Simon's conclusions are a variant of the biological observation that organisms adapt to their environment. Human adaptation is through imagination and invention, as well as through the genetic and behavioral means available to plants and animals. However, there are limits to adaptive capacity, and the ecologist will argue that this is as true for the human species as for any other.

8 Actually this response is more complex. Individuals may increase in size, fat may be stored within special tissues, reproduction may increase, the rate of development may intensify, and so on. Individuals respond physiologically to an abundance of a resource required for the relevant process.

9 Again, this is an oversimplified explanation of a complex phenomenon. The shape of the curve, the form of various segments, the capacity to reach or overshoot the asymptote may all be different under specific conditions for different species of organisms. The point is that there is assumed to be a relationship between population growth and the resource, and that relationship is expressed as the limitation of further increase in numbers at carrying capacity.

10 One limits-to-growth model is described in *Limits to Growth* by Donella Meadows and coauthors (1972). The models are applied in the Council of Environmental Quality's 1980 report to President Carter.

11 Marsh (1864, pp. 28–29) recognized the problem of overpopulation in Europe, the role of migration in response to overpopulation, and the impact of higher living standards on resources. In large part, his pronouncements remain valid today. Marsh, a Vermont farmer, lawyer, and historian, served as a US Congressman and subsequently as US Minister to the newly formed Kingdom of Italy.

12 Lester Brown et al. (1986) describe the state of the global environment each year in penetrating analyses of major problem areas.

13 Donald Worster comments: "Certainly . . . the economic revolution brought with it a glorious promise, a great utopian ambition, that was pronatalist to the core. The industrialists offered not only to make the existing population of the world infinitely rich, but also *any conceivable* increase in that population. They would fill the world to the brim with well-fed, happy, affluent human beings" (1987, p. 96). Julian Simon (1977) is a particularly eloquent advocate of this position.

14 In a report of a workshop on global ecological problems, the Institute of Ecology, representing organized ecological science in the United States, concluded: "It is clear that we are in a period of population crisis, the outcome of which can not be foreseen. It is also clear that gains in personal well being, which technology has brought to most of the world's population in some degree, are in the process of being nullified by population growth. In short, mankind is on a collision course with nature. . . . We recommend that every effort be devoted to ensuring that the world population stop growing at the earliest possible date" (1971, p. 19).

References

Allee, W. C., et al. 1949. *Principles of Animal Ecology.* Philadelphia and London: W. B. Saunders.
Brown, Lester, et al. 1986. *State of the World.* New York and London: W. W. Norton.
Carson, Rachel. 1962. *Silent Spring.* Boston: Houghton Mifflin.

Colinvaux, Paul A. 1980. *The Fates of Nations: A Biological Theory of History.* New York: Simon and Schuster.

Commoner, Barry. 1971. *The Closing Circle.* New York: Alfred A. Knopf.

Council on Environmental Quality and the Department of State. 1970. *The Global 2000 Report to the President.* Washington, D.C.: US Government Printing Office.

Ehrlich, Paul R., and Anne H. Ehrlich. 1970. *Population, Resources, Environment: Issues in Human Ecology.* San Francisco: W. H. Freeman.

———, Anne H. Ehrlich, and John P. Holdren. 1977. *Ecoscience: Population, Resources and Environment.* San Francisco: W. H. Freeman.

Everhart, W. Harry, and William D. Youngs. 1981. *Principles of Fisheries Science,* 2nd ed. Ithaca: Cornell University Press.

Gerasimov, I. 1981. "The technological revolution and trends in development in geographical research," in *Soviet Geography Today, Aspects of Theory,* ed. L. N. Kudrjasheva. Moscow: Progress Publishers, pp. 33–52.

Haeckel, Ernst. 1866. *Generelle Morphologie der Organismen. Allgemeine Grundzuge der organischen Formen-Wissenschaft, mechanisch begrundet durch die von Charles Darwin reformirte Descendenz-Theorie,* 2 vols. Berlin: Reimer.

———. 1870. "Ueber Entwickelungsgang u. Aufgabe der Zoologie," *Jenaische Z.* 5: 353–370.

Hardin, Garrett. 1968. "The tragedy of the commons," *Science* 162: 1243–1248.

The Institute of Ecology. 1971. *Man in the Living Environment: Report of a Workshop on Global Ecology Problems.* Washington, D.C.

Kingsland, Sharon. 1985. *Modeling Nature: Episodes in the History of Population Ecology.* Chicago and London: University of Chicago Press.

Krebs, Charles J. 1978. *Ecology, the Experimental Analysis of Distribution and Abundance,* 2nd ed. New York: Harper & Row.

Leopold, Aldo. 1933. *Game Management.* New York: Charles Scribner.

Liebig, Justus. 1847 (originally published 1840). *Chemistry in its Application to Agriculture and Physiology,* 4th ed. London: Taylor and Walton.

Marsh, George Perkins. 1864. *Man and Nature; or Physical Geography as Modified by Human Action.* New York: Charles Scribner.

Meadows, Donella H., et al. 1972. *The Limits to Growth.* New York: Universe Books.

Mertz, D. B., and D. E. McCauley. 1980. "The domain of laboratory ecology," in *Conceptual Issues in Ecology,* ed. E. Saarinen. Dordrecht, Boston, and London: D. Reidel Publishing Co., pp. 229–244.

Odum, Eugene P. 1953. *Fundamentals of Ecology.* Philadelphia and London: W. B. Saunders.

Pianka, Eric R. 1983. *Evolutionary Ecology,* 3rd ed. New York: Harper & Row.

Shepard, Paul, and David McKinley (eds.). 1969. *The Subversive Science: Essays toward an Ecology of Man.* Boston: Houghton Mifflin.

Simon, Julian L. 1977. *The Economics of Population Growth.* Princeton, N.J.: Princeton University Press.

Worster, Donald. 1987. "The vulnerable earth: Toward a planetary history," *Environmental Review* 11, no. 2: 87–103.

POPULATION AND SOCIAL SCIENCE

Demography and the Limits to Growth

PAUL DEMENY

"WHEN GOODS INCREASE, THEY ARE INCREASED THAT EAT THEM." These words of the Bible (*Ecclesiastes* 5:11) present a theory of population growth, unmistakably Malthusian in cast. They assert that expansion in human numbers is conditioned by the material environment not only in a permissive sense but is also mandated by it. The formulation, which displays an economy of expression that even mathematically inclined social scientists can envy, draws attention to two central issues of demography. First, what are the limits to population growth imposed by nature? Goods can increase by human exertion—to each mouth belong two hands and a brain—but in a closed system the fruits of such exertion are constrained by the availability of natural resources. Second, how close is the correspondence between population growth that is permitted by the limits of the resource environment and population growth that actually takes place? Can population increase lag behind the increase of goods so that each person can eat more?

This essay will not try to tackle these difficult and stubbornly unresolved questions. Its far more limited objective is to offer a broad-brush picture of theories, empirical findings, and intellectual debates in the field of demography that have attempted to answer them. In pursuing that objective, it would be quite inappropriate to hew to a narrow definition of demography and to focus single-mindedly on the thinking of social scientists identified professionally as demographers. The issues at hand are far too important to have remained unexamined until the very recent emergence of demography as a separate social science discipline. The word denoting that discipline in its original French version did not exist until 1855 (Kirk, 1968: 342); the first written English uses of the terms "demography" and "demographer" occurred, according to the *Oxford English Dictionary,* in 1880 and 1882. These dates, of course, are mere reference points for early linguistic coinage: it was well into the twentieth century before demography grew to be a recognized specialty within the social sciences and being a demographer became a plausible full-time occupation. Thus, at least prior to World War II, much of the intellectual effort that went into examining the issues noted above was carried out by "part-time" demographers: social scientists-at-large exercised by quantitative aspects of the growth of human populations. Consideration of their contributions is properly part of the discussion that follows.

This broader interpretation of the contribution of demography to the relationships between population and resources is appropriate also for discussing research findings and intellectual currents of more recent vintage. Card-carrying demographers cannot claim a monopoly of significant work pertinent to the questions at hand. Indeed, the ascent of demography to the rank of an independent field of study has led to an increasingly narrow definition of the discipline's scientific content and objectives. Preoccupation with the generation and refinement of demographic data and with descriptions of demographic change as a self-contained process—a process explained primarily in terms of linkages between demographic variables proper—has discouraged consideration of relationships not accommodated by that confining analytic framework and has weakened demographers' competence to analyze the resources–population nexus. Examining the state of knowledge on that topic requires continuing attention to the work of "part-time" demographers even in the post–World War II period.

The "demographic" literature that falls within the compass of an ambition so defined is vast. The overview that follows can only touch on some of the salient issues in the resources–population relationship that have dominated demographers' debates on that topic in the West. I will adumbrate themes and currents in that debate through glimpses and references to the work of some of the eminent authors who have participated in it. Even apart from limiting my references mostly to work originally written in English, my selections will be inevitably eclectic. The organization of the essay underscores this fact. The essay starts with a discussion of the current state of art concerning the notion of "carrying capacity" as applied to human populations and gives a brief overview of some recent estimates of resource limits to population growth.

It then briefly traces, in rough chronological sequence, some early views on resource limits to population growth, characterized by a shift of thinking about such limits toward optimism as the industrial revolution gathered force, and the reemergence of concerns about resources (and the counterarguments thereto) under the influence of the "population explosion" in the third quarter of the twentieth century. The discussion closes with comments on views about the prospect for a development presumed to render the issues addressed in this essay moot as a future concern for mankind: the early and orderly attainment of a stationary population.

Carrying capacity

The practical relevance of natural resource constraints to the study of human population growth in any particular historical situation is, of course, not to be taken for granted. In the Garden of Eden the goods *are* there and expansion in numbers is limited by humans' biological capacity to reproduce—a product of fertility and mortality characteristics. How much of that capacity is exercised, even in conditions of relative resource abundance, may be further limited by deliberate choice: man does not live by bread alone. Deliberate reproductive choices that rein in population growth, yet are not related to natural resource constraints, can also be the force governing demographic change. Even if goods increase, numbers need not increase proportionately.

Regardless of what factors underlie it, population growth is evidence that natural resource limits do not put a rigid ceiling on numbers. By definition, a growing population is not in a state of Malthusian equilibrium—the equilibrium elaborated in the first *Essay* (Malthus, 1966), in which limitations of the physical environment make further expansion impossible. But any positive rate of growth exhibited by a human population over an extended period of time raises the question of its sustainability. Observing the growth of fruit flies in a bottle that contains a limited supply of nutrients provides a tentative first answer: "the growth path of human populations is likely to be approximated by a logistic rather than an exponential curve." More helpfully perhaps, it suggests the application of the biological concept of carrying capacity to the analysis of the dynamics of human populations.

Paul Ehrlich (1986: 51) defines carrying capacity as "the maximum number of individuals that can be supported by a given habitat; it is usually related to the availability of a limiting resource, one that is in short supply in relation to the population's needs." Studies of animal ecology provide more plausible analogies to human demographic change than do fruit flies in a bottle, hence shed more light on carrying capacity of a given territory for humans (see, for example, Sauvy, 1969: Chapter 1). They suggest, notably, that the population of a species that attains maximum feasible size under given environmental conditions will be in an unstable equilibrium, easily upset by such events as temporary diminishment of food supply due to vagaries of the weather or to immigration of other animals to the territory who compete for the same food and living space. Predator–prey interactions may lead to long-term stabilization of an animal population's size at a level of maximum sustainable capacity, or carrying capacity proper.

As applied to human populations, the concept of carrying capacity is obviously a slippery one. Man is a toolmaking animal, capable of squeezing out of his environment more than undisturbed nature would provide for his needs. His prowess in doing so is capable of improvement and, in several periods of recorded history, has exhibited growth that can be fairly described as revolutionary. Humans also succeeded in eliminating their predators or in keeping them under control to a remarkable degree. Thus, in contrast to the case of animal ecology, the capacity of a given environment to support human populations can expand relatively rapidly. On the other hand, as already noted above, for humans, a physical definition of needs may be irrelevant. Human needs and aspirations are culturally determined: they can and do grow so as to encompass an increasing amount of "goods," well beyond what is necessary for mere survival. If men insist on satisfying needs that are continuously so redefined, the Biblical rule for growth and the strict formulation of the Malthusian population theory lose much of their relevance for assessing population size relative to the natural environment and much of their power for gauging future prospects of demographic growth.

Not surprisingly, despite the pertinence of the concept to their discipline, most demographers have tended to address the question of population carrying capacity gingerly, if at all. While they have often noted that rapid population growth does represent societal success of a tangible sort—indeed, in an evolutionary sense the success par excellence that a species can claim—they have always been acutely conscious that such success cannot last long. To hammer home this simple truth, a truth that should be evident, as Malthus noted, to anyone possessing "a slight acquaintance with numbers" (1966: 14), has been the time-honored task of demographers. The demographic literature is thus replete with reminders that population growth is a necessarily transitory experience of the human species, but is rather short on specifics as to exactly how long that passing moment in history might last. A formulation offered by Ronald Freedman and Bernard Berelson is typical:

> Projection of [present rates of] growth for very long into the future produces a world population larger than the most optimistic estimates of the planet's carrying capacity. In the long run near-zero growth will have to be restored. . . . (1974: 31)

The point can be made most memorably, yet quite legitimately, by recourse to a reductio ad absurdum. Thus, looking back on the first decade of post–World War II global population growth, Ansley Coale commented:

> No matter what technological progress the future brings, in the long run either fertility rates must be reduced or mortality rates must increase. The reason lies in simple arithmetic. Current rates of death and childbearing, if continued, would produce a substantial constant geometric increase in numbers, and the consequence of such an increase in a surprisingly short period is a population incompatible with any estimated resources, no matter how large the estimate. In about 6,500 years, if current growth continues, the descendants of the present world population would form a solid sphere of live bodies expanding with a radial velocity that, neglecting relativity, would equal the velocity of light. (1959: 36)[1]

Granted the power of exponential growth, why single out the increase in numbers of people to demonstrate that sustained growth in the long term is not feasible? The point of such a demonstration is concern with limits imposed by a finite environment. Implicitly, and sometimes otherwise, its aim is to suggest that, since population growth must eventually stop, advocating its slow-down sooner rather than later makes good sense. But, even if it were constrained by biology alone, human population growth is inherently "slow." Furthermore, observed rates of expansion of large population aggregates invariably fall short of the biological potential. Thus, when the global annual rate of population increase in the late 1960s reached what was an all-time high in recorded human history, the rate of increase was just slightly above 2 percent. For individual countries, the peak rate of natural increase ever registered is in the neighborhood of 4 percent. In contrast, it is possible to cite many recent global and national time series that depict the growth of "goods" expressed in physical quantities that show higher rates of expansion than does population size, be they consumer durables, agricultural products, metals, minerals, or fossil fuels. The same applies to the production of "negative goods," such as industrial pollutants and other waste products. Should not concern about resource limits be directed to the increase in per capita use of renewable and nonrenewable resources rather than to numbers of people?

Indeed, according to an influential line of thought, perhaps most forcefully articulated by Barry Commoner (1971), resource and environmental problems in the industrialized countries have little to do with the pace of population growth or its size but are attributable to shifts in the mix of production technologies adopted mainly since World War II. Similarly, discussions of resources and the environment in international forums are invariably accompanied by demonstrations that the one-quarter of the world's population conventionally classified as "developed" is responsible for a disproportionately high share of the worldwide use of natural resources and environmental sinks. The conclusion is then often drawn that excessive consumption levels of the rich are primarily responsible for creating problems of resource scarcity and environmental degradation, and that concerns with the rate of population growth or with population size are misplaced.

Accepting the premise that resource and environmental problems are caused by a concatenation of factors among which population is only one does not, however, relegate the demographic component to a rank of "also rans." The notions of "resources" and "environment" make sense only in relation to human numbers; concern with the relative scarcity of "goods" compared to people is the underlying rationale for most examinations of resource and environmental issues. But even if a deliberately descriptive and non–human-centered view is taken of these matters, the weight of demographic growth compared to other factors commands attention. As a rough approximation, changes in resource use and in environmental impact that take place over time may be conceptualized as the product of population change and change in resource use per capita. When population growth is even moderately rapid, and when points of time compared are reasonably distant, resource use and environmental impact so measured tend to reveal the share directly attributable to the demographic component as quantitatively highly significant.

A simple example, using data from the United States—by twentieth century standards a country of moderate population growth—serves to illustrate this point. Total primary energy consumption in the United States grew from 43.8 Quads Btu. in 1960 to 74.0 Quads in 1985. Total population during the same period grew from 179.3 million to 238.7 million (US Department of Commerce, 1988: 18 and 537). Thus the 69 percent total increase in US energy use can be decomposed as the combined result of a 33 percent increase in population and a 27 percent increase in energy use per capita. If, between 1960 and 1985, per capita energy use had increased as it did, but population size remained constant, total US energy use would have grown not by 30.2 Quads but only by 11.8 Quads. By this reasoning, 61 percent of the net increase of energy use was generated by population growth. Qualifications to calculations of this sort—that would take into account economies and diseconomies of scale in production and consumption, and consider interaction effects between population change, costs, consumption patterns, and technological innovation—would in some cases decrease and in others increase the specific numerical estimate of the resource use impact of population growth. On balance, they would rarely cast doubt on its importance.

A high initial level of material consumption (of which per capita energy use is a fairly good proximate index) makes it more likely that in various end-uses per capita resource demand levels off or even decreases. "Wasteful" base-period use reflecting resource abundance (as signaled to consumers by low relative prices) also makes possible comparatively painless adjustments in consumption if the price of a given resource rises. Adjustment in such circumstances means that the increase in resource use, which would have accompanied an increase in incomes had prices remained unchanged, will slow down (as was the case in US energy consumption in the 1970s), or may even be cut back. In either case, no major injury to welfare is likely to occur. In contrast, in situations where base-period per capita material consumption is low, reflecting low levels of average incomes, the scope for such adjustments is limited. Successful development, almost by definition, must be accompanied by rapid increase in the consumption of renewable resources, raw materials, and energy, and by increased generation of waste products. Existing population size and the speed with which accretions to it occur are therefore likely to loom large as multipliers to resource use per capita in the process of development. To argue that large population size in the developing world is associated with low effective claims on resources, energy, and the environment is merely to highlight a salient feature of the very definition of underdevelopment. To argue as if in the developing world the combination of large population size with a low per capita resource use were to remain an enduring condition is tantamount to taking the permanence of underdevelopment for granted. Should the multiplier indeed remain low, that would, in effect, certify that the existing global population is already too large for its resource base, hence precludes generalized attainment of the living standards already achieved in the developed parts of the world.

Limits to population growth

But does such a diagnosis of de facto global overpopulation—or, formulated more guardedly, of overpopulation bound to be generated by resource and environmental constraints should demographic growth continue—stand up to scrutiny? In trying to answer that question it no longer suffices to demonstrate the impossibility of sustained long-term growth. Pertinent arguments must address the present, take into account the historic experience, and venture to probe into the uncertain future that lies no further than the next few generations ahead. Attempts by demographers and other social scientists to give answers so grounded have a continuous intellectual history of several hundred years. Over this period, the answers show the coexistence of a broad range of views, including polar extremes. Between extremes, opinion of course has seldom been evenly divided: the prevailing current has been characterized by the predominance sometimes of the views of "optimists" who find no population–resources problem, and sometimes of the "pessimists" who can readily identify one. But at no time, and certainly not in the cacophonous debates of the most recent decades, has opinion on these matters converged into a narrow band of disagreements that could be expected in time to disappear as a result of improved measurements and better analytical tools. Even after due allowance for disagreements that reflect differences over values, the field, to use Jan Tinbergen's characterization (1975), remains in a prescientific state.

A highly influential modern formulation of the pessimist position asserts the unreliability of linear extrapolation from past experience to the future by noting the apparent suddenness with which exponential growth approaches a fixed limit. It recounts a French riddle for children to intimate impending resource scarcities relative to population size:

> Suppose you own a pond on which a water lily is growing. The lily plant doubles in size each day. If the lily were allowed to grow unchecked, it would completely cover the pond in 30 days, choking off the other forms of life in the water. For a long time the lily plant seems small, and so you decide not to worry about cutting it back until it covers half the pond. On what day will that be? On the twenty-ninth day of course. You have one day to save your pond. (Meadows et al., 1972: 37)

But how is it to be ascertained that we are on the twenty-ninth day and face the last chance to "save the pond"? Diagnosis is a simple matter if what is required is to look at a backyard lily pond, but is clearly less obvious in sizing up the state of the global population. On what basis can we discard the conjecture that the present corresponds, say, to the twenty-fourth day, when the global pond would be one-sixty-fourth full?

There is a certain irony in the fact that a stock example among population optimists—or, as they are sometimes labeled, "cornucopians"—also invokes the image of a body of water, albeit in a less poetic fashion. A variant of the "argument" is cited (with the dismissive scorn it clearly deserves) by Alfred Sauvy:

> [A]nti-malthusians pose the problem of the Lake of Constance: if the whole of humanity were plunged into the Lake of Constance and the outlets of the lake were blocked, by how much would the displacement raise the level of the lake? The answer (about 6 inches) astonishes by the modesty of the figure, and since the Lake of Constance takes up only a very tiny bit of the world map, the resultant feeling is that there is still plenty of room for mankind. (1961: 14)[2]

Evidently, to make such arguments more than metaphorically suggestive, numbers of people have to be related to specific resources. At the very least, the image invoked in making the point that people are too numerous or, alternatively, that there is plenty of room to spare, ought to be more closely related to everyday experience than lilies on a pond or human bodies dumped into a body of water. A noted optimist,[3] Herman Kahn, also impressed by the relative scarcity of people compared to the existence of much hospitable land, offered a more humanized, although on its face also plainly fanciful mental picture. Speculating on limits to population growth during the "next 200 years," he wrote:

> [T]here is plenty of room in almost all countries for everybody to have a suburban lifestyle. For example, in such places as Holland, Bermuda or Westchester County (all of which are considered almost ideal areas in which to live) we find that population densities range between 1,000 and 2,000 per square mile. This means that in 10 percent of the United States we have enough room for from 300 to 600 million people, and thus we have 90 percent of the land left over for recreation, agriculture, industry and various other purposes. This conclusion even applies to the more populated countries in Asia, where the population densities are not unduly high (about 500 per square mile in India). (Kahn et al., 1976: 32)

At the other end of the opinion spectrum, a book-length commentary on the lily pond riddle by Lester Brown opens with gloomy prepossessions, stated in an only slightly hedged fashion, on the same subject. Belaboring the metaphor, he comments:

> The global lily pond in which four billion of us live may already be at least half full. Within the next generation it could fill up entirely. Occasional clusters of

> lily leaves are already crowding against the edge, signaling the day when the pond will be completely filled. The great risk is that we will miss or misread the signals and fail to adjust our lifestyles and reproductive habits in the time available. (1978: 1–2)

The conventional candidates for playing the role of the limiting resource that (again using Ehrlich's words) is "in short supply in relation to the population's needs" are energy, metals and minerals, and food. On the global level, existing energy resources do not appear to constitute a limiting factor for many generations to come. Even if renewable energy sources (hydroelectric and geothermal energy, energy from wood and agricultural products, and wind- and solar-electric-energy) as well as nuclear energy are ignored (and, clearly, they have a potentially important and even dominant role to play in supplying future energy needs), proven reserves of fossil fuels are adequate to match the demand of a much larger global population at a significantly increased per capita level. A typical calculation, presented by Roger Revelle (1982), assumes roughly a tripling of per capita energy consumption in the developing world by 2025 (to 2 tons of coal-equivalent per year per capita), a leveling-off of consumption in the developed countries, and a total world population of 8.2 billion, also by 2025. Continuation of these conditions, it is claimed, would deplete fossil fuel reserves in 280 years. Such calculations, given the inevitable arbitrariness of the underlying assumptions, are both merely illustrative and, even on their own terms, subject to sizable error. Nevertheless, their logic clearly indicates that in terms of global energy supplies the twenty-ninth day is still far away.

Given the availability of adequate energy sources, metals and minerals need not be a limiting factor for a very long time to come. This is a point on which in the "age of substitutability" (Goeller and Weinberg, 1976) there is a virtual consensus of expert opinion.

It is quite otherwise with respect to the third candidate for the role of limiting resource, food. Famine was recognized as a potential check to population growth long before Malthus made it the centerpiece of his population theory. Assessments of the carrying capacity of the Earth have also remained focused on the problem of food since Malthus. The first modern quantitative formulation of the problem, by E. G. Ravenstein (1891), is prototypical of many calculations performed since, albeit with widely differing assumptions and with widely differing results.

What is "the number of people whom this earth of ours would be capable of supplying with food and other necessaries of life, once it had been fairly brought over cultivation," Ravenstein asked. Although this formulation of the question was global, he proceeded to divide the world into broad regions, assuming self-sufficiency in each. He also assumed continuing differences in standards of food consumption between regions, taking as given estimated ratios of population to area. Ravenstein was evidently anxious to protect the advantages European populations already possessed with respect to diets:

> I observe . . . . that there are present some vegetarians. These, if their opinions were asked, would maintain that if man returned to nature, and fell in with their peculiar views, three men could live where one lives now, and six men might take the place of one of our larger domestic animals, which would, of course, become extinct, once their dietary value became a thing of the past. Views like these have met with considerable support from certain "hygienists," one of the most prominent of whom has even held out a hope that the day would come when food, as toothsome as meat and equally nutritious, might be grown in our fields, thus obviating the necessity of keeping up large herds of cattle and sheep. I am not sufficiently utopian to believe that mankind generally will ever be prepared to accept these principles, or, that, having accepted them, man would not degenerate. (1891: 28–29)

The question of what represents an adequate or, in some formulations, an optimal nutritional standard remained a key issue of later calculations of this sort, with major influence on the outcome expressed in terms of population supporting capacity. Could people be expected to change their consumption habits, shifting from a meat-rich diet to a diet in which cereals are consumed, without "wasteful" transformations? Might such changes occur voluntarily, without the inducement of scarcity and the consequent increase of prices? Conversely, and with even more far-reaching implications for estimated global supporting capacity, should calculations assume that, as incomes rise in the developing world, elasticities of demand for food will be similar to those observed in the past, hence patterns of food consumption will converge toward patterns now prevailing in the developed countries? In this latter group of countries, current average per capita consumption of cereals, direct and indirect, is three times as high as in the rest of the world.

Other crucial elements in calculations of food supporting capacity are assumptions concerning the cropped area and the average yields per unit of land expected to be obtained. Between the middle of the nineteenth century and 1980 the global cropped area nearly tripled, from somewhat above 0.5 billion hectares to 1.5 billion hectares (World Resources Institute, 1987: 272). Differences between countries in yields per hectare attributable to the technology and intensity of cultivation rather than to differences in climate and land quality remain striking (ibid.: 276–277). What is the scope of further extension of the cultivated area that can be effected at the expense of forests and grasslands without ultimately deleterious consequences to agriculture and to the world's ecosystems? How far can future progress in technology and management permit further increases in food yields in areas under the most advanced methods of cultivation, and to what extent and how speedily can yields be brought up to the best attainable standards elsewhere? There is a wide scope for differences between experts concerning the right answer to these questions. Combinations of assumptions that tend to pull in the same direction can lead to strikingly different results.

Ravenstein, for example, assumed substantial extension of the cultivated area but was highly conservative in anticipating improvements in yields:

> [I]t has been asserted that our present methods of cultivation are capable of vast improvement; that the earth might be made to yield much larger harvests than it yields now; and that population might thus be permitted to increase without correspondingly increasing the cultivated areas. This no doubt is true as respects many countries, but it is hardly true of the world at large. In the United States, for instance, and generally-speaking in all newly settled countries, where large tracts of unoccupied land are still available, agriculture is carried on in a wasteful style, the cultivator looking only to immediate returns and having no thought of the prosperity of his descendants. If you travel from Montreal to Washington [D.C.] you pass through millions of acres of land, which were once most productive and are still lovely to look upon, but which nevertheless produce nothing. The forests have been devastated in the most reckless style, and swamps and sandy wastes have taken the place of trees. These things, however, will be mended in course of time; the exhausted soil of the eastern states will recover; and the forests, where wantonly destroyed, will be replanted. In proportion as the population increases, so will the resources of the country be more carefully husbanded. (ibid.: 29)

The end result of Ravenstein's calculations for the "total possible" population of the Earth, bravely provided for 4 significant digits, was 5.994 billion—a size that will be attained, according to current United Nations medium projections (1986: 140), in the late 1990s.

Post–World War II estimates benefited from the statistical and scientific knowledge accumulated in the more than half a century after Ravenstein's effort, but they carried conflicting messages. The ecologist William Vogt, the most widely read author on the subject in the 1940s and 1950s, ventured no numerical estimate of carrying capacity, but argued that world population size was already past a sustainable optimum. "Agricultural land," Vogt wrote at a time that was to be followed by a rapid increase of crop yields and total food production, "now amounting to little more than an acre per person and shrinking fast, as populations rise and the land is destroyed, is every year producing less food. . . . As we look ahead toward a falling carrying capacity over most of the earth and toward a sharp increase in world populations, we must also look for a marked decrease in our material standard of living" (1948: 78–79).

Writing in 1953 from the opposite end of the pessimist–optimist spectrum, Colin Clark offered a strikingly different opinion, albeit cast, as is often the case in such arguments, in the form of a near-tautology: "Most of the world .... is populated at far below its potential density. . . . [A]t Danish standards of cultivation and consumption [it] could support 12,000 million people, as opposed to the 2,300 million people it supports now" (1958: 42). Later (1967: Chapter 4), Clark presented detailed supportive calculations. He proceeded to estimate the amount of land required, "using good farming techniques now known, to feed people at the standards now prevailing in the United States." The estimate, prepared in terms of square meters of land per person, was disaggregated according to main food categories. Thus, for example, to produce the 42 kg. pig and poultry meat called for by the "US-type" diet required 500 square meters of land per person, 12 kg. eggs required 200 square meters, and so on. All told, this US-type diet—a "maximum standard" according to Clark—was equivalent to about 11 times the basic subsistence-level diet. (The latter was defined as 250 kg./person/year grain-equivalent. Estimated current annual grain production per capita in the developing world happens to be 250 kg.) Clark concluded that at maximum standards, requiring 2000 square meters per head, the world could feed 47 billion people. He also presented a calculation for less comfortable provisions: "For people living at Japanese standards of food consumption and Asian standards of timber requirements only 680 sq.m./person is required, and the world's potential agricultural and forest land could supply the needs of 157 billion people" (ibid.: 153). Finally, for good measure, Clark offered a "sort of science-fiction picture of how agriculture might be conducted if we really were extremely short of space," which is summed up by the "interesting conclusion that the full support of one person requires the continuous cultivation of an area no larger than 27 sq.m." (ibid.: 155–157). The logic of this conclusion would suggest a carrying capacity of the order of several trillion people.

Some years earlier, geophysicist Harrison Brown, a member of the pessimist camp, made estimates not unlike Clark's, but presented them in a properly grim light:

> There are, of course, physical limitations of some sort which will determine the maximum number of human beings who can live on the earth's surface. But at the present time we are far from the ultimate limit of the number of persons who could be provided for. If we were willing to be crowded together closely enough, to eat foods which would bear little resemblance to the foods we eat today, and to be deprived of simple but satisfying luxuries, such as fireplaces, gardens, and lawns, a world population of 50 billion persons would not be out of the question. (1954: 220–221)

In the same jaundiced vein Brown added that with the construction of floating islands and algae farms perhaps 100 billion persons could be provided for, and if caloric requirements were kept at very low levels, that figure could be raised to 200 billion.

Nowadays, extravagant estimates of this kind are less frequently presented, perhaps because they are considered plainly pointless. Well before such ultimate limits to food supplies[4] could become operative, other constraints to growth would be expected to set in. An often-cited estimate by Revelle (1976: 177) puts global carrying capacity at "nearly 40 billion people." This figure assumes an average gross food production (that is, including food, feed, and seed) per capita of 2,500 kilocalories (kcal) per day: a minimum standard that compares with 15,000 kcal prevailing in the United States and a number of high-income countries. Bernard Gilland, who reviewed this and other recent estimates, has commented that Revelle's figure "cannot be regarded as anything but a nightmare to be avoided at all costs" (1983: 206). Gilland's own calculations are predicated on an assumed dietary allowance of 9,000 kcal: that is, a standard roughly at midpoint between the minimum and current high consumption levels. This medium standard, in combination with his assumptions about cultivable area and crop yields (which Gilland characterized as reflecting "technological realism"), gives 7.5 billion as the estimate for global carrying capacity. The construction of the estimate implies that a much larger population could well be supported but only at the price of lower dietary standards.

An elaborate set of calculations on "potential population supporting capacities of lands" was carried out recently under the auspices of the Food and Agriculture Organization. This project, however, was less than global in scope: it was limited to 117 developing countries, not including China. Each country estimate was prepared as a set of alternative assumptions on levels of agricultural inputs. Using the high input variant, and assuming that all cultivable areas are devoted to food production, and, finally, setting a daily allowance of somewhat above 3,000 kcal per person (that is, well below the 4,000 kcal present average level in the area covered by the FAO study) yields an estimate of 33 billion as carrying capacity (Higgins et al., 1983: 100–105). This compares with a 1985 population of 2.6 billion for the area in question. The contrast, however, is greatly narrowed once more realistic estimates are selected as to the average production technology likely to prevail in the next few decades, and as to the area likely to be cultivated for food. Upgrading the dietary standard from the bare minimum reflected in the calculation would have the same effect.[5]

A merit of detailed area-specific estimates of carrying capacity is that their validity can be more readily subjected to scrutiny. For example, the FAO study's result, which claims 7 billion as Brazil's population supporting capacity (with high inputs), would seem to call for critical reevaluation. Most salutarily, however, area-specific estimates highlight the great differences that exist between individual countries with respect to prospective self-sufficiency in food production. Like the notion of "world population," for many purposes the concept of "global food supplies" is a figment of the statistician's imagination. This is not to suggest that countries are the all-important units of analysis, or that each country must necessarily rely on its domestically produced food supplies, or that being a net food importer is somehow reprehensible. Such propositions and judgments evidently do not apply to countries like Japan or Switzerland: in principle, they need not apply to any other country either. In a trading world, national self-sufficiency in food production is not a precondition for prosperity, much as the prosperity of New York or Bangkok does not depend on their inhabitants' success in growing corn or rice.

Countries that wish to rely on international trade to secure an adequate supply of food must make sure, however, that their ability to compete in the international markets for their nonfood exports is well established. In peacetime, when international commerce is largely unhindered, this condition is easily met by countries on the cutting edge of technological innovation. Alternatively, countries may derive market strength from possession of natural resources that make them competitive exporters of raw materials, or enable them to maintain a large and profitable tourist industry. In contrast, countries that become dependent on net food imports to a significant degree, yet are less advantageously situated in the competition for international markets, can find themselves in a precarious situation. Major reliance on imported food can be particularly problematic in the case of countries with large populations. The magnitude of export earnings from the sale of industrial goods or raw materials that such countries would have to seek to pay for their food imports may be large enough to shift the international terms of trade against them significantly, or elicit protectionist countermeasures from their trading partners.

For many countries, therefore, achievement and maintenance of self-sufficiency in food production, broadly defined, is an eminently desirable objective. For them, adequacy of food supplies on a global level is not a guarantee of food security. By the same token, the need to keep domestic population growth in balance with domestic ability to expand food production is not obviated by the proposition that there is no technological reason why global food supplies could not keep up with world population growth for a long time to come.[6] Presumably these considerations underlie the interest of the FAO study in country-level estimates of carrying capacity in the developing world. They also explain why, despite the optimistic interpretation that may be warranted by global-level findings on food production prospects, the detailed picture that emerges is somber. The adequacy of global supplies is likely to have limited relevance to the food problem facing a large number of individual countries. For these countries, carrying capacity on the country level could become a check to population growth even if global food supplies are plentiful, and even if their rate of expansion keeps pace with global population growth.

The special and even exclusive attention paid in most discussions of resource problems to food as the most likely limiting factor to population growth has been occasionally challenged. The British astronomer Fred Hoyle (1963) persuasively argued that the classic Malthusian-type equilibrating mechanism—which works through a rise in the death rate due to shortage of food—cannot apply to a technologically complex society whose operation is inconceivable on a near-starvation level. Indeed, such a society can support more people well-nourished than an inefficient community can support at the starvation level. Modern technological civilization has passed the stage of biological control that directed evolution in the past. But, according to Hoyle, the inclination of the human species to increase its numbers whenever the environment permits it to do so can be expected to persist.[7] Since growth cannot continue indefinitely, a new equilibrating mechanism is certain to be brought into play. This new mechanism will be organizational overload, Hoyle suggested, leading to a sudden catastrophic collapse of civilization. But human history will not end. Collapse will set the stage for a process of recovery, initiating a cyclical pattern of evolution characterized by recovery–collapse sequences. Hoyle did not describe these cycles in terms of numerical estimates, but his graphical illustration pictures the first catastrophic breakdown as occurring in the twenty-third century, when world population size may be about 25 billion. That prospect is remote enough to suggest that the scenario depicted by Hoyle may be characterized as one of qualified technological optimism.

Qualifications of a somewhat different sort are attached to conjectures about mankind's growth prospects set forth by the mathematician John von Neumann (1955). In many respects an extreme technological optimist—among other futuristic developments, he predicted free energy and human control of the climate as realistic medium-term options—he nevertheless identified space as an absolute limiting factor: not in a remote future when the Earth becomes filled with an ever-growing population, but as a constraint operating already in the second half of the twentieth century. Von Neumann saw the success of the industrial revolution as tied to the existence of the safety valve represented by an expanding geographical and political *Lebensraum,* and he argued that the interaction of technology, geography, and political organization now sharply inhibits this safety mechanism. Due to the finiteness of the globe and the size of the existing political units, further acceleration of technological progress can no longer be absorbed, as it was in the past when leading countries and industries could readily extend their area of operation; hence spatial limits become a source of instability and deepening crisis. "[L]iterally and figuratively, we are running out of room" (ibid.: 106). In this frame of analysis the question of how many people can be fed on how many hectares of land seems somewhat parochial, indeed, beside the point.

Limits discovered and contested

Yet the seeming novelty of the point of view expressed by von Neumann, and its distance from the mundane debate about food and other garden-variety resources, are deceptive. We can find countless early manifestations of the dialectic apparent in von Neumann's thought. A sense of limits and confinement alternates with awareness of opportunities for conquest and expansion, sometimes in a tightly knit package, laden with unresolved contradictions, in a single person's oeuvre. More commonly, the dialectic takes the form of debates between representatives of distinct schools of thought, one inclined to stress the limits to growth, the other bent to dispute them. Before returning to the mid–twentieth century scene, a few glimpses at some prominent early actors in that debate should be instructive.

The recognition of the conflict between human numbers and their limited environment so prominent in Malthus's work was first articulated with clarity in the writings of the sixteenth century Jesuit, Giovanni Botero. Joseph Schumpeter pays well-deserved homage to Botero as the originator of modern population theory:

> Divested of non-essentials, the "Malthusian" Principle of Population sprang fully developed from the brain of Botero in 158[8]: populations tend to increase, beyond any assignable limit, to the full extent made possible by human fecundity (the *virtus generativa* of the Latin translation); the means of subsistence, on the contrary, and the possibilities of increasing them (the *virtus nutritiva*) are definitely limited and therefore impose a limit on that increase. . . . [Botero's] path-breaking performance. . . . came much before the time in which its message could have spread; it was practically lost in the populationist wave of the seventeenth century. But about two hundred years after Botero, Malthus really did no more than repeat it, except that he adopted particular mathematical laws for the operation of the *virtus generativa* and the *virtus nutritiva.* (1961: 254–255)

Apart from setting out a theory à la Malthus (a feat of which Malthus was not aware), Botero gave early vent to the erroneous view—much repeated later by writers of the era of Enlightenment—that population growth in ancient times (at least for a limited period) was rapid, and the numbers attained as large as, or larger than in the contemporary world. Botero also believed that Europe's population and the population of the world at large had ceased to grow. His presumed understanding of the factors that limited population growth went hand-in-hand with a strong desire to see those limits removed:

> [A]lthough men were as apt for generation in the height of Rome's greatness as in the beginning thereof, yet the multitudes of people augmented not by proportion. For the *virtue nutritive* of the city had no force to pass any further,

> because the inhabitants, in process of time, not having greater commodity of victuals, either never married or, if they married, their children, through misery or necessity, came to nothing; but forsaking their country, endeavored to better their fortune by transmutation of place. . . . For the same reason mankind being increased to a certain multitude has not proceeded any further. And for three thousand years since, and more, the world was as fully replete with men as now at this present, for the fruits of the earth and abundance of victual comports not with greater number of people. . . . [T]here is not any thing for which men fight more furiously than for territory, food, and convenience of habitation. (1635: 338–339)[8]

It was not until David Hume's 1742 essay "On the populousness of ancient nations" that the belief about the ancient world's demographic edge over the modern one was vigorously rejected. While persuasive, Hume's case was based primarily on deductive reasoning. He compared the domestic and political situations of the ancients and moderns, and argued that the social institutions of the ancients were less conducive to large populations than modern social conditions. This methodology in part reflected the rudimentary state of statistical information available even on contemporary European populations until the late eighteenth century. The earliest modern calculation of the world's population, published originally in 1682 by Sir William Petty (1698), father of modern political economy, put that number at 320 million. That was a badly flawed estimate: about one-half of the actual figure. The way it was derived deserves greater credit than the estimate itself. Since knowledge about the world's land areas was more accurate than knowledge about the number of inhabitants, Petty proceeded with a carrying capacity calculation that took into account the ability of differing qualities of lands to support populations. He also estimated the rate of growth, astutely assuming that the path of population followed a geometric progression. The estimate itself was a poor fit: Petty arrived at a "doubling time" of 360 years, implying an annual rate of growth of 0.0019. Understandably, with such quantitative notions holding sway, Europeans, with plenty of room to spare in and outside their Continent, evinced little concern about rapid population growth or resource limits thereto. In contrast, they saw many reasons to desire demographic expansion, firmly associated in most informed minds with increased power and prosperity. Petty, nevertheless, did manage to engage in a mental exercise that later became a favorite pastime of demographers: long-range forecasting. The world's population, he reasoned, "will within the next 2000 years so increase as to give one Head for every two Acres of Land in the Habitable part of the Earth." At that density (implying a total population of some 10 billion persons) Petty expected "Wars and great Slaughter &c."—a deduction that has inspired numerous followers ever since.

A few years later (1695), the statistician Gregory King produced more accurate estimates than Petty's, but in a work that remained in manuscript form, unknown until 1973. King also proceeded by positing population supporting capacities per unit of territory in various climatic zones, and arrived, with a measure of luck, at a quite correct estimate of the size of the contemporary world population. Characteristically, he assumed that that size was generated by progressively slower rates of growth since the time of the Flood. Consequently, a population projection he prepared was unduly cautious: it yielded a population of 0.78 billion by the middle of the twenty-first century.

By the late eighteenth century, such pioneering efforts were superseded by an increasingly sure grasp by scholars of the quantitative aspects of population growth, at least in the European and North American settings. Johann Süssmilch's *Göttliche Ordnung* (1765) and the second edition of Malthus's *Essay* (1803) were major milestones in this development, reflecting the accumulation of information from vital statistics, censuses, and also records of economic activity. Süssmilch's orientation was mercantilist-populationist, as was the orientation of most contemporary writers on the subject. This line of thinking remained influential on the Continent even after the ascendancy of the English classical school of economics, shaped by Smith, Malthus, and Ricardo. Classical economics represented a superior intellectual achievement, but its message was dismal. In the classical system, the long-term implication of development, and of its inevitable concomitant, population growth, was the cessation of both. After the happy days of progress, growth was expected to come to a halt when natural resource limits, and especially the limit imposed by the scarcity of land, became strictly confining. This meant that the final equilibrium of the economic system was characterized by acute resource scarcities and, consequently, by a subsistence standard of living.

As was often remarked, the empirical validity of these conclusions remained essentially untested in the century and a half following the construction of the Malthusian model. The technological revolution that gathered force after 1800 and was largely unanticipated by Malthus seemed forever to postpone the day when diminishing returns in the economy would set in. Rapid population growth—"rapid," as defined by historical comparisons—thus proved to be consistent with improvements in the standard of living. It was possible to argue that such gains were only temporary, leaving the long-term prospect of a subsistence-level equilibrium intact. Less grimly, the claim could be advanced that per capita gains would have been higher, had population growth been slower. Nevertheless, resource limits to population growth and the impact of demographic growth on living standards were seldom matters of concern during the period bracketed by 1800 and 1950. When population–resource issues were addressed, the prevailing opinion was anti-Malthusian, as can be illustrated with reference to such prominent nineteenth century writers on the question of population as Frédéric Bastiat in France, Henry George in the United States, or Walter Bagehot in England.

The menace of resource scarcities caused by expanding populations could be further discounted once voluntary limitation of fertility began to spread rapidly among populations of European origin. Indeed, by the 1920s and 1930s, Western preoccupations in population matters came to be centered on the unwelcome prospect of the cessation of population growth and of eventual population decline. Some prominent economists—such as John Stuart Mill in the nineteenth century and John Maynard Keynes in the twentieth—did point out the potential economic, esthetic, and cultural advantages and opportunities offered by a voluntarily chosen stationary population. Their views on this matter, however, were not especially influential.

Outside the Western world—meaning Europe and its overseas demographic outposts—the dynamics of fertility and mortality patterns typically remained traditional, and living standards were generally low. In these areas, an acceleration of population growth, such as generated by slowly declining mortality rates, could more readily activate Malthusian pressures, particularly when population–resource ratios were already high. This was occasionally recognized and discussed as a problem for colonial administrators to worry about, without, however, occupying an important place in Western discourses about social and economic issues.

This state of affairs changed dramatically in the aftermath of World War II. Decolonization, the Cold War, and recognition of the stake of the West, and in particular of the United States, in the political stability and economic progress of the Third World, directed attention to the precariousness of the natural resource base relative to population size in some of these countries, hence to rapid population growth as a potential hindrance to development. Beginning roughly in 1950, efforts to articulate population and resource problems and to develop solutions for such problems intensified. Before describing some of the intellectual underpinnings of these efforts, the point just made may be illustrated with reference to an atypical case: that of Japan.

Today it is difficult to think of Japan as a less developed country, one suffering a bad case of overpopulation to boot. Yet, writing as recently as 1956 Julian Huxley could compare the demographic predicament of India and Japan and conclude that "[India's] immediate future is not quite as desperate as Japan's." Huxley speculated, however, that if population policy measures, recommended in 1954, are successfully put into practice, "they will save Japan from disaster" (p. 68).

In an article published a few years earlier (1950), Warren Thompson—a prominent demographer and a longtime student of the Pacific region—was less optimistic. "I do not believe," said Thompson, "that the means of relieving the pressure of population on resources . . . will do a great deal to help Japan within the next decade or two. I do not see how increased productivity, expanded foreign trade, and emigration can add to the per capita production of the Japanese enough to improve their level of living substantially as long as their numbers increase from 1.0 percent to 1.5 percent per year." Thompson went on to conclude that "a real catastrophe involving millions of persons may be in the making" (p. 153).

While Thompson's formulation was perhaps more extreme than most, his view was far from atypical of those routinely expressed in discussions of Japan's economic prospects in the early 1950s. The actual course of events, as we know from the benefit of hindsight, was quite different. Even after its postwar recovery was largely completed, Japan went on to sustain annual real rates of aggregate economic growth that approximated, and often exceeded, 10 percent per year for some two decades.

Posed in the simplest terms, the economics of population reduces to a race between two rates of growth: that of population and that of economic output. Obviously there is no population problem that a sustained economic growth of, say, over 5 percent per year could not solve. At such a rate, at worst, the population problem is a modest hindrance to economic betterment, but is certainly not an issue to be overly agitated about. While treating demographic growth and economic expansion as independent of each other is not formally correct, when the two rates differ as much as they did in the Japan of the post–World War II economic boom, such cavalier treatment is quite permissible. The problem of explaining the error in assessing the magnitude of Japan's population problem is then reduced to the problem of explaining what caused the gross misjudgment of the prospects for economic growth as seen from the vantage point of the early 1950s. What went wrong in assessing Japan's economic prospects? There were several sources of misjudgment. Thompson—and other writers of similar persuasion—failed to foresee the productivity gains that were to be achieved by Japanese agriculture; exaggerated the importance of raw materials and mineral resources in industrial development; and greatly underestimated the qualities of the labor force and of Japanese entrepreneurship and organizational ability. The most crucial failure of foresight, however, concerned the framework in which international relations were to be conducted in the years to come. Thompson assumed that international trade would be largely confined to bilateral arrangements between countries, and he foresaw the continuation and even a worsening of the protectionism of the interwar years. Failing to anticipate the rapid economic growth and technological change that the 1950s and the years beyond were to witness, he also assumed that Japanese industrial exports would consist of "bicycles, rubber shoes, flashlights" and such.

Today these errors seem egregious. But early postwar analyses of population–development interactions, and their dependence on natural resources, were of course still under the experience of the three-and-a-half decades that preceded 1950. That period was characterized by two major wars and an economic depression of unprecedented severity. Average productivity growth was extremely low, and aggregate income growth remained well below the 2 percent annual level, including growth in the leading industrial countries. However, in shaping views about population problems, perhaps most important in the interwar years were the policies of nation-states aimed at achieving greater degrees of economic autarky. International trade, the great potential resolver of national-level resource constraints, grew as a consequence at the snail's pace of 0.5 percent per year. Undoubtedly, the anticipated continuation of similar performance in the post–World War II period cast an ominous light on the economic prospects of all resource-poor countries even if their rates of population growth were relatively moderate, such as the one percent per year cited in the case of Japan.

Indeed, under the circumstances it was perhaps fortunate that the early postwar years were also characterized by estimates of future demographic growth prospects that in their erroneousness nearly matched the "rubber shoes and flashlights" concept of the expected future composition of Japanese industrial exports. Ironically, gloomy assessments of the population problem often rested on forecasts of what were then considered rapid rates of demographic growth but that in fact soon proved to be excessively modest expectations. To cite one example, in a contribution to the 1954 Rome World Population Conference, E. F. Schumacher (later the author of the book *Small is Beautiful*) examined the global prospects for energy use in the next 26 years, that is, up to 1980. He anticipated a per capita growth of total energy use of 2 percent per year, not far below the 2.4 percent level that was actually recorded during the period.

Schumacher's estimate of total energy use was far off the mark, however. In line with then commonly shared assumptions about future global population growth, Schumacher posited a total world population of 3 billion in 1980. The actual population turned out to be some 50 percent higher. Such a margin of error is extraordinary in view of the presumed glacial slowness with which demographic aggregates change. In retrospect, it is clear that the assumptions of the fertility levels and trends underlying the global population forecast were far too low and there was an almost total failure to foresee the spectacular postwar mortality decline, even though at the time of Schumacher's writing that decline was already well under way. A more accurate anticipation of the magnitude of the unprecedentedly rapid world population growth that was to follow would have further darkened the already pessimistic forecasts based on the widely shared notion of a growing scarcity of natural resources and, in particular, on the perceived narrowness of the physical limits to expanding food production.

Examples of forecasts that exhibited what later turned out to be underestimates of both demographic and economic growth are numerous but are well worth pondering since they offer valuable lessons for those undertaking similar efforts. Brief reference to a few instances should suffice. Thus, the

Census Commissioner of India in his report on the 1951 census (which counted a population of just over 350 million) flatly declared that efforts to keep pace with the growth of population by increasing food production were bound to fail once the population passed 450 million. India's population has now exceeded that mark by some 80 percent, and India at present is said to be self-sufficient in food.

In an analysis of China's population prospects, Frank Notestein and Irene Taeuber correctly identified the huge demographic growth potential of China but expressed doubt that sustained increases of over one percent per year could occur (Balfour et al., 1950). They foresaw demographic growth between 1950 and 1980 in the 0.5 percent range, and, assuming the then current population as only 400 million, put the plausibly anticipated absolute increase by 1980 between 65 and 140 million. The actual increase of China's population between 1950 and 1980—precipitous fertility decline during the latter part of the period notwithstanding—was somewhat over 400 million.

Kingsley Davis, in his encyclopedic study of the Indian Subcontinent (1951), refrained from making formal predictions or forecasts concerning future demographic trends and their economic implications. As a gesture toward demographic prognostication, however, Davis did make a logistic projection for India, fitting the curve to adjusted census data for the prepartition territory up to 1941. Davis commented that in the exercise he found it satisfactory to posit 700 million as the upper asymptote, to be approximated by the middle of the twenty-first century. In the actual course of events, by 1985 the population of the Subcontinent had exceeded this envisaged ultimate upper limit by at least a quarter of a billion persons, and today projections issued by the World Bank (Zachariah and Vu, 1988) envisage an eventually stabilized population of nearly 2.4 billion.

As the 1950s unfolded, the excessive conservatism that characterized such demographic forecasts became gradually apparent. This was true globally as well as for all national populations of significant size in the less developed world. As the standard projections took into account such factors as upward-corrected base population figures, the typically higher levels of fertility than were previously estimated, and most of all, the spectacular dimensions of the ongoing mortality decline, the accuracy of the projected population figures increased markedly, at least for the short and medium run. Since the 1960s the ex post record of population projections (notably those prepared by the United Nations) has been impressive.

Parallel to this development in demographic forecasting, the need for a raising of sights as to aggregate economic performance has also arisen. It was discovered that economic growth in the postwar period represented a clean break with the depressed interwar years. Technological change was rapid and growth was widely if unevenly diffused in the world system through an extraordinary and sustained expansion of international trade. In the quarter century preceding 1973, exports and imports grew at annual rates well in excess of 5 percent.

All in all, the pace of economic growth in the developing world accelerated greatly. Not all developing countries made rapid progress; indeed many (including some of the most populous countries) continued to perform quite poorly, but many others did remarkably well when measured by any realistic historical yardstick. Existing differentials in income per head within the less developed world thus showed a tendency to widen, despite relatively modest differentials in demographic patterns. As noted above, demographic growth has turned out to be far more rapid than was expected in the early 1950s. But where economic conditions were favorable, average economic improvement could be fast even when the demographic discount was severe. The point may be illustrated by an example of failed medium-term forecasting for Brazil. Herman Kahn and Anthony Wiener in a projection published in 1967, and at that time considered highly optimistic, had forecast that Brazil's per capita income would grow from US$280 in 1965 to $372 in 1985 (measured in 1965 dollars). The modest rate of improvement over time implicit in that forecast reflected in no small part the strong deflating effect of rapid population growth in the country (Kahn and Wiener, 1967: 165). Yet, while Brazil's population increased by more than 50 million between 1965 and 1985, average income per capita in 1985 (also in 1965 dollars) was nearly $700.

As a result of this combined upward shift of both economic performance and demographic growth in less developed countries, the ground was gradually prepared for a far-reaching reassessment of the role of the population factor in economic development. The most important change was the shift away from an emphasis on natural resource scarcities. Ricardian economics was all but expurgated from the analysis of the effects of population change on economic betterment. Absolute population size and absolute population increase entered the picture, if at all, by reference to their effect on economies of scale; but, relegated to that role, and applying the conventional frame of analysis that emphasizes economies tied to the technology of production, population size as such was usually found to be of little or no consequence. The main beneficiaries of the shift in analytic emphasis were, instead, two interrelated demographic variables: the rate of population growth (in particular the rate of growth of the population in the labor force ages) and the age composition of the population. Reflecting the then dominant view in development economics that savings and capital accumulation were the engines of economic growth, changes in demographic growth and in age distribution were seen as affecting economic performance through their effects on savings, on capital accumulation, and on the level of per capita investment needed to equip a growing labor force and to support the population in the ages of economic dependency.

The most important work that expressed this new way of thinking about the economics of population in the less developed world was the study of the development prospects of India and Mexico by Ansley Coale and Edgar Hoover (1958). Positing alternative assumptions as to the future course of fertility, Coale and Hoover investigated the relative economic prospects of low-income countries under contrasting demographic scenarios. Their model yielded the confident prediction that a demographic slowdown brings economic benefits, regardless of the socioeconomic characteristics and resource endowments of individual countries. But the expected magnitudes of the economic gains consequent upon even major reductions of fertility were shown in these predictions to be rather modest. By the logic of the aggregate models from which such gains were calculated, the effects of a precipitous drop in fertility on income per head over time could be also achieved, as was shown by Simon Kuznets (1967), by a fairly minor improvement in economic efficiency, say, as reflected in a slightly lower capital–output ratio.

Some students of demographic–economic interaction objected, however, that the modesty of the predicted effect of even a dramatic slowdown of demographic growth on development performance reflected incomplete model specification rather than the real nature of the relationship. Thus, the break in thinking with the earlier tradition that stressed absolute resource limits to population growth, rather than just relative income gains that might result from slower population growth, has never become fully complete. Parallel to the approach epitomized by the Coale–Hoover analysis, there continued a current of literature, produced mostly by ecologists and biologists, that emphasized natural resource scarcities as constraints to growth (see Hardin, 1968; and Daly, 1980). While in the 1950s the influence of this literature on demographers and economists remained marginal, by the late 1960s analyses of economic–demographic relationships once again displayed a distinctly Ricardian hue. Efforts were also begun to incorporate in Coale and Hoover-type models more promising areas of demographic–economic interaction than the relationship between demographic structure and savings and investment, and to extend the analysis to investigation of the differential impact of demographic change by sector, region, and social stratum. The end of the great postwar boom and the sudden darkening of the economic horizons after the 1973 oil crisis gave a powerful impetus to both of these developments.

But intellectual currents were also flowing in the opposite direction: toward discounting the significance of rapid population growth and natural resource scarcities as influences retarding economic development. The influential work of Albert Hirschman (1958) and Ester Boserup (1965, 1981) emphasized the stimulus population pressure can give to economic development through inducing technological and organizational improvements. The positions taken by prominent modern resource economists (representative examples are Barnett and Morse, 1963; Smith, 1979; and Ridker and

Watson, 1980) have long been distanced from the Malthusian orientation of much of mainline population economics. This more relaxed view on the severity or, indeed, existence of resource constraints on development was eventually extended to the interpretation of population–resources issues at large. The works of P. T. Bauer (1971, 1981) and of Julian Simon (1977, 1981) are representative of this current and have received the most attention, but theirs are by no means isolated voices. Close reading of the final report of the National Research Council committee that discusses the issue of population growth and economic development (1986) provides a case in point. Compared to the strong "Malthusian" orientation of a similar report issued 15 years earlier (National Academy of Sciences, 1971), the NRC report is a thoroughly "revisionist" document, especially if judged by its analysis of population–resources issues. Another ambitious review of demographic–economic interactions, one carried out by the World Bank (1984), on balance defends the thesis that rapid population growth retards economic progress, yet it, too, could be characterized by Colin Clark (1985: 120) as "Malthusianism in retreat." Thus, in the late 1980s, despite the long history of intellectual efforts invested in the population and resources issue, the field appears to be in disarray, with little prospect for the emergence of scholarly consensus. Indeed, Geoffrey McNicoll's penetrating examination (1984) of the economic consequences of rapid population growth reveals the inadequacy of existing analytic frameworks for settling the controversies that surround the subject.

Limits made moot: The promise of demographic stasis

Demographers' most distinctive claim to participation in discussions concerning resource constraints on development rests on their presumed ability to make authoritative statements about the likely future course of population change. In a purely technical sense, the algorithms and the statistical inputs needed to calculate future population size and distribution are sufficiently intricate to give demographers a quasi-monopolistic hold on the supply of population projections. The potential usefulness of such projections in discussing prospective trends in economic and social change is evident. Human numbers constitute the most crucial inputs to modeling future economic and social development and to calculating indicators of its success. They also represent one of the few elements of the development process in which change is inevitable yet about which it is possible to offer relatively reliable long-term forecasts.

Or at least so it came to be assumed by many nondemographers, with consequences that strongly color the tone of the contemporary debate on the limits to growth. That assumption is not unfounded. Population growth and structure both have considerable momentum if only because of human longevity and because of the considerable inertia that characterizes change in important facets of human behavior, such as fertility, in any large population. This makes demographic prognostication relatively robust for the short and medium term—yielding, as Nathan Keyfitz has shown (1981), usable forecasts for the next five to 20 years. But beyond that time span the reliability of population forecasts rapidly decreases: according to Keyfitz (p. 590), forecasts provide "virtually no information at all on population 100 years hence." Very few demographers would take exception to this judgment. They, nevertheless, continue to make long-range population projections. Prestigious institutional backing of that activity, in turn, gives wide currency to the enterprise.

What is the excuse for this seemingly questionable practice? A cynic might point to the eager demand for long-term population projections as a sufficient explanation. But there is a more respectable and valid answer. Such projections do have a potentially valuable truth content: they show the implications for population size and structure of well-specified assumptions regarding the future course of fertility and mortality. Such calculations, albeit tautological, thus transform one kind of information (inputs expressed in terms of indicators of fertility and mortality change) to a different set of indexes (one depicting population size and distribution), more appropriate for many of the analytic purposes at hand. The projected alternative population trajectories are useful as reference points in monitoring ongoing demographic change, and in related population policy discussions. Such discussions might compare the relative desirability of the various population trajectories, assess the plausibility of their attainment, and consider the costs and benefits of possible policy measures aimed at alterations in fertility and mortality trends that may be judged necessary.

In practice, however, there is a strong tendency on the part of the "consumers" of long-run population projections to perceive them as true forecasts. Indeed, demographic practice—the way in which projections are presented and explained—often fails forcefully to discourage this erroneous perception. This is least likely to be the case when the projections are based on stylized assumptions concerning the most crucial element of the calculation: the envisaged future course of fertility. Thus, for example, the influential set of long-range projections prepared by Tomas Frejka (1973a)—a deliberately mechanistic exercise aimed at illustrating alternative possible time paths to a hypothetical stationary population—started with a projection incorporating the explicitly unrealistic assumption that fertility everywhere instantaneously falls to replacement level, and thereafter remains constant. Such a projection was counterfactual yet evidently meaningful: it demonstrated that even such a precipitous decline would imply that, starting with a population size of 3.6 billion in 1970, the global population would still grow by more than 2 billion. Other projections presented by Frejka were less prima facie implausible, but their schematic construction alone clearly indicated that none of them was intended as a forecast.

The common element in each of Frejka's projections, and in projections of this type in general—that is, incorporating the assumption of fertility converging to replacement level and remaining constant thereafter—nevertheless can carry a message open to misinterpretation.[9] It may be taken as implying not only that demographers see no alternative to zero population growth as the end point of demographic evolution, but also that such an outcome is foreordained in the not-too-remote future. Such a perception is erroneous. Attainment of a stationary population following a suitably specified time path may be an eminently arguable normative proposition, but as a predictive postulate it lacks a defensible theoretical, empirical, or historical foundation.

Failure to realize this fact has had unfortunate consequences for the framing of the population–resources issue in the contemporary debate. To illustrate, the notion that populations everywhere *are* converging to a stationary state is incorporated in the work of Herman Kahn and his associates in discussing global development prospects and, in particular, issues of population growth and resource adequacy. Kahn's overall position on these matters had always been highly optimistic. Nevertheless he was acutely aware that sustained population growth would undercut the credibility of his rosy portrayal of long-run trends in economic and social development. Invoking demographic authority regarding the presumed certainty of a coming stationary population therefore became a crucial foundation of Khanian development scenarios. The "proof" that the requisite demographic preconditions would be fulfilled was embodied in each of his last three books exploring long-run development trends. The proof was presented as a diagram depicting the evolution of the rate of population growth over the long stretch of human history—including its anticipated future course, taken as an assured fact (Kahn et al., 1976: 29; Kahn, 1979: 9; Kahn, 1982: 30). Kahn refers to the diagram as the "spike diagram": it shows a sudden rise of the growth rate in the modern era from a near-zero level to its peak of 2 percent per year around 1970, followed by a precipitous fall again to zero or near-zero. Repeatedly, Kahn invoked demographers' authority in support of this picture: demographers, he asserted, believe that the curve "reasonably describes the past, present, and future history of population growth."

The "spike diagram," however, is a stylized construct, based on demographers' more than "slight acquaintance with numbers" (to use again Malthus's expression), hence on their well-taken endorsement of the proposition that growth cannot proceed indefinitely. Beyond that, the theoretical, empirical, or historical arguments that would help to draw the descending (i.e., future) segment of the population growth curve and delineate its long-run resting point with accuracy are at best threadbare, at worst nonexistent.

Yet, seemingly modest variations in the tempo with which fertility might decline toward replacement level (even if, unjustifiably, one allows that replacement level *is* the most likely spontaneous final resting point of fertility) could generate startlingly different trajectories of future population size. The massive long-run uncertainty as to which of these trajectories will materialize is concealed only by demographers' natural inclination to be "reasonable"—to play it safe. At mid-century, demographers dismissed as patently unreasonable the notion that by the 1980s the population of China or of the Indian Subcontinent might be on the order of one billion. Analogously, assumptions made today as to the future course of fertility and mortality are selected to assure that they generate a population trajectory that common sense suggests is both desirable and necessary: an early and orderly convergence to the stationary state.

The best example of this tendency is provided by the most widely known and cited set of long-range projections, those issued by the World Bank. Unlike the more sophisticated and complex projections of the United Nations (1986), the Bank's projections consist of a single variant for each of the country components of the global total, and, over time, they stretch as far as the middle of the twenty-second century. In their most recent version (Zachariah and Vu, 1988), they envisage a rough doubling of the present size of the world's population—that is, attainment of a stationary population slightly above the 10 billion level.

Acceptance of such projections as depictions of the most likely, and indeed highly probable, outcome of the long-run demographic evolution seems to be common among professionals interested in such matters—ironically, with the notable, though largely unnoticed, exception of demographers themselves. But belief in the reliability of such long-range forecasts short-circuits the debate over the possible implications of population change for development, and over the relationships between population and resources. In particular, narrowing the likely evolution of population size to a single series—or, rather, to a single set of country projections, each leading to a plausible demographic stasis—tends to render the issue of potential limits moot. Such a view of the population future combines a seeming pretense to perfect foresight with the implicit suggestion that although the anticipated population trajectory may be less than optimal, it can probably be accommodated in a manner consistent with improvements in average living standards.

To a significant degree, however, such a relatively comforting outcome is achieved by a sleight of hand. The assumptions that enter the calculations bear the marks of feedback from the anticipated results: within the broad limits of freedom available, the projections are constructed to offer the least offending combination of inputs and outputs. The particular combinations selected may well prove correct ex post; indeed, the argument that they represent the most likely demographic outcome may be, at any given time, eminently defensible. But, then, a different scenario may triumph, inducing a continual revision and readjustment of projected demographic trends. In time, it may be discovered that such adjustments are systematic, rather than random—revealing, perhaps, the operation of a ratchet-principle. As development progresses, levels of population size that once seemed beyond reasonable bounds may prove capable of being accommodated. As goods increase, they will increase that eat them. Alternatively, in some places a less benign Malthusian mechanism may assert itself, necessitating new projections revised in the opposite direction. At any given time, then, the single "most probable" set of projections will reflect a certain harmony between population and resources, both, by definition, in the present, at the projections' starting point, and, by construction, in the future. But tracking demographic drift over the course of development is an exercise that should satisfy only historians. Ex ante, demographers should insist on the multiple degrees of freedom inherent in any population pattern as it unfolds over time. The population–resources debate ought not to center on what demographic changes can be accommodated by development and with what consequences for human welfare. Its proper subject, instead, should be an exploration of demographic choices open to societies that aim not just to muddle through, but to reach the best of all possible worlds.

Notes

1 In a footnote to the quoted passage, Coale remarks that "calculations of this sort are scarcely original," and specifically disclaims being the source of the "expanding sphere idea." A comment in Vogt (1960: 49–51) suggests that it may have originated with Harrison Brown. In their study of India's development prospects, Coale and Hoover (1958: 331) offer another vivid illustration of the impossibility of sustaining demographic growth in the long run, calibrated to a more modest time scale: "In 1200 years a continuation of 1951 fertility levels and projected 1986 mortality risks would produce an Indian population heavier than the entire mass of the earth."

2 A book by Sauvy written about a decade later retells the Lake Constance story with the difference that the water now rises by nine inches (1969: 409). Apparently the assumption made in the calculation about average human bodymass had increased from about 28 kg. to about 36 kg.

3 The labels "optimist" and "pessimist" introduced above and used here recommend themselves only by their simplicity. Plainly, a crude dichotomy can hardly accommodate the many shades that differentiate the positions of various writers concerning the population–resources issue. Herman Kahn himself uses a more subtle classification (Kahn et al., 1976: 9–20), distinguishing four positions: "Convinced Neo-Malthusian," "Guarded Pessimist," "Guarded Optimist," and "Technology-and-Growth-Enthusiast." In that classification Kahn sees himself in the third category.

4 It should be noted, however, that the figures cited for supporting capacity may be considered understatements, since none of them makes appeal to possible future advances in genetic engineering or allows for synthetic production of food.

5 For a critical discussion of the FAO study, see the book review by Bernard Gilland

in *Population and Development Review* 10, no. 4 (1984): 733–735.

6 A significant share of the unexploited capacity for increasing food production is located in countries in which prospective demand conditions can be expected to leave these potentials dormant. Kenneth Blaxter's remarks, made with reference to analyses dating from the early 1980s that called for a rapid expansion of world food production so as to improve global food adequacy (1986: 51–52), are well taken: "To the farmers within the European Economic Community the idea that there is a need to increase food production by 75% in the short space until the year 2000 or to double it in the next quarter of a century must seem bizarre, when their essentially parochial problem is one of surplus agricultural production. It must seem so too to farmers in the United States and Canada, and in Australia and New Zealand."

7 Hoyle was persuaded about the de facto inadequacy of fertility control as a long-term effective check on population growth by the book of Charles Galton Darwin on the future evolution of man (1952).

8 The page numbers refer to the excerpts that appear in Vol. 11 of *Population and Development Review.*

9 When Frejka summarized his projections in an article in *Scientific American,* the editors apparently could not resist the temptation to suggest that what the reader was being offered were indeed predictions, even though no such claim was advanced in the text. The article appeared under the exquisitely ambiguous editorial headline: "The human population is now about 3.6 billion. An extrapolation of present world demographic trends that lies between two extreme projections shows it leveling off at some 8.4 billion by the year 2100" (Frejka, 1973b: 3). It is interesting to note that the 8.4 billion figure roughly coincides with the current United Nations medium projection of the global population in the year 2025.

References

Balfour, M. C., F. R. Evans, F. W. Notestein, and I. B. Taeuber. 1950. *Public Health and Demography in the Far East.* New York: The Rockefeller Foundation.

Barnett, Harold J., and Chandler Morse. 1963. *Scarcity and Growth: The Economics of Natural Resource Availability.* Baltimore: The Johns Hopkins University Press.

Bauer, P. T. 1971. *Dissent on Development: Studies and Debates in Development Economics.* London: Weidenfeld and Nicolson.

———. 1981. *Equality, the Third World, and Economic Delusion.* Cambridge, Mass.: Harvard University Press.

Blaxter, Sir Kenneth. 1986. *People, Food and Resources.* Cambridge: Cambridge University Press.

Boserup, Ester. 1965. *The Conditions of Agricultural Growth: The Economics of Agrarian Change Under Population Pressure.* Chicago: Aldine.

———. 1981. *Population and Technological Change.* Chicago: University of Chicago Press.

Botero, Giovanni. 1635 [1588]. *The Cause of the Greatness of Cities* (tr. Sir T. Hawkins). London. Excerpts reprinted in *Population and Development Review* 11, no. 2 (1985): 335–340.

Brown, Harrison. 1954. *The Challenge of Man's Future.* New York: The Viking Press.

Brown, Lester R. 1978. *The Twenty-Ninth Day: Accommodating Human Needs and Numbers to the Earth's Resources.* New York: W. W. Norton.

Clark, Colin. 1958. "Population growth and living standards," in *The Economics of Underdevelopment,* ed. A. N. Agarwala and S. P. Singh. London: Oxford University Press, pp. 32–53.

———. 1967. *Population Growth and Land Use.* New York: St. Martin's Press.

———. 1985. "World Development Report 1984: Review," *Population and Development Review* 11, no. 1: 120–126.

Coale, Ansley J. 1959. "Increases in expectation of life and population growth," in *International Population Conference, Wien 1959.* Vienna: IUSSP, pp. 36–41.

———, and Edgar M. Hoover. 1958. *Population Growth and Economic Development in Low-Income Countries.* Princeton, N.J.: Princeton University Press.

Commoner, Barry. 1971. *The Closing Circle: Nature, Man, and Technology.* New York: Alfred A. Knopf.

Daly, Herman E. (ed.). 1980. *Economics, Ecology, Ethics: Essays Toward a Steady-State Economy.* San Francisco: W. H. Freeman and Co.

Darwin, Charles Galton. 1952. *The Next Million Years.* London: Rupert Hart-Davis.

Davis, Kingsley. 1951. *The Population of India and Pakistan.* Princeton, N.J.: Princeton University Press.

Ehrlich, Paul R. 1986. *The Machinery of Nature.* New York: Simon and Schuster.

Freedman, Ronald, and Bernard Berelson. 1974. "The human population," *Scientific American* (September): 31–39.

Frejka, Tomas. 1973a. *The Future of Population Growth: Alternative Paths to Equilibrium.* New York: John Wiley and Sons.

———. 1973b. "The prospects for a stationary world population," *Scientific American* (March): 3–11.

Gilland, Bernard. 1983. "Considerations on world population and food supply," *Population and Development Review* 9, no. 2: 203–211.

Goeller, H. E., and Alvin M. Weinberg. 1976. "The age of substitutability," *Science* 191 (20 February): 683–688.

Hardin, Garrett. 1968. "The tragedy of the commons," *Science* 162 (13 December): 1243–1248.

Higgins, G. M., A. H. Kassam, L. Naiken, G. Fischer, and M. M. Shah. 1983. *Potential Population Supporting Capacities of Lands in the Developing World.* Rome: FAO.

Hirschman, Albert O. 1958. *The Strategy of Economic Development.* New Haven, Conn.: Yale University Press.

Hoyle, Fred. 1963. *A Contradiction in the Argument of Malthus.* University of Hull Publications. Reprinted in *Population and Development Review* 12, no. 3 (1986): 547–562.

Huxley, Julian. 1956. "World population," *Scientific American* (March): 64–76.

Kahn, Herman. 1979. *World Economic Development.* Boulder, Colo.: Westview Press.

———. 1982. *The Coming Boom: Economic, Political, and Social.* New York: Simon and Schuster.

——— and Anthony J. Wiener. 1967. *The Year 2000: A Framework for Speculation on the Next Thirty-Three Years.* New York: Macmillan.

———, William Brown, and Leon Martel. 1976. *The Next 200 Years: A Scenario for America and the World.* New York: William Morrow and Co.

Keyfitz, Nathan. 1981. "The limits of population forecasting," *Population and Development Review* 7, no. 4: 579–593.

King, Gregory. 1695. *A Manuscript Notebook.* Reproduced in *The Earliest Classics.* Gregg International Publishers Limited, 1973.

Kirk, Dudley. 1968. "The field of demography," in *International Encyclopedia of the Social Sciences,* ed. David L. Sills. New York: The Macmillan Co. and The Free Press. Vol. 12, pp. 342–349.

Kuznets, Simon. 1967. "Population and economic growth," *Proceedings of the American Philosophical Society* 111, no. 3: 170–193.

Malthus, Thomas Robert. 1966 [1798]. *First Essay on Population 1798* (A Reprint in Facsimile). London: Macmillan.

McNicoll, Geoffrey. 1984. "Consequences of rapid population growth: An overview and assessment," *Population and Development Review* 10, no. 2: 177–240.

Meadows, Donella H., Dennis L. Meadows, Jorgen Randers, and William W. Behrens III. 1972. *The Limits to Growth.* New York: Universe Books.

National Academy of Sciences. 1971. *Rapid Population Growth: Consequences and Policy Implications.* Baltimore: The Johns Hopkins University Press.

National Research Council. 1986. *Population Growth and Economic Development: Policy Questions.* Washington, D.C.: National Academy Press.

Neumann, John von. 1955. "Can we survive technology?" *Fortune* (June): 106–108 and 151–152. Reprinted in *Population and Development Review* 12, no. 1 (1986): 117–126.

Petty, Sir William. 1698 [1682]. *An Essay Concerning the Multiplication of Mankind* . . . London: Robert Clavel and Henry Mortlock.

Ravenstein, E. G. 1891. "Lands of the Globe still available for European settlement," *Proceedings of the Royal Geographic Society.* New Monthly Series 13: 27–35 and 64.

Revelle, Roger. 1976. "The resources available for agriculture," *Scientific American* (September): 165–178.

———. 1982. "Resources," in *Population and the World Economy in the 21st Century,* ed. Just Faaland. New York: St. Martin's Press, pp. 50–77.

Ridker, Ronald G., and William D. Watson. 1980. *To Choose a Future: Resource and Environmental Consequences of Alternative Growth Paths.* Baltimore: The Johns Hopkins University Press.

Sauvy, Alfred. 1961. *Fertility and Survival: Population Problems from Malthus to Mao Tse-Tung.* London: Chatto and Windus.

———. 1969. *General Theory of Population* (tr. by C. Campos). New York: Basic Books.

Schumacher, E. F. 1954. "Population in relation to the development of energy from coal," *Proceedings of the World Population Conference, Rome 1954.* New York: United Nations. Vol. 5.

Schumpeter, Joseph A. 1961. *History of Economic Analysis.* New York: Oxford University Press.

Simon, Julian L. 1977. *The Economics of Population Growth.* Princeton, N.J.: Princeton University Press.

———. 1981. *The Ultimate Resource.* Princeton, N.J.: Princeton University Press.

Smith, Kerry V. 1979. *Scarcity and Growth Reconsidered.* Baltimore: The Johns Hopkins University Press.

Thompson, Warren S. 1950. "Future adjustments of population to resources in Japan," in *Modernization Programs in Relation to Human Resources and Population Problems.* New York: Milbank Memorial Fund, pp. 142–153.

Tinbergen, Jan. 1975. "Demographic development and the exhaustion of natural resources," *Population and Development Review* 1, no. 1: 23–32.

United Nations. 1986. *World Population Prospects: Estimates and Projections as Assessed in 1984.* New York.

US Department of Commerce. 1988. *Statistical Abstract of the United States 1988.* Washington, D.C.: US Government Printing Office.

Vogt, William. 1948. *Road to Survival.* New York: William Sloane Associates.

———. 1960. *People! Challenge to Survival.* New York: William Sloane Associates.

World Bank. 1984. *World Development Report 1984.* New York: Oxford University Press.

World Resources Institute. 1987. *World Resources 1987.* New York: Basic Books.

Zachariah, K. C., and My T. Vu. 1988. *World Population Projections: 1987–88 Edition. Short- and Long-Term Estimates.* Baltimore: Published for the World Bank, The Johns Hopkins University Press.

Social Science Approaches to International Migration

KINGSLEY DAVIS

AMONG THE MAJOR ASPECTS OF HUMAN DEMOGRAPHY, migration across national borders stands out as perhaps one of the most resistant to scientific analysis. Involving painful and sometimes catastrophic changes in people's lives, it is a subject fraught with emotion and strong opinion, and the literature devoted to it is vast. Yet the topic is usually handled descriptively and historically, with little effort to generalize, or is fitted with a model so simplified by assumptions as to be unrecognizable in real-world terms.

In the present essay, then, we shall start by trying to explain why international migration is so opaque to theoretical reasoning in general, and to formal models in particular. This in turn should indicate why efforts to formulate a general science of migration have failed even while historical studies of population movements have succeeded. In the last part of the essay, we offer a brief historical analysis of four centuries of world migration.

It should be noted that internal migration, not discussed here, presents quite different issues in theory and manifestation (see, e.g., Ross, 1982; Davis, 1973).

Peculiarities of international migration as a topic

At first glance, international migration as a topic seems straightforward. It resembles mortality and fertility in being part of the fundamental balancing equation in demography, which says that any population change is a function of natural increase (births minus deaths) and net migration (immigration minus emigration). This gives migration equal billing with natural increase and implies that a migrant is like a birth, arithmetically speaking. But in fact migration is a totally different phenomenon. Unlike mortality and fertility, it has no biological constraints and hence no built-in limits. There is no "normal" or "natural" rate of migration, and no potential minimum or maximum other than zero and 100 percent. Also, to a much greater extent than birth and death, migration is a creature of policy. For example, strong constraints exist on what the modern state can do about mortality and fertility, but only weak constraints on what it can do about movement across its borders. It can decree a closed border, letting no one in or out; it can cause a mass exit or encourage a mass entry; or it can permit entry only to people in certain ethnic or economic categories.

International migration becomes even more complicated and unpredictable when one takes into account the interests involved. First, there are the interests of the migrant himself. He may or may not be responsible for his move, but he is certainly the agent through whom the various other interests are served. Second, there are interested parties in the country or region where the migratory move originated (the "O" country or region). These include recruiters, relatives, friends, employers, officials, and others who stand to gain or lose by the migrant's move. Third, there are interested parties at the place of destination (the "D" region or country), including potential employers, religious leaders, teachers, police, welfare officials, health workers, friends, relatives, and the public at large.

With so many interests involved, it is virtually impossible to formulate theoretical principles that apply to international migration in general. As a consequence, social scientists usually confine themselves to delineating streams of migration and developing ad hoc explanations as needed. They often concentrate on the one or two interests that seem crucial in the migratory stream under discussion or that at least fit their scheme of analysis. Empirical models at best fit particular circumstances that will not be repeated. The history of thought about migration therefore turns up no grand synthesis or set of fundamental principles. It boasts no revolutionary discoveries, no cumulative advances in knowledge comparable to Lotka's stable population theory.

This explanation of why the study of migration is so amorphous is confirmed, I think, by the failure of deliberate attempts to produce a science of migration. Two such attempts—one to formulate "laws" of migration and the other to develop a labor-supply theory—deserve particular attention. Let us review them.

The "laws" of migration

The remarkable achievements in the physical sciences during the seventeenth and eighteenth centuries naturally gave rise to the hope that similar breakthroughs, using analogous methods, could be made in the social sciences. So it is not surprising that a century ago a determined effort was made to formulate general principles governing migration. The author of this effort, E. G. Ravenstein, published two papers in the *Journal of the Royal Statistical Society,* one in 1885 and the other in 1889, each running to 60 pages and both entitled "The laws of migration." The first paper, using data exclusively from the British Isles, dealt with internal migration. The second also dealt with internal migration but with reference to other countries. Both papers made careful and extensive use of data to illustrate the generalizations, giving the two articles a modern flavor in spite of the old-fashioned purpose of discovering "laws."

Upon examination, the so-called laws of migration turn out to be of two types: simple regularities that Ravenstein feels he has found in the data, and abstractions that can be deduced from arbitrary assumptions. Characteristically, he does not distinguish between these empirical and deductive propositions, nor does he have the same list in both papers. If we follow the list at the end of the second paper, we can get a reasonably clear notion of what he had in mind. The first rule is what is now called, after Samuel Stouffer (1940, 1960), the law of intervening opportunities—namely, that migrants move no farther than they have to. This is clearly a deductive proposition, derived from the assumption that men are rational and therefore will avoid waste of effort. As a corollary or consequence of the first rule, the second states that there are more short-range than long-range migrants. The third rule—that a migratory stream always produces a counter-current of lesser strength—is evidently a rough rule-of-thumb; stated in a broad and unqualified manner, without any particular rationale, the proposition is hard to confirm or deny. Certainly, not many slaves brought to the Americas made their way back to Africa. Not many Jews who managed to leave the Soviet Union ever went back, and not many Jews driven out of Hitler's Germany returned. By definition, a refugee is someone who will probably not return. How large must a counter-stream be to qualify as a stream?

The fourth rule, that "in all settled countries" the towns grow at the expense of the rural parts, is also so broadly stated as to be virtually meaningless. In the late stages of national development, there is hardly any strictly rural population left, and what there is may grow by virtue of migration from cities and towns (Long, 1983). The fifth rule is more precise but not more convincing. "Females," Ravenstein says, "tend to predominate among short-journey migrants." He admits exceptions to this rule, but says the violations are numerically insignificant. However, we could hardly call the examples found in Asia, the Middle East, and most of Africa insignificant. In these regions, men tend to predominate in both long and short migration. The general principle is that when women are restricted to the home and excluded from the labor market (as is the case in most Middle Eastern countries even today), they receive less education and consequently have less opportunity to move. When, as in most industrial countries of Europe and the Americas, women not only are allowed to enter the labor market but also receive an education, they tend to be more numerous than men in rural-to-urban migration but not necessarily in distant movement (Davis, 1951, 1974; Youssef,

1974). The sixth and last rule—that migration tends to increase with the development of manufacture and commerce—has about the same validity as the fourth rule. It sounds plausible, but Ravenstein does not tell us why the regularity should exist or why the exceptions should occur.

Under criticism for calling his rules "laws," Ravenstein admits they are not laws in the scientific sense. They are characterized by unexplained exceptions and are not logically connected with other propositions in a system of reasoning. They are like the familiar rules-of-thumb about the physical world that we all carry in our heads but do not fully understand. A knowledge of such rules is useful if not necessary in everyday life, but it hardly constitutes science. Ravenstein's work contains no systematic reasoning that could be called a conceptual framework or even a "school of thought" about migration. We thus find nothing that could be employed as an ideological basis for migration policy.

That the search for "laws of migration" is a blind alley is confirmed by the failure of scholars to follow up or to build upon Ravenstein's painstaking work. His articles are widely referenced, but only because there is no one else in this genre to cite. With only one exception, subsequent scholars have not seriously used Ravenstein's "laws" as a springboard for further theoretical development.

The one exception was Everett Lee (1966). Writing nearly a century after Ravenstein, with an armory of better data and newer techniques, and trained at a center of population research that featured the study of migration, Lee deliberately set out to build on Ravenstein's foundations. Like Ravenstein, he thought of his task as setting forth empirical generalizations about the "volume" of migration. Leaving "volume" undefined and hence ambiguous as to whether total or net, absolute or relative migration is meant, he says that a high volume is caused by a large diversity among areas and people, by an absence of intervening obstacles, and by rapid progress in technology. Since, like Ravenstein, he thinks of these as empirical generalizations rather than deductive propositions, he fails to develop a systematic or logical analysis of why they should be true. He points out that migration occurs mainly within well-defined streams and that the rate of return migration is low if the stream arises from negative factors in the place of origin. He also calls attention to the selectivity of migration: if the movement is motivated primarily by opportunities in the area of destination, it selects positively; if not, it selects negatively.

Lee deserves credit for increasing the number of rules and classifying them, but he falls into the same trap as Ravenstein by confusing empirical rules-of-thumb with deductive propositions. As a result, many of his rules (he has 18 all-told) seem trivial, ambiguous, or redundant. Sometimes the same proposition is treated at one place as an invariant scientific law and at another place as a common observation with known exceptions. Instead of

"A theory of migration," his article might better be entitled "Miscellaneous regularities with respect to migration."

The fundamental problem with the approach of Ravenstein and Lee is that it misconstrues the task. The task is not to arrive at a list of rules-of-thumb with respect to migration. Such rules are of mild interest, especially when a field of knowledge is in an early stage of development, but they have little value for science. The question is not whether a given regularity is true or not, but why it could be expected to be true. For instance, Lee (pp. 52–54) states several rules that seem identical. "The volume of migration," he says, "is related to . . . the intervening obstacles." It is also related to "fluctuations in the economy," and it tends to "increase with time" and to "vary with the state of progress." These statements seem to say that migration increases with economic development. If so, the important question is not only whether this proposition is generally true, but why. What is it about development that spurs migration? The answer obviously requires a theory of development, which Lee does not offer.

Migrants as workers

If the search for "laws" is a false trail, what is the alternative? Has any other approach done better in bringing order to the subject of international migration? Since the Mercantilists, and possibly before, economists have viewed immigration as a source of labor. As such, it is a factor in production along with capital, land, native labor, and other resources. Migration can thus be analyzed in terms familiar to labor economists. The migrant is a worker who finds he can get higher wages and better working conditions by moving.

The liberal tradition

In the approach of laissez-faire classical economics, attention is centered on the migrant himself, who is assumed to be free to follow his own best interest. When, however, attention is shifted to the countries involved, the theory becomes more complex. On a global scale, the law of comparative advantage in international trade can be invoked. Labor will go to those areas able to pay higher wages. When not distorted by governmental intrusion, the net effect of international migration is to distribute labor more efficiently around the world.

But as Brinley Thomas (1973, p. 2) points out, when it came to international migration, the classical economists abandoned laissez-faire. Like the Mercantilists, they "believed that migration should be regulated by the State. It was one of the few exceptions to the general rule of laissez-faire."

Why was this exception made? Could it be that the interests of migrants, sending countries, and receiving countries were all different, and that any assumption of automatic harmony, such as the invisible hand of Adam Smith, was patently unrealistic? The economists of the time lived mostly in Britain, a country of considerable outmigration. When they assessed the role of migration, it was from the standpoint of that country. But Britain had some important peculiarities. For one thing, it headed an empire that stretched around the world. Some of the dependencies were very sparsely settled by European standards, and it was thought that they needed immigrants. According to Edward Wakefield, the chief proponent of emigration (1833; cited in Thomas, 1973, p. 4), the overall purpose was colonization. This, he said, "would confer three advantages on an old society: it would increase the market for its products, give relief from overpopulation, and promote foreign investments."

Every author had his own view of how migration should be regulated. Most thought that emigration should be subsidized or otherwise encouraged, and that it should be directed to those overseas possessions most in need of European settlement.

Not surprisingly, the rising exodus of Europeans to the New World led to a considerable literature on emigration, which Thomas (1973, Part 1) has thoroughly summarized. One finds oneself in a squirrel cage of highly abstract reasoning. Often it is unclear whose interests are being served. The high level of abstraction makes it difficult to test hypotheses. Clearly, despite all the writing about it, no one has produced an integrated study of international migration. There is no work that serves as a benchmark, or point of departure, for the entire subject. In other words, international migration has not yet had its Thomas Malthus or its Adam Smith.

The favorable or liberal view of migration persists among intellectuals with remarkable tenacity. Despite millions of refugees and displaced persons from two world wars, despite chronic ethnic and religious strife, despite closed borders and forced exchanges of minorities, the predominant theory treats migration as the result of free individuals (the migrants) pursuing their own economic interests.

A twentieth century example of the liberal view

To account for this hiatus between abstraction and reality, let us examine a particular book embodying the liberal tradition. *Economics of Migration* was published in 1947 by Julius Isaac and had a wide impact. Isaac starts by making clear that he is dealing only with free migration. Indeed, he defines migration as "the movement of free individuals" (p. 3). By this definition, a great many, perhaps a majority, of migrants throughout history are excluded. They are people who, for one reason or another, were not free to move as they pleased—for instance, political, religious, and ethnic refugees, slaves, coolies, children and wives, and convicts. Isaac was of course aware of forced migration and frequently discussed it in his book, but he left it out of his theoretical reasoning because it did not fit his analytic framework, while free migration did. Among the "causes" of migration, then, he considers the "predominant" one to be "the desire to become better off" (p. 23). Indeed, he seems to regard the individual's pursuit of that goal as both an explanation and an ethical right. The liberal attitude toward migration, he says, "is based mainly on two propositions: (1) Individual free migration is determined by the economic interest of the migrant. (2) The economic self-interest of the individual coincides with the general interest" (p. 70). For the society as a whole, "the optimum point for a population with a given amount of capital and natural resources is reached under conditions of free competition when the marginal product of labor is equal to the average output per head. So long as the marginal product of labor is greater than the average output an increase in the working population would raise the output per head" (p. 71). In a free international system, workers would move to where their skills were most rewarded. Any interference with migration is therefore of questionable validity.

A critique of laissez-faire

According to Isaac, laissez-faire as a doctrine had a powerful influence in rationalizing migration from Europe to the New World, but as a theory about international migration in general, I believe it is flawed. As noted already, a large share of such migration is involuntary and therefore beyond the scope of decision theory, and the essential decisionmaker is not the migrant him- or herself. Indeed he (for simplicity) is not exclusively the decisionmaker even in free migration. Migrants can move from one country to another only because they are permitted to do so. Of course, they may enter or remain in a country illegally, but if they do so it is because the receiving country has decided not to invest the money and manpower required to stop illegal immigration. Further, the immigrant can get a job only because an employer decides to hire him or he has the capital necessary for self-employment, and he can bring in his wife and children only because he is allowed to do so. In other words, the basic decisions governing the volume of supposedly free migration are made by interested parties in the "O" and "D" countries. Migrants make the decision to move or to remain within the confines of decisions made by others. Unless the latter decisions are favorable to migration, no movement will take place. Accordingly, an adequate theory of migration must include an analysis of how migration affects, or is thought to affect, interests and policies in the "O" and "D" countries—interests that are not accidental or minor constraints, but important controls that must themselves be explained.

This is not to belittle the role of the migrant himself. He has some important characteristics. For instance, he is possessed of considerable inertia because he has to make the personal adjustments required by a durable change of residence. He has to leave relatives, friends, and familiar surroundings. He has to cope with a new climate and often with a new language. For all of these reasons, he does not want to move, certainly not far. That is why, in the history of migration, he has seldom been the principal decisionmaker. Left to his own devices, he would not move, but he has been led or forced to move by unfavorable conditions or the interests of others.

Having focused his theoretical analysis on "free" migration, Isaac easily falls into the trap of viewing the migrant as exclusively a worker. Although this assumption simplifies the analytical task by treating migration theory as an extension of labor economics, it has the disadvantage of ignoring important aspects of migratory behavior. For instance, it allows one to overlook the possibility that the migrant may not be a worker at all, or if he is a worker, that he is variously other things as well—a voter, a member of ethnic, linguistic, religious, and political groups, a devotee of arts or sports, a child or an adult, and so on.

Absorption power and migration policy

The narrowness of this view can be seen in Isaac's treatment of migration policy. "To determine for any country the desirable volume of immigration or emigration," he says (pp. 105–106), two concepts are useful—the "absorption power" and the "carrying capacity" of a region or nation. The absorption power, he writes, can be visualized by thinking of a firm rather than a country. "If an industrial firm utilizes for its current output only 70 percent of its productive capacity, it is easy to calculate how many hands the firm would employ if it worked at full capacity." The policy required to raise the firm to full employment depends on the causes of the deficiency, but in any case "employment with the firm at full capacity corresponds to the carrying capacity of a country," that is, "the size its population would have if all its resources were fully utilized." The capacity to absorb immigrants, Isaac says, is the difference between the actual population and the potential carrying capacity. When the difference is large, the absorption potential is high. For example, an ideal rate of population growth in Australia would be 2 percent per year, guaranteed by immigration (pp. 111–116).

Underlying such reasoning is the idea that migration must be judged in terms of its effect on population growth and, through such growth, on economic development. Liberal political and economic leaders tend to believe that a movement from areas of high population density to areas of low density is not only natural but desirable. On the other side, their opponents point out that the Earth is already too crowded, that migration, by helping to fill the last remaining open spaces, is making the crowding worse. Further, they argue that overcrowding, especially in the less developed countries, is hindering economic development because development depends on the quality, not the size, of the labor force. Finally, they note that migration is no longer predominantly from crowded to less crowded areas, but rather from poor agrarian to advanced industrial nations, giving rise to problems attendant on the influx of ethnic minorities.

Resting migration policy on alleged carrying capacity has the additional flaw that it overlooks international trade. Further, "capacity" is highly sensitive to the level of living assumed. If one insists on a high level and ignores foreign trade, the carrying capacity of a given area will be smaller than it will be if a low level of living is assumed. In most discussions of carrying capacity, per capita income is assumed to be quite modest; indeed, all too often the concept implies that to sustain life in an area, all that is needed is sufficient food and shelter. I call this the "bread-alone fallacy" because I know of no society whose members are satisfied to get just enough to eat and wear, who ignore all wants except for bare necessities, and who thus eschew ceremony, religion, recreation, art, and other cultural preoccupations and amenities. Since the human species is distinguished precisely by its cultural mode of adaptation, any estimate of carrying capacity that ignores cultural needs is bound to be misleading as well as unrealistic.

It is hard to avoid the conclusion that the liberal laissez-faire reasoning about migration—reasoning prevalent among officials and intellectuals for a century or more—was inadequate. Isaac illustrates the problem. Stated at a time when mass involuntary dislocations of people were already occurring in the aftermath of World War II, his approach seems narrow and anemic. It gives scant attention to the sentiments, interests, and group structure of the public at large. Yet, for whatever it is worth, this remains the most widely used theoretical approach to the science of migration.

Migration in the modern world

Let us now see how the subject of migration is clarified or deepened by a historical approach. By such an approach we mean an analysis in which the questions posed and the answers given refer to a specified time and place and to other events happening simultaneously. With respect to migration, for example, one might assess the rationale and effectiveness of United States migration law and policy since World War II, a period during which illegal immigration flourished, by placing the discussion in a wider social and economic context. For purposes of illustration, however, I prefer to take a longer period and a wider scope—world immigration since 1500. No matter where we start, we encounter an inherent weakness of the historical approach, namely that there is no systematic cutoff point or criterion of relevance. A theme or context must be introduced from the outside, so to speak, to organize and limit the historical material.

For the period after 1500, three signal developments must have greatly affected migration: the European discovery of the New World, the industrial revolution, and the onset of the demographic transition. A priori, one might have expected the first of these—the Age of Discovery—to have produced a formidable movement of people from crowded Europe to the sparsely inhabited lands abroad. Later, one might have expected the industrial revolution to have pulled rural inhabitants into the burgeoning cities of Europe while slowing the frontier settlements abroad. Finally, more recently, one might have thought the less developed countries would experience only slow population growth because their poverty would keep the death rate high (Thompson, 1942).

In actuality, most of these expectations proved wrong, at least in part. For three centuries after Columbus the movement of Europeans to areas abroad was a mere trickle; and the spread of industrialism in Europe in the nineteenth and early twentieth century, while it pulled people into the cities in Europe, also pushed them into the New World. Finally, after World War II, extremely rapid population growth came to characterize the world's impoverished countries, driving their people to migrate in unprecedented numbers.

An advantage of the historical approach is that one already knows what happened. One may therefore remedy an error of interpretation by going into finer detail. In the present case, for example, the new lands opened up by the Age of Discovery were not uniformly amenable to settlement. Some were tropical and others temperate. Some were virtually free of inhabitants, others were densely populated. In general, Europeans tended to settle permanently only in temperate and sparsely inhabited regions, but these, in the absence of cheap labor, were rough frontier areas that usually required hard physical effort by the cultivator. Further, the costs—in both psychic and monetary terms—of moving to a new area were extremely high. On the other hand, the tropical areas were assumed to be unsuitable for permanent European settlement. In them, agriculture was carried out on plantations managed by Europeans but with forced non-European labor brought from other tropical areas. Finally, in the heavily populated colonies, such as India and Java, the Europeans, remarkably few in number, were satisfied to become rulers and managers.

Such facts explain why, for nearly three centuries after Columbus, migration from Europe to the new lands was not large, and why it was more than matched by the importation of forced and quasi-forced labor from Africa, Asia, and the Pacific. They also help to explain why outmigration from Europe, though small, was nevertheless strategic in establishing European dominance over more than half the globe.

The early European migrants turned to slavery because their new settlements had vast resources but few workers. In general, labor had to be imported from elsewhere, either because native labor was too sparse or because, governed by its own customs and economic organization, it was notoriously unreliable. The slave trade flourished until the mid-nineteenth century (Curtin, 1969). When it was abolished in the British Empire in 1834 and in other areas around that time, slavery was replaced by expansion of the next most compulsory form of labor migration—indentured and contract labor. Many areas of the world received immigrant workers during the century and a half before the Great Depression.

The term "contract labor" was misleading, because the contracting parties were completely unequal. The overwhelming majority who signed up to work were illiterate and ignorant. They had no clear idea of their destination, the dangers they faced, the rights they had, or the specific kinds of work they would do. All they knew was that money could be earned.

In this worldwide transport of workers, why did the slave trade mainly involve Africans and the contract-labor system Asians? I think the answer lies in geography and timing. Europe was closer to Africa than to Asia, yet Africans were more untutored than Asians. Further, the tribal organization of African peoples facilitated the selling of slaves: slavery was an established institution in Africa when the Europeans first explored the continent.

Regardless of whether the migrants were African or Asian, they were clearly not the decisionmakers. Instead, the decisions were made by European managers, entrepreneurs, and officials. Frequently, the same managerial enterprise operated in both the sending and the receiving countries, thus facilitating firm control over the labor supply. The contract system transferred millions of Asians around the globe. Thus the Age of Discovery generated a substantial non-European migration managed by Europeans but not manned by them.

By the early nineteenth century, however, several developments had led to greater settler migration from Europe. First, the previous increase of Europeans in the sparsely inhabited temperate regions of the New World, though slow by subsequent standards, had nevertheless built up sufficient numbers to make the new lands reasonably civilized. Second, steamships began crossing the Atlantic in 1850, sharply reducing the cost of shipping goods to Europe and of bringing people back. Third, Europe was experiencing a rise in natural increase because of a falling death rate. This, in spite of emigration, was making Europe the most densely settled of the continents. Since, as we have just seen, Europeans controlled most of the world's sparsely inhabited areas, it was almost inevitable that growing numbers of people would leave crowded Europe, where land was dear and labor cheap, for the temperate New World areas, where the reverse was true and where European culture was already established. Indeed, under the circumstances, the puzzle is not why so many left Europe, but why so few did. The answer, already given, is that until the nineteenth century, life in the new lands was hard and the costs of getting there were substantial. Further, although the governments concerned—those in the sending and receiving countries—generally favored overseas migration, they actually did little to defray the costs. Finally, the "snowball" effect (the more immigrants of a given nationality in the "D" region, the more who wanted to come) took time to develop.

Eventually, the movement from Europe to the New World became a stampede. From the mid-nineteenth century to the Great Depression, tens of millions of Europeans departed, chiefly to the United States. This flood dwarfed the previous movement in numbers and popular interest, but not in significance, for the earlier movement had already determined that the temperate parts of the New World would be overwhelmingly European in language and culture.

Europe, however, was not the only crowded continent. The bulk of humanity lived in Asia, where poverty was endemic. It was therefore inevitable that Asians, too, would move to the New World, not only as contract labor under the direction of Europeans, but also as individuals with the same rights as Europeans. It was also inevitable that the rise of Asia as a source of migrants should alarm the New World countries, which, as noted already, were by then overwhelmingly European in race and culture. Indeed, "The first definite change in the American policy of free immigration was the restriction of Oriental immigration" (Bernard, 1950, p. 11). The national-origins quota acts of 1921 and 1924 in the United States, and similar restrictive legislation in other New World areas, ushered in a period of vacillating policy with respect to the number and national origin of immigrants who should be admitted.

The final chapter in this brief history of modern migration may turn out to be the most spectacular. Beginning with World War II, it potentially involves tens of millions of people. It stems mainly from the difference in population growth between the developed and the less developed countries, a difference that is wider now than ever in the past. Between 1980 and 1985, the United Nations *Demographic Yearbook* shows the less developed countries of the world growing approximately three times as fast as the developed countries. This disparity creates strong pressure for migration from the poor to the rich nations, a movement not likely to please the wealthy nations. If the developed nations were to receive as immigrants only the excess natural increase of the less developed nations—that is, if they admitted enough immigrants to give the less developed countries zero population growth—they would have to absorb approximately 70 million immigrants per year. This would be more migrants in each single year than left Europe during the entire period following the discovery of the New World. Although in the 1950s and 1960s the industrialized nations accepted a record number of foreign workers from the Third World, they became noticeably less hospitable in the 1970s and 1980s (Werner, 1986). They often tried to send the "guestworkers" back home, but not with full success. As the world becomes increasingly conscious of the plight of poor nations, the pressure on the rich countries to accept migrants will become greater, and of course the desire of individuals to migrate to escape poverty will be extreme, giving rise to illegal as well as legal migration.

Given the last two centuries of wholesale transfer of people from Europe, Asia, and Africa to the New World, one would expect to find an ideology justifying such a transfer. Isaac (1947, pp. 13–24) views the demise of mercantilism and the rise of liberalism as the ideological basis for pro-migration policies. Adam Smith, with his interest in free trade, "stressed the necessity of removing all obstacles to the free mobility of labor" (ibid., p. 21). The political philosophy of Locke and his followers, the ideologues of the American and French revolutions, and the constitutions of many new nations all talked of the rights of man, with the freedom to move either stated or clearly implied. The same stance is taken by many economists today. According to Charles Kindelberger (1978), for instance, "Restrictions on migratory flows have the effect of distorting both the optimal economic allocation of labor and the international distribution of income" (p. 24).

The trouble with such reasoning lies in its omissions. First, it assumes an existing misallocation of labor without explaining the misallocation. Second, it assumes that migrants are exclusively workers and that they move in order to get more income. Third, the usual justification offered by receiving countries is that immigration provides needed labor or that it is humanitarian (giving disadvantaged people a new environment). But these are short-run goals. A labor shortage this year may be followed by a surplus next year. Refugee status may change from one year to the next with a change in relations between the countries of origin and destination. In other words, the long-run consequences of migration are seldom considered, much less made the basis of policy. For instance, by sending millions of persons abroad, Europe kept its rate of population growth moderate. As a result, the continent's population was reduced in size relative to the New World, as the following comparison with the United States shows:

	Population (thousands)		**US population as a percent of Europe's**
	Europe	**United States**	
1800	187,693	5,308	2.8
1850	266,228	23,192	8.7
1906	424,634	84,308	19.9

SOURCE: Gustav Sundbarg, *Aperçus Statistiques Internationaux* (New York: Gordon and Breach Science Publishers, no date; first published in 1908 by Imprimerie Royale, Stockholm), Tables 1, 9, 17.

As for the receiving countries, their stake in the migratory stream was greater than that of the sending countries, because migrants tended to become permanent residents. Also, the migrants were more numerous measured against the populations of the receiving countries than against those of the sending countries. During the decade 1890–1900, for example, the rate of migration into the United States was approximately ten times the rate of emigration from Europe. Such high rates gave the receiving countries major problems of assimilation.

The demand for cheap labor continued to drive the colonies and eventually the new nations to welcome immigrants. This motive led to improved transportation and to the use of seasonal workers. It also led to the establishment of recruiting offices in regions from which migrants could embark and eventually led to massive immigration from crowded impoverished countries.

What were the consequences? One looks back and wonders at the flimsiness of reasons for policies that affected hundreds of millions of people during four centuries. What did the officials and elite members of European societies abroad think they were doing? Did they ever consider the long-run effects of their short-term need for workers? One can see why the elite of an agrarian society might wish to bring in immigrants to cultivate their fields. The proprietors benefit directly. But why a nation's officials should favor immigration is less clear, except insofar as they identify with the proprietary class. As national economies have become more complex, the attitude toward immigration has been increasingly guided by the assumption that something variously called "development," "growth," or "progress" is an overarching goal by which the desirability of virtually all activities, including immigration, can be judged. The importation of labor, it is assumed, necessarily expands the labor force and thus contributes to growth.

There are several problems with this justification. In the first place, as an ultimate goal, sheer growth is meaningless. Presumably one is thinking about economic growth, an increase in production and consumption, but surely there is a point beyond which people are surfeited with goods and services—a point where new growth is used simply to overcome the pollution and congestion created by past growth. In the second place, an increase in total economic activity can occur simultaneously with a decline in per capita output. Foreign workers, if poorly qualified, add more to the total labor force than to the skilled labor force. A weakness of pro-immigration policies has been their tendency to emphasize the number of bodies to be admitted without reference to skills. Under a pending proposal to reform rules governing US immigration laws, a point system would be used to distribute a portion of new visas. Points would be allocated according to such factors as immigrants' education, job skills, and work experience. In the third place, the justification of immigration on economic grounds is short-run, but the consequences are not. To say there is a demand for labor that is not being met by the native citizenry is to speak from the standpoint of employers, whose fortunes vary from month to month and year to year, whereas immigrants tend to stay permanently in their country of destination. Even guestworker policies evolve into de facto immigration policies, with attendant problems of longer term integration. Therefore, even if immigration is regarded as meeting a current shortage of labor, it may not be justified over the long term. It may, for example, give rise to religious, linguistic, or ethnic conflict. European guestworkers have extended the average length of residence in their countries of destination, and increasing numbers are deciding against returning home. When strenuous efforts are made to send temporary labor back home, the fact that laborers are also human beings makes it difficult to treat them as commodities to be shipped back and forth as the needs of employers dictate.

Conclusion

In this essay I have speculated on why international migration is so resistant to systematic analysis. I have concluded that, as a subject, it contends with too many aspects of human behavior that have little logical connection one with another. Unlike fertility and mortality, immigration has virtually no biological constraints. To an exceptional degree, it is a creature of policy and of accidental or arbitrary rules.

Attempts to formulate theories of migratory behavior—efforts to find "laws" of migration, for instance—produce little more than empirical rules-of-thumb. Similarly, attempts to use economic reasoning to account for migratory behavior commonly treat the migrant himself as the decisionmaker, ignoring the interested parties in the sending and receiving countries. The migrant is not always a worker, nor is his role in society completely dependent on his labor.

A historical approach captures more of the complex reality of international migration than other approaches. To illustrate such an approach, I briefly outlined the history of world migration during the modern period when international migration was dominated by at least three great developments: first, the discovery and early exploration of the New World by Europeans, which led to European control of much of the globe; second, the invention and spread of the industrial revolution, which started in Europe but soon diffused to overseas countries and exercised an influence nearly everywhere; and third, the demographic transition in industrial countries, whereby continuing rapid population growth came to be associated with poverty, slow growth with prosperity.

In the early stages of European colonization, the use of involuntary labor was understandable. Europeans suddenly had vast natural resources available to them but almost no labor. To acquire reliable labor, they could depend on their own high rate of natural increase, but this solution meant postponing exploitation of new resources for several generations; so they turned to slavery and so-called contract labor. As industrialization got under way, the need for skilled labor increased disproportionately. By the second half of the nineteenth century, the movement of people from Europe to the New World became a stampede. It was a move largely by the poor, from advanced countries to less advanced countries where they became better off. In time, however, the European countries neared the end of their demographic transitions while the less advanced countries were rapidly entering theirs. As a result, following World War II the direction of international migration reversed itself. Instead of going from more developed to less developed nations, it proceeded in the opposite direction. How long this will continue, and with what volume, is hard to say, but its potential effect in the future is enormous.

References

Bernard, William S. 1950. *American Immigration Policy—A Reappraisal.* New York: Harper and Brothers.

Curtin, Philip D. 1969. *The Atlantic Slave Trade: A Census.* Madison: University of Wisconsin Press.

Davis, Kingsley. 1951. *The Population of India and Pakistan.* Princeton, N. J.: Princeton University Press.

——— (ed.). 1973. "Cities: Their origin, growth, and human impact," Readings from *Scientific American.* San Francisco: W. H. Freeman.

———. 1974. "The migrations of human populations," *Scientific American* 231, no. 3 (September): 93–105.

———. 1976. *World Urbanization, 1950–1970,* Vol. II: *Analysis of Trends, Relationships, and Development.* Westport, Conn.: Greenwood Press.

Isaac, Julius. 1947. *Economics of Migration.* New York: Oxford University Press.

Kindelberger, Charles P. 1978. "Migration, growth and development," *OECD Observer,* No. 93 (July): 24.

Lee, Everett S. 1966. "A theory of migration," *Demography* 3 (1966): 47–57.

Long, Larry H. 1983. "Population redistribution in the U.S.: Issues for the 1980's," *Population Trends and Public Policy,* No. 3. Washington, D.C.: Population Reference Bureau.

Ravenstein, Ernest G. 1885. "The laws of migration," *Journal of the Royal Statistical Society* 48, part 2 (June): 167–227.

———. 1889. "The laws of migration, second paper," *Journal of the Royal Statistical Society* 52 (June): 241–301.

Ross, John A. (ed.). 1982. "Urbanization," in *International Encyclopedia of Population,* Vol. 2. New York: Free Press, pp. 649–664.

Stouffer, Samuel A. 1940. "Intervening opportunities: A theory relating mobility and distance," *American Sociological Review* 5: 845–867.

———. 1960. "Intervening opportunities and competing migrants," *Journal of Regional Science* 2: 1–26.

Thomas, Brinley. 1973. *Migration and Economic Growth: A Study of Great Britain and the Atlantic.* Cambridge: Cambridge University Press.

Thompson, Warren S. 1942. *Population Problems.* New York: McGraw-Hill.

Werner, H. 1986. "Post-war labor migration in Western Europe: An overview," *International Migration* 24, no. 3 (September): 543–557.

Youssef, Nadia H. 1974. *Women and Work in Developing Societies.* Westport, Conn.: Greenwood Press.

Population Factors in Development Economics

Kenneth E. Boulding

Virtually all the basic concepts of development economics originate with Adam Smith, especially in *An Inquiry into the Nature and Causes of the Wealth of Nations,* first published in 1776, and perhaps in the long run the most important event of that distinguished year. Almost 100 years before, Sir William Petty had observed the importance of the division of labor and specialization in making goods cheaper, but not until Adam Smith did the concept of economic development as an ongoing, total system emerge. This is perhaps because economic development itself, while noticeable, had been very slow and sporadic before the eighteenth century. After the development of agriculture and the production of a food surplus with which to feed the people who could build cities and form armies, and so create civilization, civilizations came and went, with each one not much more developed than the last and often followed by an age of decline. Even in the seventeenth and eighteenth centuries in Europe, debate waxed strong between those who looked back on a golden age from which the present had been in long retreat, and those who saw the beginnings of a great upsurge of human knowledge and productive capacity. Adam Smith's lifetime, however, especially in Britain, witnessed great improvements in agriculture, the beginnings of the industrial revolution, and a surge of elegance in the building of cities, like the New Town in Edinburgh. The population of Britain seems to have been actually declining in the 1730s. Then a noticeable rise in overall comfort and nutrition, largely a result of the improvements in agriculture, produced a great decline in infant mortality, especially between about 1740 and 1760, which led to a very substantial rise in population, and indeed is one reason why so much of the world now speaks English. The birth rate, however, did not decline until about 1880, and so we have about 120 years of what might be called the first population explosion of modern times. This explosive growth permitted—and indeed encouraged—a great deal of migration, especially to North America and Australasia, which in turn may have produced a general improvement in the standard of living in Britain, in spite of the population increase. It is not surprising, therefore, that Adam Smith was so much interested in the concept of improvement.

The first two sentences of *The Wealth of Nations* set the tone for the whole work:

> The annual labour of every nation is the fund which originally supplies it with all the necessaries and conveniences of life which it annually consumes, and which consist always either in the immediate produce of that labour, or in what is purchased with that produce from other nations.
>
> According therefore, as this produce, or what is purchased with it, bears a greater or smaller proportion to the number of those who are to consume it, the nation will be better or worse supplied with all the necessaries and conveniences for which it has occasion. (Smith, 1981 [1776]: 10)

There is some confusion here, which has a long history in subsequent economics, between stocks and flows, in that total wealth is identified with income and Smith's measure of the wealth of a nation is what today we call per capita real income.

Development, therefore, is essentially identified with increase in per capita real income. This idea has dominated economic thought for over 200 years. One can raise questions about it. I have argued for many years that the capital stock with which we are surrounded and from which we derive satisfaction and enjoyment is more significant in many ways than its production and consumption, which constitute income (Boulding, 1950: 135). I gain satisfaction from enjoying my house, driving my car, wearing my clothes; I gain very little satisfaction from the fact that my house, my car, and my clothes are wearing out and being consumed. One can perhaps justify taking income—that is, rates of production and consumption of goods—as a surrogate measure of wealth or riches. If goods have a fairly constant length of life, as measured by the interval between their production and consumption, the ratio of capital stock to income will be fairly constant. These considerations, however, are rarely noted today, and Smith's concepts still dominate the field.

Adam Smith goes on to say:

> But this proportion [that is, per capita real income] must in every nation be regulated by two different circumstances; first, by the skill, dexterity, and judgment with which its labour is generally applied; and, secondly, by the proportion between the number of those who are employed in useful labour, and that of those who are not so employed. [T]he abundance or scantiness of this supply must, in that particular situation, depend upon those two circumstances. (ibid., p. 10)

In other words, the average productivity of those employed determines the total product, which then has to be divided by the total number of people.

An increase in the percentage of the population employed will, of course, increase this ratio, but such an increase cannot go on for long. There are sharp limits to the proportion of the population in the potential labor force. A persistent, long-run increase in per capita incomes can only result from a persistent, long-run increase in the productivity of the employed, that is, the productive powers of labor, labor being defined as human activity devoted to production. The very title of Book I reads "Of the Causes of Improvement in the productive Powers of Labour, and of the Order according to which Its Produce is naturally distributed among the different Ranks of the People" (ibid., p. 13). This nails down the two major dimensions of economic development: the increase in the per capita product, and the way in which per capita product is distributed. Thus, we could have two nations with the same per capita product, but in one this is largely consumed by, say, 5 percent of the population, leaving 95 percent in starvation and misery, while in the other the product is widely distributed among the entire population. We would be strongly tempted to say that the second was more developed than the first. Smith suggests that the distribution among the different ranks of the people is "natural," that is, somewhat determinate. There is some evidence for this. The relative proportions of the population in the various "ranks" are another matter.

On the conditions for economic development

So much for "nature." Now let us examine "causes." Smith is clear that the rise in the productivity of labor, which is the major cause of development, is a result of what we might call a "positive-feedback process." In the first place, it is clear that the increase in the productivity of labor is the result of a learning process, which in turn is a result of the division of labor, or specialization. When we stay at one job we unquestionably increase our skill and dexterity, though only up to a certain point. More important is "judgment," which is essentially a specialization in the learning process itself. A very well-known passage is worth quoting at length:

> All the improvements in machinery, however, have by no means been the inventions of those who had occasion to use the machines. Many improvements have been made by the ingenuity of the makers of the machines, when to make them became the business of a peculiar trade; and some by that of those who are called philosophers or men of speculation, whose trade it is, not to do any thing, but to observe every thing; and who, upon that account, are often capable of combining together the powers of the most distant and dissimilar objects. In the progress of society, philosophy or speculation becomes, like every other employment, the principal or sole trade and occupation of a particular class of citizens. Like every other employment, too, it is subdivided into a great number of different branches, each of which affords occupation to a

> peculiar tribe or class of philosophers; and this subdivision of employment in philosophy, as well as in every other business, improves dexterity and saves time. (ibid., p. 21)

This is an astonishing insight at a time when modern science was in its infancy and applied science was still 100 years off. Economics, I have argued, is the second or third oldest of the sciences, dating from 1776. Even modern chemistry, after all, only really emerged with John Dalton in 1808.

The next question, of course, is what creates the division of labor and increases it? The answer comes through in Chapters II and III of Book I of *The Wealth of Nations.* It is the opportunities to exchange that permit the division of labor. There is no point in specialization if we cannot exchange our products for things we want that other specialists produce. Robinson Crusoe, after all, could not specialize, for he had no opportunities for trade, at least until Man Friday appeared. Both trade and productivity then develop in what today we might call a "double positive-feedback process": an increase in trade produces opportunities for further specialization, which increases productivity and production; the increase in production provides further opportunities for trade. Given favorable social conditions, this process can presumably continue until either the potential for increasing productivity is exhausted or the potential for expanding trade comes to an end.

One can distinguish at least five underlying conditions in society that help to determine the rate at which development may take place, and even whether this rate is positive, zero, or negative. The first is a political and social condition that Smith describes as "order and good government." This involves the widespread legitimation and security of property. For exchange to take place, there must be ownership of the articles exchanged, although this ownership may be corporate and governmental as well as private. Exchange cannot take place unless this ownership is recognized by all parties, and until it is relatively certain that the exchangeables involved are not threatened by theft, social disruption, or public seizure.

Another social consideration is what Adam Smith calls the "habit of subordination," which enables hierarchy to be developed and larger organizations to form. To this factor he attributes the success of the European invaders of America in displacing the culture of the indigenous populations, which were too individualistic to form large organizations and larger societies. It is somewhat ironic perhaps that Smith sees capitalism arising from an individualism strictly modified by hierarchy, social organization, and social identification. The collapse of "order and good government" or its absence may easily prevent the double feedback process that produces development and an expansion of trade and productivity.

Adam Smith was very much aware of the complexity and the heterogeneity of the development process, unlike some of his more macroeconomic successors. He saw not only that productivity would increase at very different rates in different occupations and industries, thus producing changes in the relative price structure, but he saw also that some of these occupations and industries—particularly transportation and agriculture—were much more significant than others from the point of view of overall development.

The second condition for economic development is improvement in transportation, which is particularly important because of its effect on the extent of the market. The extent of the market depends on how many people can participate in exchange; this is determined by people's proximity and the cost of transport between them. A diminution in the cost of transport, therefore, is fundamental to the development process, for it not only reduces economic distance between potential exchangers, but also permits the aggregation of people into larger towns and cities, again increasing the extent of the market. This is why, Smith argues, economic development in ancient civilization was contingent on water transportation, for instance, on rivers like the Nile, the Tigris and Euphrates, the Indus, the Ganges, and the great rivers of China. An interesting exception to this rule, which Smith does not mention, is the Inca and Aztec civilizations of the Americas, which developed routes of transportation on high, fairly open mountains. There is something perhaps corresponding to this in the empires of the Mongols. Forests indeed are the great enemy of cheap transportation; perhaps the main reason why the Mississippi valley did not produce an early civilization, as one might have expected, is that it was too densely forested, as the Amazon was, for trade to penetrate very far from the river itself.

The development of worldwide ocean transportation, which was well on its way in Smith's day, is what created the world economy. It would be instructive to draw a map (which could be done on a polar projection from a particular place) in which the distances between various locations were in proportion to the cost of transport, not to the global distances. It would be a very strange map. The oceans would collapse almost to a puddle, with the great seaports forming a single world city around it, and the hinterlands stretching out beyond the sea and river ports. Even in our own day, the container revolution in ocean-going transportation has spawned a remarkable expansion in world trade and may well have had much greater economic effects than some more dramatic technological changes.

A third significant condition for economic development is the increase in productivity in food production, especially, of course, in agriculture. Thus, Smith observes that

> when by the improvement and cultivation of land, the labour of one family can provide food for two, the labour of half the society becomes sufficient to provide food for the whole. The other half, therefore, or at least the greater part of them, can be employed in providing other things, or in satisfying the other wants and fancies of mankind. (ibid., p. 180)

He observes in the previous sentence that among savage and barbarous nations, 99 percent of the labor is needed to provide food and only 1 percent goes into "cloathing and lodging." This would certainly explain why such societies do not develop cities and record very little capital improvement.

All the classical economists—even as late as William Stanley Jevons (1970 [1911])—had what might be called a "food chain" theory of the economy, which goes back perhaps in the more extreme form to the Physiocrats and the "Tableaux Economique." Thus, the farmer produces "corn"—almost in those days a synonym for food—but grows more corn than the farmer and his family alone can eat. This results in a surplus. If this is fed to cattle it produces meat and milk, which improve human nutrition and perhaps enable the farmer to produce more food, another positive feedback. Food and leather "fed" to shoemakers produce shoes. Food and some implements "fed" to miners produce iron ore. Food and iron ore "fed" to a smelter produce iron. Food and iron "fed" to a blacksmith produce tools or, fed to a machinist, machines. Then the tools and machines "fed" back to the farmer produce more food, another positive feedback. This process has been much neglected in modern economics, although the Austrian economists are somewhat aware of it in their capital theory, in the concept of the "period of production." This hierarchy of the food chain, including raw materials and half-finished goods and machinery as economic "food," is something lost in Walrasian equations, in which all commodities have an equal status, and is not even explicit in Wassily Leontief's input–output analysis.

Curiously enough, one of the most striking historical examples of this food chain process was occurring in Adam Smith's lifetime, although he did not take very much notice of it. This was the so-called agricultural revolution in Britain in the early eighteenth century especially. This was partly the result of the enclosure movement, which created modern farms and permitted the development of the four-course rotation, such as wheat, turnips, barley, and clover in successive years, as against the medieval pattern of wheat, barley, and fallow. The medieval fallow fields were needed to get the weeds out, which could not be done in grain fields sowed broadside. Root crops could be planted in rows, so that the weeds could be gotten out while still producing a crop. Then the use of clover increased the fertility of the soil. The enclosure movement and the creation of the modern farm is an interesting example of a change in property institutions that, while it had considerable social costs in terms of displaced people, nevertheless permitted a large expansion in agricultural productivity, both in quantity and in quality. The root crops especially were mainly used for livestock feed, which permitted keeping more livestock through the winter and therefore permitted the improvement in livestock, which also improved human nutrition in protein production. This agricultural revolution created a marked diminution in infant mortality in Britain by the middle of the eighteenth century. The laborers released from agriculture by this increasing productivity and the great increase in the number of surviving children together provided the workers for the industrial revolution of the latter half of the eighteenth century.

An aspect of agricultural improvement, rather neglected even by the classical economists, is improvement in product per acre. This may not have been quite so striking in the eighteenth and nineteenth centuries, but it has been very important in the twentieth, with the development of high-yielding hybrids, and may be even more important in the twenty-first century with direct genetic manipulation. One trembles to think of the possible impact of a technology that will permit a family to grow all the food it needs on its own rooftop. Increased productivity per acre, of course, is important as an offset to the Ricardian nightmare of all surplus being gobbled up in rent with the population increase. The increase in product per acre, indeed, has been equivalent to an enormous expansion of land, which we used to think was so limited. This is important also in cities with the development of skyscrapers, and in air travel, which requires fewer roads, and so on. At the macro level, economists have paid surprisingly little attention to this phenomenon.

The food-chain theory leads easily to a fourth underlying condition for economic development, which is the demographic situation, particularly in terms of what checks the increase in population. Demography was a fledgling discipline at the time of Adam Smith, and data on population were scattered and woefully incomplete. Nevertheless, Smith has some acute observations about population dynamics, which formed a very important part of his general system. He observes, for instance, that both poverty and riches seem to discourage population increase for different reasons, so that it is mostly the middle classes that add to the population. Thus, in regard to riches, he says: "Luxury in the fair sex, while it enflames perhaps the passion for enjoyment, seems always to weaken, and frequently to destroy altogether, the powers of generation" (ibid., p. 97). Whereas, in regard to poverty, he observes: "It is not uncommon, I have been frequently told, in the Highlands of Scotland for a mother who has borne twenty children not to have two alive" (ibid.).

A long-run demographic distribution model implicit in these observations (although never clearly formulated) may have considerable significance for some societies. If the rich do not propagate, their numbers will decline and their per capita wealth in terms of net worth will increase unless they marry their daughters off to the rising middle class. The middle class may increase demographically, but as this is the saving class, especially saving for its children, its per capita net worth may even increase. The size of the poor population earning a mere subsistence wage remains fairly constant, a fundamental concept in classical economics, though a little ambiguous in Smith himself. In Thomas Malthus, of course, this becomes the famous "dismal theorem," that if the only check to the increasing population of the poor is misery, the population will increase until it is miserable enough to check the increase, like the Highland Scots of Adam Smith. This implies a perfectly elastic supply of labor at some subsistence level, above which the laboring population will increase, below which it will diminish. The classical economists, especially David Ricardo, recognized that this was a socially determined level rather than a physiological one, and indeed he argues that "The friends of humanity cannot but wish that in all countries the labouring classes should have a taste for comforts and enjoyments" (Ricardo, 1969 [1817]: 51).

Adam Smith, however, has moments of at least short-run optimism. Thus, he says, "The same cause, however, which raises the wages of labour, the increase of stock, tends to increase its productive powers, and to make a smaller quantity of labour produce a greater quantity of work (Smith, 1981: 104). ("Work" in Adam Smith means "the product of labor," as in the phrase "a work of art.") Smith also thinks that a rise in real wages, by improving the health and perhaps the ambition of the laborer, will make him work harder and thereby increase his productivity, thus producing more positive feedback. There is something realistic about Adam Smith's ambiguity on this subject. Historical examples abound of societies that have developed by increasing real wages in spite of a considerable expansion of the total population. It is an interesting question whether the "demographic transition" to a stationary or even to a declining population, by expanding per capita income, is not a result of both wage earners and the middle class rising to a "level of riches" at which luxury inhibits propagation.

A fifth condition of development in classical economics is the increase in "stock," or capital, as reflected in both the quantity and the value of physical assets, including buildings, machines, equipment, tools, all stocks of raw materials, half-finished goods, and finished goods, to which one should add money. Classical economists assumed almost without exception that the increase in productivity of the laborer, as measured by the quantity of goods he could produce, say, in an hour of work, was a result not only of an increase in "skill, dexterity, and judgement," but also an increase in the capital goods and equipment with which he worked. It is probably true that the idea of capital-saving improvements hardly ever occurred to the classical economists, perhaps because in their time such improvements were very rare. Today, of course, with the development of computers, the possibilities for solar cells, and both energy- and materials-saving improvements in the methods of production, capital-saving improvements are quite common, although they still have not received much attention from economists. With a few dollars today one can buy a small solar-powered calculator, the performance of which would have required rooms full of equipment costing thousands of dollars 40 years ago. Over the last 200 years there has been a noticeable reduction in the relative price of most raw materials as a result of great economies in their use, more than offsetting increased costs of mining and extraction. This dominance of know-how over "stuff," which Adam Smith dimly perceived, has only become a striking phenomenon since the time of the classical economists. They can hardly be blamed for not having noticed it, although many modern economists have scarcely been more perceptive.

If the accumulation of stock is necessary for development, an important question arises as to who accumulates it. The classical economists on the whole thought that the laboring class would be too poor to accumulate anything and, even if they became rich enough, would devote these riches to an increase in their numbers, which would soon reduce them again to the poverty and nonaccumulating level. Ricardo, especially, thought that it was only the capitalists of the middle class who would accumulate. The tastes of the landlords and the aristocrats were too expensive, and they would devote their income to fancy houses and servants, which Adam Smith thought, perhaps rightly, was unproductive and could even lead to the "Rake's Progress" depicted in William Hogarth's famous sketches, a "progress" from riches to poverty.

The whole question of the relation of the size and perhaps the composition of the capital stock to wages has a very curious and unsatisfactory history, but a theory of the "wages fund," for which Adam Smith has some rather confused responsibility, probably arose from the observation that in order to be an employer one had to possess money to pay wages. This money paid in wages, of course, was eventually returned to the employer when the product of the labor was finally sold. But this might take some time, so an employer had to have enough money to continue paying wages until the product of the labor of the initial week was sold. Hence arises the theory that the return to capital is a payment for "waiting," in Alfred Marshall's term, a better term perhaps than Nassau Senior's original concept of "abstinence." This view was reinforced by the observation that in agriculture there had to be enough accumulated food at the beginning of the growing season to feed the workers who produced the harvest at the end of the season.

Relying on the theory of equilibrium, when development is disequilibrium

Here we encounter the usual tangle over stocks and flows, a perennial confusion in economics. Real wages in income terms cannot exceed the flow of "wage goods" that the workers buy. If there is a fixed production of such goods, as there was in any one year when what the workers bought was mostly food, it was not wholly unrealistic to suppose that a rise in money wages would simply increase the price of the "corn" that the workers bought, leaving real wages unchanged. This is at least one of the origins of the famous "Iron Law of Wages" of the classical economists. In certain times and places it is not unrealistic. In a war economy, for instance, real wages cannot rise above what is produced in the civilian sector of the economy, allowing for some siphoning off by the rich. There are very important questions here related to the distributional aspects of development that are still by no means solved. The crude "wages fund" theory was discredited quite early by Henry Thornton. What replaced it, however—the marginal productivity theory of wages, originating with John Bates Clark in the 1890s—saw the labor market simply as an exchange of a quantity of money paid to the laborer in wages, in return for the value of the increase in the quantity of goods produced by the laborer's activities. This theory triumphed, but it completely neglected the capital aspect of the problem and led to disastrous misunderstandings of the nature of the labor market.

One very important element in development theory that is missing in classical economics is a consensus on what we have come to think of as the macroeconomic problems, especially those of inflation and unemployment and their impact on development. Adam Smith was interested in the history of inflation; indeed, he traced the price of wheat back several hundred years. He was also concerned about its measurement, although he did not have the device of index numbers, which was not developed until nearly 100 years later. So his solutions to the problem of how one allows, for instance, in long-term contracts for changes in the value of money were quite inadequate. He tried two measures: the labor-commanded measure, something like a labor clause instead of a "gold clause" in long-term contracts, which might read "I will pay you in the future so many times the dollar value of an hour of common labor"; and the "corn measure," which would read "I will pay you so many times the dollar value of a bushel of corn." Unfortunately, both common labor and corn fluctuate in their prices in ways that can diverge sharply from the general price level. The labor-commanded clause would have been very hard on debtors over the couple of hundred years since Smith, as the relative price of labor has risen. The corn clause would have been very hard on creditors, as the relative price of corn has fallen. Smith did not have very much to say, however, about the impact of inflation or deflation on development. This is not surprising, because on the whole he lived through a period of relative stability in price levels, despite great changes in relative prices.

Similarly, there is virtually no mention in *The Wealth of Nations* of unemployment in the modern sense, perhaps because it was not a very important phenomenon in the eighteenth century. The business cycle was not supposed to have started until about 1760 in Britain. Adam Smith is aware of fluctuations in the demand for labor, but thinks on the whole this should be taken care of by fluctuations in real wages, due, for instance, to the high price of food in years of bad harvests.

Until John Maynard Keynes, the theory of unemployment resided largely in an underworld of economic thought. The most famous exponent of the theory, of course, is Malthus, in his *Principles of Political Economy* (1964 [1817]) in which he posits the existence of a "general glut" of commodities that would produce unemployment, something Ricardo vehemently denied. In this context Keynes remarked, "If only Malthus, instead of Ricardo, had been the parent stem from which nineteenth-century economics proceeded, what a much wiser and richer place the world would be today!" (Keynes, 1972b [1933]: 100).

Karl Marx was also concerned about what he called the "reserve army of the unemployed" as an indicator of the failure of capitalism and a potential source of revolutionary fervor. But his account of the problem was so confusing that even his condenser and interpreter, Julian Borchardt, felt obliged to write a chapter of his own (Borchardt, 1932: 302–314) explaining the theory rather than rely on Marx's own words.

It is hard to think of any major improvement on Adam Smith's view of economic development until the Great Depression of the 1930s and Keynes. It is surprising that 150 years of very dramatic and striking development should have produced so little literature on the subject. The Marxists might object that Marx's dialectical materialism and his theory of history is an improvement on Smith. Non-Marxists might well regard this as a step backward. Marx, indeed, recognized that capitalism did produce economic development, but he thought that certain internal contradictions in the system would bring this development to an end, would create increasing unemployment, would create an "immiseration" of the working class. There are deep inconsistencies in Marx's thought here. He did think, like Adam Smith, that the accumulation of capital would lower profits and thereby cause unemployment, which would then lower wages. But how Marx reconciles an increase in the total product with a decline both in profits and in wages is ambiguous, as he does not even fall back on Ricardo's recourse to the landlord as the major beneficiary. Certainly his predictions about income distribution have been completely falsified by the history of the temperate zone, although there is some evidence of "immiseration" in the tropics. Even Smith observed that the wages of labor in Great Britain have been continually increasing since Henry VIII and that the profits of stock have been diminishing (Smith, 1981: 106). With some interruptions, this process continues to the present day. In the United States, for instance, the proportion of national income going to labor has increased from about 59 percent in 1929 to well over 70 percent today. On the other hand, the whole question of whether capitalism can survive a stationary state in which net investment is zero and per capita incomes do not increase, and conversely whether capitalism requires a developing economy for its survival, remains unresolved. It was never really faced by the classical economists, and it is certainly very confusing in Marx, where the anticipated demise of capitalism seems to come much more from political than from economic sources.

The long gap in development economics following Adam Smith can be explained perhaps only by the obsession of economists with equilibrium theory. This theory, too, perhaps originates with Smith, on whose theory of relative prices, again, not much improvement has been made. Smith and virtually all his successors have had two concepts of relative price theory: the theory of market price, which rests fundamentally on the assumption that over the short haul changes in the relative structure of market prices—the actual prices at which commodities are exchanged—are a function of the stocks of exchangeables in the market and of the preferences of the owners of these exchangeables; and an equilibrium set of market prices at which everybody in the market is willing to hold what is there to be held (Boulding, 1944: 55–63). If the actual market prices differ from this equilibrium set, some prices will be "too high," meaning that buyers are not as eager to buy as the sellers are to sell. This will bring down the price. Other prices will be "too low," meaning that buyers want to buy more than sellers want to sell, and this will raise the price. This is at least a useful way of looking at the phenomenon.

Then we recognize that commodities are produced and consumed and hence that the stocks in the hands of the market are continually changing. This leads to the concept of an equilibrium set of "normal," or, as Smith calls them, "natural" prices. This concept depends on the fact that the relative market prices determine a set of rewards for different occupations. For instance, if the market price of wheat exceeds the natural price, the producers of wheat will be unusually well rewarded. If the price of oats is below the natural price, the producers of oats are unusually badly rewarded. This also means, however, that some producers will stop growing oats and begin growing wheat. Similarly, consumers may increase their consumption of oats and diminish their consumption of wheat. As a result the stocks of wheat will fall and, with the same preferences, the market price will rise. Conversely, the stocks of oats will rise and the market price will fall. This, again, is a useful way of looking at things, even though, of course, it abstracts from such considerations as speculation, expectations, and so on. This equilibrium theory has passed almost unscathed from Adam Smith to the present day, suffering mathematization on the way, somewhat to its detriment, with oats and wheat turned into x and y.

Whether this obsession with equilibrium is related to an obsession with the stationary state is hard to say, but it is at least a hypothesis. Adam Smith certainly thought that development could not continue forever and that it would have to end in something like a stationary state. He saw history as a succession of progressive, stationary, and declining states, irregularly spaced. In a famous passage he says,

> It deserves to be remarked, perhaps, that it is in the progressive state, while the society is advancing to further acquisition, rather than when it has acquired its

> full complement of riches, that the condition of the labouring poor, of the great body of the people, seems to be the happiest and the most comfortable. It is hard in the stationary, and miserable in the declining state. The progressive state is in reality the cheerful and the hearty state to all the different orders of society. The stationary is dull; the declining, melancholy. (Smith, 1981: 99)

Perhaps the nineteenth century simply took the progressive state for granted, as even the stationary state seemed such a long way off. Indeed, John Stuart Mill, in his *Principles of Political Economy,* praises the stationary state: "The best state for human nature is that in which, while no one is poor, no one desires to be richer, nor has any reason to fear being thrust back by the efforts of others to push themselves forward" (Mill, 1965 [1848]). Keynes also has some praise for the stationary state in his essay on "The economic world of our grandchildren" (1972a [1931]).

New pathways in development economics

The mathematization of economics, which began seriously with Jevons and Leon Walras in the 1870s (Jevons, 1970 [1911]; Walras, 1954 [1871]), also perhaps diverted attention from development theory, which is less subject to elegant mathematization than is equilibrium theory. The new surge in development theory begins in earnest following World War II. In part this may be the result of the dissolution of Europe's colonial empires and the development of a "Third World" of independent but poor countries. In part the interest may come from the development of national income statistics, which began about 1929, and expanded to a world scale after World War II, enabling analysts to perceive more quantitatively which countries were developing and which were not, at least by rather crude and inaccurate measures.

From about the mid-1950s on, development literature virtually explodes. Perhaps four such explosions can be distinguished. One is on the left wing, somewhat to the left of center. A second might be described as the "mainline." The third is a more right-wing approach, emphasizing the importance of the free market, with an extreme position on supply-side economics, although I find it hard to take this one seriously. We might add a fourth approach, of a descriptive and statistical nature, that seeks to summarize what has actually been happening in different societies, with some emphasis on a comparative approach.

The left-wing approach begins perhaps with Paul Baran's *The Political Economy of Growth* (1957). There is a certain harking back here, of course, to Lenin's theory of imperialism as a necessary concomitant of capitalist expansion. Other contributors to this literature include Raúl Prebisch (1962), Andre Gunder Frank (1969), and Samir Amin (1972). Several themes run through this literature. One is the attribution of the failure to develop to unfavorable terms of trade imposed by the monopolistic power of the rich countries on the poor ones, a doctrine particularly associated with Prebisch. Another theme is the psychological dependency of the postcolonial world on its previous imperial masters, joined to a considerable pessimism about prospects for what might be called "indigenous revolution."

Even for non-Marxists like myself this literature cannot be lightly dismissed, simply because the conditions for successful capitalist development are not universally present and certainly need to be identified when they are absent. The situation of the so-called Third World, however, is immensely complex. I argue that there is no such thing as the Third World, that there is 3.01, 3.02, and so on, for every country and even every region is different. The fact that some postcolonial societies, like Singapore of the old British Empire, and Taiwan and even South Korea of the old Japanese Empire, have experienced fairly successful economic development in the last generation, and the even more remarkable success of Hong Kong, which is still officially a British colony, certainly indicate that colonialism and postcolonialism cover a great variety of cases, about which it is hard to generalize. The terms of international trade fluctuate so widely that they can hardly be reduced to a simple explanation of underdevelopment. The various psychological dependency theses have something to recommend them, but here again, the cases vary tremendously. Even within Latin America, Costa Rica is extraordinarily different from El Salvador. Mexico is a case by itself. Argentina, Uruguay, and Chile fell off the development bandwagon after World War II, whereas the postcolonial societies of Australia and New Zealand stayed on. The only safe conclusion that seems to be drawn from the left-wing critique is that it is very hard to generalize.

The mainline literature goes back to the late 1940s. The first sign of the revival of interest in economic development comes with what might be called "mechanical economic dynamics," using differential or difference equations. Paul Samuelson's *Foundations of Economic Analysis* (1947) was a pioneering work, as was Roy Harrod's *Toward a Dynamic Economics* (1948). Jean Fourastie's *The Causes of Wealth* (1951) opened up the subject on a broad scale. Gerald Meier and Robert Baldwin (1957) contributed *Economic Development: Theory, History, Policy.* Evsey Domar (1957), Nicholas Kaldor (1960), and Michal Kalecki (1954) followed suit. All of these authors tend to assume stable macroeconomic parameters for the economic system, often of a rather arbitrary nature. If these are limited enough, only one "best" path of development emerges, according to what Samuelson has called the "turnpike theorem." Otherwise, cycles of unemployment will develop. The Harrod–Domar type of theory assumes a constant relationship between the amount of investment and the capacity output of the economy, say, in the following year, with given consumption and government functions: a full-employment level of investment will create an additional capacity the next year, which will necessitate a still larger amount of investment to guarantee full employment. The fact that development is usually characterized by fluctuations, often very irregular, suggests that these "turnpikes" are very rarely traveled and that while these theories may be useful as indicating certain limiting conditions of development, they throw very little light on the actual process. Allen Kneese's essay in the present volume points to some excellent criticisms of this type of theory.

The barrenness of mainline development economics goes back to the neoclassical concept of a production function, in which production is regarded as a function primarily of labor and capital, perhaps occasionally of land. This is what I have called the "cookbook" theory of production—we mix land, labor, and capital in given proportions and out come potatoes. Statistical investigations, of course, have revealed that this relationship is very incomplete, if it can be measured at all, the incomplete factor, of course, being what Adam Smith knew about all along—human knowledge or know-how. I have argued myself that production always begins with a genetic factor of know-how, whether this resides in the genes of the fertilized egg or in an inventor's mind (Boulding, 1978). Production, then, is essentially the process by which the genotype turns into the phenotype: how the egg becomes a chicken, how a plan becomes a house. To effect this transformation, the genotype has to control energy in certain specific forms in order to select, transport, and transform materials into the structure of the phenotype. This genetic factor is the missing component of the mainline production function.

There is, furthermore, what might be called a "fallacy of taxonomy" in the neoclassical production function. Both labor and capital are extremely heterogeneous aggregates, labor perhaps a little less so. Capital, especially, in real terms is an aggregate of buildings, machines, tools, and raw materials. And, of course, we should also include the labor force itself. Production is part of the ecosystem of the world and cannot be understood except as a system of the interaction of a great variety of species. Neoclassical production theory is analogous to what ecological theory would be if we classified all the objects in an ecosystem by their color. Trying to understand the economic system as the alchemists tried to understand the chemical system, in terms of earth, air, fire, and water, can only be described as "economic alchemy."

This profound weakness of the mainline theory of production emerges somewhat in the so-called Cambridge capital controversy between Cambridge, England, and Cambridge, Massachusetts, which there is not time to go into here, but in which the "winner" in my view was Joan Robinson of Cambridge, England, who suggested almost indelicately that capital might be measured in "leets," this being steel spelled backwards (Boulding, forthcoming). This is not to deny, of course, that the value of the total stock of valuable artifacts can be expressed in terms of a monetary unit. But then this goes for human capital as well. The monetary value of all capital is mixed up in very complex ways with rates of return and rates of time discounting. There is a host of unresolved problems here, certainly going back to Bohm-Bawerk and the Austrian economists.

This is not to argue that there is no such thing as wages, profit, and rent. The different forms of capital—human, material, land, even financial—emerge as factors of distribution. Furthermore, there is substitution among these different forms of capital, which is not unrelated to relative price structures. The real problem is that production is affected profoundly by what might be called "limiting factors," which limit the realization of the potential implied in some genetic factor. The lack of energy in the right forms, materials in the right forms, space, and time, all may operate as limiting factors. Where there are limiting factors it is the *most* limiting one that is significant. If we are climbing a mountain it is the first cliff we come to that stops us. In the biosphere, for instance, energy is probably the most limiting factor in the tundra; water is the limiting factor in the desert. Even the absence of a trace element might prevent the growth of certain plants. How we identify these limiting factors in the process of development has been very little explored. Actually, political uncertainty is sometimes a more important limiting factor than any of the conventional factors of production. I suspect we will look back on this period of mainline economics as productive of very little.

As far as the theory of production goes, John Maynard Keynes does not vary much from the mainline. Nevertheless, he did make an important contribution to the theory of development, chiefly in *A Treatise on Money* (1930), by pointing out the impact of inflation and deflation, particularly on the distribution of income as between profit and other forms of income. Development results from new ideas, but new ideas do not emerge if their realization in the form of human artifacts and organizations is not profitable. In a capitalist system this means that the expenditure in realizing these artifacts and organizations must bear a positive rate of return. Under the communist system, of course, it means that their realization must be profitable to some bureaucrat or planner in terms of prestige or promotion, which may be even more difficult to guarantee. If the rate of profit is negative, as it was in the United States in 1932–33, it is extremely unlikely that any innovations will be realized. Keynes saw in what he called the "widow's cruse" theory that the proportion of national income going to profit depended in part, at least, on the willingness of profit receivers to buy household goods that were being produced. This I have called the "K Theory," which goes back to Keynes, Kaldor, and Kalecki (whose famous remark, apparently in the Cambridge oral tradition, was that "capitalists get what they spend, workers spend what they get") (see also Boulding, 1985: 4–10). It certainly seems quite impossible to explain the disappearance of profit in 1932–33 in terms of conventional production function theory. This would suppose that capital suddenly became fantastically plentiful and labor extremely scarce.

Keynes pointed out that deflation tended to destroy profits, which got gobbled up by interest increasing in real terms, whereas inflation tended to expand profits. Profit arises fundamentally from buying something at one time and selling it, or its product, later for more than its original cost. If all prices are rising, this is much easier to do than if all prices are falling. Thus, Keynes attributed the extraordinary explosion of the European economy and culture after Columbus to inflation due to American gold and silver, and attributed the decay of ancient empires to deflation following a decline in the quantities of metallic money. Now, of course, money has been liberated from metals and has become indefinitely expandable, so we have to worry much more about inflation than deflation. Inflation, when it gets out of hand, can also be very destructive, as it makes all economic calculations extremely difficult. But even hyperinflation, as in Hungary in 1946, may assist the formation of real capital.

Somewhat on the right side of the mainline we have Walter Rostow (1971), who tries to put economic development in terms of "stages," an idea that really goes back to Adam Smith, and that has something to recommend it as a simplification of some extremely complex processes, but it can easily be misleading if taken too literally. The Chicago School, whose principal mentor is Milton Friedman, with its almost unqualified enthusiasm for the free market, has not done much theoretically in the development field, although it has not hesitated to give advice, for instance, in Chile, which has not been too beneficial.

A contribution which is hard to classify is that of the anti-Malthusians, among whom Julian Simon (1981) is the most spectacular example of "outrageous optimism." It is valid to recognize that the "ultimate resource" is the human mind and its learning capacity. Nevertheless, the optimists tend to assume that this resource is without limits, and this seems too optimistic. Simon argues that every increase in population will increase the number of Einsteins and so increase the ultimate resource. But there must be some point in population growth at which we reach standing room only on Earth. On the other hand, we cannot rule out the possibility of humans going into the solar system with self-reproducing space colonies, mining the asteroids, developing nanotechnology, which might use protein-like substances to build airplanes out of diamonds, and other preposterous notions. All this may be science fiction, but still it is sometimes the poets and the science fiction writers who are the best guides to the future.

Finally, there has been a steady volume of descriptive and statistical work. The first is the work of Gunnar Myrdal (e.g., 1968), which certainly added to our information if not always to our understanding. In this connection the reports of the World Bank are an outstanding source of valuable information. An expanding data base that recognizes the enormous variety of the world, even though at times it may be overwhelming, is at least a platform on which future improvements and understanding can be built.

If any consensus emerges from the voluminous literature on economic development, it is that economics is not enough. Development is a process involving the dynamics of whole societies. The conditions that encourage or discourage development are often found in the political culture, the educational culture, the family culture, the communications culture, and so on. Development perhaps is the outstanding example of where economists need to go beyond economics.

References

Amin, Samir. 1972. "Underdevelopment and dependence in Black Africa," *Journal of Peace Research* 2.

Baran, Paul A. 1957. *The Political Economy of Growth.* New York: Monthly Review Press.

Borchardt, Julian. 1932. "The theory of crises," in Karl Marx, *Capital, the Communist Manifesto, and Other Writings,* ed. Max Eastman. New York: Random House/Modern Library.

Boulding, Kenneth E. 1944. "A liquidity preference theory of market prices," *Economica,* NS 11, no. 42 (May). Reprinted in Kenneth E. Boulding, *Collected Papers,* Vol. 1. Boulder: Colorado Associated University Press, 1971.

———. 1950. *A Reconstruction of Economics.* New York: Wiley.

———. 1978. *Ecodynamics: A New Theory of Societal Evolution.* Beverly Hills, Calif.: Sage Publications.

———. 1985. "Puzzles over distribution," *Challenge* 28, no. 5 (November/December).

———. Forthcoming. "A personal note on Joan Robinson," in *Joan Robinson and Modern Economic Theory,* ed. George R. Feiwel. London: Macmillan.

Domar, Evsey. 1957. *Essays in the Theory of Economic Growth.* New York: Oxford University Press.

Fourastie, Jean. 1960 [1951]. *The Causes of Wealth,* trans. and ed. by Theodore Caplow. Glencoe, Ill.: Free Press.

Frank, Andre Gunder. 1969. *Latin America: Underdevelopment or Revolution?* New York: Monthly Review Press.

Harrod, Roy. 1948. *Toward a Dynamic Economics.* New York: Macmillan.

Jevons, William S. 1970 [1911]. *The Theory of Political Economy,* 4th ed. Harmondsworth, England: Penguin/Pelican Classics.

Kaldor, Nicholas. 1960. *Essays on Value and Distribution.* New York: Free Press.

Kalecki, Michal. 1954. *Theory of Dynamic Economics: An Essay on Cyclical and Long-Run Changes in Capitalist Economy.* New York: Rinehart.

Keynes, John M. 1930. *A Treatise on Money.* London: Macmillan.

———. 1972a [1931]. "The economic world of our grandchildren," in *Essays in Persuasion.* New York: St. Martin's Press, for the Royal Economic Society.

———. 1972b [1933]. *Essays in Biography.* New York: St. Martin's Press, for the Royal Economic Society.

Malthus, Thomas R. 1964 [1820]. *Principles of Political Economy.* New York: Augustus M. Kelley.

Meier, Gerald M., and Robert E. Baldwin. 1957. *Economic Development: Theory, History, Policy.* New York: Wiley.

Mill, John Stuart. 1965 [1848]. *Principles of Political Economy,* ed. J. M. Robson. 2 vols. Toronto: University of Toronto Press.

Myrdal, Gunnar. 1968. *Asian Drama: An Inquiry into the Poverty of Nations,* 3 vols. New York: Twentieth Century Fund and Pantheon Books.

Prebisch, Raúl. 1962. "The economic development of Latin America and its principal problems," *Economic Bulletin for Latin America* 7, no. 1 (February).

Ricardo, David. 1969 [1817]. *The Principles of Political Economy and Taxation.* London and New York: Everyman's Library.

Rostow, Walter W. 1971. *The Stages of Economic Growth: A Non-Communist Manifesto,* 2nd ed. London: Cambridge University Press.

Samuelson, Paul. 1947. *Foundations of Economic Analysis.* Cambridge, Mass.: Harvard University Press.

Simon, Julian. 1981. *The Ultimate Resource.* Princeton, N.J.: Princeton University Press.

Smith, Adam. 1981 [1776]. *An Inquiry into the Nature and Causes of the Wealth of Nations,* Book I. Indianapolis: Liberty Press/Liberty Classics.

Walras, Leon. 1954 [1871]. *Elements of Pure Economics,* 4th ed., trans. by W. Jaffe. Homewood, Ill.: Irwin. Reprinted, Fairfield, N.J.: Augustus M. Kelley, 1977.

The Economics of Natural Resources

Allen V. Kneese

Economists have studied natural resources from the earliest days of the profession and for good reason. Resources are seen as the basis for national prosperity, power, and wealth. For example, the ability to harness energy resources in new ways is recognized as perhaps the major factor underlying the industrial revolution. Even more fundamental, food supplies depend on forests, fisheries, and agricultural land.

Yet only relatively recently have broad theories been developed specific to natural resources and energy economics. Previously, examination of these fields relied upon the general economic theories used to analyze other commodities. Now, however, economists recognize that certain special characteristics of natural resources require theories that account explicitly for these characteristics.

Only in the last generation have agricultural land, forests, and fisheries been perceived and described as renewable resources. Of course, this does not imply unconditional renewal. Such resources are self-renewing at a limited rate, which may itself depend on the size of the stock in existence at any given time and on the extent and nature of human intervention into the stock dynamics. Regardless, *renewable resources* is an apt and useful term.

In contrast, minerals and many energy commodities now are seen as depletable or nonrenewable resources—resources for which only a limited, concentrated stock exists for allocation over all time. For these resources, a central issue involves when they should be extracted and used. Using a given portion of a stock at one time precludes the option of using that portion at another time.

Even more recently have the environmental resources—air, water, open space—also been seen as renewable or, in some cases, depletable resources. The image of environmental resources, fisheries, and wild animal stocks as common property resources owned by everyone and hence by no one has played an enormous role in economic reasoning about these resources in recent decades. Furthermore, economists systematically have incorporated concepts of materials balance into theories of the flow of physical materials from the natural environment, through the economy, and back into the natural environment. And only since the early 1970s have energy resources been given major attention as a matter for theorizing, empirical testing, and policymaking.

Thus, there now exists a set of concepts that unite the field of natural resource economics. While these concepts also are finding application in other branches of economics, their formalization has been motivated by the need to better understand natural resource issues.

Economics may be necessary to understand the use and abuse of natural resources, but it is not sufficient. Indeed, most important energy and natural resource issues are inherently interdisciplinary, requiring integration of information from some combination of physics, engineering, chemistry, biology, ecology, political science, and law.

Current theories reflect this interdisciplinary reality. Materials balance concepts from physics now are fundamental to economic theories of the environment. Population dynamics concepts from biology and ecology are intertwined with economic concepts in renewable resources theories. Thermodynamic concepts and concepts of energy conservation are basic to theoretical work on natural resources.

Resource economics: The state of the art

The study of resource economics thus has required and motivated researchers to reach out beyond their own disciplines and to integrate ideas from other fields. In some of the most recent work this has extended, at least in an experimental manner, to such fields as formal ethical theory and concepts from information theory.

I address these ideas in the second part of this essay, which deals with frontier issues in the field. In that section I hope to show that the era of theory building is not over in resource economics, that in fact the field is in a considerable state of ferment.

In the first part of this essay I discuss what I see as a half dozen of the main themes in the received body of resource and environmental economics. The underlying problem that animates all of them is a concern with resource scarcity. Indeed, all of economics is concerned with scarcity, for in a world without scarcity (of labor, capital, information, natural resources) there is no economic problem. The problem of scarcity of natural resources may be exacerbated by rapid population growth. Let us start therefore with a classical statement of the problem of scarce natural resources.

1 Diminishing returns and resource scarcity: The Malthusian debate

Thomas Malthus could be viewed as the first natural resource economist, even though he is most widely known for his work on population. In 1798, he published his *Essay on Population,* a clear and forceful version of the seminal idea of diminishing returns to increased effort in the presence of a scarce resource. The scarce resource, in his view, was the stock of agricultural land, which he took to be absolutely limited. (David Ricardo later built a theory of scarcity on the assumption that land was not absolutely limited but progressively declined in quality as more of it was exploited.)

Harold Barnett and Chandler Morse (1963) succinctly state the basic Malthusian proposition:

> Malthus' famous *Essay on Population* may be credited with having widely propagated the belief that natural resource scarcity impairs economic growth. His doctrine is based on presumed natural law. That natural resources are limited and population multiplies continuously, subject to a biological restriction, are taken as nature-given facts. In the absence of social preventive checks, population increases to the limits of subsistence. The limits of nature constitute scarcity. The dynamic tendency of population to press continually to the borders of subsistence is the driving force. The incompatibility of a finite amount of agricultural land with provision of subsistence to a continually increasing population entails an eventual decline in output per capita and cessation of growth. This is the economic scarcity effect. (p. 52)

The idea of diminishing returns to effort expended upon the land became generally accepted in economics. The concept was accepted for generations as intuitively obvious. Perhaps the most famous English economist of the late nineteenth and early twentieth century, Alfred Marshall (1920), wrote:

> . . . our law [of diminishing returns] states that sooner or later (it being always assumed that there is meanwhile no change in the arts of cultivation) a point will be reached after which all further doses will obtain a less proportionate return than the preceding doses. (p. 153)

But by the middle of the twentieth century, it became clear that a great deal of growth in fact had occurred in the developed world without an apparent diminishing return to effort. Part of this growth was simple expansion as new geographic regions were occupied and developed and labor and capital were applied to them. But it also was apparent that the "arts of cultivation" or, more generally, technological progress in man's ability to find and exploit resources had much to do with it. In 1963, Barnett and Morse's

Scarcity and Growth was published, to less notice than it merited. In this now classic work, the authors explored the importance of technological change and resource substitution in combating resource scarcity. They also reported an empirical test to determine whether real resource costs have risen over the long term, which would indicate scarcity in an economic sense. Their methods and data need not detain us here, but the authors concluded:

> Our empirical test has not supported the hypothesis—let us call it the "strong hypothesis"—that economic scarcity of natural resources, as measured by the trend of real cost of extractive output, will increase over time in a growing economy. Observing the extractive sector in the United States from 1870 to 1957, we have found that the trend in the unit cost of extractive goods as a whole has been down—not up. (p. 199)

A later extension of the time series confirms the conclusion (Barnett, 1979, p. 175).

Thus, one main theme in resource economics involves the question of whether resources are becoming more scarce. Almost two centuries ago, Malthus and others thought such increasing scarcity to be imminent and obvious. But so far, in an economic sense (rising real cost of resources), this scarcity is not apparent. Whether one believes it will become so in the future depends heavily on whether one views the world through the eyes of a technological optimist or a technological pessimist. But in the very long run, as I point out in the Frontiers section, even technological optimists must contemplate profound changes in the way natural resources are used.

2 Optimal depletion

As suggested, the economic theory of natural resource use commonly distinguishes between depletable or exhaustible resources and nondepletable or renewable resources. But the distinction is not always clear. A renewable resource can be exhausted, as with the extinction of a species. Indeed, Hans Landsberg has argued that when time, space, quality, and considerations of reversibility are taken into account, few if any resources are inexhaustible (Landsberg, 1983). But the distinction has played a large role in economic theorizing concerning natural resources, and I will adhere to it, at least for now.

In the late nineteenth century, the problem of resource depletion came to the attention of economists in a somewhat different context than it had to Malthus, as Britain, France, Germany, and Russia competed ever more strenuously to establish colonies and spheres of influence. In considerable measure, colonialism sought to gain control over resources seen to be inherently scarce. The question then raised by economists was: Is there an optimal depletion path for an exhaustible resource? The models developed in this field of study were, and are, "macro" in the sense that typically it is assumed that there is a single undifferentiated resource stock (perhaps of varying quality) for an entire economy. Alternatively, it may be assumed that there is a single extractive industry composed entirely of identical competitive firms.

In the first reasonably widely known article on the economics of exhaustible resources, L. C. Gray (1914), using the graphical methods characteristic of the time, recognized that a depletable resource was different from an ordinary good in that it is limited in total quantity and is not producible. As we have seen, one outcome of this point is that a unit of such a resource used today leaves a unit less of it to use tomorrow. In other words, using it today involves not only the cost of contemporary extraction but also an additional cost—that of not having it available for use in the future. This additional opportunity cost is referred to variously in the literature, perhaps most commonly as a user cost. The practical result of defining such a cost is that unlike a producible resource, for which the efficiency condition is that price equal incremental production cost, the condition for an exhaustible resource is that price equal incremental production cost plus user cost. But how should user cost vary over time? Gray perceived that the answer hinged, in a key way, on the interest rate or, equivalently, on the rate of discount. He anticipated a general result for the simplest case. Given a well-defined quantity of the exhaustible resource, assuming extraction costs do not rise with increased extraction, and assuming demand continues until exhaustion, user cost must rise over time at the rate of interest.

To see this, consider the following situation. If user cost—the difference between incremental production cost and price—rises less than the rate of interest in period two, it would have paid to increase extraction in period one and to invest the additional proceeds at the market rate of interest. Conversely, if user cost promised to rise at a rate higher than the rate of interest, it would pay to reduce production in the present period and to borrow money at the rate of interest to increase production in the second period. Equilibrium occurs when the two rates are equal.

For this extraordinarily simple example, intuition seems adequate to derive the answer. But more realistic cases require more powerful methods. For example, what happens when extraction costs increase as the resource is depleted and the quality of the remaining stock declines? The method of calculus of variations was applied to this type of question by Harold Hotelling (1931) in a classic article. The problem of optimal depletion addressed by Hotelling is one of a class of optimization problems in which the quest is not for a number (scalar) but for an optimal path (function) through time or across space. Hotelling's approach and results were relatively neglected until recently, probably because the mathematics were difficult and most economics curricula did not include much mathematical training for at least a generation after his article appeared. His work and most subsequent work assumed no technological change.

Economists revived interest in the matter of optimal depletion theory in the 1960s, and this interest greatly accelerated in the 1970s. Most newer work addresses the "optimal-path" problem using contemporary mathematical (optimal control) methods. A key question in the newer work is how to handle technological change. I will return to this subject in the section on Frontiers.

3 How quickly to use a renewable resource

Living natural resources experience a life cycle. In some cases, as with most field crops, this cycle is annual and not much under the control of man. With others, like fish or, particularly, forests, the life span is longer and the stock is manageable through the scheduling of harvest. In the classic example of when to cut a standing forest, the manager faces conflicting choices. If the forest is not mature and still growing, he can wait another year and produce more lumber from a given stand. But if he does this he will forgo the interest he could have earned on the income he would receive if he cut now. Moreover, he would forgo interest on all earnings from future cuttings that would be similarly delayed if harvesting is done in a succession of cycles of equal length.

The problem is, given that the forest tends to grow more slowly as it ages, when is the optimum time to cut if one wishes to maximize the present value (discounted future income) from managing the forest? In a seminal 1849 paper, Martin Faustmann derived the solution for a simple situation in which the forest is used exclusively for timber production, and with prices, costs, the growth function, and the interest rate known and unchanging over time. The rigorous derivation requires the use of calculus. But if we simplify the problem further by concentrating on a single harvest and neglect all costs and gains that may occur in the future as a result of the harvest decision, the solution becomes intuitive. Again, as in the case of optimal depletion, the solution depends in a pivotal way on the interest rate.

Under the circumstances postulated, the manager should harvest at the time (year) at which the additional gain from delay—the value of additional timber growth—exactly equals the interest he could earn on the money he gets for harvesting now, minus harvesting costs. The period from the start of regeneration of a harvested forest to another harvest is known as the rotation period. When future forgone interest is considered, the solution indicates a slightly shorter rotation time.

Over the years, the Faustmann solution has, until quite recently, stood fast along with several published interpretations and extensions (Gaffney, 1957; Samuelson, 1979). For example, in analyzing the Faustmann solution vis-à-vis the maximum sustained yield criterion beloved of foresters, Paul Samuelson defined maximum sustained yield as based on the assumption of an even flow of harvest aimed at producing the greatest average flow of value per year. He showed that such a policy results in the selection of longer rotation periods than the economically optimum policy and amounts to ignoring the interest rate.

Despite its long tenure, the Faustmann solution has only very limited relevance to the conditions under which multiple-use forestry management is conducted by public agencies in the United States. One of the main reasons is that the managers of these lands must, in addition to considering timber harvests, consider the various nonmarket amenity services such as recreation, water flow, and wildlife that are influenced by alterations in the standing stocks of timber. When these are considered, the problem becomes immensely more complicated.

Michael Bowes and John Krutilla (1985) have recently addressed the problem of multiple use. Their methodology, which involves a rather advanced mathematical technique known as dynamic programming, produces conclusions that are interesting, if somewhat disillusioning, in the light of Faustmann's simple and straightforward outcome:

> The general multiple use harvesting policy is seen to be complex. No simple rule of thumb is likely to describe the harvest. We see that sometimes younger stands are harvested, leaving older ones uncut. We may choose to briefly delay regeneration. We rarely cut a particular stand at the same age twice in succession during the initial periods. The forest areas may be managed with some areas set aside for specialized purposes—old growth or clearing for wildlife. We may choose to specialize over time with the land producing high timber yields in some periods and high recreation benefits in others. Even flow policies are not inherently desirable long-run goals. The optimal harvest age is unlikely to be at the age of maximum sustained yield. Indeed, long even flow rotations, far from being the desirable compromise policy for multiple use management, may simply provide both uneconomic timber and a poor balance of age classes for nontimber use. Perhaps most importantly we see, from these examples, that the harvesting decision can be extremely sensitive to factors about which we have little empirical knowledge. (p. 566)

4 Models of economic growth and natural resources

The development of economic growth models is among the more significant accomplishments by economists, including some resource economists, since

World War II. These models are "aggregative" in the sense that they deal with total measures of such variables as labor, capital, income, saving, investment, and (sometimes) resource depletion for entire national economies.

Some early versions of aggregative growth models are often referred to as Keynesian because a number of the seminal ideas underlying them stem from J. M. Keynes's great work, *The General Theory of Employment, Interest, and Money.* Keynes himself did not advance a formal model of economic growth, but basic ideas of the early aggregative growth models, like the "multiplier" and the "accelerator," stemmed from his thought.

The first generation of such models are usually referred to as Harrod–Domar models.[1] They were based on what Lawrence Klein (1962) has called "the great ratios of economics," including the savings–income ratio (propensity to save) and the capital–output ratio (acceleration principle).

It is not my intent to review these early efforts in detail, but merely to give the reader unfamiliar with them an impression of their nature. A basic proposition of the Harrod–Domar models is that a change in the rate of investment flow will have two effects. On the one hand, it will affect aggregate demand through its effect on national income (the multiplier effect); on the other hand, it will affect the productive capacity of the economy (the acceleration effect).

In this type of model, equilibrium is defined as a situation in which investment stimulates aggregate demand just enough to use up the potential capacity it generates. In other words, generated demand must equal productive capacity and vice versa. The basic question for this type of model is the following: Is there a time path of investment that will satisfy this equilibrium requirement, and, if so, what is it? The basic result of the Harrod–Domar models is proof that such time paths do exist and can be defined for various capacity–capital ratios and marginal propensities to save.

These early, highly simplified models could be criticized on a number of grounds. One is that they do not take into account the time lags—for example, between investment and capacity expansion—that characterize the real world and that may give rise to cyclical phenomena. One line of further development, therefore, was to build models containing explicit time lags and employing difference equation techniques for their solution.

Another line of early criticism pertained to the extremely simple form of the production function (that is, the mathematical function relating outputs to inputs) embodied in the model, which simply posits production capacity to be proportional to invested capital. One result of this simplistic assumption is an inherent instability in the behavior of the Harrod–Domar models. To avoid either surpluses or shortages of productive capacity, investment growth must be carefully guided along a "razor's edge."

In later work, Robert Solow (1956) showed that the razor's edge result is an artifact of the particularly simple (and unrealistic) form of the production function in Harrod–Domar models. Because output in the model is stated as a function of capital alone, it is implicitly assumed that labor is combined with capital in a fixed proportion. Solow analyzed a growth model in which labor and capital can be combined in varying proportions. Thus, in general form his production function is

$$\pi = f(K, L)$$

where π is aggregate output, K is the capital stock, and L is the labor force. Solow showed that for a linearly homogenous production function (in which an increment of a fixed set of inputs always yields the same increment in output regardless of the scale of output) containing both labor and capital, a growth pattern of investment could result that represents an equilibrium with inherent stability properties. For present purposes, it is important to note that natural resources played no role in the Harrod–Domar models.

The traditional economic view, as exemplified by the Harrod–Domar models (and their relatives and offspring), and building on the much older concept of a production function, attributes output to "factors of production," notably labor and capital. Resource flows are not normally regarded as essential factors of production. Yet, this seems to flagrantly contradict the fact that the economic system could not function for a minute without a large flow of available energy (essergy)[2] and materials.

Some economists have faced this issue and offered a rebuttal of sorts. They argue that one can suppose without major error that resources are, in effect, infinitely substitutable by labor and/or capital. This assumption is, in fact, implied by the choice of two favorite forms (Cobb–Douglas and constant elasticity of substitution—CES) of production functions. Moreover, an important attribute of the assumed free market is that impending scarcity "casts a shadow," so to speak, in the form of rising prices. This, in turn, automatically triggers technological substitution of capital—or of other resources—for the scarce resource on the supply side and the altered consumption patterns on the demand side. Increased supply, coupled with decreased demand, brings supply and demand back into balance, and the market clears. Thus, actual shortages never occur in a perfectly functioning free market, provided the elasticity of substitution between reproducible capital and exhaustible resources is sufficiently large. It follows, incidentally, that in the received paradigm, economic growth can, in principle, continue indefinitely without resource constraints. Certainly there are many well-documented historical examples of technological substitutions that have "come to the rescue" in the above sense. Moreover, plausible nonscarce substitutes for most—if not all—so-called scarce resources can be identified by any competent technologist. (For instance, see the well-known article "The age of substitutability," by H. E. Goeller and Alvin Weinberg, 1976).

But the standard view of the resource situation noted above is not shared by all economists. For instance, it has been noted by Robert Ayres (1978) and others that substitution of capital for scarce resources has physical limits if scarce resources (either mass or energy) must be embodied in the capital itself. They show that if energy is embodied in capital, the first law of thermodynamics—conservation of mass/energy—precludes boundless economic growth unless a limitless supply of energy (essergy) is available. On the other hand, if the production function is constrained by the availability of some scarce material species, even constant consumption is impossible unless the critical scarce materials can be recovered and recycled with 100 percent efficiency either from waste or from the Earth's crust. The former possibility appears to be ruled out by the second (entropy) law of thermodynamics. Indeed, it is on this basis that Nicholas Georgescu-Roegen (1979a and b) denies even the possibility of a steady-state economy in the long run, still less a perpetually growing one. These considerations take us to the boundaries of our understanding of relationships between scarce resources and economic growth.

I will discuss these issues further in the section on Frontiers. But before doing so, I will address two more main themes. One is the emergence of environmental economics, as a part of natural resource economics, and its relation to classical welfare theory. The second is the application of an applied economics technique, benefit–cost analysis, to resource and environmental issues.

5 Economic welfare and the emergence of environmental economics

Coincident with the rise of the modern national state there arose a body of doctrine called mercantilism, which held that money was a store of wealth and that the overriding object of a state was to earn money abroad by importing as little as possible. The mercantilists sought to serve the purposes of monarchies, which in turn sought the political and economic supremacy of their nation.

In the eighteenth, nineteenth, and twentieth centuries, however, especially in Britain, France, the Scandinavian countries, and the United States, a body of economic doctrine arose that called into question the main premises of mercantilism. Moreover, this body of thought has displayed an enduring fascination with market processes. The result is an elaborate structure of theory that explains and evaluates the functioning of market processes under highly idealized conditions. Today, therefore, when economists speak of the market, they usually have a particular intellectual construct in mind—not the corner grocery store or even the stock exchange. This conceptual, or in recent decades, mathematical, model is the product of an evolutionary process going back at least as far as Adam Smith's *Wealth of Nations*, which was published at the close of the eighteenth century.

The model derived from the observation of a curious phenomenon. Economic activities such as farming, mining, industrial production, selling, and finance were unplanned and, on the surface at least, apparently entirely uncoordinated. Yet, in the end there seemed to be order in the results (the often-used modern illustration of this rather amazing situation is that the right number of cartons of milk wind up in the right number of households in New York every day, yet the whole process starts with the conception of a calf, perhaps in Wisconsin). Adam Smith saw clearly that prices—the powerful signaling and incentive (information) forces generated by private exchange in markets—were at the core of a process that, through the decisions of many independent economic units, transformed resources into products and distributed them to consumers: hence, his famous reference to "the invisible hand." Clearly, in spite of occasional spectacular failure, markets do display an orderly and directed production process. But economists also have been very interested to discover whether this order was purely orderly or whether it might have other desirable or normative properties as well.

Welfare economics, which has nothing to do with welfare programs in the ordinary sense, concerns itself with such questions. Its practitioners have found that the results of an ideal market process are not only efficient but also desirable if a basic value judgment is accepted and if the market-exchange economy has certain structural characteristics.

The value judgment is that the personal wants of the individuals in a society should guide the use of society's resources. This is also the premise at the root of Anglo-American political theory.

The three structural characteristics are that:

1 All markets are competitive: no particular firm or individual can affect any market price significantly by decreasing or increasing the supply of goods and services offered. In this sense, all participants in the market-exchange process must be small units. A good example is an individual grain grower. He can sell or hold his crop as he wishes, his decision having no effect on the market price for grain.

2 All participants in the market are fully informed about the quantitative and qualitative characteristics of goods and services and the terms of exchange. This can, of course, be only approximately true in any market.

3 And, as is usually implicit, all valuable assets can be individually owned and managed without violating the competition assumption. This, plus competitive market exchange, implies that all costs of production and consumption are borne by the producer and consumer.

If these conditions hold, it could be concluded that the best social solution to the problem of allocating society's scarce resources to alternative ends is to limit the role of government to deciding questions of income distribution, providing rules of property and exchange, and enforcing competition, while allowing exchange of privately owned assets in markets to take care of the rest.

Market exchange, under these circumstances, with each participant pursuing his own private interest, will lead to a "Pareto optimum," named for the Italian economist and sociologist who first stated it. Perhaps the simplest way of intuitively grasping the meaning of such an optimum is to regard it as a situation where all possible gains from voluntary exchange have been exhausted. Money is the medium of exchange, and prices are the terms of exchange at which real goods and services of all kinds are traded. Under the conditions postulated, an exchange takes place only when both parties feel they benefit by it. When no one can be better off without someone else being worse off, the optimum has been reached. Pareto optimality has been demonstrated to result from exchange in theoretical competitive market models that contain labor markets, markets for intermediate goods, and markets for consumer goods—or, in other words, from a reasonably complete if highly abstract characterization of the functions performed in an actual market economy. The proof that ideal markets can achieve a Pareto optimum may be regarded as the basic theorem of modern welfare economics.

We must be careful to note the exact sense in which a Pareto optimum can be equated with a maximum position of economic welfare in a society. A Pareto optimum is efficient in fulfilling consumer wants. This means, to put it in a slightly different way, that if the use of any productive service were changed, or if any consumer good or service were made available to a consumer other than the one who had a claim to it, someone would have to be made worse off. This concept of the efficiency of a whole economic system is a rather subtle idea but a vastly important one. But we must be clear that a Pareto optimum is the highest welfare position for the society only in relation to the particular distribution of rights to assets that exists. It says nothing about the justice of the distribution of claims. I will return to this point in the Frontiers section.

For some decades a few economists, voices in the wilderness, argued that while the model provided a highly useful insight into the functioning of market processes, in reality there were serious departures from the model. Of particular pertinence for environmental concerns, they claimed (although they did not quite put it that way in their day), was that the third structural assumption indicated above—the holding of all valuable assets in discrete units of private property—was a severe simplification of reality for existing economies. At the turn of the present century, Alfred Marshall in his *Principles of Economics* (already cited under theme 1) had introduced, along with most of the other major ideas found in contemporary market theory, the notion of external costs and benefits. These terms describe instances in which the activities of one fiscally independent economic unit, let us say a firm, directly affected the position of another fiscally independent unit, say a consumer, without the intervention of the market. Early examples were offered that were environmental in nature—sparks from a locomotive engine setting fire to a farmer's field, or, on the external benefit side, a beekeeper's bees pollinating an orchard owner's apple trees. In the last four or five decades, writers like A. C. Pigou, in Britain, and William Kapp and William Baumol, in the United States, called attention to what they regarded as the importance of such phenomena in actual economic systems.

While well taken, it is fair to say that their warnings carried very little weight within the profession. Perhaps it was because the structure of market theory—welfare economics—was so tightly and elegantly developed that there was a great reluctance to modify it, especially if those modifications were to be "messy."

During the 1960s and especially toward the end of that decade, a number of economists began to come to grips with environmental problems. A fair amount of theoretical development ensued, as well as a substantial amount of applied work. Both lines of activity have continued to accelerate in the 1970s and the 1980s. What happened to make people, including economists, suddenly so acutely aware of environmental pollution? I believe three things that have come upon us slowly, but more or less simultaneously, are chiefly responsible.

First, recent decades have seen immense increases in industrial production and energy conversion. Associated with these are massive flows of materials and energy from concentrated states in nature to degraded and diluted states in the environment. This has begun to alter the physical, chemical, and biological quality of the atmosphere and hydrosphere on a truly massive scale. Furthermore, scientists and technicians now have the means to detect even very small changes in these natural systems so that we are much more aware of what is happening.

Second, "exotic" materials are being introduced into the environment. The near-alchemy of modern physics and chemistry has recently subjected the world's biological systems to strange, unnatural inputs to which they cannot adapt (or at least not quickly); or adaptation may occur in some species but not in others, and thus the balance of species is upset.

Third, because of general affluence, ordinary folk have come to expect standards of cleanliness, safety, and wholesomeness in their surroundings that were the exclusive province of the well-born or rich in earlier times.

What is to be done in the face of these profound new forces in the world? And why did existing market institutions not cope with them at all well? To answer, we must try to understand the basic causes of the pollution problems that affect the economies of most of the nonsocialist industrialized world (the socialist world has its own set).

As a first step toward gaining insight into the origins of this growing divergence between private ends and social ends, it is useful to invoke one of the most basic physical principles—that of mass balance (the first law of thermodynamics).[3] When minerals, fuels, gases, and organic materials are extracted and harvested from nature and used by producers and consumers, their mass is not altered except in trivial amounts. The mass of material residuals (commonly, wastes or by-products) generated in production and consumption activities must be about equal to that extracted initially from nature.

Market exchange works to allocate the services of material objects to those who desire them most, but their physical substance remains intact. This fact has important implications for the allocation of resources in a market system: namely, while most extractive harvesting, processing, and distributional activities can be conducted relatively efficiently through the medium of exchange of private ownership rights, the inevitable residual mass returned to the environment goes heavily into what economists call common property resources. The same is true of residual energy. Common property resources are those valuable natural assets that cannot, or can only imperfectly, be reduced to private ownership. Examples are the air mantle, watercourses, the oceans, complex ecological systems, large landscapes, and the electromagnetic spectrum. The nature of all these resources violates the third structural assumption for an efficient market—that all valuable assets can be individually owned and managed without violating the competition assumption.

One need not ever have heard of the discipline of economics to know what will happen when open and unpriced access to such resources is permitted, and careful study of particular common property or common pool problems confirms that intuition: unhindered access to such resources leads to overuse, misuse, and the degradation of quality. Market forces are marvelously efficient in allocating owned resources, but they work to damage or destroy common property resources.

The laws of conservation of mass and energy have always existed. But at lower levels of population and economic activity, the return of "used" materials and energy to the environment has only local effects, most of which can be dealt with by local government measures to improve sanitation in the immediate vicinity of cities. Thus, butchers can be moved, sewers can be installed, and streets can be cleared of trash and offal.

But, as economic development proceeds, more and more material and energy are returned to the environment. Indeed, some forces press in the direction of increasing the proportion of residual waste to final usable output; the need to mine progressively lower quality ores or to use shales for the production of oil is a case in point. Larger areas or "problem sheds" are affected, and greater numbers of people more remotely located in both space and time suffer adverse impacts. Common property assets, which cannot enter into market exchange, are progressively degraded because industries and individuals use them as dumps at no cost to themselves, even though important assets associated with other uses are degraded or destroyed.

In summary, a great asymmetry has developed in the effectiveness and efficiency of economic incentives inherent in market systems. On the one hand, the market works well in stimulating the exploitation of basic resources and in processing and distributing them, but it fails completely in the efficient disposal of residuals to common property resources.

Seen from this perspective, it is clear that Marshall's external costs are not freakish random effects. They are a systematic part of the economic development process in economies where common property resources have become increasingly scarce, and they present a problem of collective management that different governments have undertaken in various ways.

What I have described here could fairly be represented as today's conventional view of environmental economics. In the Frontiers section I will raise some questions about this viewpoint.

6 Benefit–cost analysis

An applied welfare economics technique called benefit–cost analysis has played a very large role historically in natural resource economics and, more recently, in environmental economics as well. This mode of analysis initially was developed to evaluate water resources investments made by federal water agencies in the United States, principally the US Bureau of Reclamation and the US Army Corps of Engineers. The general objective of benefit–cost analysis in this application was to provide a useful picture of the costs and gains from making investments in water development. The intellectual father of the technique is often said to be Jules Dupuit, who in 1844 wrote a frequently cited study, "On the measure of the utility of public works." In this remarkable article, Dupuit recognized the concept of consumer's surplus[4] (a central concept in the modern application of benefit–cost analysis) and saw that consequently the benefits of public works are not necessarily equal to the direct revenues that the public works projects will generate.

Early contributions to benefit–cost analysis generally came from the federal agencies responsible for water development. In fact, such agencies have long been aware of the need for economic evaluation of projects, and the benefit–cost procedure is now embodied in agency policy and in government legislation. As examples, in 1808 Albert Gallatin, President Jefferson's secretary of the treasury, issued a report on transportation programs for the new nation in which he stressed the need to compare the benefits and the costs of proposed waterway improvements. The Federal Reclamation Act of 1902, which created the Bureau of Reclamation and was aimed at opening the American West to irrigation, required analysis to establish the repayment capacity of projects. The Flood Control Act of 1936 proposed a feasibility test based on utilitarian welfare economics that requires that the benefits to "whomsoever they accrue" must exceed costs. This directive told the agencies to ignore the distribution of benefits and costs and give attention only to their total amounts.

In 1946, the US Federal Interagency River Basin Committee appointed a subcommittee on benefits and costs to reconcile the practices of federal agencies in making benefit–cost analyses. In 1950, the subcommittee issued a landmark report entitled "Proposed practices for economic analysis of river basin projects." While never fully accepted either by the parent committee or the federal agencies, this report was remarkably sophisticated in its use of economic analysis and laid such an intellectual foundation for research and debate as to set it apart from other major reports in the realm of public expenditures. This document also provided general guidance for the routine development of benefit–cost analysis of water projects that persists to the present day.

Following this report came some outstanding publications from the research and academic communities. Several books appearing over the past quarter century have clarified the welfare economics concepts applicable to water resources development and use and have explored the fundamental rationale for government activity in the area. For example, Otto Eckstein's 1958 book, *Water Resources Development: The Economics of Project Evaluation*, is outstanding for its careful review and critique of federal agency practice with respect to benefit–cost analysis.

A clear exposition of principles together with applications to several important cases was prepared by Jack Hirschleifer and collaborators in 1960. Other reports appeared during the early 1960s. One, which was especially notable for its deep probing into applications of systems analysis and computer technology within the framework of benefit–cost analysis, was published in 1962 by a group of economists, engineers, and hydrologists at Harvard University (Maass et al.). The intervening years have seen considerable additional work on the technique and its gradual expansion to areas outside the field of water resources.

The most striking development in benefit–cost analysis in recent years has been its increasing application to the environmental consequences of new technologies and scientific and regulatory programs. For instance, the Atomic Energy Commission used the technique to evaluate the fast breeder reactor research and development program, and the technique has also been applied to other potential sources of hazard and environmental pollution. Its development and application to environmental issues were accelerated by a Reagan administration directive requiring the benefit–cost analysis of "major" federal regulations.

Even while benefit–cost analysis was limited largely to the relatively straightforward problem of evaluating investment in water resources, economists actively debated the proper way of handling both empirical and conceptual difficulties with the technique. Some of the discussion centered primarily on such technical issues as ways of computing consumer surplus and how best to estimate demand functions for various outputs. Other issues were more clearly related to questions of value and equity, including whether the distribution of benefits and costs among individuals needed to be accounted for or whether it was adequate to consider, as the Flood Control Act directed, only aggregates, and the question of the appropriate rate of time discount to use on water projects.

Application of the technique to issues like the development of nuclear energy, the storage of atomic waste, man-induced climate change, and the regulation of toxic substances complicates both the empirical and value issues found in water resource applications. There are several reasons for this.

First, while water resource applications often involve the evaluation of public goods[5] (in the technical economic sense of goods exhibiting jointness in supply), most outputs pertain to such things as irrigation, navigation, flood control, and municipal and industrial water supplies, which usually can be reasonably evaluated on the basis of market price information. But in the newer applications, we are dealing almost entirely with public goods, where market surrogates are much more difficult to establish—for example, a magnificent vista obscured by air pollution.

Second, such matters as nuclear radiation and toxic materials relate to exposure of the entire population or large subpopulations to very subtle influences of which they may be entirely unaware. It is difficult to know what normative value individual preferences (upon which the economic theories of demand and consumer surplus are built) have under these circumstances.

Third, the distributional issues involved in these applications entail not only monetary benefits and costs, but also the distribution of actual physical hazard. While it is not impossible that monetary equivalents to these risks could be developed, the ethical issues appear to be deeper than just the economic returns involved. This is especially so if compensation is not actually paid to losers, as in practice it is unlikely to be.

Fourth, we are in some cases dealing with long-term effects that could extend to hundreds of thousands of years and to great numbers of human generations. This raises the question of how the rights and preferences of future generations can be represented in the decision process. Realistically, the preferences of the existing generation must govern. The question is whether simple desires of existing persons are to rule or whether it is necessary to persuade the present generation to adopt some ethical rules of a constitutional nature in considering costs imposed on future generations.

The new applications of benefit–cost analysis bristle with ethical and value issues. I turn to a further discussion of these in the next section.

Frontier issues in resource economics

7 Ethical foundations

Much of the recent questioning by resource economists about the ethical foundations of their subject (see, for example, Page, 1977 and Kneese and Schulze, 1985) stems from the types of concerns just expressed. For instance, standard benefit–cost analysis discounts the future and therefore gives little regard to events beyond a few decades hence. This has led economists and (lately) moral philosophers to question the nature of our obligations to future generations in the face of resource depletion and potential environmental degradation. These concerns fall under the heading of sustainability.

The idea of managing resources so as to maintain a sustainable yield has appealed to many conservationists, but the concepts they have put forward have often drawn the criticism of economists, as is explained under theme 3 above. Some economists, however, have been attracted to close relatives of the sustainable yield concept in considering questions about our obligations to the "further future," as some philosophers put it. In an early instance, S. V. Ciriacy-Wantrup (1952) advocated requiring a "safe minimum standard of conservation" as a matter of resource and environmental policy: "A safe minimum standard of conservation is achieved by avoiding the critical zone—that is those physical conditions, brought about by human action, which would make it uneconomical to halt and reverse depletion" (p. 253).

In more recent writings, Talbot Page (1982) has elaborated a related idea. He argues that preserving opportunities for future generations is a commonsensical minimal notion of intergenerational justice. He writes:

> It seems sensible to focus on and limit our responsibility to what we can foresee and control. As future opportunity is more in our control than future utility, it would seem that opportunity is a more sensible object of intergenerational justice. With some effort we can control the form of the heritage to be passed on to the next generation. It is beyond the control of the present generation to ensure that the next one will be happy or hardworking. It is beyond our control to increase their welfare; we can only assure them of certain opportunities for happiness that we foresee will be essential. But we *can* preserve certain essentials, such as the valuable parts of the cultural and natural resource base. If we cannot ensure that these will in fact be passed on to future generations, we can at least keep from ensuring that they will not be passed on. (pp. 53–54)

From his writings, it is clear that Page includes environmental resources in his concept of the "resource base."

The idea of sustainability might also find support in the ideas of the moral philosopher John Rawls, whose *A Theory of Justice* (1971) has been exceptionally widely noted and commented upon. Rawls's just society is based on principles contracted with the mutual consent of all of society in an "original position," behind what he calls a "veil of ignorance." Behind the veil, everyone has the general knowledge for determining what principles of justice will regulate society, but lacks knowledge about his own individual case. Rawls writes:

> [N]o one knows his place in society, his class position or social status; nor does he know his fortune in the distribution of natural assets and abilities, his intelligence and strength, and the like. Nor, again, does anyone know his conception of the good, the particulars of his rational plan of life, or even the special features of his psychology such as his aversion to risk or liability to optimism or pessimism. More than this, I assume that the parties do not know the particular circumstances of their own society. That is, they do not know its economic or political situation, or the level of civilization and culture it has been able to achieve. The persons in the original position have no information as to which generation they belong. (p. 137)

Rawls goes on to formulate principles of justice that he thinks would be chosen by society behind the veil of ignorance, so that: "each person is to have an equal right to the most extensive basic liberty compatible to similar liberty for others"; and "social and economic inequalities are to be arranged so that they are both: (a) reasonably expected to be to everyone's advantage, and (b) attached to offices and positions open to all" (p. 150).

These are principles for intragenerational justice. To the extent that he treats the intergenerational question at all, Rawls views it primarily in terms of the present generation's duty to save. But this is unsatisfactory because in an intergenerational context, one of the important ideas of the "original position" is that it links all generations together with a common perspective. In the original position, there is no shift in time perspective from one generation to another. It seems plausible that if those in the original position did not know which generation they were going to be part of, they would emphasize intergenerational equity for the same reasons that Rawls supposed that they would do so in developing principles of intragenerational justice. Rawls's theory may be taken to imply an egalitarian system of values.

I proceed now to a discussion of two other systems of ethical beliefs that have dominated the discussion of welfare and justice in economics. These are utilitarianism in its various forms and the Pareto criterion or libertarianism.

In classical utilitarianism, individual or collective actions were to be taken in such a manner as to maximize the good of the whole society. Thus, it is quite possible that a person would be called upon to take an action injurious to himself for the good of the whole. By contrast, neoclassical utilitarianism requires that the individual maximize only his own utility. As indicated under theme 6, neoclassical welfare economics demonstrates that, under certain very restrictive conditions, this results in a welfare maximum for the whole economic system, for a given distribution of claims to assets. Thus, neither classical nor neoclassical utilitarianism is concerned with the distribution of income, but they are indifferent to it in distinct ways. Classical utilitarianism is indifferent to the overall distribution of income as long as measured utility is maximized; neoclassical utilitarianism does not claim to be able to measure utilities or to compare them across individuals. Therefore, neoclassical utilitarianism must take the distribution of income as fixed in proving its welfare theorem and must also admit that there is a welfare maximum that corresponds to every conceivable income distribution and, as such, it cannot choose among them. Choice of income distribution must be based on concepts other than utility, such as justice. Page (1982) comments on these matters in an illuminating way:

> To state the matter a little more soberly, many economists rejected classical utilitarianism in favor of its neoclassical version when they decided that utility was entirely nonobservable. At the same time it became clear that most of the structure in economics could be preserved by thinking in terms of preference orderings instead of quantitative utilities. Preference orderings have the advantage of being, at least in principle, observable by choices actually made.
>
> If interpersonal comparisons of utility are impossible, then we are no longer able to maximize the sum of utilities across people. So the neoclassical utilitarian defends a weaker kind of maximization process in which each one maximizes his own utility. The classical utilitarian's moral principle, which says to maximize the sum of utilities, is strong in the sense that it sometimes directs people to act against their own selfish interests. The corresponding, weaker neoclassical utilitarian's moral principle says that we should move toward Pareto optimality. This principle is weaker in not requiring individuals to act against their own selfish interests. It is also weaker because in many situations it does not tell us what to do (it is a partial ordering). (p. 45)

Thus, the most modern versions of economic welfare theory are said to be ordinal utility theories, while the classical utility theories assume measurable or cardinal theory. It is now possible to see where benefit–cost analysis (theme 6) sits in all this. Actually, it is an amalgam of classical and neoclassical ideas. It is neoclassical in assuming the maximization of individual utilities rather than the utility of the whole, but it is classical in that in actual quantitative application it must, contrary to the neoclassical tradition, assume both measurable and comparable utility. However, it cannot actually measure utility, and to get around this fact—to exclude considerations of income distribution and to maintain its logical integrity—it must make some very strong assumptions. For example, in its simplest form benefit–cost analysis must assume that the marginal utility of income is constant and equal for everyone. Under this assumption, in terms of maximizing net total utility, it does not matter who gets a dollar's worth of benefit or who bears a dollar's worth of costs. In this simple but very unrealistic case, the to-whomsoever-they-accrue criterion of the Flood Control Act corresponds to neoclassical welfare maximization.

The second ethical system is an amalgam of a number of ethical principles embodied in part in a Christian ethic (the Golden Rule) as well as in the US Constitution (individual freedoms prevail except where other persons may be harmed). These views emphasizing individual rights have been formalized by Robert Nozick (1974) in a strict libertarian framework. We are not concerned here with changing the initial position of individuals in society to some ideal or at least acceptable state, as was the case in the ethical systems discussed earlier, but rather in benefiting all or at least preventing harm to others, even if those others are already better off. This ethic has often been embodied by economists in the form of a criterion requiring "Pareto superiority"—that is, an unambiguous improvement in welfare requires that all persons be made better off by a change in resource use or at least as well off as before. Any act is then immoral or wrong if anyone is worse off because of it. Any act that improves an individual's (or several individuals') well-being and harms no one is then moral or "right."

This criterion, while seemingly weak—it does not call for redistribution—can block many possible actions if they redistribute income so as to make anyone worse off, however slight the effect may be and regardless of intent. To satisfy a libertarian or Pareto criterion requires that gainers from a particular social decision must actually compensate losers. In practice, this rarely occurs in public policy decisions, at least not fully, and in some important situations it is technically impossible. This criterion, while appealing strongly to a sense of fairness, is often rejected because it tends to paralyze public decisionmaking.

In a recent article, William Schulze and I (Kneese and Schulze, 1985) define these utilitarian, neo-utilitarian, and libertarian ethical systems more rigorously, developing a model that permits their illustrative application to some large issues in environmental economics. The one we chose to elaborate was the storage of nuclear wastes. The most we can claim is to have taken a step toward making ethical issues an explicit and integral part of the economic analysis of resource problems. This is truly a frontier area.

8 Economics, thermodynamics, and information

Economists normally do not think of economic activities and relationships in thermodynamic terms. When economists talk about equilibrium, they refer to a balance between supply and demand, or (looking at it another way) between prices, wages, and profits. Neoclassical economic models consider labor, capital goods, and services to be abstractions (see theme 3). The exception is resource/environmental economics, where some physical properties (e.g., mass, toxicity), as we have seen, cannot be neglected (see theme 4).

The proof of the existence of a static equilibrium (conjectured by Leon Walras and finally proven by Kenneth Arrow and Gerard Debreu), as I have also noted under theme 4, is one of the great achievements of neoclassical economics because it seems to provide a theoretical explanation of Adam Smith's price-setting "invisible hand." Unquestionably, the operation of a money-based free competitive market generates a kind of coherence, or long-range order, in contrast to the unstable price/wage anarchy that prevails, for instance, in a barter society. The static competitive free-market–based economic system described in textbooks does reflect a kind of order very similar to cooperative phenomena in physics and other realms of reality. It has also been proven, again as noted under theme 4, that an idealized market-based system tends toward a Pareto optimum—a situation where no one can be better off without making somebody else worse off—although it does not necessarily allocate resources equitably. (Equity, as indicated, is a moral concept.) Finally, the market system is, in theory, self-regulating and capable of recovering from a perturbation in demand, for instance.

Even this very abstract model of the economic system depends on resource inputs, although in most general equilibrium models, resources are assumed to be generated by labor and capital or neglected altogether. Thus, the neoclassical system is, in effect, a perpetual-motion machine. (This was emphatically pointed out in 1922 by F. Soddy, a chemist, who was ignored or ridiculed by virtually all economists of his time.) Among the first economists to stress the dissipative nature of the economic system was Georgescu-Roegen. The relevance of mass/energy conservation to environmental and resource economics was emphasized particularly by Kneese, Ayres, and d'Arge (1971).

In reality, the resource inputs to the economic system are physical: they include air, water, sunlight and material substances, fuels, foods, and fiber crops, all of which embody thermodynamically available work (essergy). Outputs, on the other hand, are "final goods" whose utility is ultimately used up and thrown away or, sometimes, recycled. Available work is expended at every stage—extraction, refining, manufacturing, construction, and even final consumption. Although total energy is always conserved, essergy, as we have seen, is not. Energy inputs like fossil fuels are rich in essergy, while energy residuals are mostly in the form of low-temperature waste heat, oxidation products, or degraded materials. Thus, the economic system in reality is absolutely dependent on a continuing flux of essergy from the environment and knowledge from structures, centrally including man. In preindustrial times, the sun provided almost all essergy in the form of wood, food crops, animals, water power, or windpower. Today, the major source, by far, is fossil fuels: petroleum, natural gas, and coal from the Earth's crust. These resources are of course exhaustible.

Evidently, the real economic system looks somewhat like a "dissipative structure," in the sense described by Ilya Prigogine and Isabelle Stengers (1984): it depends on a continuous flow of essergy (the sun or fossil fuels) as well as information in more familiar form—not instantly recognized as essergy (although the two can be proven to be equivalent). And the system exhibits coherent, orderly behavior. In fact, it is self-evidently capable of growth. Economic growth can be of two distinct kinds. First, an economic system can, in principle, expand like a balloon without technological or structural change. It simply gets bigger, as capital and labor inputs increase proportionally. This kind of quasi-static growth can lead to increased final consumption per capita while maintaining its equilibrium, but only by producing more of everything, in fixed ratios. (This is possible only if there are no economies or diseconomies of scale, which is an unrealistic but common economic assumption.) Also, there has to be a nonscarce input, "nature," in order for this process to continue indefinitely. (Most growth models, as we have seen, contemplate this kind of growth.)

The second kind of economic growth adds evolutionary changes in structure. These changes are driven by innovations—new products, new processes—that result not only in quantitative increases in per capita consumption, but also in qualitative changes in the mix of goods and services generated by the economy. In general, this kind of growth involves increased complexity and organization.

Quasi-static growth of the first kind can be modeled theoretically as an optimal control problem with aggregate consumption (or welfare) as the objective function. The control variable is the rate of savings diverted from immediate consumption to replace depreciated capital and add new capital to support a higher level of future consumption. The rate of growth in this simple model is directly proportional to the rate of savings, which, in turn, depends on the assumed depreciation rate and an assumed temporal discount rate to compare present and future benefits. Note that assumptions about the operation of the market play almost no role in this type of growth model. Savings, in this model, can be voluntary or enforced by government. These are the types of growth models discussed under theme 3.

It is noteworthy (and unfortunate) that most economic development programs in the Third World for at least two decades following World War II were based on the generalized Harrod–Domar models; this approach assumed a primary role for aggregate capital investment and depended on central planners to maintain balance between the capital needs of various sectors. Harrod himself called this balancing process "walking on the razor's edge." As I noted, however, Solow later showed that the Harrod–Domar models' extreme sensitivity to balancing is an artifact of their particular choice of production function. But empirical research carried out as early as the 1950s by Moses Abramovitz, Solomon Fabricant, Robert Solow, and others established quite clearly that economic growth in the United States cannot be accounted for primarily in terms of increased capital inputs. In fact, the linked notion of increased factor productivity as a reflection of technological progress was introduced into economics at this time, for example by John Kendrick. The relatively poor performance of most centrally planned economic development programs is probably due in part to their focus on investment per se, to the neglect of structural adjustments and innovation (production and embodiment of knowledge).

Dynamic growth of the second, evolutionary, kind is less dependent on savings and/or capital investment. It cannot occur, however, without capital investment because new production technologies, in particular, are largely embodied in capital equipment. Technological innovation drives this kind of dynamic growth. There is ample evidence that technological progress is not an autonomous (self-organizing) process, as often assumed in economic growth models (when it has been included at all). On the contrary, knowledge and inventions are purposefully created by individuals and institutions in response to incentives and signals generated within and propagated by the larger socioeconomic system.

An actual example of the importance of knowledge and intelligence, as I have defined them, in economic development may be illuminating. This is the so-called German economic miracle following World War II. In less than a decade, the German economy recovered fully from a condition so severe that many doubted it could ever again compete in the world economy. This recovery was made possible by knowledge and intelligence, in the information theory sense, embodied in human skills, organizations, and infrastructure. Far greater amounts of capital became available to other countries—such as Iran—with far different results. This illustrates that financial capital and raw labor (the focus of most economic models) are feeble engines of development compared with embodied knowledge and skills.

It is axiomatic that technological progress is based mainly on an expanding knowledge base embodied in structures, including man. Several themes following from the prior discussion can now be summarized in terms of their implications for economic growth. First, because the economy is a dissipative structure, it depends on continuous energy (essergy) and material flows from (and back to) the environment. Such links are precluded by closed neoclassical general equilibrium models, whether static or quasi-static. Second, the energy and physical materials inputs to the economy have shifted, over the past two centuries, from mainly renewable sources to mainly nonrenewable sources. Third, dynamic economic growth is driven by technological change (generated, in turn, by economic forces or deliberate government policy) that also results in continuous structural change in the economic system. It follows, incidentally, that a long-term survival path must sooner or later reverse the historical shift away from renewable resources. This will be feasible only if human technological capabilities rise to levels much higher than current ones. But, since technological capability is endogenous, it will continue to increase only if the pace of deliberate investment in research and development is continued or even increased. In short, the role of knowledge-generating activity in retarding the global entropic increase seems to be growing in importance.

In a recent article, Robert Ayres (1987) develops a formal model that endeavors not only to include central concepts from thermodynamics and information into economic growth theory but also to move them to center stage. As we try to explain long-term growth in modern economic systems, such concepts are much more deserving of attention, in my view, than are the static or quasi-static traditional concepts of capital and labor that have dominated the economic growth and natural resources literature. A step has been made in this direction, but we still are at the frontiers of understanding.

A closing comment

Natural resource economics is an enormous subject, and I have merely sampled from it, but I trust not randomly. I hope, as a result, that the reader will see that resource economics displays plenty in the way of ideology and intellectual traditions, as well as more than a little science.

In addition to theory, a vast body of empirical work exists in the area of natural resource economics. I have chosen to neglect this almost entirely (the exception is the discussion of Barnett and Morse under theme 1, where the concern about natural resource scarcity stemmed directly from population growth) since our main concern here has been with ideas and principles, but the reader should be aware of this additional dimension.

Notes

In the preparation of this essay, the author acknowledges a special debt to Robert Ayres (Carnegie-Mellon University and International Institute for Applied Systems Analysis) and William Schulze (University of Colorado). Both have been frequent collaborators with me in various writings (published and unpublished), and I have borrowed freely from them in this article.

1 The basic publications on which this designation is based are R. F. Harrod (1936, Chapter 2) and E. D. Domar (1956). The mid-1930s also saw the development of "sectoral" growth models that disaggregate the economy by industrial sector. The basic article was published by the Hungarian-born John von Neumann in 1937; an English version appeared in 1945 (von Neumann, 1945).

2 Essergy is a relatively new concept in thermodynamics, although it is a close relative of some older ones. It depends on a set of subtle ideas about the nature of energy. Suffice it to say, it is a measure of energy available to do "work." Work in this conception is inherently a dissipative process (see Prigogine and Stengers, 1984). Therefore, while energy is strictly conserved, because of entropy, essergy is not. If full thermal equilibrium is achieved, no energy is lost but essergy becomes zero and no work can be performed because there can be no heat gradients. Rudolf Clausius, one of the originators of the entropy concept, envisaged a cosmology in which the entire universe would reach equilibrium and the result would be the famous *Wärmetod*, or heat death of the universe.

3 One speaks freely of "conservation of mass," as I have just done, although it is now realized that mass per se is not rigorously conserved. In fact, mass is totally interconvertible with energy via Einstein's famous equation $E=mc^2$. In practice, however, mass–energy conversion is insignificant except in nuclear reactions or at relativistic velocities close to the speed of light. Hence, since total energy is conserved and the mass–energy interconversion is negligible under normal terrestrial circumstances, mass can also be regarded as a separately conserved quantity in virtually all cases of economic interest.

4 The basic idea of consumer's surplus is that, if a consumer pays a price for a good or service that yields an amount of revenue less than he would have been willing to pay rather than go without the good or service, he gets an extra benefit from that good or service not reflected in the revenue yield; and that an effort should be made to include this extra benefit in the evaluation of public works.

5 Economists distinguish between private goods and public goods. Private goods exhibit a quality known as separability. To take a mundane example, if I buy and eat a banana you cannot buy and eat that same banana. The most extreme example of a public good is national defense. If it is provided for one citizen, it is simultaneously and unavoidably provided to all others in the same amount. This phenomenon, termed "jointness in supply," is the central characteristic of public goods. Many aspects of environmental quality exhibit jointness in supply.

References

Arrow, K. J., and G. Debreu. 1964. "Existence of an equilibrium for a competitive economy," *Econometrica* 22, no. 3: 265–290.

———. 1968. "Applications of control theory to economic growth," in *Mathematics of the Decision Sciences,* ed. G. Dantzig and A. Veinott. American Mathematical Society.

Anderson, K. 1972. "Optimal growth when the stock of resources is finite and depletable," *Journal of Economic Theory* 4 (April): 251–267.

Atkins, P. W. 1984. *The Second Law.* Scientific American Library (distributed by W. H. Freeman and Company).

Ayres, Robert U. 1978. *Resources, Environment and Economics.* New York: John Wiley and Sons.

———. 1987. "Optimal growth paths with exhaustible resources: An information-based model." Laxenberg, Austria: International Institute for Applied Systems Analysis, mimeographed.

———, and A. V. Kneese. 1969. "Production, consumption and externalities," *American Economic Review* 69 (June): 282–297.

Barnett, Harold J., and Chandler Morse. 1963. *Scarcity and Growth: The Economics of Resource Scarcity.* Baltimore: Johns Hopkins University Press, for Resources for the Future.

Barnett, Harold J. 1979. "Scarcity and growth revisited," in *Scarcity and Growth Revisited,* ed. V. Kerry Smith. Baltimore: Johns Hopkins University Press, for Resources for the Future.

Baumol, William J., and Wallace E. Oates. 1975. *The Theory of Environmental Policy: Externalities, Public Outlays, and the Quality of Life.* Englewood Cliffs, N.J.: Prentice-Hall.

Bentham, Jeremy. 1789. *Introduction to the Principles of Morals and Legislation.* London.

Berndt, E. R., and D. W. Jorgenson. 1973. "Production structure," in *U.S. Energy Resources and Economic Growth,* Ford Foundation Energy Policy Project, October.

Berry, R. S., Geoffrey Heal, and Peter Salamon. 1978. "On a relation between economic and thermodynamic optima," *Resources and Energy* 1 (October): 125–127.

Bowes, Michael D., and John Krutilla. 1985. "Multiple use management of public forest lands," in *Handbook of Natural Resources and Energy Economics,* ed. Allen V. Kneese and James L. Sweeney, Vol. 2. Amsterdam: North Holland.

Brillouin, Leon. 1956. *Science and Information Theory.* New York: Academic Press.

Ciriacy-Wantrup, S. V. 1952. *Resource Conservation: Economics and Policies.* Berkeley and Los Angeles: University of California Press.

Committee of the National Academy of Sciences. 1974. "Air quality and automotive emissions control," in vol. 4, *The Costs and Benefits of Automotive Emissions Control,* serial no. 19-24. Washington, D.C.: US Government Printing Office.

Daly, Herman. 1973. *Toward a Steady State Economy.* San Francisco: W. H. Freeman.

Dasgupta, P., and G. Heal. 1974. "The optimal depletion of exhaustible resources," *Review of Economic Studies,* Symposium on the Economics of Exhaustible Resources.

———, G. Heal, and M. Majundar. 1977. "Resource depletion and research and development," in *Frontiers of Quantitative Economics,* ed. M. Intrilligator. North Holland Press.

Denison, E. F. 1967. *Why Growth Rates Differ.* Washington, D.C.: Brookings Institution.

Domar, E. D. 1956. "Capital expansion, rate of growth and employment," *Econometrica* 14:137–147.

Dorfman, Robert, Paul Samuelson, and Robert Solow. 1958. *Linear Programming and Economic Analysis.* New York: McGraw-Hill.

Eckstein, Otto. 1958. *Water Resources Development: The Economics of Project Evaluation.* Cambridge, Mass.: Harvard University Press.

Ehrlich, P. R., and A. H. Ehrlich. 1970. *Population, Resources, Environment: Issues in Human Ecology.* San Francisco: W. H. Freeman.

Faustmann, Martin. 1849. "On the determination of the value which forest land and timber stands possess for forestry," English version in M. Gane (ed.) 1968, *Martin Faustmann and the Evolution of Discounted Cash Flow,* Institute Paper 42, Commonwealth Forestry Institute, Oxford University.

Fisher, I. (n.d.). *Nature of Capital and Income.* New York: A. M. Kelley.

Fisher, A. C., J. V. Krutilla, and C. J. Cicchetti. 1972. "Alternative uses of natural environments: The economics of environmental modification," in *Natural Environments: Studies in Theoretical and Applied Analysis,* ed. J. V. Krutilla. Washington, D.C.: Resources for the Future.

———. 1981. *Resource and Environmental Economics.* Cambridge: Cambridge University Press.

Forrester, J. W. 1971. *World Dynamics.* Cambridge, Mass.: Wright-Allen.

Frautschi, S. 1982. "Entropy in an expanding universe," *Science* 217 (August): 593–599.

Gaffney, M. M. 1957. "Concepts of financial maturity of timber and other assets," Agricultural Economics Information Series no. 62, North Carolina State College, Raleigh.

Georgescu-Roegen, N. 1971. *The Entropy Law and the Economic Process.* Cambridge, Mass.: Harvard University Press.

———. 1979a. "Energy analysis and economic valuation," *Southern Economic Journal* (4 April).

———. 1979b. "Comments," in *Scarcity and Growth Reconsidered,* ed. V. K. Smith. Washington, D.C.: Resources for the Future.

Goeller, H. and A. Weinberg. 1976. "The age of substitutability," *Science* 191 (February): 560–567.

Gray, L. C. 1914. "Rent under the assumption of exhaustibility," *Quarterly Journal of Economics* 28: 466–489.

Guggenheim, E. A. 1949. "Statistical basis of thermodynamics," *Research* 2: 450–454.

Harrod, R. F. 1936. *The Trade Cycle.* Oxford: Oxford University Press.

Herfindahl, O. 1967. "Depletion and economic theory," in *Extractive Resources and Taxation,* ed. M. Gaffney. Madison: University of Wisconsin Press.

Hirschleifer, Jack, James De Haven, and Jerome Milliman. 1960. *Water Supply: Economics, Technology, and Policy.* Chicago: University of Chicago Press.

Hotelling, H. 1931. "The economics of exhaustible resources," *Journal of Political Economy* 39: 137–175.

Huettner, David A. 1976. "Net energy analysis: An economic assessment," *Science* 192 (April): 101–104.

Jackson, Clement, et al. 1976. "Benefit–cost analysis of automotive emissions reductions," General Motors Research Laboratory GMR 2265.

Jaynes, E. T. 1957. "Information theory and statistical mechanics, I," *Physical Review* 106: 620.

Kamien, M., and N. Schwartz. 1978. "Optimal exhaustible resource depletion with endogenous technical change," *Review of Economic Studies* 45.

Kantor, F. W. 1977. *Information Mechanics.* New York: John Wiley and Sons.

Khinchin, A. L. 1957. *Mathematical Foundations of Information Theory.* New York: Dover.

Klein, L. R. 1962. *An Introduction to Econometrics.* Englewood Cliffs, N.J.: Prentice-Hall.

Kneese, A. V., and B. T. Bower. 1968. *Managing Water Quality: Economics, Technology, Institutions.* Baltimore: Johns Hopkins University Press.

———, R. Ayres, and R. d'Arge. 1971. *Economics and the Environment.* Baltimore: Johns Hopkins University Press.

———, and B. T. Bower. 1979. *Environmental Quality and Residuals Management.* Baltimore: Johns Hopkins University Press.

———, and W. P. Schulze. 1985. "Ethics and environmental economics," in *Handbook of Natural Resources and Energy Economics,* ed. Allen V. Kneese and James L. Sweeney, Vol. 1. Amsterdam: North Holland.

Knight, F. H. 1921. *Risk, Uncertainty, and Profit.* New York: A.M. Kelley.

Krutilla, John V. 1972. *Multiple Purpose River Development Studies in Applied Economic Analysis.* Baltimore: Johns Hopkins University Press.

———, and Anthony C. Fisher. 1975. *The Economics of Natural Environments: Studies in the Valuation of Commodity and Amenity Resources.* Baltimore: Johns Hopkins University Press.

Lansberg, Hans H. 1983. "Some thought on exhaustibility," unpublished manuscript, Resources for the Future, Washington, D.C.

Maass, Arthur, et al. 1962. *Design of Water Resource Systems.* Cambridge, Mass.: Harvard University Press.

Mäler, Karl-Goran. 1974. *Environmental Economics: A Theoretical Inquiry.* Baltimore: Johns Hopkins University Press.

Malthus, T. R. 1826. *An Essay on Population,* reprint of 6th ed. London: Ward, Lock and Company.

Manne, Alan S., Richard G. Richels, and John Weyant. 1979. "Energy policy modelling: A survey," *SRSA Journal* (January–February): 1–36.

Marshall, Alfred (1890) 1920. *Principles of Economics,* 8th ed. London: Macmillan.

Meadows, D., et al. 1972. *The Limits to Growth: A Report for the Club of Rome's Project on the Predicament of Mankind.* Universe Books.

Nicolis, Gregoire, and Ilya Prigogine. 1977. *Self Organization in Non-Equilibrium Systems.* New York: John Wiley and Sons.

Nozick, Robert. 1974. *Anarchy, State, and Utopia.* New York: Basic Books.

Odum, Howard T. 1971. *Environment, Power and Society.* New York: John Wiley and Sons.

Page, Talbot. 1977. *Conservation and Economic Efficiency.* Baltimore: Johns Hopkins University Press, for Resources for the Future.

———. 1982. "Intergenerational justice as opportunity," in *Energy and the Future,* ed. Douglas MacLean and Peter Brown. Totowa, N.J.: Rowman and Littlefield.

Pielou, E. C. 1969. *An Introduction to Mathematical Ecology.* New York: Wiley-Interscience.

Pigou, A. C. 1920. *The Economics of Welfare,* 1st ed. London: Macmillan and Company, Ltd.

———. 1952. *Economics of Welfare.* London: The Macmillan Company.

Prigogine, Ilya, and Isabelle Stengers. 1984. *Order out of Chaos.* New York: Bantam Books.

Ramsey, F. P. 1928. "A mathematical theory of saving," *Economic Journal* 38, no. 152 (December): 543–559.

Rawls, John. 1971. *A Theory of Justice.* Cambridge, Mass.: Harvard University Press.

Rifkin, Jeremy. 1980. *Entropy: A New World View.* New York: Viking Press.

Samuelson, P. A. 1979. "Wildlife habitats in managed forest: The Blue Mountains of Oregon and Washington," Agricultural Handbook no. 533. Washington, D.C.: US Department of Agriculture, Forest Service.

Shannon, C. E., and W. Weaver. 1949. *The Mathematical Theory of Information.* Urbana: University of Illinois Press.

Siebert, Horst. 1981. *Economics of the Environment.* Lexington, Mass.: D.C. Heath.

Soddy, F. 1922. *Cartesium Economics.* London: Hendersons.

Solow, R. M. 1956. "A contribution to the theory of economic growth," *Quarterly Journal of Economics* 70 (February): 65–95.

———. 1974a. "The economics of resources or the resources of economics," *American Economic Review* 64, no. 2 (May): 1–14.

———. 1974b. "Intergenerational equity and exhaustible resources," *Review of Economic Studies:* 29–45.

Stiglitz, J. 1974. "Growth with exhaustible natural resources: Efficient and optimal growth paths," *Review of Economic Studies* 41: 25–36.

———. 1979. "A neoclassical analysis of the economics of natural resources," in *Scarcity and Growth Revisited,* ed. V. K. Smith. Baltimore: Johns Hopkins University Press, for Resources for the Future.

Theil, H. 1967. *Economics and Information Theory.* Amsterdam: North Holland.

Tribus, M., P. T. Shannon, and R. B. Evans. 1966. "Why thermodynamics is a logical consequence of information theory," *American Institute of Chemical Engineering Journal* 244 (March): 55–67.

———, and E. C. McIrvine. 1971. "Energy and information," *Scientific American* 225 (September): 179–188.

US Atomic Energy Commission, Division of Reactor Development and Technology. 1972. *Updated 1970 Cost–Benefit Analysis of the US Breeder Reactor Program.* Washington, D.C.

von Neumann, J. 1945. "A model of general economic equilibrium," *Review of Economic Studies* 13:1–9.

Wan, H. J. 1971. *Economic Growth.* New York: Harcourt Brace Jovanovich.

Wicksteed, Philip. 1894. *An Essay on the Coordination of the Laws of Distribution.* London: Macmillan and Company.

Wright, P. G. 1970. "Entropy and disorder," *Contemporary Physics* 2, no. 6: 581–588.

AUTHORS

KENNETH E. BOULDING is Distinguished Professor of Economics Emeritus, and Research Associate and Project Director, Institute of Behavioral Science, University of Colorado at Boulder.

KINGSLEY DAVIS is Distinguished Professor of Sociology, University of Southern California, and Senior Research Fellow, Hoover Institution, Stanford University.

PAUL DEMENY is Vice President and Director, Center for Policy Studies, the Population Council, New York.

FRANK B. GOLLEY is Research Professor, Institute of Ecology and Department of Zoology, University of Georgia.

JACQUELINE HECHT is Maître de Recherches, Institut National d'Études Démographiques, Paris.

SHARON KINGSLAND is Associate Professor, Department of the History of Science, Johns Hopkins University.

ALLEN V. KNEESE is Senior Fellow, Resources for the Future, Washington, D.C.

WILLIAM PETERSEN is Robert Lazarus Professor of Social Demography Emeritus, Ohio State University.

ANTOINE PROST is Director, Research Center for the History of Social Movements and the Trade Unions, and Professor, Université de Paris I.

MICHAEL S. TEITELBAUM is Program Officer, Alfred P. Sloan Foundation, New York.

SYLVANA TOMASELLI is Research Fellow, Newnham College, University of Cambridge.

PAUL WEINDLING is Interim Director, Wellcome Unit for the History of Medicine, University of Oxford.

JAY M. WINTER is University Lecturer in History and Fellow of Pembroke College, University of Cambridge.

E. A. WRIGLEY is Senior Research Fellow, All Souls College, Oxford, and Associate Director, Cambridge Group for the History of Population and Social Structure.

QMW Library
23 1056796 7